Modern
human relations
at work

second edition

Modern human relations at work

second edition

Richard M. Hodgetts
Florida International University

The Dryden Press
Chicago   New York   Philadelphia   San Francisco   Montreal   Toronto   London   Sydney   Tokyo   Mexico City
Rio de Janeiro   Madrid

Acquisitions Editor: Anne Elizabeth Smith
Project Editor: Russell Hahn
Managing Editor: Jane Perkins
Design Director: Alan Wendt
Production Manager: Mary Jarvis

Text and cover designer: Margery Dole
Copyeditor: Kathy Richmond
Compositor: G & S Typesetters, Inc.
Text type: 10/12 ITC Garamond

Library of Congress Cataloging in Publication Data

Hodgetts, Richard M.
    Modern human relations at work.

    Rev. ed. of: Modern human relations. © 1980.
    Includes indexes.
    1. Personnel management. 2. Organizational
behavior. 3. Management. I. Title.
HF5549.H5192   1983   658.4   83-11547
ISBN 0-03-062482-7

Printed in the United States of America
    6-039-987654

First edition published as *Modern Human Relations*, copyright 1980
The Dryden Press
Copyright 1984 CBS College Publishing
All rights reserved

Address orders to:
383 Madison Avenue
New York, New York 10017

Address editorial correspondence to:
One Salt Creek Lane
Hinsdale, IL 60521

CBS College Publishing
The Dryden Press
Holt, Rinehart and Winston
Saunders College Publishing

To Sara and Emilio

The Dryden Press Series in Management
Arthur G. Bedeian, Consulting Editor

preface

In writing this second edition of the book, I have again attempted to capture the dynamic elements of human relations by incorporating the most significant developments that have occurred over the last few years. At the same time, I have tried to remain faithful to my initial objective in writing the book, namely that of providing an up-to-date text that is geared toward a reader who is a novice in the area of human relations or a practitioner with little formal training in the subject.

Major revisions

This edition contains approximately 35 percent new material and incorporates some of the most interesting human relations developments of the 1980s. Many of these, not found in most other human relations texts, relate to topics and issues discussed in today's newspapers and magazines. Examples include changing work values, quality circles, Theory Z, industrial democracy, the management of stress and burnout, how to dress for success, how to organize your office so that it conveys the image you want it to present, and how to effectively answer employment ads. These topics are action-oriented. The purpose of including them in this book is to bridge the gap between human relations theory and human relations practices. Theory helps explain why things are done the way they are; practice describes what is being done. No study of human relations can be effective without consideration of both areas. In this regard, I have also included in each chapter a self-examination exercise, designed to give the reader personal feedback on a human relations topic. Again, the objective is to provide an opportunity both to learn and to use the information in respective chapters.

Distinguishing features

The field of human relations is a very broad one. For this reason I have concerned myself with only the most important topics and concepts. Drawing upon the kinds of topics discussed above, I have attempted to present the material in an interesting and easy-to-read style. In so doing, I have relied heavily on the following features.

Organization   The book is organized into six parts. In Part I the foundations of human relations are examined. The parts of the book that follow focus on the social system (individuals, groups, the informal organization), the technical system (the formal organization structure, technology, job enrichment, and job design), the administrative system (leadership, appraisal, and rewards), organizational effectiveness (communication, management of change, organizational development), and human relations and you. I have used this approach because I believe it is a very logical one, moving from the human element to the environment in which people work to the ways of achieving an effective fit between the people and the organizational system to how readers can use these ideas to help manage their careers.

Exhibits   A large number of tables, charts, and illustrations are employed in this textbook to highlight important concepts and to present them in an easy-to-understand manner.

Self-examination exercises   In each chapter I have included a self-examination exercise designed to provide the reader with personal insights. These exercises complement the material in the chapter by helping the reader think more deeply about some of the concepts and how they apply to him or her.

Short cases   All too often, students learn theories without ever understanding their practical application. For this reason, I have included two short cases at the end of each chapter, providing an opportunity for the reader to apply the concepts discussed in the chapter and thus reinforcing the major ideas.

Glossary of terms   At the end of the text, a glossary of terms identifies or describes many of the concepts presented in the book. This glossary is more comprehensive than that contained in any other human relations text in the field and should provide the reader with a definition or explanation of its most important topics.

Supplement

An *Instructor's Manual* containing a synopsis of the goals and materials in each chapter as well as recommendations for teaching the material has been prepared. In addition, there are answers to the review and study questions and case questions and a large pool of true-false and multiple-choice questions for testing purposes.

acknowledgments

Many individuals have played a decisive role in helping me write this book, although I accept full responsibility for any errors of omission or commission. In particular, I would like to thank Drs. Steven Altman and Enzo Valenzi, both of Florida International University, who provided continued encouragement in this effort. I would also like to thank those who read, reviewed, and commented on portions of the text including David Klein and Arthur Moyer of Stark Technical College; Desmond D. Martin, University of Cincinnati; and Barbara M. Weinel, Greenville Technical College; and to acknowledge Dr. Fred Luthans of the University of Nebraska for his unfailing assistance and encouragement. I would also like to acknowledge Jerre J. Kennedy, Brevard Community College, Cocoa campus, and Robert O. Nixon, Pima Community College, West campus. Thanks also go to the staff at the Dryden Press who provided me assistance and guidance, including Anne Smith, Debbie Karaszewski, Russell Hahn, Jane Perkins, Mary Jarvis, Alan Wendt, and Margery Dole. Finally, thanks go to Ruth Chapman and Sharon Quigley for their typing of the manuscript.

Richard M. Hodgetts
Coral Gables, Florida
May 1983

contents

Modern
human relations
at work

second edition

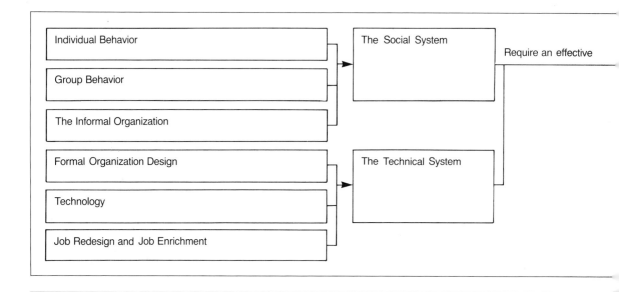

Introduction

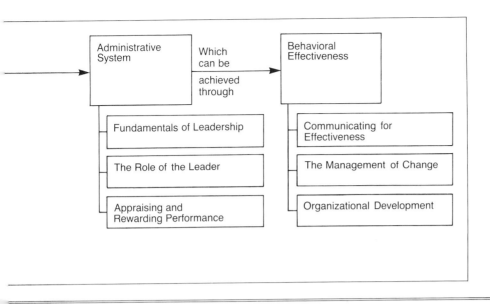

The overall goal of this part of the book is to introduce you to the area of human relations. We do so by first examining the nature of human relations. In Chapter 1, we define the term *human relations* and trace the evolution of human relations thinking from industrialism through scientific management up to the current day. In our historical analysis, we examine some of the important human relations studies that have been conducted during the last five decades. We also compare and contrast the classical model of the workers with the modern human resources model. Finally, we identify the steps in the scientific method and discuss the role of behavioral science in human relations. When you are finished reading Chapter 1 you will know where modern human relations is today, who the people are who study and investigate human relations problems, and how they go about conducting their investigations. We also present a systematic model for the remainder of our study of human relations.

In Chapter 2 our attention is directed to one of the overriding questions in human relations today: "How do you get people to do things?" In answering this question we study the fundamentals of motivation. We begin by describing the two sides of motivation, movement and motive, and then we move on to identify the five basic needs that all people have and to explain each of these needs and its importance in the motivation process. We then study the now-famous two-factor theory of motivation and its relevance for the practicing manager. Finally, in the last part of the chapter we deal with a new theory in motivation—expectancy theory—and explain how this theory can help you understand the fundamentals of motivation.

When you have finished reading this part of the book you should have a solid understanding of the nature of human relations. You should also know a great deal about motivation and its role in directing, influencing, and channeling behavior at work.

The nature of human relations

Goals of the chapter

The initial goal of this chapter is to explain what is meant by the term *human relations*. In doing so, we address both what human relations is and what it is not.

Our second goal is to trace the evolution of human relations from the emergence of industrialism up to the present day. We review the behavioral challenges that confronted management and the progress that was made in meeting them. Particular attention is given to current thinking in human relations.

Our final goal is to examine the impact of behavioral science on human relations. A great deal of human relations training and practice in successful modern organizations is based on empirical findings. Less reliance is now being placed on intuition and "gut feeling," and more attention is being given to the systematic observation and analysis of behavior at work. The scientific method is replacing seat-of-the-pants theory.

When you have finished reading this chapter you should be able to:

1. define the term *human relations*
2. trace the evolution of human relations thinking from industrialism through scientific management up to the current day
3. explain the findings and impact of the Hawthorne studies on human relations thinking
4. compare and contrast the classical model of the worker with the modern human resources model
5. identify the steps in the scientific method
6. discuss the role of behavioral science in human relations
7. explain how this book can be of value to you.

What is human relations?

Management is the process of getting things done through people. At the very heart of this process is a concern for the organizational personnel; this is where human relations enters the picture. ***Human relations*** is a process by which management brings workers into contact with the organization in such a way that the objectives of both groups are achieved. The organization is concerned with such objectives as survival, growth, and profit. The worker is concerned with such objectives as good pay, adequate working conditions, a chance to interact with the other personnel, and the opportunity to do interesting and meaningful work. Human relations, then, is concerned with four major areas: the individual worker, the group, the environment in which the work is performed, and the leader responsible for seeing that everything is done properly. As can be seen in Figure 1.1, each of the four areas influences the others and, in turn, is influenced by them. In this book we study human relations from the standpoint of the leader or manager who must influence, direct, and respond to both the people and the work environment. Before we begin our study of human relations, however, two points merit attention.

Human relations implies a concern for the people, but the effective manager never loses sight of the organization's overall objectives. He or she must be interested in the people, the work, *and* the achievement of assigned objectives. Some managers are so interested in pleasing their people that they never get the work done. Others are overly concerned with the work and spend very little time trying to understand the psychological and sociological aspects of the job. The effective manager balances concerns for people and work. In addition, he or she draws upon experience and training in deciding how to use many of the ideas presented in this book. The effective manager realizes that human relations

Figure 1.1
Human relations in action

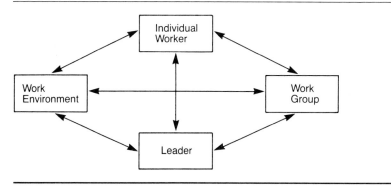

Table 1.1
What human relations is and is not

Human Relations Is:	Human Relations Is Not:
People-oriented	Exploitive of the workers
Work-oriented	An attempt to manipulate people
Effectiveness-oriented	An erosion of the manager's authority
Based on empirical experience as opposed to intuition and common sense	An infringement on the workers' personal lives
Useful at all levels of the hierarchy	Used in the same way at all levels of the hierarchy

is important at all levels of the organization but that the way the ideas are applied is *not* always the same. The situation dictates the right way to use human relations ideas. Table 1.1 sets forth some of the truths and common misconceptions about human relations.

Much of what we know about people in organizations is a result of careful study. If we were to trace the development of human relations in industry, we would see that 200 years ago managers knew very little about how to manage their human assets. The next section of the chapter examines the evolution of modern human relations and sets the stage for our study of this area. Before going on, however, take the true-false quiz and see how much you initially know about human relations.

The evolution of human relations

In industry today it is common to hear a great deal of talk about human relations and its importance to management. However, a concern for human relations is largely a modern development. This should become clearer as we discuss the three major stages through which business has progressed on its way to developing a philosophy for managing human assets: (1) the emergence of industrialism, (2) the scientific management movement, and (3) the behavioral management movement.

The emergence of industrialism

Industrialism emerged in England in the latter half of the eighteenth century. New inventions enabled wealthy proprietors of this period to invest their money in efficient machinery that could far outpace people doing similar work by hand. For example, no weaver could hope to match the speed and accuracy of the power loom. The age of machine-made goods had begun. These machines were placed in factories, and a work force was hired to run the equipment. The same pattern emerged as industrialism spread to the United States.

Human relations in organizations: an initial quiz

The following 10 true-false questions are designed to give you some initial insights regarding your current knowledge of human relations in modern organizations. Read each statement carefully and then choose the correct answer. The key, along with explanations, is provided at the end of the chapter.

T **F**   1. When asked what motivates them, most workers put money at the top of their list.

T F   2. In the long run, a work group with high morale and a basic understanding of job requirements will always outperform a work group with moderate morale and a basic understanding of its job requirements.

T F   3. While in physics it is true that opposites attract, in human relations just the reverse occurs, i.e. people tend to associate with others who do the same jobs, have the same training, or work in the same unit.

T **F**   4. The most efficient employees report that they do their best work when placed under high stress.

T F   5. When it comes to getting and giving information along informal lines, managers tend to use the grapevine more than workers.

T **F**   6. Most top managers are not very intelligent, but they have terrific personalities.

T **F**   7. The reason why many managers do not get all of their daily work done is that the boss overloads them with assignments.

T F   8. The higher up the organization you go, the greater the amount of job-related stress you will encounter.

T **F**   9. The major reason why workers do not have high productivity is that they are lazy.

T F   10. Most managers say that they are very effective two-way communicators, but their subordinates report that the managers seldom listen and are usually interested in only one form of communication—downward.

Early factory owners used a paternalistic style.

The primary concern of the factory owners was increased output. However, there was a great deal the owner-managers did not understand about this new work environment. For example, they knew very little about machine feed and speed, plant layout, and inventory control. Nor were they very knowledgeable about the management of people. Some tended to use a paternalistic style, in which they told the workers what was expected of them and rewarded those who "toed the line" by giving them more money than their less cooperative counterparts. Others simply exploited their people in the name of efficiency and profit.

In the United States the people who helped the factories and industrial establishments develop more efficient work measures for increasing output brought about what is known as the scientific management movement. Today, of course, we can fault them as being shortsighted. However, they simply did not understand how to manage a factory, so they sought to solve the technical (work) problems facing them, which are simpler to resolve than the human (people) problems.

Scientific management movement

The scientific management movement in America had its genesis in the post–Civil War era. The scientific managers were, for the most part, mechanical engineers. Applying their technical expertise in factories and industrial settings, they tried to *scientifically* merge the people and the work environment so as to achieve the greatest amount of productivity.

The interest of these managers in people involved identifying the "one best man" for each job. For example, in a task requiring heavy lifting, they would select that person who had the best combination of strength and endurance. If a machinist was needed to feed parts into a machine, a scientific manager would choose that person with the best

---

Figure 1.2

These rules were posted in 1872 by the owner of a carriage and wagon works

Starting The New Year Right

1. Office employees will sweep the floors and dust the furniture, shelves, and showcases every day.
2. Each clerk will bring a bucket of water and a scuttle of coal for the day's business.
3. Clerks will fill the lamps, clean the chimneys, and trim the wicks every day and wash the windows once a week.
4. Make your pens carefully. You may whittle the nibs to your own individual taste.
5. This office will open at 7 A.M. and close at 8 P.M. daily, except on the Sabbath, when it will remain closed.
6. Male employees will be given an evening off each week for courting purposes, or two evenings a week if they attend church regularly.
7. Every employee should put aside some of his pay so as to provide for himself in later years and prevent becoming a burden on others.
8. Any employee who smokes Spanish cigars, uses liquor, gets shaved at a barber shop or frequents pool or public halls will give the employer good reason to suspect his worth, integrity and honesty.
9. Any employee who has performed his labors faithfully for a period of five years, has been thrifty, attentive to religious duties, and is looked upon by his fellow workers as a substantial and law-abiding citizen, will be given an increase of 5¢ per day in his pay, providing profits allow it.

Scientific managers tried to increase efficiency.

hand-eye coordination and the fastest reflexes. If someone lacked the requisite physical skills for a job, he would be scientifically screened out.

The scientific managers sought to increase work efficiency by employing such measures as plant design, plant layout, time study, and motion study. By placing the machinery and materials at strategically determined points on the shop floor, they sought to reduce the amount of time needed to move goods from the raw materials stage to the finished products stage. By studying the rate at which the machines were run and the way in which material was fed in, they attempted to achieve optimum machine speeds while eliminating excessive time taken and motion used by the machinists.

Frederick Taylor   Frederick Taylor, the most famous of the scientific managers, conducted a number of important studies, the best known being the pig iron experiments carried out at Bethlehem Steel. Taylor's objective was to increase the number of steel ingots being loaded into an open railroad car by the workers. The ingots weighed approximately 92 pounds each, and the average worker was loading 12.5 long tons per day (1 long ton = 2,240 pounds). After studying this job in depth, Taylor and his associates estimated that a scientifically trained worker could load 47 long tons a day.

Choosing one of the workers, to whom he gave the pseudonym Schmidt, Taylor taught the man how to pick up, carry, and load the ingots. Using this training, Schmidt loaded 47.5 long tons of pig iron the first day! Soon Taylor had many of the other men in the yard loading just as much as Schmidt. As you can see, Taylor was able to get an increase of over 300 percent in production by scientifically engineering the job. Much of this success he attributed to the *task concept.*

The task concept was central to scientific management.

Perhaps the most prominent single element in modern scientific management is the task idea. The work of every workman is fully planned out by the management at least one day in advance, and each man receives in most cases complete written instructions, describing in detail the task which he is to accomplish, as well as the means to be used in doing the work. And the work planned in advance in this way constitutes a task which is to be solved . . . not by the workman alone, but in almost all cases by the joint effort of the workman and the management. This task specifies not only what is to be done but how it is to be done and the exact time allowed for doing it.[1]

The pig iron experiment is representative of the work that scientific managers did. By studying the worker and the physical environment, they were able to design a "best fit" between the two, so that output was increased. In carrying out their work, there were four principles of scientific management to which they adhered. Taylor described them this way:

---

[1] Frederick Winslow Taylor, *Principles of Scientific Management* (New York: Harper & Brothers Publishers, 1911), p. 39.

1. **Develop a science for each element of a man's work, thereby replacing the old rule-of-thumb method.**
2. **Scientifically select and then train, teach, and develop the workman, in contrast to having the individual choose his own work and train himself as best he can.**
3. **Heartily cooperate with the men so as to insure all of the work being done in accordance with the principles of the science that has been developed.**
4. **Divide work and responsibility equally between management and the workers, with each doing that for which they are best suited.**[2]

Principles of scientific management.

Those workers who cooperated with management and followed the directives set forth by the scientific managers were rewarded with increased pay. It was common, for example, to find that men were offered incentive payment plans giving more money for more output. The average worker in Taylor's pig iron experiment, for example, increased his pay from $1.15 per day (under the old system in which 12 long tons were loaded) to $1.85 daily (for loading 47 long tons).

Yet scientific management had its problems. Primarily, they stemmed from the tendency to view all workers as factors of production rather than as human beings. Many of the scientific managers saw the hired help as mere adjuncts of the machinery, who were to be carefully instructed in how to do the job and then offered more money for productivity increases. Quite obviously, this behavioral philosophy is shallow. While scientific managers may have known a lot about machinery and equipment, they knew very little about human relations in a work setting.

Behavioral management movement

If business and industrial organizations were to continue expanding, investigations of individual and group behavior were imperative. It was obvious that management knew a great deal more about its production facilities than it did about the people staffing them. By the 1920s, breakthroughs began to occur.

As scientific management moved into its heyday, an interest in the behavioral side of management started to grow. It was becoming obvious that concern for production brought about people-related problems and that the effective manager had to be interested in *both* the personnel and the work.

Many people believe that modern behavioral management had its genesis in the Hawthorne studies. These studies were started as scientific management experiments designed to measure the effect of illumination on output and wound up lighting the way for much of the behavioral research that was to follow.

---

[2] *Ibid.*, pp. 36–37.

The Hawthorne studies   The Hawthorne studies were begun late in 1924 at the Hawthorne plant of Western Electric, located near Cicero, Illinois. In all there were four phases to these studies.

The relationship between illumination and output was studied.

Phase 1.   The researchers first sought to examine the relationship between illumination and output. Was there an ideal amount of lighting under which workers would maximize their productivity? The researchers sought to answer this question by subjecting some employees to varying amounts of illumination (the test group) while others kept on working under the original level of illumination (the control group). To the surprise of the researchers, the results of these experiments were inconclusive, because output increased in *both* the test group and the control group. They concluded that variables other than illumination were responsible for the increases. At this point, Elton Mayo and a number of other Harvard University researchers took an interest in the problem.

A small group of workers was isolated and studied.

Phase 2.   In order to obtain more control over the factors affecting work performance, the researchers isolated a small group of female workers from the regular work force and began to study them. The women were told to keep working at their regular pace because the purpose of the experiment was not to boost production but to study various types of working conditions in order to identify the most suitable environment. During this period the researchers placed an observer in the test room. This observer was chiefly concerned with creating a friendly atmosphere with the operators so as to ensure their cooperation. He also took over some of the supervision, conversed informally with the women each day, and tried to dispel any apprehensions they might have about the experiment. In turn, the women began to talk more freely among themselves and formed much closer relationships with one another than they had in the regular factory setting. The researchers then began introducing rest breaks to see what effect they would have on output. As productivity increased, the researchers believed that these work pauses were reducing fatigue and thereby improving output. Shorter work days and work weeks were instituted, and output again went up. However, when the original conditions were restored, output still remained high. This proved that the change in physical conditions could not have been the only reason for the increases in output. After analyzing the possible cause of the results, the researchers decided that the changes in the method of supervision might have brought about improved attitudes and increased output.

The interviewers used indirect questioning.

Phase 3.   At this point the investigators began to focus on human relations. Over 20,000 interviews were conducted, in which the interviewers were primarily interested in gathering information about the effect of supervision on the work environment. Although the interviewers told their subjects that everything would be kept in strict confidence, the workers often gave guarded, stereotypical responses. This led the interviewers to change from direct to *indirect* questioning, allowing the employee to choose his or her own topic. The result was a wealth of information about employee attitudes. The researchers started to realize that an individual's performance, position, and status in the organization were determined by both the person and the group members. In order to study this impact more systematically, another test group was chosen.

Phase 4.   In the fourth phase of the studies, the investigators decided to examine a small group engaged in one type of work. They chose the bank wiring room, in which the workers were wiring and soldering bank terminals. No changes in their working conditions were made, although an observer was stationed in the test room to record employee interactions and conversations. During these observations, several behaviors were noted. First, the group had an informal production norm that restricted output. Second, there were two informal groups or cliques in the room, and individual behavior was partially dictated by the norms of the groups. Third, to be accepted by the group one had to observe informal rules such as not doing too much work, not doing too little work, and never telling a superior anything that might be detrimental to an associate.

Norms of group behavior were discovered.

Results of the Hawthorne studies   From their work the researchers were able to arrive at some conclusions about human behavior in organizations. However, it should be noted that some of their findings were not developed until years later because more information was needed, while other conclusions were only partially accurate.

The organization is a social system.   The data revealed that organizations were not just formal structures in which subordinates reported to superiors; they were *social* networks in which people interacted, sought acceptance from and gave approval to fellow workers, and found enjoyment not only in the work but also in the social exchange that occurred while doing the work. Commenting on the second phase of the Hawthorne studies, Mayo concluded that the increases in output were achieved not by scientific management practices (rest periods) but by sociopsychological phenomenon (the structuring of social networks in which the women became friendly with one another). This finding indicated the importance of understanding both individual and group behavior in a work setting.

Organizations are social networks.

The Hawthorne effect.   A second interesting finding was the "Hawthorne effect": people will act differently when they know they are being observed. Some behavioral scientists claim that worker output increased in Phase 2 not because of the changes that were introduced (work breaks, shorter work weeks) but because the women liked the attention being given to them. This finding points out the need for distinguishing the impact of psychological factors. It also helps explain why some

People act differently when they are being observed.

changes introduced by management result in short-run increases in output followed by a return to the status quo. When novelty wears off, the workers go back to their old levels of production. For sustained, long-run increases there must be some permanent psychological reward, such as a feeling of accomplishment or the opportunity for meaningful work, that is available day after day.

The supervisory climate.

A third outcome of the Hawthorne studies was the attention it focused on supervisory climate. The women in Phase 2 of the studies liked the supervision they received. Could this have been the causal factor accounting for their increased output? Mayo himself believed that this might indeed have been the case, noting that when workers are

> **getting closer attention than ever before, the change is in the quality of the supervision. This—the change in quality of supervision—is by no means the whole change, but it is an important part of it.**

The researchers began to study supervisory and leadership style.

The result was a growing interest in supervisory and leadership style. Sparked by the light from Hawthorne, human relations theorists began to investigate these areas further. Since 1934, when the studies ended, a great deal has been learned about behavior in organizations, and many of the simple, erroneous assumptions about people in the work place have been replaced by more accurate concepts. In particular, the practice of human relations is now in what is called the "human resources" era. Before examining this era, however, we should note some of the refinements that have occurred in human relations thinking between the end of the Hawthorne studies and the present day.

Refinement of human relations theory

The Hawthorne research generated a great deal of interest in human relations. However, some misunderstandings also arose from the findings of both these studies and subsequent research.

Happiness and productivity.

Many behaviorists have attacked some of the Hawthorne findings, calling them naive and, in certain cases, erroneous. One of the most vigorous attacks has been made against the supposedly Hawthorne-generated finding that happy workers will be productive workers.

Happy workers are not necessarily productive workers.

> **Many managers seemed to equate job satisfaction with "happiness"; therefore, they set out to make their employees happy. Apparently, the managers felt that it was not necessary to worry about productivity; all they needed to do was keep the employees happy and the productivity would take care of itself. This was not what the research**

---

[3] Elton Mayo, *The Human Problems of an Industrial Civilization* (New York: The Macmillan Co., 1933), p. 75.

indicated. Happiness and satisfaction and the entity of which it is part—job satisfaction—are not the same thing. Employees may be happy in this sense whether or not they perform.[4]

This stinging attack has so stigmatized human relations that in many colleges of business the term is no longer used because it carries the connotation that "happiness automatically leads to productivity"; the term *organizational behavior* is used instead.

The role of participation. A second misunderstanding revolved around the role of participation. Do workers want to participate in decision making, and will their participation engender higher output? For many of the post-Hawthorne human relationists, participation was viewed as a lubricant that would reduce resistance to company directives and would ensure greater cooperation. In their naive way, they regarded participation as a manipulative device for ensuring worker support of organizational objectives.

Over the past 50 years this view has changed. Human relationists realize that it is important to allow people to participate, feel important, "belong" as members of a group, be informed, be listened to, and exercise some self-direction and self-control. However, this is not enough. All these things ensure that the workers will be treated well, but modern human relationists now realize that the personnel do not want to be treated well, they want to be *used well.* The very subtle yet important difference between these two philosophies is that the latter views people as vital human resources who *want* to contribute to organizational goals and, under the proper conditions, will do so. This is why it has been said that human relations is in a "human resources" era.

Modern workers want to be used well.

Human resources era

The scientific managers had a philosophy of management. Its basic ideas constitute a *traditional model.* Today this philosophy has given way to a **human resources model** that, in essence, sees the personnel as untapped resources containing unlimited potential. Through the effective application of human relations ideas, these resources can be released and used for the overall good of both the organization and the personnel. Table 1.2 provides a summary of the points of contrast between the traditional (scientific management) and human resources models.

We are now in a human resources era.

How can the human resources model be used by modern managers? An answer can be found through an analysis of Rensis Likert's four systems of management:

System 1: Exploitive autocratic. Management has little confidence in the subordinates, as seen by the fact that they are seldom involved in

---

[4] Aubrey C. Sanford, *Human Relations: The Theory and Practice of Organizational Behavior*, 2nd ed. (Columbus, Ohio: Charles E. Merrill Publishing Co., 1970), p. 33.

Table 1.2

The traditional and human resource models

Traditional Model	Human Resources Model
Assumptions	*Assumptions*
1. Work is inherently distasteful to most people.	1. Work is not inherently distasteful. People want to contribute to meaningful goals which they have helped establish.
2. What workers do is less important than what they earn for doing it.	
3. Few want or can handle work which requires creativity, self-direction, or self-control.	2. Most people can exercise far more creative, responsible self-direction and self-control than their present jobs demand.
Policies	*Policies*
1. The manager's basic task is to closely supervise and control his subordinates.	1. The manager's basic task is to make use of his "untapped" human resources.
2. He must break tasks down into simple, repetitive, easily learned operations.	2. He must create an environment in which all members may contribute to the limits of their ability.
3. He must establish detailed work routines and procedures and enforce these firmly but fairly.	3. He must encourage full participation on important matters, continually broadening subordinate self-direction and control.
Expectations	*Expectations*
1. People can tolerate work if the pay is decent and the boss is fair.	1. Expanding subordinate influence, self-direction, and self-control will lead to direct improvements in operating efficiency.
2. If tasks are simple enough and people are closely controlled, they will produce up to standard.	2. Work satisfaction may improve as a "byproduct" of subordinates making full use of their resources.

From Raymond E. Miles, *Theories of Management* (New York: McGraw–Hill Book Company, 1975). Copyright © 1975 by McGraw–Hill Book Company. Used with the permission of McGraw–Hill Book Company.

decision making. Management makes most of the decisions and passes them down the line, using threats and coercion when necessary to get things done. Superiors and subordinates deal with each other in an environment of distrust. If an informal organization develops, it usually opposes the goals of the formal organization.

    System 2: Benevolent autocratic.   Management acts in a condescending manner toward the subordinates. Although there is some decision making at the low levels, it occurs within a prescribed framework. Rewards and some actual punishment are used to motivate the personnel. In superior-subordinate interaction, the management is condescending and the subordinates appear cautious and fearful. Although an informal organization usually develops, it does not always oppose the goals of the formal organization.

    System 3: Consultative democratic.   Management has quite a bit of confidence and trust in the subordinates. Although important decisions

are made at the top of the organization, the subordinates make specific decisions at the lower levels. Two-way communication is evident, and there is some confidence and trust between superiors and subordinates. If an informal organization develops, it either gives support or offers only slight resistance to the goals of the formal organization.

System 4: Participative democratic.   Management has complete confidence and trust in the subordinates. Decision making is highly centralized. Communication flows not only up and down the organization but among peers as well. Superior-subordinate interaction takes place in a friendly environment and is characterized by mutual confidence and trust. The formal and the informal organization are often one and the same.[5]

Quite obviously, System 1 represents the traditional model, while System 4 presents the human resources model. At the present time there appears to be a decided swing toward the use of Systems 3 and 4. Modern managers are realizing that the way to handle personnel has changed dramatically since the heyday of the scientific managers. One reason is because today's employee has a much different view of work than the employee of the past. The very meaning of work is changing.

The meaning of work

Work is the use of physical and/or mental effort that is directed toward the production or accomplishment of something. Do people today work as hard as they used to work? Some individuals say no, arguing that many workers do just enough to get by. Others challenge this contention, pointing out that the American work ethic is alive and well in many organizations. Both groups are partially right and partially wrong. This can be seen by examining the meaning of work along a continuum ranging from those who regard work as highly desirable to those who see it as highly undesirable. The most extreme example of the individual who sees work as a "good thing" is the workaholic; the most common example of the individual who sees work as a "bad thing" is the person who subscribes to the leisure ethic.[6]

Work defined.

The workaholic

The *workaholic* obtains satisfaction from continual work. The individual enjoys having something to do at all times. Many people confuse the workaholic with the efficient worker. Actually there is quite a difference

---

[5] Adapted from Rensis Likert, *The Human Organization* (New York: McGraw–Hill Book Company, 1967), pp. 4–10.

[6] For an excellent in-depth discussion of the work ethic and the meaning of work see: David J. Cherrington, *The Work Ethic* (New York: American Management Association, 1980).

between the two. In particular, a workaholic has an uncontrollable compulsion to work. He or she obtains enjoyment from being busy at all times; if there were no more work to do the individual would feel nervous or guilty.

When examined from a human relations standpoint, the workaholic presents a major challenge to the manager. Unless this worker can be made to see that his or her meaning and purpose of work is distorted, the individual is highly likely to eventually suffer a heart attack, high blood pressure, and/or job burnout. While more will be said about workaholics later in the book, it is important to remember that the development of workaholic practices is bad for the worker and should be discouraged by the manager.

Workaholism should be discouraged.

The work ethic

The *work ethic* holds that work is a desirable activity. Those who subscribe to this ethic believe that:

Work ethic beliefs.

1. it is acceptable to work long and hard every day;
2. one should strive to be highly productive on the job;
3. one should take pride in their work;
4. commitment and loyalty to one's profession, organization, and work group are to be encouraged; and
5. people should be achievement-oriented and constantly striving for advancement and promotion.

Many successful people believe in the work ethic. In large part, they feel that this philosophy has helped them to succeed in life.

When examined from a human relations standpoint, the manager has to keep in mind that not everyone subscribes to the work ethic. Many people work hard but do not attach extreme importance to the job. In managing these individuals the manager has to be careful not to foist his or her work values on them. If the workers are doing an acceptable job, this may be all the manager can expect.

The worth ethic

The *worth ethic* is held by those who work because they want to achieve something of worth or value. These people fall into one of two groups. The first group works because their jobs give them feelings of competence and job mastery. They like what they do because they feel in command of the situation. They also have feelings of self-esteem as reflected in their belief that they do a good job. These beliefs are often shown by such statements as: "I am a very competent worker." "I am a valuable member of this organization." or "I can really get things done

Self-esteem is important.

around here." These people like to work because of the psychological satisfaction it provides to them.

The second group of people that subscribes to the worth ethic does so because of the personal, tangible rewards. The rewards come in such forms as money, status, recognition and/or promotion, and they help the individual meet the desire for tangible rewards. The worker who can point to a new car, a house, a boat, a large office, or a key to the executive washroom falls into this second group of individuals.

So are personal, tangible rewards.

Both of the rewards discussed above (self-esteem and personal, tangible rewards) can be successful motivators. The important thing for the manager to remember is that in many cases he or she has no authority to give out additional money or provide special promotions. The manager can merely encourage the personnel to work hard and try to provide them with feelings of self-esteem by giving them continuous positive feedback. In this case, those seeking personal, tangible rewards will not be as satisfied as those desiring self-esteem. Yet this is all the manager can do. It is a problem with which the organization must live.

The leisure ethic

Many workers today subscribe to the ***leisure ethic***. These people fall into one of two groups. The first group sees work as an unfortunate obligation. However, they are willing to work because they know that it is the only way for them to maintain a desirable lifestyle. These individuals cannot be counted on to do much more than the minimum needed to keep their job. If they do work hard in an effort to earn a promotion or advancement, it is only because they want to use the money to pursue nonwork activities.

Many people dislike work.

The other group which subscribes to the leisure ethic believes that work is totally undesirable and punishing. There are no rewards associated with it. An individual who fits into this category was well described by Studs Terkel in his book *Working*, when he reported the comments of a steelworker.

Others hate it.

The first thing happens at work: When the arms start moving, the brain stops. I punch in about ten minutes to seven in the morning . . . at seven it starts. My arms get tired about the first half-hour. After that they don't get tired any more until maybe the last half-hour at the end of the day. I work from seven to three-thirty. My arms are tired at seven-thirty and they're tired at three o'clock. I hope to God that I never get broke in, because I always want my arms to be tired at seven-thirty and three o'clock (laughs). 'Cause that's when I know there's a beginning and there's an end. That I'm not brainwashed. In between, I don't even try to think. . . . Unless a guy's a nut, he never thinks about work or talks about it. . . . I'd say one out of a hundred will actually get excited about work.[7]

---

[7] Studs Terkel, *Working* (New York: Avon Books, 1972), p. 5.

"Good morning, Miss Ferguson. I'd like to leave a 5 P.M. wake-up call."

Drawing by Leo Cullum: © 1982
The New Yorker Magazine, Inc.

But there are ways of dealing with these people.

The challenge presented to the manager by individuals who believe in the leisure ethic is the most difficult to meet. However, it is not an impossible task. One of the most effective approaches, used in many jobs, is to redesign the work so that it becomes more challenging and meaningful. This can help greatly. Of course, if the workers do not like challenge and meaningful work, the redesign effort is a waste of time. A second, and often complementary, approach is to develop a system of positive reinforcement designed to encourage work output and discourage loafing. If used for an extended period of time, it is possible to turn some of these leisure ethic people around and move them into the category of worth ethic. This book examines some of the ways that this can be done.

Before we begin our study of how this is possible, however, there is one final point that merits consideration. It relates to human relations and the scientific method. Much of what we now know about people in organizations is based on systematic analysis. Although the study of human relations is not a true science, it is far less an art than it was 50 years ago. Much of this progress can be attributed to the rigorous application of scientific measures in answering the question: "Why do people behave as they do?"

Behavioral science and human relations

A great deal of what people know about human relations is a direct out-growth of what they have heard, read, or experienced. Many try to classify this information into the form of rules or principles of behavior. For example, just about everyone knows Murphy's first law: "If anything can go wrong, it will." Another commonly cited behavioral adage comes from Parkinson, who holds, "The time spent on the discussion of any agenda item is in inverse proportion to the sum involved."[8] Other illustrations are contained in Figure 1.3.

Are these laws scientific or are they generalizations that make for an interesting discussion but little else? Human relations experts opt for the latter view, noting that such rules are too broad in coverage to provide much operational assistance. Furthermore, since nothing is more dangerous than generalizing behavioral findings from one situation to another without systematically studying the facts, modern human relationists prefer to use the scientific method in developing their theories and rules about human relations.

The scientific method

The greatest barrier to our understanding of human relations can be found within ourselves. Biases, personal opinions, inaccurate perceptions, and errors of judgment all combine to give us our own views of the world. Sometimes these factors lead us to see things as we would like them to be rather than as they really are. For example, a manager who dislikes the union may easily regard the shop steward as a mouthpiece for union dissension and may discount anything the steward says as mere "union rhetoric."

Practitioners of modern human relations know that they must step outside themselves and try to study human behavior in the work place from an *objective* standpoint. In analyzing behavioral problems, for example, they must rely on the scientific method, because, as Kerlinger has noted:

The scientific method has one characteristic that no other method of attaining knowledge has: self-direction. There are built-in checks all along the way to scientific knowledge. These checks are so conceived and used that they control and verify the scientist's activities and conclusions to the end of attaining dependable knowledge outside himself.[9]

---

[8]C. Northcote Parkinson, *Parkinson's Law* (Boston: Houghton Mifflin Company, 1957), p. 24.

[9]Fred N. Kerlinger, *Foundations of Behavioral Research*, 2nd ed. (New York: Holt, Rinehart and Winston, 1973), p. 6.

Figure 1.3
Laws of work and nature

The First Two Rules of Work

Rule One: The boss is always right.
Rule Two: When the boss is wrong, refer to Rule One.

The Army General's Law

Nothing is impossible for the man who does not have to do it.

Adler's Law

Warranties cover only those things that do not break down.

The Buttered-Side-Down Law

An object will fall in such a way as to do the most damage.

Weaver's Law

When several reporters share a taxi cab, the reporter in the front seat pays for everyone.

Doyle's Corollary

No matter how many reporters share a cab, nor who pays, everyone puts the full fare on his or her expense account.

Rowe's Rule

The odds are 5 to 6 that the light at the end of the tunnel is the headlight of an oncoming train.

O'Brian's Rule (the $357.73 theory)

Auditors always reject an expense account with a bottom line that is divisible by 5 or 10.

Horner's Five-Thumb Postulate

Experience gained is directly proportional to the amount of equipment ruined.

Nieberg's Law

Progress is made on alternate Fridays.

The Harvard Law

Under the most rigorously controlled conditions of pressure, temperature, volume, humidity, and other variables, the organism will do as it darn well pleases.

Cahn's Axiom

When all else fails, read the instructions.

Man's Law

No matter what happens, there is someone who knew it would.

The following are generally regarded as the basic steps in the scientific method:

Identify the problem. What exactly is the objective of the entire investigation?

Obtain background information. Gather as much data as possible about the problem under study.

Pose a tentative solution to the problem. State a hypothesis that

can be proved to be either right or wrong and that is most likely to solve the problem.

Investigate the problem area. Using available data, as well as any information gathered through experimentation, examine the problem in its entirety.

Steps in the scientific method.

Classify the information. Take all the data and classify them in a way that expedites their use and helps establish a relationship with the hypothesis.

State a tentative answer to the problem. Draw a conclusion regarding the right answer to the problem.

Test the answer. Implement the solution. If it works, the problem is solved. If not, develop another hypothesis and repeat the process.

Behavioral research in human relations

It is quite obvious that practitioners of human relations do not have time to make a systematic study of human behavior at work. They are too busy being operating managers. However, there are people in academia and industry who do have time for scientific, behavioral research, including psychologists, who are interested in individual behavior, and sociologists, who are most concerned with group behavior. These highly skilled people are known as ***behavioral scientists***, and they are responsible for a great deal of what we know about human relations in industry.

How is the scientific method applied in the study of human relations? There are numerous ways: One is to set up *test* and *control groups*, to subject the former to some behavioral change, and then to study what happens in both groups. This, of course, is exactly what researchers did during Phase 2 of the Hawthorne studies. Behavioral scientists also obtain important human relations information through the use of formal questionnaires; ***structured interviews***, in which specific questions are asked in a predetermined order; and ***unstructured interviews***, in which the interviewer has questions to be asked but follows no set format, allowing the interview to develop on its own. All these approaches are designed to gather data about workers and working conditions. Through analysis of this information and study of the environment in which the subjects work, it is often possible to draw conclusions about factors that affect communication, attitudes, and work habits.

Behavioral research in industry uses the scientific method.

It is important to remember that modern human relations is based, not on generalizations, hunches, opinions, and "gut feeling," but on empirical information that is systematically gathered and analyzed by trained scientists. Much of what you will study in this book is a direct result of their investigations.

How this book will help you

Having discussed the nature of human relations, let us now examine the way in which this text can be of help to you. The primary objective of the book is to familiarize you with the field of human relations, pointing out ways in which this information can be of personal value. For the most part the text is written from the standpoint of human relations in organizations, since this is where most adults have the greatest need for this information. However, much of the material is also applicable in your own life. In particular, there are four major benefits that this book will provide to you.

Scientific findings will be reported.

1. *Fact Not Intuition.* The information in this book is based on fact. Research studies and reports from industry, government, and other major organizations have been drawn upon in gathering together the material in each chapter. While the art of human relations is not overlooked, it is not allowed to get in the way of proven, scientific findings.

Thorough coverage will be employed.

2. *Comprehension.* This book is thorough in its coverage of the field of human relations. All of the major areas of concern to the modern manager, as well as many minor ones, are addressed. Additionally, this edition has been thoroughly updated and revised so as to contain the very latest available human relations material.

There will be an emphasis on practicality.

3. *Application.* Information that is too theoretical has limited value for practicing managers and others who are interested in learning about human relations. In this book, every effort has been made to show how the information can be applied.

Personal insights will be increased.

4. *Personal Insights.* In all of the chapters, there are short quizzes or workshop projects assigned to provide feedback on your own personal human relations style or philosophy. The purpose of these projects is to supplement the text material and get you involved in further analysis of the concepts under discussion, thereby increasing your personal insights.

Some of the information we will be studying will be of value to you almost immediately, as in the case of material related to communication effectiveness. Some of the material may be of more value to you a little bit later in your career, as in the case of the material related to performance evaluation and appraisal. Yet, regardless of where your career path takes you, the material in this book is designed to help you meet the human relations challenges you will face in the world around you.

Model for this book

In studying human relations in industry, we start with the most fundamental question asked about working personnel: "How do you motivate people?" In Chapter 2 we discuss the fundamentals of motivation and how these fundamentals can be applied on the job.

Chapters 3, 4, and 5 address human behavior at work, or what is commonly called the *social system*. Initial attention is given to individual

Figure 1.4
Model for this book

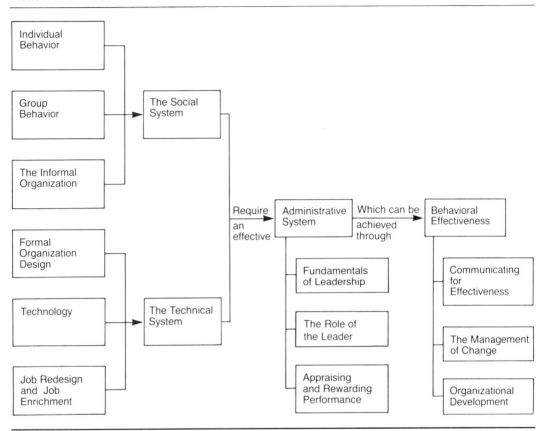

behavior in organizations. Then, in Chapter 4, our focus switches to group behavior, addressing such questions as: "Why do people join groups?" "Is a highly cohesive group always productive?" Finally, Chapter 5 is concerned with the informal organization, including the nature of the organization, how it works, and its advantages and disadvantages.

Chapters 6, 7, and 8 deal with the areas of organizational environment and behavior, or what is commonly called the *technical system*. In Chapter 6, we study organization design, with attention to both basic and contingency factors. Chapter 7 focuses on the impact of technology, structure, and behavior. Finally, in Chapter 8, we examine job design and job enrichment.

Chapters 9, 10, and 11 are concerned with leadership of organizational personnel, or what is commonly called the *administrative system*. In Chapter 9 the fundamentals of leadership are reviewed, and in Chapter

10 the role of the leader is studied. Chapter 11 is concerned with evaluating and rewarding performance.

In Chapters 12, 13, and 14, we study how *behavioral effectiveness* can be achieved. Chapter 12 examines communication with specific attention to the communication process, communication barriers, and the steps for promoting communication effectiveness. In Chapter 13, the topic of consideration is the management of change. Here we learn why change is inevitable, how resistance to change develops, and how effective managers introduce change successfully. Chapter 14 is concerned with human resource development, with particular consideration of organizational climate, organizational development (OD), and a discussion of some common OD interventions.

Finally, in Chapter 15 we take a look at human relations and you. Here you will learn some of the key questions that should be asked in carrying out a self-evaluation, find out how to obtain some initial insights into your own degree of creativity, learn how to write an effective resume and carry out a successful job hunt, and learn some of the major steps you should follow in managing your career effectively. You will also learn some of the basic rules for dressing for success and how to organize your office properly. Finally, we will examine the characteristics that successful executives must possess in the future and discuss the challenges that face the human relationist manager of the 1980s.

Summary

Management is the process of getting things done through people. At the heart of this process is a concern for the organizational personnel, and this is where human relations enters the picture. Human relations is a process by which management brings workers into contact with the organization in such a way that the objectives of both groups are achieved. Human relations is people-oriented, work-oriented, effectiveness-oriented, based on empirical experience as opposed to relying solely on intuition and common sense, and useful at all levels of the hierarchy.

The modern manager has to be concerned with human relations if he or she hopes to be effective. When industrialism emerged in the latter half of the eighteenth century, however, the owner-managers were more interested in efficient production than in their employees. This concern for efficiency continued through the nineteenth century and was vigorously promoted by the scientific managers. Employing their engineering skills in a work setting, these managers studied plant design, plant layout, machine feed and speed, and a host of other factors that could bring about increases in productivity. The greatest weakness of the scientific managers, however, was that they knew very little about the management of people.

As the scientific management movement progressed, an interest in the behavioral side of management started to grow. It was becoming obvious that concern for production brought about people-related problems and that the effective manager had to be interested in both the personnel and the work. The Hawthorne studies revealed the work organization to be a social system and pointed to the need for consideration of psychological and sociological aspects of organizational behavior. The Hawthorne studies helped light the way for much behavioral research. Since then, the behavioral movement has made great progress. The classical model of the worker has been replaced by a human resources model. In addition, behavioral scientists have entered the field and, via the scientific method, are helping to unravel many of the mysteries of human behavior at work. One of these is how to deal with workaholics and those who subscribe to the leisure ethic. Managers are finding part of the answer in the effective use of motivation. This subject will be the focus of our attention in the next chapter.

Key terms in the chapter

management	System 4
human relations	workaholic
scientific management	work ethic
Hawthorne studies	worth ethic
social network	leisure ethic
Hawthorne effect	scientific method
classical model	behavioral scientist
human resources model	test group
System 1	control group
System 2	structured interview
System 3	unstructured interview

Review and study questions

1. What is meant by the term *human relations*? Put it in your own words.

2. How much did the owner-managers of factories in the latter half of the eighteenth century know about human relations?

3. Did the scientific managers know anything about human relations? What were their shortcomings in this area?

4. The Hawthorne studies had four phases. What happened in each?

5. What were some of the principal findings of the Hawthorne studies? Cite them.

6. Are happy workers also productive workers? Explain.

7. Will participation always bring about increased output? Explain.

8. How does the classical model differ from the human resources model? Compare and contrast the two models.

9. How does a System 1 manager differ from a System 2 manager? How does a System 3 manager differ from a System 4 manager? Which of these systems is most reflective of the human resources philosophy?

10. In analyzing behavioral problems, practitioners of modern human relations must rely on the scientific method. What is the logic behind this statement?

11. What are the steps in the scientific method? Describe them.

12. Who are these people known as behavioral scientists? Explain.

13. How do each of the following view work: a workaholic, a work ethic advocate, a worth ethic advocate, a leisure ethic advocate?

Answers to human relations in organizations: an initial quiz

1. False. While money is certainly an important motivator, most workers place it in fourth or fifth position. The most commonly cited factors include recognition for a job well done, a chance to succeed, a feeling that the work is important, and an opportunity to contribute to the accomplishment of worthwhile objectives.

2. False. The work group with high morale will outperform the work group with moderate morale only if the first group's objectives or goals call for higher output than the second group's. If the first group sets low output goals because it is in a conflict with the management, the group's output will be low.

3. True. Workers who do the same job, belong to the same union, or are members of the same unit are more likely to associate with each other than they are to associate with individuals who do none of these things.

4. False. The most efficient workers perform best when placed under moderate stress. Under high stress their output slows because they have to adjust to job-related tension and anxiety.

5. True. Managers tend to use the grapevine far more than workers both in terms of sending and receiving information.

6. False. Top managers tend to be more intelligent than the average of their subordinates. Additionally, while personality is important, it is no substitute for intelligent problem solving and decision making.

7. False.   Many managers do not get all of their work done because they fail to establish priorities and do not delegate enough of the minor work to the subordinates.

8. False.   While job-related stress does increase as one goes up the hierarchy, it is greatest at the middle to upper-middle ranks. After this it tends to decrease because the executive can delegate many stress-creating tasks to subordinates.

9. False.   The major reason is that the organization's machinery is inefficient, the workers are not trained as well as they should be and/or the rewards associated with high output are not sufficiently motivational to encourage personnel to maximize their output.

10. True.   Research reveals that eight out of ten managerial communications are downward while only one out of ten involves an upward flow of information.

Scoring:*

9–10	Excellent. Your score is in the top 4 percent of all individuals taking this quiz.
8	Good. Your score is in the top 26 percent of all individuals taking this quiz.
7	Average. Your score is just about in the middle. Thirty-seven percent of all individuals taking this quiz received this score.
6 or less	Below average. Thirty-seven percent of all individuals taking this quiz received this score.

Totally unpredictable

Tom Bernardino graduated from State University last year with an undergraduate degree in engineering. His uncle Andy immediately offered him a job in the family business, and he accepted. The family owns a manufacturing firm that makes auto parts under a subcontracting agreement with one of the big three auto makers.

Tom is the oldest of all the children in his generation, and his uncle, who is president of the company, is interested in seeing Tom eventually enter top management and carry on the

*Regardless of your score, you should use this initial quiz only as an indication of the amount of general human relations knowledge you now have. You will be learning a great deal more as you read this book. If your score was lower than you would have liked, do not be discouraged. You will have an opportunity later in the book to take another quiz similar to this one. By then you should be able to improve your score.

family tradition. Right now, however, he wants Tom to get some experience down on the line.

A few weeks ago the company moved into its busiest season. Everyone who wanted overtime and weekend work was given it. Additionally, on the basis of a suggestion from Tom, the management announced a new incentive plan providing for a 5 percent increase in pay for overtime worked during the week, 10 percent on Saturday, and 15 percent on Sunday. Despite this added incentive, however, the number of people volunteering for overtime was 11 percent less than last year.

The president told Tom that his incentive idea was a good one, because even though the number of people asking for overtime was down, some of the workers said that they like the increased financial incentive and would not have taken overtime without it. "At least you stopped things from getting even worse," Andy told his nephew.

Nevertheless, Tom is not happy. He does not understand why everyone will not work a few hours overtime each day and at least half a day on Saturday. "Heck," he exclaimed to his uncle, "these guys don't know a good thing when they see it. Why, most people would give their eye teeth for a chance to increase their overall salary by 20 to 30 percent."

Yesterday, the production manager made a report on output to the president. It seems that the firm is falling behind in meeting new orders and, if they cannot get any more overtime from the current work force, will have to hire more people and go to a second shift for a couple of months. The president has asked all the managers for suggestions about how to increase output without hiring more help.

Tom has promised that he, too, will think about how the problem can be solved. However, he is really disappointed about the failure of his earlier suggestion. "I guess I just don't understand human relations," he told his friend Gary. "Machines do what they are told, but these workers are just totally unpredictable."

Questions

1. Why did Tom's idea not create more interest in overtime?
2. How might Tom's educational background prevent him from understanding much about human relations?
3. In order to overcome this deficiency what would you recommend that Tom do now? Explain.

Is it all predetermined? [10]

One of the greatest challenges for the modern manager is knowing how to deal with personnel. Having insights into each person, such as background information that might apply to their being lazy or "self-starters," could greatly help. In this regard, some people have suggested the use of birth-order rank analysis in determining what people are like. For example, is the oldest brother of brothers more likely to be a hard worker than the youngest child? Is the youngest sister of sisters going to be spoiled and hard to manage or a joy to work with? The following summary offers eight short birth-order rank profile sketches.

Oldest brother of brothers (OBB).   The OBB is considered to be a good worker when he wants to be. He can inspire and lead others competently, and he often takes the greatest hardship upon himself. He can accept the authority of a male supervisor, however, only if he identifies with that authority. Otherwise, he is likely to look for loopholes in the boss's position and try to undermine the latter's power. Ultimately, the OBB wants the power for himself.

Youngest brother of brothers (YBB).   The YBB is seen as an irregular worker, sometimes quite excellent in his achievements and at other times very unproductive. He is at his best in scientific or artistic endeavors where his environment is taken care of by others. He not only accepts authority, he loves it. However, he tends to be careless with his money and often squanders it.

Oldest brother of sisters (OBS).   The OBS is a responsible worker and likes to do things well. He will accept authority as long as it does not interfere with his private affairs. In a position of authority, he is a live-and-let-live person who thinks his subordinates should have fun. However, he will not let the workers goof off.

Youngest brother of sisters (YBS).   The YBS is not a very regular or systematic worker. However, when his abilities and interests are great, he is capable of accomplishing a great deal. He is not particularly popular with his male peers, however, because they

---

[10] The data in this case can be found in: Walter Toman, "Birth Order Rules All," *Psychology Today*, December 1970, pp. 45–49.

resent the way he takes help and support for granted, having been used to this treatment from his early home life. He gets along best with men who are junior to him in the organization.

Oldest sister of sisters (OSS). The OSS is the female counterpart of the OBB: assertive, dominant, and somewhat bossy. She is a good worker when in a position of leadership. She is also competent and responsible, and she gets things done efficiently. However, she likes to have other women defer to her authority and will usually heed only the authority of older males.

Youngest sister of sisters (YSS). The YSS can be any kind of worker—erratic or excellent. She is best at jobs that require high (but somewhat automatic) skills and decision making. A typist or interpreter are illustrations. She may attempt to be creative, but such efforts are usually too rushed or chaotic to do her much good. Overall, she is charming, pretentious, gullible, emotional—and a brat.

Oldest sister of brothers (OSB). The OSB does not excel in speed and diligence at work, but colleagues like to have her around. She mediates with quarreling parties and intercedes with the boss, tactfully calming a belligerent male. If she considers the work to be unimportant, however, she may tend to be patronizing.

Youngest sister of brothers (YSB). At work the YSB is the ideal employee if she is under somebody's guidance. She gets along with male coworkers, who often find her to be considerate, funny, and charming, although the same cannot be said for the female coworkers. However, this does not bother her, as she is not on their side; she is on the boss's side.

Others. If a person falls into any other category, he or she will tend to be a mixture. For example, a male with more brothers than sisters will be more like the OBB; if he has more sisters than brothers, he will be more like the OBS. Finally, if a person is precisely in the middle, he or she may be a little confused as to identity.

Questions

1. Find yourself or one of your close friends in the above description. How accurate was the description?

2. Is birth-order ranking a scientific way of gathering information about people? Explain.

3. In addition to the above information, what else would you want to know about someone in deciding how to manage them? Explain.

Fundamentals of motivation

Goals of the chapter

One of the most important questions in human relations today is: "How do you get people to do things?" The answer rests in an understanding of what motivation is all about, for it is motivated workers who ultimately get things done, and without such people no organization can hope to be effective.

In this chapter we examine the fundamentals of motivation at work. Our first goal is to look at both how and why people act as they do. We then study the need hierarchy and its relevance to motivation. Finally, we focus attention on expectancy theory and try to answer the question: "What motivates an individual to act in a given way?"

When you have finished reading this chapter, you should be able to:

1. describe the two sides of motivation: movement and motive
2. identify the five basic needs in Maslow's need hierarchy
3. explain each of the basic needs and its importance in the motivation process
4. describe the two-factor theory of motivation and explain its relevance to the practicing manager
5. discuss expectancy theory, noting how both valence and expectancy influence motivational force
6. explain how expectancy theory helps one understand motivation at work.

What is motivation?

The word *motivation* comes from the Latin word *movere*, "to move." When we see people working very hard we say they are motivated, because we can see they are moving. This is as true for a secretary typing 100 words a minute as it is for an executive slowly reading a complex legal document. Yet motivation involves more than just movement. A student staring at some notes on a piece of paper may be memorizing this information, but we see virtually no movement occurring. Thus, motivation involves both physical *and* mental movement.

In addition, any systematic analysis of motivation must be concerned with both *how* and *why* people act as they do. The former may be easy to pinpoint, but the latter often is not easy to identify. For example, Ralph has been offered time and a half to work on Saturdays and he has agreed to do so. We can, therefore, respond to the question, "How do you get Ralph to work on Saturday?" by answering, "Money." However, we cannot say with certainty why he is willing to work on Saturday. It may be

---

What motivates you?

There are many things that motivate people. The list below contains 10 work-motivating factors. Read the list carefully and place a 10 next to the factor which has the greatest work-motivating potential for you. Place a 9 next to the second most important work-motivating factor. Continue until you have rank-ordered all ten. If you do not currently work, mentally choose a job for yourself and use it in completing the list.

_8_	**1.** interesting work
_10_	**2.** job security
_6_	**3.** up-to-date equipment
_9_	**4.** a feeling of doing something important
_10_	**5.** good wages
_10_	**6.** challenging work
_5_	**7.** effective supervision by the boss
_10_	**8.** a chance for advancement
_9_	**9.** pleasant working conditions
_9_	**10.** the opportunity to succeed at what you are doing.

The interpretation of your answers can be found in the back of the chapter.

Figure 2.1
Motives and goals

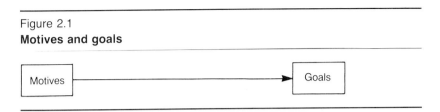

because he wants to buy a boat, go on a vacation, put aside some money for a rainy day, or help pay some hospital bills for an elderly aunt. The "why" is currently unclear, and if we want to know the answer, we must investigate his motives. Motivation, therefore, has two sides: *movement* and *motive*. The former can be seen; the latter can only be inferred. Before reading on, take the quiz "What Motivates You" and then read interpretation of the results at the back of the chapter. This quiz should provide some insights to your own job-related motivation.

Motivation has two sides: movement and motive.

Motives and motivation

Motives are the "whys" of behavior. Oftentimes they are defined as needs, drives, wants or impulses within the individual. Regardless of how they are defined, however, motives arouse and maintain activity as well as determine the general direction of an individual's behavior. This is why motives or needs are commonly referred to as the "mainsprings of motivation."

In studying how motives prompt people to action, we must first examine two related topics: motive strength and goals. *Motives are directed toward goals.* For example, a person who needs money (motive) will opt for overtime (goal). An individual who desires recognition (motive) will strive for promotion to the top ranks of the organization (goal). It is easy to picture the relationship between motives and goals (Figure 2.1).

Motives are directed toward goals.

Of course, an individual often has many motives or needs and cannot actively pursue all of them simultaneously. To determine which motives the person will attempt to satisfy through activity, it is necessary to examine *motive strength*. In Figure 2.2, a diagram of relative motive strengths, Motive 7 has the greatest strength and will receive the most activity. The individual will work hardest to satisfy this motive. On the other hand, Motive 2 has a very low strength and will be given the lowest priority. Finally, once a motive or need is satisfied, it will no longer motivate the individual to seek goal-directed behavior. Therefore, after Motive 7 is satisfied, the individual will direct behavior toward activities to help fulfill Motive 3. Once that motive is satisfied, the individual will proceed to seek satisfaction for Motives 5, 4, 8, 6, 1, and finally 2, in that order.

Motive strength determines behavior.

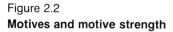

Figure 2.2
Motives and motive strength

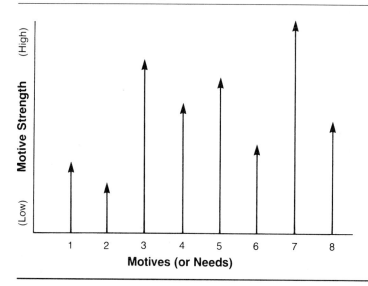

The need hierarchy

We have examined motives or needs in very general terms. What kinds of needs do people have that in turn result in goal-directed behavior? Abraham Maslow, the noted psychologist, has set forth five needs that he believes are universal: *physiological, safety, social, esteem*, and *self-actualization*.

Physiological needs

Physiological needs include food, clothing, and shelter.

The most fundamental of all needs, according to Maslow, are *physiological*. Some common examples are food, clothing, and shelter. A person deprived of everything would want to satisfy these basic needs first. Safety, social, esteem, and self-actualization needs would be, at least for the moment, of secondary importance.

In the work place many organizations try to satisfy these needs by providing cafeterias, vending machines, adequate ventilation, lighting, heating, and other physical facilities. In addition, the firms pay the workers a salary with which they can meet these needs by purchasing food and clothing for their families.

Figure 2.3
Maslow's need hierarchy when physiological needs are dominant

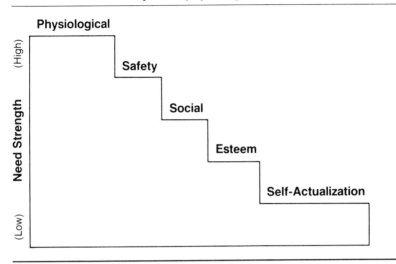

Figure 2.4
Physiological needs and need strength

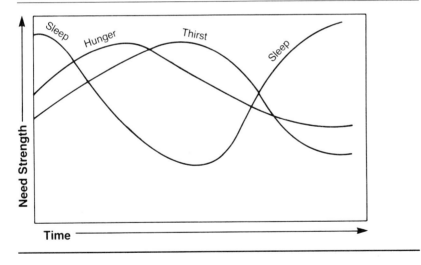

Although there are many physiological needs, the most basic would get prime attention until fulfilled and then would be replaced by other physiological demands with greater need strength. Figure 2.4 is a graphic representation of the relative strengths of physiological needs that might be felt by a person who has come home from work totally fatigued. The individual decides first to take a nap. After awakening, the person has supper, eating and drinking until full. Then, it is off to bed for a good night's sleep.

Safety needs

Once physiological needs are basically satisfied, *safety needs* replace them. These are of two types. First, there is the need for *survival*; this need is so great that many of the laws in our society are designed to protect the life of the individual. Second, there is the need for *security*; this need has both physical and psychological dimensions. On the physical side, businesses often provide safety equipment and safety rules for protecting the worker on the job. They also provide accident, health, and life insurance to help meet safety needs. The psychological aspect of safety is evident in workers' desire for secure jobs in a predictable environment. Individuals who work in government bureaucracies often fall into this category. They want guaranteed employment. Their pay may not be very high, but they are assured of a steady job. Other people find such safety in business bureaucracies where the firm may not pay well, but it just about guarantees continued employment to anyone with minimum performance.

Many people start off their business careers uncertain of how much security they should seek in a job. Peter F. Drucker, one of the most famous writers in the management field today, has recommended that people ask themselves some important questions when choosing work: Do I belong in a job that calls for faithfulness in the performance of routine work and promises a great degree of security? Do I like to know what I am supposed to be doing both today and tomorrow? Do I like to have my relationships with people throughout the organization well defined? Would I feel happiest in a routine job, or do I prefer work that offers the opportunity to employ my imagination and ingenuity, even though it is accompanied by penalty for failure? It is not always easy to answer these questions, since security needs can be conscious or subconscious. Most people prefer some degree of security in their work, but they also welcome the opportunity for challenge. For example, many sales people like a job where they are paid a certain percentage of their monthly gross sales. However, they also welcome the company's rule guaranteeing a minimum salary of $500 a month. The salespeople know that their monthly salaries will never be below $500 and may be a lot higher.

Often in a discussion of the safety need as it functions in the business world, there is an implication that safety is a less respectable motive for work behavior than the other needs. A person's need for safety is regarded as "anti-achievement" or as an encouragement to laziness. This attitude is unfair, however, because the need for safety is one of the most fundamental needs human beings have. In one way or another, everyone has to satisfy this motive.

Social needs

When physiological and safety needs are basically satisfied, *social needs* become important motivators. The need involves interaction with others for the purpose of meaningful relationships. On the job, interaction often occurs among people who work near one another and come into frequent daily contact. Over time they build up friendships and look forward to the interaction. In their home lives, people fulfill social needs when they meet their neighbors and socialize with them on a regular basis.

Social needs are satisfied through interaction with others.

In this interaction people give and receive friendship, affection, and acceptance. "Stroking" or a verbal pat on the head in the form of praise and kindness makes people feel good. They need this form of interaction; if it is refused them, they actually suffer. For example, in prison, an inmate who breaks a rule is put into solitary confinement. This denial of social interaction punishes the person psychologically for misconduct. Many times, psychological punishment has a greater effect on motivating the person to obey the rules than physical punishment would have.

Business firms try to meet this need in their workers by allowing them to interact and talk with each other. On assembly lines, workers know that they can do their routine jobs and interact at the same time. In retail and banking firms, there is an increased opportunity for interaction, since the workers carry out their jobs by socializing to some degree with the customers.

If such social interaction is denied, as when organization rules forbid "talking on the job" or "fraternization with other employees," the workers circumvent these rules. One of the most common means of circumvention is the emergence of the *informal organization*, which is the focus of attention in Chapter 5. These groups help workers fulfill social needs. Additionally, although management is often suspicious of such informal groups, they are inevitable, and management is often wiser to accommodate them than to fight their existence.

It is important to note that in boring, routine work, social affiliation helps make the job more bearable. When such interaction occurs, morale is higher and productivity tends to remain at least within tolerable ranges. However, when social interaction is denied, workers tend to fight the system by restricting work output or by doing no more than is required by their job descriptions. Allowing the personnel to fulfill social needs on the job often helps prevent these negative behaviors.

Esteem needs

When social needs are basically satisfied, *esteem needs* come into play. People need to feel important, and self-esteem and self-respect are vital in this process. Esteem is much more *psychological* in nature than the other three needs we have discussed. We can give a person food, clothing, shelter, protection, and social interaction. However, the esteem with which in-

People need to feel important.

dividuals regard themselves is mostly a function of what they allow themselves to believe. For example, a person who is told by his boss that he does an excellent job will only be motivated by this praise if he accepts the laudatory comments. If the individual believes that the manager is only complimenting his work as a matter of course and really does not mean it, the praise has no motivational effect. Thus, self-esteem and self-respect come from *within* the person.

Organizations cannot give out esteem the way they do money, but they can create the right *climate* for allowing people to satisfy this need. Research shows that two motives related to esteem are prestige and power, and to the degree that these motives can be satisfied, the esteem need can be met.

Prestige carries with it respect and status.

Prestige   For many people, prestige means "keeping up with Joneses," or perhaps getting ahead of them. In any event, prestige carries with it respect and status and influences the way people talk and act around the individual. A company president has a lot of prestige and is treated with great respect by organizational members. Out on the golf course, however, the company president may have limited prestige among the players, and the country club's golf pro is given the greatest amount of respect. Thus, one's prestige varies depending on the situation.

In their business lives many people seek prestige through promotion or gaining reputations as hard workers. Off the job, many try to attain prestige through the purchase of material status symbols like a big house, a new car, or a boat. Obviously, salary and other financial benefits are of great importance in satisfying this need. Additionally, many people set a level of prestige for themselves and, once it is attained, feel that they "have arrived."

Power is the ability to influence or induce behavior.

Power   Power is the ability to influence or induce behavior in others. Power can be of two kinds: position and personal. *Position* power is derived from the individual's position in the company. The president has a great deal more position power than a middle manager in the same organization. *Personal* power derives from an individual's personality and behavior. Anne may have a pleasing personality and an easy-going manner, which results in her being able to cut across departmental lines and get support for her proposals; Andy, however, is considered hard-nosed and bossy and is unable to secure such cooperation. Within bounds, people like power because it provides them with feelings of self-esteem.

Self-actualization needs

When all the other needs are basically satisfied, *self-actualization* needs manifest themselves. Because people satisfy this need in so many different ways, behavioral scientists know less about it than the other needs. However, research reveals that there are two motives related to self-actualization, *competence* and *achievement.*

Competence   Competence is similar to power in that it implies control over environmental factors. At a very early age children begin illustrating their need for competence by touching and handling objects so as to become familiar with them. Later on, they begin trying to take things apart and put them back together again. As a result, children learn tasks at which they are competent.

Competence implies control over environmental factors.

On the job, the competence motive reveals itself in the form of a desire for job mastery and professional growth. The individual begins matching his or her abilities and skills against the environment in a contest that is challenging but that can be won. Organizations that provide meaningful, challenging work help their people meet this need. In some companies, such as those using assembly lines, such jobs are not in abundance, and the competence motive often goes unsatisfied.

Achievement   Over the last 25 years, a great deal of research has been conducted on people's desire to achieve. One of the leading researchers, David C. McClelland of Harvard University, has been particularly interested in this urge.[1] On the basis of his research, he has set forth the following characteristics of high achievers. People who are high achievers: (1) like situations in which they can take personal responsibility for finding solutions to problems, (2) tend to be moderate-risk takers, as opposed to high-risk or low-risk takers, and (3) like concrete feedback on their performance so that they know how well they are doing.

Characteristics of high achievers.

Although only about 10 to 15 percent of the population in the United States have the desire to achieve, high achievement can be encouraged and developed. McClelland has recommended several methods for individuals who want to become high achievers:

1. **Strive to obtain feedback, so that your successes can be noted and you can make them serve as reinforcement for strengthening your desire to achieve even more.**
2. **Pick out people you know who have performed well and use them as models to emulate.**
3. **Modify your self-image by imagining yourself as someone who needs to succeed and to be challenged.**
4. **Control your daydreaming by thinking and talking to yourself in positive terms.**

Ways to develop high achievement.

Are you a high achiever? Margaret H. Harmon, a university psychologist, has recently claimed that the way people decorate their homes,

---

[1] See David C. McClelland, J. W. Atkinson, R. A. Clark, and E. L. Lowell, *The Achievement Motive* (New York: Appleton-Century-Crofts, Inc., 1953); and David C. McClelland, *The Achieving Society* (Princeton, N.J.: D. Van Nostrand Company, Inc., 1961).

Figure 2.5

For interpretation of answers, see end of chapter. Reprinted with permission of PEI Books, Inc. from *Psycho-Decorating* by Margaret H. Harmon. Copyright 1977 by Margaret H. Harmon.

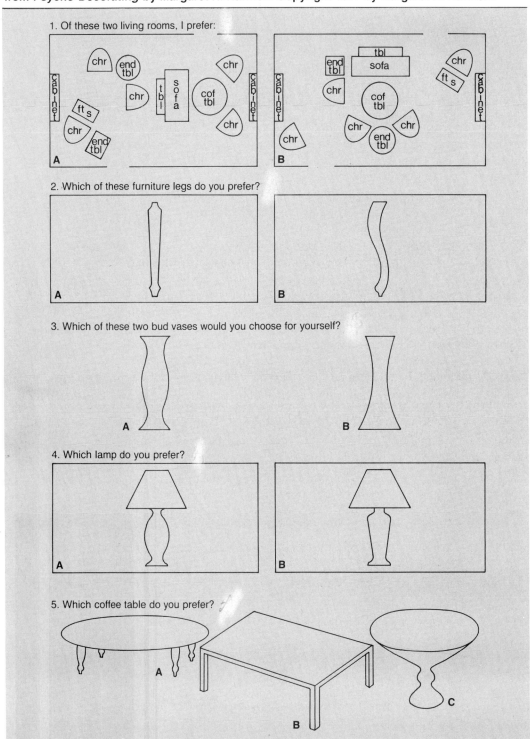

1. Of these two living rooms, I prefer:

2. Which of these furniture legs do you prefer?

3. Which of these two bud vases would you choose for yourself?

4. Which lamp do you prefer?

5. Which coffee table do you prefer?

from the coffee table they buy to the shape of the chair legs, tells something about their personality and achievement drive.[2] Figure 2.5 lists some questions from a quiz in her book on the subject. Before reading further, take the quiz and see what it reveals about you. The interpretations are provided at the end of the chapter.

On the job, business firms can help create the proper climate for developing high achievement by giving people jobs that provide feedback, increase personal initiative, and allow individuals to take moderate risks. However, while the company can encourage high achievement in its people, to a large degree this drive is something that develops in early childhood. Also, high achievers get things done themselves, but they are often ineffective in managing others, so organizations do not want all their employees to possess high achievement drive.

Need mix

An important premise of the need hierarchy is that as one need is basically fulfilled, the next most important need becomes dominant and dictates individual behavior. Note that we say "basically fulfilled." This is because most people in our society are *partially satisfied* at each level and *partially unsatisfied*. Greatest satisfaction tends to occur at the physiological level and least satisfaction at the self-actualization level. Maslow put it this way:

People are partially satisfied and partially dissatisfied at each level of the hierarchy.

> In actual fact, most members of our society who are normal are partially satisfied in all their basic needs and partially unsatisfied in all their basic needs at the same time. A more realistic description of the hierarchy would be in terms of decreasing percentage of satisfaction as we go up the hierarchy of prepotency. For instance, if I may assign arbitrary figures, . . . it is as if the average citizen is satisfied perhaps 85 per cent in his physiological needs, 70 per cent in his safety needs, 50 per cent in his [social] needs, 40 per cent in his self-esteem needs, and 10 per cent in his self-actualization needs.[3]

As a result, the Maslow need hierarchy cannot be viewed as an all-or-nothing framework. Rather, to understand the fundamentals of human behavior we should regard the hierarchy as useful in predicting behavior on a high or low probability basis. For example, among people who come from abject poverty, the need mix pictured in Figure 2.6 is probably highly representative. However, most people in American society are characterized by strong social or affiliation needs, relatively strong esteem and safety needs, and somewhat less important physiological and self-actualization needs; this need mix is illustrated in Figure 2.7. For indi-

---

[2] M. H. Harmon, *Psycho-Decorating: What Homes Reveal About People* (New York: Wyden Books, Inc., 1977).

[3] Abraham H. Maslow, "A Theory of Human Motivation," *Psychological Review*, July 1943, pp. 388–389.

Figure 2.6
**Need mix when physiological and
safety needs have the highest strength**

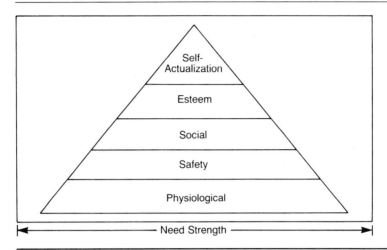

Figure 2.7
Need mix when social needs have the highest strength

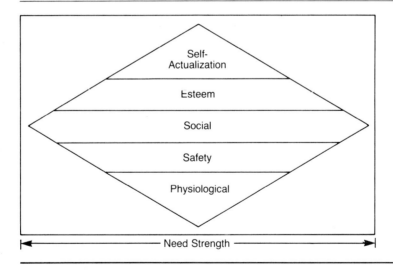

viduals whose physiological, safety, and social needs are greatly satisfied, esteem and self-actualization are most important. A person born to great wealth would fit into this category. So would a top management executive. The need mix for these people is pictured in Figure 2.8. Of course, these configurations are intended only as examples. Different configura-

Figure 2.8
**Need mix when esteem and self-actualization
needs have the highest strength**

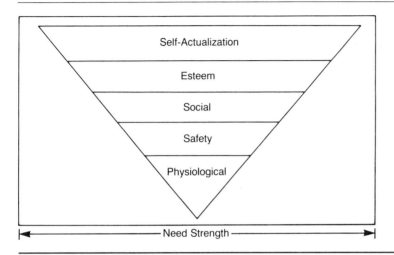

tions would be appropriate for different people, since in reality the need mix changes from one individual to another. Keith Davis has observed the following about American workers:

> Since 1935, the need distribution has been shifting upward, and by 1995 we may assume that esteem needs will dominate, followed by self-actualization. Employees whose dominant needs are physiological should be rather rare by that date . . . . We are moving from economic to social to self-actualized persons.
>
> It should not be assumed that once the labor force reaches the fifth need level there is no further room for progress. Level five is a broad classification of needs, and it would be possible to reclassify it into five more steps for improvement. Needs can never be fully satisfied. People are beings who perpetually want. The sports figure who makes $1 million dollars has achieved all that was wanted when earnings were only a few thousand, but now this person's wants have increased to $2 million or $5 million. The conclusion that we must reach is that need satisfaction is a continuous problem for organizations. It cannot be permanently solved by satisfying a particular need today.[4]

Maslow's theory is interesting but its practical value is limited. In order to see its application to the motivation of personnel, we must turn to Frederick Herzberg's two-factor theory.

[4]Keith Davis, *Human Behavior At Work: Organizational Behavior*, 6th edition (New York: McGraw–Hill Book Company, 1981), p. 50.

Table 2.1
The two-factor theory

Hygiene Factors (Environment)	Motivators (Work itself)
Salary	Recognition
Technical supervision	Advancement
Working conditions	Possibility of growth
Company policies and administration	Achievement
Interpersonal relations	Work itself

The two-factor theory

The two-factor theory of motivation is a direct result of research conducted by Herzberg and his associates on job satisfaction and productivity among 200 accountants and engineers.[5] Each subject was asked to think of a time when he or she felt especially good about his or her job and a time when he or she felt particularly bad about the job and to describe the conditions that led to these feelings. The researchers found that the employees named different types of conditions for good and bad feelings. This led Herzberg to conclude that motivation consists of two factors: hygiene and motivators (Table 2.1).

Hygiene factors

Hygiene factors were those associated with negative feelings. Illustrations included salary, technical supervision, working conditions, company policies and administration, and interpersonal relations. When the subjects of Herzberg's study were asked what made them feel exceptionally bad about their jobs, typical answers included: "I'm really not satisfied with the salary I'm being paid; it's much too low." "My boss is always too busy to offer me any technical supervision." "The working conditions around here are really poor." All the responses have one thing in common: They relate to the environment in which the work is performed.

Hygiene factors are environmentally related.

Herzberg called these environment-related factors *hygiene* because, like physical hygiene, they prevent deterioration but do not lead to growth. For example, if you brush your teeth (a hygienic step) you can prevent cavities, but your teeth will not become stronger nor will a chipped tooth grow back to its original size. Thus, you have two alternatives: brush your teeth and prevent further damage, or do not brush your

[5] Frederick Herzberg, Bernard Mausner, and Barbara Bloch Snyderman, *The Motivation To Work* (New York: John Wiley & Sons, Inc., 1959).

Figure 2.9
The result when hygiene factors are not satisfied

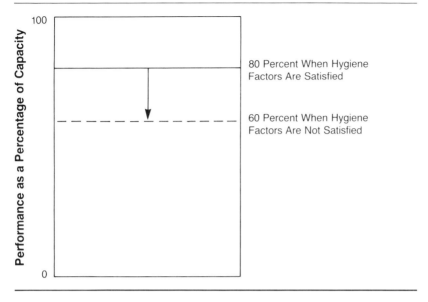

80 Percent When Hygiene
Factors Are Satisfied

60 Percent When Hygiene
Factors Are Not Satisfied

teeth and end up losing them. Analogously, Herzberg felt that if you give people hygiene factors you will not give them motivation but you will prevent dissatisfaction.

Using our own percentages as examples, Figure 2.9 provides an illustration of how Herzberg believes hygiene can affect performance. Note that when hygiene factors are satisfied, the workers perform at less than capacity. When these factors are not satisfied, performance drops. Thus, hygiene will not bring about an increase in productivity, but it will prevent a decline.

Motivators

The factors associated with positive feelings Herzberg called *motivators*. Examples are recognition, advancement, the possibility of growth, achievement, and the work itself. When the subjects were asked what made them feel exceptionally good about their jobs, typical answers included: "My job gives me a feeling of achievement." "I like the recognition I get for doing my job well." "The work is just plain interesting." All these responses have one thing in common: they relate to the work itself. Additionally, they are psychological in nature and relate to upper-level need satisfaction.

Herzberg termed these factors *motivators* because he felt that they caused increases in performance. Using our own percentages as exam-

Motivators are associated with positive feelings.

Figure 2.10
The effects of motivators on employee performance

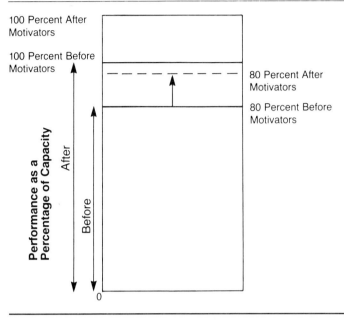

ples, Figure 2.10 provides an illustration of how Herzberg believes motivators can affect performance. Note that the employees represented are performing at 80 percent of capacity. When they are given motivators such as recognition, advancement, and the possibility of growth, their capacity for performance increases by 80 percent of this new amount. In short, as performance potential increases, output goes up.

Motivation-hygiene theory and managers

One of the major reasons that Herzberg's two-factor theory has been so well accepted by managers is that the theory applies Maslow's need concept to the job. For example, Herzberg suggests using hygiene factors to help people attain their lower-level needs. Conversely, he recommends motivators to meet upper-level needs. Figure 2.11 integrates these two concepts. As you can see, Herzberg suggests that physiological, safety, social, and, to some degree, esteem needs can be satisfied with hygiene factors. The remainder of the esteem needs and self-actualization needs can be satisfied with motivators.

A second reason for the popularity of Herzberg's theory is that practicing managers agree with it. In a recent study designed to learn more about work motivations of men and women, 128 managers were asked to

Figure 2.11
Motivation-hygiene and Maslow

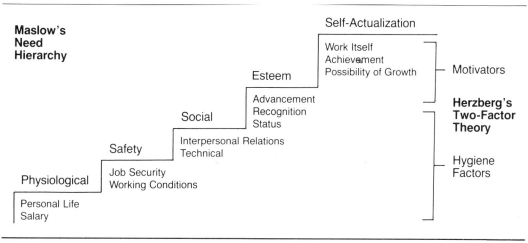

"What makes you think you're not appreciated here?"

From the *Wall Street Journal*, permission Cartoon Features Syndicate.

rank eight motives for pursuing a managerial career. The results are reported in Table 2.2. Notice that the top two choices correspond to Herzberg's motivators, illustrating the value of his theory. Also the lists for both groups are quite similar, revealing the application of his theory to managers in general.

Table 2.2

A comparison of career motivations for female and male managers on a scale of 1 (highest) to 8 (lowest)

Motivation	Females	Males
Sense of achievement	1.68	2.10
Challenge	2.91	2.55
Money	3.45	4.04
Independence	3.48	3.96
Power	5.53	5.71
Security	5.58	5.38
Opportunity to meet interesting people	5.80	5.24
Opportunity to travel	7.00	7.00

Source: Benson Rosen, Mary Ellen Templeton, and Karen Kichine, "The First Few Years on The Job: Women in Management," *Business Horizons*, November–December 1981, p. 27. Copyright 1981 by the Foundation for the School of Business at Indiana University. Reprinted with permission.

Motivation-hygiene theory in perspective

Many business people who read about the motivation-hygiene theory are likely to accept it as totally accurate. Certainly, to the extent that it encourages the manager to provide upper-level need satisfaction, the theory is relevant to our study of motivation. However, the theory has several serious shortcomings that merit attention.

First, Herzberg contends that something is *either* a hygiene factor *or* a motivator. The two are independent of each other. Additionally, a lack of hygiene will lead to dissatisfaction, but its presence will not lead to satisfaction. Satisfaction results only from the presence of motivators. We can diagram the relationship as in Figure 2.12. If you give people hygiene factors, you will not motivate them, but you will prevent dissatisfaction. Thus hygiene, according to Herzberg, creates a zero-level of motivation.

Research, however, reveals that some people are indeed motivated by hygiene factors. For example, many individuals say that money is a motivator for them. Some people report that recognition and the chance for advancement lead to dissatisfaction. For them, these are not motivators. Also, researchers have found that some factors are satisfiers some of the time and dissatisfiers the rest of the time. For example, many people want a chance to achieve, but not every minute of the day. If it is offered too often, they will be unhappy, believing that too much is expected of them. On the basis of findings such as these, Herzberg's critics claim that his initial theory has not been supported well by further investigation.

Motivation-hygiene theory has some shortcomings.

A second major criticism centers on the way in which the original data were gathered. The researchers asked accountants and engineers what they particularly liked and disliked about their jobs. Critics say that

Figure 2.12
Motivation-hygiene continua

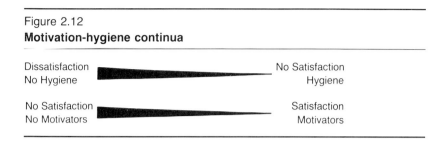

| Dissatisfaction | No Satisfaction |
| No Hygiene | Hygiene |

| No Satisfaction | Satisfaction |
| No Motivators | Motivators |

the answers are biased because people tend to give socially acceptable responses when asked such questions. What would you expect people to say that they disliked about their jobs? Stereotyped answers would include salary, supervision, and working conditions. Likewise, people could be expected to say that they liked recognition, advancement, and achievement. A close analysis of these two groups of answers shows that things people dislike about their jobs are related to the work environment, a factor the employee cannot control. The aspects of their jobs that people like are related to their own achievements and accomplishments, and are factors they can control. It is therefore possible that Herzberg's methodology may have encouraged stereotyped answers.

Despite such problems, however, Herzberg's theory sheds some important light on the subject of motivation. In particular, it stresses the importance of helping personnel fulfill *all* their needs, not just lower-level needs.

Expectancy theory

While a study of the need hierarchy and blocked need satisfaction is one way of examining motivation, there is now a great deal of interest in *expectancy theory*. Developed by Victor Vroom,[6] and based on earlier work by others, expectancy theory has been expanded and refined by individuals such as Lyman Porter and Edward Lawler.[7] Vroom's motivation formula is a simple, yet powerful one that can be expressed as follows:

Motivation $=$ Valence $\times$ Expectancy

To understand the theory we must examine the concepts of valence and expectancy.

[6] Victor H. Vroom, *Work and Motivation* (New York: John Wiley & Sons, Inc., 1964).

[7] Lyman W. Porter and Edward E. Lawler III, *Managerial Attitudes and Performance* (Homewood, Ill.: Richard D. Irwin, Inc. and the Dorsey Press, 1968).

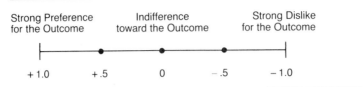

Figure 2.13
Range of an individual's valence

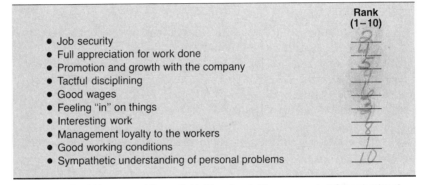

Table 2.3
What do workers want from their jobs?

	Rank (1–10)
● Job security	8
● Full appreciation for work done	4
● Promotion and growth with the company	5
● Tactful disciplining	9
● Good wages	6
● Feeling "in" on things	3
● Interesting work	2
● Management loyalty to the workers	8
● Good working conditions	1
● Sympathetic understanding of personal problems	10

Reported in Paul Hersey and Kenneth H. Blanchard, *Management of Organizational Behavior: Utilizing Human Resources*, 3rd ed. (Englewood Cliffs, N.J.: Prentice-Hall, Inc., 1977), p. 47.

Valence

Valence is a person's preference for a particular outcome.

A person's preference for a particular outcome can be expressed as a *valence*. For example, Bob wants a promotion to the New York office. On a scale from −1 to +1, his valence is +1. Suzy, meanwhile, is indifferent to the idea of promotion to the New York office. Her valence is 0. Tom, however, will not take a promotion to the New York office under any conditions. His valence is a −1. Figure 2.13 illustrates the valence range.

Note that expectancy theory forces the manager to answer the question: what motivates the individual? By examining the preference of the workers for various outcomes, ranging from increased salary to a feeling of accomplishment, the manager is in a good position to offer the workers what they want. However, it is important to realize that most managers do *not* know what motivates their workers. In Table 2.3 is a list of qualities of their jobs for which workers would have varying degrees of preference. This list was given to workers and managers all around the country. The workers were asked to rank the factors from most important to least important. The managers were asked to rank the factors the way they thought the workers would. Before reading further, take time to rank the items on this list by placing a 1 after the item that you think workers said was most important to them, a 2 after the item you think they ranked second, down to a 10 after the item you think the workers ranked last. Then compare your answers to those given at the end of the chapter.

You may find that your list was closer to that of supervisors in industry than to that of the workers themselves. Most students' lists are, because like many managers, they do not know the valences workers actually have for various qualities of the work environment.

Expectancy

A person's perception of the probability that a specific outcome will follow from a specific act is termed *expectancy*. For example, what is the likelihood that Bob will get a promotion to the New York office if he receives the highest efficiency rating in his department? If Bob thinks the chances are very good, he will assign a very high probability such as .99. If Bob believes the likelihood of the promotion is fair (efficiency ratings help, but it really depends most heavily on how well the boss likes you personally), he may assign it a probability of .50. Finally, if Bob believes the high efficiency rating will knock him out of consideration for the New York position (if you are that good they will keep you here rather than let you get away to New York), he will assign it a very low rating, such as .01.

Expectancy is the perceived probability that a specific outcome will follow a specific act.

People do not strive for goals they feel are unattainable. A man may have a high valence for saving $2 million in his lifetime. However, if his job pays only $300 a week, he will not be motivated toward accumulating this amount of money, because there is virtually no chance of reaching the goal. After taxes and living expenses, $300 a week may net the most frugal of people $150 a week, or $7,800 a year in savings. If he can save at this rate for 30 years, the gross savings would be $234,000, and with interest from tax-free municipal bonds or bank savings accounts, it might approach $500,000. Clearly the goal of $2 million should be beyond his expectations and he will have little motivation, if any, toward attaining it.

Motivational force

Motivation is a function of both valence and expectancy. One without the other will not produce motivation. This becomes clearer if we apply some illustrations to the expectancy theory formula. Also, let us use the term *motivational force* rather than just motivation, since force or effort is what we are interested in measuring. The formula is:

Motivational force = Valence × Expectancy

If either expectancy or valence is 0, the motivational force will be 0. Likewise, if one is high and the other is low, the motivational force will be low.

Let us take an example. The vice president of sales has just announced that the salesperson with the best sales record for next month will get an all-expenses-paid trip to Hawaii for two at Christmas. The three top salespeople are Charles, Fred, and Maureen. In order to determine each one's motivational force, we have to look at the valence and expectancy each has regarding the free trip.

Charles has a very high valence for his trip (valence = 1.0). He has never been to Hawaii, and he knows his wife would love to go. However, the last time the vice president made a promise like this he was overridden by the company comptroller, who said the firm could not afford to send two people to Paris for a week. Instead, the winner was given a check for $250. Charles remembers this incident vividly, since he was the winner. As a result, he believes that the possibility of the winner's going to Hawaii is good but not certain (expectancy = .5). We can determine Charles's motivational force as follows:

Motivational force $= V(1.0) \times E(.5) = .5$

Fred would also like to win the free trip to Hawaii. However, as luck would have it, Fred took his wife and family there four months ago for their vacation. Nevertheless, his valence for this trip is still quite high (valence = .7). Furthermore, while he also remembers that the vice president was prevented from awarding an all-expenses-paid trip last time, Fred believes that this time the contest was probably cleared with the company comptroller and that the winner will indeed travel to Hawaii (expectancy = .9). Fred's motivational force is the following:

Motivational force $= V(.7) \times E(.9) = .63$

Maureen is the only one who is not delighted with the prospect of the trip. Last week she and her fiance decided that their date for their wedding would be on December 22. They plan to spend the next two weeks honeymooning in Switzerland. The bridegroom's father has a chalet there, right near one of the finest ski resorts in the country. Maureen knows there is simply no way she can take the trip. As a result, she is indifferent about the prize (valence = 0), although she does believe that the winner will be sent to Hawaii (expectancy = 1.0). Her motivational force can be computed this way:

Motivational force $= V(0) \times E(1.0) = 0$

Of the three, Fred is most motivated toward attaining the highest sales record. A close look at the motivational force computations shows that he had neither the highest valence for the Hawaiian trip (Charles did) nor the highest expectancy (Maureen did). However, the *combination* of the two produced a greater motivational force than that for the others.

Expectancy theory and motivation

It is obvious that no manager is going to spend time trying to determine the motivational force of each worker for each objective. However, expectancy theory is helpful in understanding motivation, for several reasons.

First, the expectancy model urges us to look at motivation as a *force* or strength of drive directed toward some objective. As a result, we no longer consider *if* a person is motivated toward doing something, but *how great* the motivation may be. Just about every worker is motivated by money, but some workers are more highly motivated by it than others.

Second, although Maslow's need hierarchy can be applied to everyone in general, it really does not address *individual motivation* and its specific aspects. Expectancy theory does.

Third, the model suggests that people learn what kinds of rewards they like and dislike through *experience*. They also learn to determine the probabilities of their attaining these rewards. Thus, both valence and expectancy are a result of individual experiences, and what highly motivates one person may create no motivational force in another.

The expectancy model is helpful in understanding motivation.

Fourth, to a large extent, motivation is determined not only by rewards available but by their degree of *equity*. If a worker has a higher efficiency rating than anyone else in her department and everyone is given the same raise, she may well stop trying to be so efficient because higher efficiency does not pay off. This issue was indirectly covered in our discussion of valence (the valence for a high efficiency rating declines), but it warrants discussion here, since *equity theory* is a major topic in modern motivation theory.

Fifth, if we accept the expectancy model, it follows that to motivate an individual to work we can do only two things. First, we can increase the positive value of outcomes by increasing rewards. Second, we can strengthen the connection between the work and the outcomes.[8]

Finally, expectancy theory postulates the relationship between a person's valence and expectancy for a particular outcome and his or her satisfaction with this outcome. The relationship can be pictured as in Figure 2.14. Note that goal attainment leads to satisfaction. For example, if Fred wins the trip to Hawaii and is satisfied with the prize, what can we say about Fred's motivation in the future? Certainly it will be high any time the company offers rewards he desires. The same can be said for every other individual in the organization. In short, if people are motivated to attain given objectives and they succeed in their efforts, a "closed loop" is established: they are much more likely to continue to strive for desired objectives. When this process occurs over and over again, we have a highly motivated work force. The process depends, as we noted earlier, on making the desired rewards available to those who attain organizational goals.

---

[8]Davis, *op. cit.*, p. 67.

Figure 2.14
A model of expectancy theory

Valence × Expectancy → Motivational Force → Action toward the Goal → Goal Attainment → Job Satisfaction

Summary

In this chapter we examined the fundamentals of motivation. It was noted that motivation has two sides: movement and motive. The former can be seen and the latter can only be inferred. Yet motives are important, for they constitute the "whys" of behavior.

Motives are directed toward goals. That goal that has the highest motive strength is the one the person will attempt to satisfy through goal-directed behavior. Having satisfied that goal, the individual will then go on to the goal with the next highest motive strength.

In examining motives or needs in greater depth, we focused attention on Maslow's need hierarchy. The most fundamental of all needs, according to Maslow, are physiological ones, such as food, clothing, and shelter. When these are basically satisfied, safety needs replace them. Safety needs are of two types: survival and security. Next in the hierarchy are social needs, such as the desire for friendship, affection, and acceptance. The fourth level of the hierarchy contains esteem needs, such as the need to feel important and respected. Research shows that prestige and power are two motives closely related to the esteem need, and to the degree that these motives can be satisfied, the esteem need can be met. At the top of the hierarchy are self-actualization needs. Because people satisfy this need in so many different ways, behavioral scientists know less about it than the other four. However, research does reveal that there are two motives related to self-actualization: competence and achievement. If individuals can satisfy these motives, they can fulfill their drive for self-actualization.

Frederick Herzberg has also found that people desire upper-level need satisfaction. In his famous two-factor theory of motivation, he divided all job factors into two categories: hygiene factors and motivators. Into the former he placed those things that he found do not motivate people but stop them from becoming unmotivated: salary, technical supervision, working conditions, and interpersonal relations. Into the second category he grouped all the factors that motivate people to increase their contribution to the organization: recognition, advancement, the possibility of growth, and achievement. Herzberg contends that hygiene factors do not produce motivation but do prevent dissatisfaction. Conversely, motivators can give satisfaction but never give dissatisfaction. Today the two-factor theory is criticized as incomplete and erroneous. For example, some researchers report that money is a motivator for many people despite Herzberg's claim that it is a hygiene factor. Similarly, some researchers report that workers regard recognition and the chance for advancement as dissatisfiers. At best, then, the two-factor theory is a controversial approach.

The last part of the chapter examined expectancy theory, which holds that motivation can be expressed as the product of valence and expectancy. *Valence* is the measure of a person's preference for a particular outcome. *Expectancy* is the perceived probability that a specific outcome will follow from a specific act. By multiplying the values of valence and expectancy, one can arrive at a motivational force number; the higher the number, the greater the motivation.

Expectancy theory is very helpful in understanding motivation for several reasons. The expectancy model urges us to look at motivation as a force greater in some people than in others. The model suggests that valence and expectancy are a result of individual experiences, and what will highly motivate one person may create no motivational force in another. Expectancy theory makes it possible to study the issue of equity in motivation among specific individuals as opposed to examining general motivation of groups.

Key terms in the chapter

motivation	high achiever
motive	need mix
physiological needs	hygiene factors
safety needs	motivators
social needs	expectancy theory
esteem needs	valence
self-actualization needs	expectancy
prestige	motivational force
competence	equity theory
achievement	

Review and study questions

1. Motives are the "whys" of behavior. What does this statement mean?
2. How does motive strength determine goal-directed behavior? Explain.
3. What are physiological needs? Give some illustrations.
4. How important are safety needs to people just starting their busi-

ness careers? To top executives in large organizations? If your answers differ, what accounts for the difference?

5. How do people attempt to meet their social needs? Cite some examples.

6. Research shows that two motives related to esteem are prestige and power. What are these two motives, and how do people try to satisfy them?

7. One of the ways in which individuals try to satisfy the self-actualization need is through the development of competence. How do they go about doing this?

8. What are the characteristics of high achievers? How can high achievement drive be developed?

9. Maslow states that everyone in our society is partially satisfied at each level of the hierarchy and partially unsatisfied. What does he mean?

10. In your own words, what are some of the questionable aspects or concepts associated with the need hierarchy?

11. Of what value is the need hierarchy approach in the study of motivation?

12. In Herzberg's terms, what are hygiene factors? Give some illustrations.

13. In Herzberg's terms, what are motivators? Give some illustrations.

14. According to the two-factor theory, if you give people hygiene factors, you will not motivate them but you will prevent dissatisfaction. Conversely, if you give people motivators you may get satisfaction but you will never get dissatisfaction. What is meant by these two statements?

15. In what way did Herzberg apply Maslow's need hierarchy to the work place?

16. What are some of the major criticisms launched against the two-factor theory? Explain them.

17. The two major terms in expectancy theory are *valence* and *expectancy*. What is meant by each of these terms?

18. Using the expectancy theory formula, compute the motivational force for Mr. A, whose valence (V) is .8 and expectancy (E) is .7. Compute the motivational force for three other individuals who had the following respective valences and expectancies: Ms. B, $V=.7$, $E=.4$; Mr. C, $V=1$, $E=.5$; Ms. D, $V=.9$, $E=.5$. Which of the four has the greatest motivational force?

19. Of what value is expectancy theory in understanding the fundamentals of motivation? Explain.

Interpretation of What motivates you

Remember that you gave a 10 to the most important factor and a 1 to the least important factor. So high scores indicate greater motivating potential than low scores. With this in mind, fill in below the number you assigned to each of the 10 factors and then add both colums.

Column A

  _8_ **1.**   8   4   10
  _9_ **4.**   2   10   8
  _10_ **6.**   5   8   6
  _10_ **8.**   7   6
  _9_ **10.**   9   4
  _46_ **Total**   38   29

Column B

  _10_ **2.**   3   3   5
  _6_ **3.**   10   2   9
  _10_ **5.**   8   5   1
  _5_ **7.**   1   3
  _9_ **9.**   6   2
  _40_ **Total**   17   26

If your total in Column A is higher than that in Column B, you derive more satisfaction from the psychological side of your job than from the physical side. Notice that the five factors in Column A are designed to measure how you feel about the job. These factors are internal motivators. If your score in Column A is over 30, you are highly motivated to succeed and achieve at your current job. Individuals who are most successful in their careers have jobs with higher psychological value than physical value.

If your total in Column B is higher than that in Column A, you derive more satisfaction from the physical side of your job than from the psychological side. Notice that the five factors in Column B all relate to the environment in which you work or the pay you receive for doing this work. These factors are external to you and you have limited control over them. A score of 30 or more indicates that you do not particularly care for the job, but you do like the benefits the company is giving you. Most people who have a higher total in Column B than in Column A rank good wages as one of their top two choices. If you are under 40, it is likely that you will either be promoted to a job with greater psychological value or you will leave the organization. If you are over 40, you may find that your job mobility is reduced, the money is too good to pass up, and you will stay with the organization because of these financial rewards.

Interpretation of Figure 2.5[9]

1. If you chose A, it indicates you are achievement-oriented, and exhibitionistic, doing your best to attract attention to yourself by

[9]Reprinted with permission of PEI Books, Inc., from *Psycho-Decorating* by Margaret Harmon. Copyright 1977 by M. H. Harmon.

appearance, speech and manner. If you chose B, you are practical, nurturing and affiliation-oriented, sharing things with friends and forming attachments to them, assisting those less fortunate and giving moral support to others.

2. Again, A is indicative of orientation toward achievement. If you chose B, it indicates that you have become socialized, being conscientious and socially mature and endeavoring to fulfill your duties.

3. If you chose bud vase A, you are practical, socialized and tend toward abasement, feeling yourself blameworthy and inferior to others and experiencing timidity. If you chose bud vase B, you are achievement-oriented, dominant and have esthetic interests, interested in things related to music, art, literature and drama.

4. If you prefer lamp A, you are practical and tend toward self-abasement. If you prefer lamp B, you are dominant and tolerant, with permissive, accepting and nonjudgemental beliefs and attitudes.

5. Coffee table A is oval, the choice of people who need to help others and have a very active conscience—not achievers. Coffee table B is rectangular, the choice of people who like to achieve things and those who have a good deal of endurance; square corners seem to echo the firmness with which they control themselves and bring projects to the desired conclusion. Coffee table C, the circle, is the favored shape of people who enjoy receiving support from others; curves seem to reflect the wish to avoid rough edges in dealing with others.

Answers to Table 2.3

	As ranked by:	
	Workers	*Supervisors*
Job security	4	2
Full appreciation for work done	1	8
Promotion and growth with the company	7	3
Tactful disciplining	10	7
Good wages	5	1
Feeling "in" on things	2	10
Interesting work	6	5
Management loyalty to the workers	8	6
Good working conditions	9	4
Sympathetic understanding of personal problems	3	9

Why do people work?

Harry Barrett is the department manager of a well-known retail chain. Harry has been with his store for 23 years, but he has been passed over for promotion three times in the past five years. As a result, he will undoubtedly remain a department manager for the rest of his career.

This development does not greatly concern Harry. He believes that he does the best job he can, and if he is unable to be promoted any higher in the organization, that is all right with him. Some of Harry's friends, however, feel that Harry killed his chances of moving up by failing to understand human relations. They think Harry does not know how to manage his people very well.

One of their biggest complaints is that Harry misunderstands why people work. He believes that salary, working conditions, and security are the three most important objectives. One day during a coffee break with one of the other department managers, Harry remarked that people work only to make a living and then go home to enjoy their lives. The other manager claimed that this simply was not so. "People want more out of a job than just an opportunity to satisfy their psychological and safety needs," he told Harry. "They want to interact with other workers on the job, feel that what they are doing is important, and contribute to the overall good of the organization."

Harry disagreed with this point of view, claiming that his friend had been to too many management courses. "You know, ever since you started working on your master's degree in business, you've come out with some really wild ideas. I'll tell you this: I've been a department manager here for over 10 years and I certainly don't let people socialize on the job. When they are not selling, I want them standing around the counters, alert to the needs of any passing customer. If they get into conversations, they'll lose half their business. And as far as the rest of your ideas about doing important work and contributing to the organization's overall good, that's all philosophical nonsense. People work to make a living and that's all."

Having finished their coffee, the two men stood up to leave. "Harry," said his friend, "you've had the poorest performance record now for almost two years, and evaluations among your personnel reveal that you are considered below average. I've heard some of your workers say that you don't care anything about human relations."

"Oh, I've heard that stuff, too," Harry said. "It's all just sour grapes because I won't buckle under and let them get away with breaking the rules the way some other department managers do."

The two men then returned to their jobs.

Questions

1. What types of needs does Harry think people satisfy on the job?

2. What did the other manager mean when he said that people want more from a job than the opportunity to satisfy their physiological and safety needs?

3. In what way can Harry's beliefs help account for his department's performance? How could an understanding of Maslow's need hierarchy be of value to Harry? Explain.

What do you really want? [10]

Regardless of whom you ask, you are likely to get different answers to the question, "How satisfied are you with your job?" Nevertheless, *Psychology Today* (PT) has reported that what psychologists have been saying for some time is true—people work for a lot more than money. Personal satisfaction is also important. For example, when asked to rank 18 items in the order of their importance, respondents in a PT study gave the following answers:

Rank	Job Features
1	Chances to do something that makes you feel good about yourself
2	Chances to accomplish something worthwhile
3	Chances to learn new things
4	The opportunity to develop your skills and abilities
5	The amount of freedom you have on your job
6	The chances you have to do things you do best
7	The resources you have for doing your job
8	The respect you receive from people with whom you work
9	The amount of information you get about your job performance
10	Your chances for taking part in the making of decisions
11	The amount of job security you have
12	The amount of pay you get
13	The way you are treated by the people with whom you work
14	The friendliness of people with whom you work
15	The amount of praise you get for a job well done
16	The amount of fringe benefits you get
17	Chances for getting a promotion
18	The physical surroundings of the job

---

[10] Reprinted from *Psychology Today* Magazine, Copyright © 1978 Ziff-Davis Publishing Company.

Questions

1. Using the two-factor theory of motivation as your guide, decide where the motivators on this list are, at the top or bottom. Where are the hygiene factors?

2. Does the survey reported in this case support or refute Herzberg's two-factor theory? Explain your answer.

3. The amount of pay was ranked as number 12. How do you account for this? What might it tell you about the types of people who were surveyed in this study?

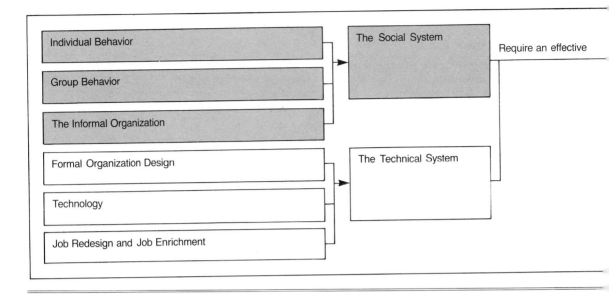

The social system

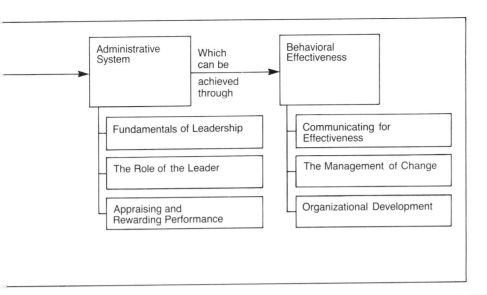

The overall objective of this part of the book is to study the *social system* of organizations. How and why do people act as they do? In answering this question we must explore three major areas: individual behavior, group behavior, and the informal organization. The individual is the primary unit of behavior in the work place, and studying workers one by one provides a basic understanding of worker behavior. However, it is really not possible to isolate the individual from the group. The individual influences the group and in turn is influenced by it. In short, group behavior is more than the sum of the behaviors of the members. Finally, we need to consider the informal organization. Sometimes people act as formal representatives of the organization, and at other times they resort to informal networks to "get things done." Study of the informal organization provides important insights into the dynamics of behavior in the work place. In this part of the book we examine all three of these areas.

In Chapter 3 we study individual behavior in organizations. We discuss some of the behavioral continua that can be used in describing the individual and then move on to the area of values and perceptions, examining how individual values influence a person's perception. Next we turn to other major components of individual behavior, including attitudes and personality. Finally, we examine some of the ways in which managers can improve their understanding of interpersonal behavior via an understanding of FIRO theory, transactional analysis, assertiveness training, and encounter groups.

Chapter 4 is concerned with group behavior. We define the term *group* and then describe the most common types of groups, including functional groups, project groups, and interest-friendship groups. From here we turn to the major characteristics of groups, including roles, norms, status, and cohesiveness. In particular we try to answer the question: "Are highly cohesive groups always high-producing groups?" Then we examine some of the benefits of group decision making vis-à-vis individual decision making, define the *risky-shift phenomenon*, and describe the ways in which this problem can be prevented. The next part of the chapter is concerned with the major factors upon which intergroup performance depends. The last part of the chapter is devoted to an examination of the role, functions, advantages, and disadvantages of committees and how committees can be effectively used in modern organizations. In our analysis of this area, we study some of the ways in which groups try to gain power over other groups and describe some of the strategies that managers can use in resolving intergroup conflict.

In Chapter 5 we examine the informal organization. We start by comparing and contrasting the formal and informal organizations. Then we describe the differences between authority and power and identify which is of greater importance in the informal organization. Next we discuss some of the controls used by members of the informal organization to ensure compliance with group norms. From here our attention is focused on the informal communication network: how it operates, some of the conditions under which people are most likely to be grapevine-active, and some of the primary benefits and disadvantages associated with the informal organization. In the last part of Chapter 5 we discuss some of the ways in which a manager can deal with the informal organization.

When you are finished reading Part II, you should have a solid understanding of human behavior at work. In particular, you should know a great deal about individual and group behavior in organizations and should be aware of how both individuals and groups use the informal organization to accomplish their objectives.

Individual behavior

3

Goals of the chapter

At the very heart of human relations is the need for an understanding of human behavior. In this chapter we examine this topic. The first goal of this chapter is to review the nature of individual behavior. The second goal is to study some of the major components of individual behavior, including values, perception, attitudes, and personality. The third goal is to examine some of the ways in which managers can improve their understanding of interpersonal behavior.

When you have finished reading this chapter, you should be able to:

1. discuss some of the common behavioral continua used in describing individual behavior
2. identify and describe some of the common values held by all individuals
3. describe the term *perception* and explain why it is a determinant of individual behavior
4. explain how stereotyping can influence a person's view of another's behavior
5. define *attitude*, explain its basic components, and describe its impact on worker output
6. define *personality* and discuss the major forces affecting personality development
7. describe how FIRO theory, transactional analysis, assertiveness training, and encounter groups can help both managers and subordinates improve their understanding of interpersonal behavior.

The nature of the individual

The individual is a complex being, but this complexity does not stop most people from trying to generalize about human behavior by summing up individuals with a descriptive cliché such as, "People are basically good," or "Everybody has his price; it's just a matter of how much." Some clichés are totally accurate, some partially accurate, and the rest erroneous. In human relations, however, we need to be much more scientific in our analysis of individuals and to realize that people are a *blend of many different types of behavior.* For example, sometimes people are very rational and at other times they are highly emotional; sometimes they are controlled by their environment and at other times they control their environment; sometimes they are interested in economic objectives and at other times they are more concerned with self-actualizing.

Continua of behavior

There are occasions when an individual is highly rational. When faced with a complex problem he or she will analyze all the available information, gather background and supplemental data for further understanding of the problem, determine the possible courses of action, and choose the one that offers the best cost-benefit ratio. On this occasion the individual is acting in a deliberate, serious, and highly computational manner. In fact, sometimes people like this scare us because they appear to be "computerized" and not sufficiently human. On the other end of this continuum is the emotional individual. Highly controlled by his or her unconscious drives, this person always seems to be "flying off the handle." The individual appears to have adjustment problems, is highly anxious and nervous, and never seems to have a moment of calm. We all know people like this and often find it hard to deal with them, because they seem incapable of slowing down and approaching a problem with the required amount of seriousness and deliberation. It seems that continual action is more important to them than careful thought.

Then there are people whose behaviors appear to have been shaped by their environment and who are unable to have any independent thought. When we observe them, they remind us of little children who are still being directed by their parents. They do not like a new challenge because it is too threatening. They want to stay with what is familiar. On the other end of this continuum are those people who are individuals in the true sense of the word. They seem always to control their own destiny and to have unlimited potential. People we admire often fit into this category, if only because we like to see them as models of hope and comfort. Far from being controlled by their environment, they shape the environment to their own needs and expectations.

Finally, we have the economic–self-actualizing continuum. On the one end are those people whom we judge to be motivated by money and

Figure 3.1
Continua of individual behavior

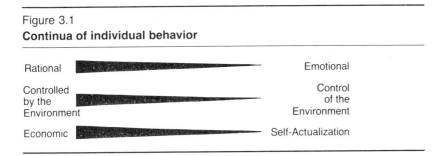

Rational	Emotional
Controlled by the Environment	Control of the Environment
Economic	Self-Actualization

low-level need satisfiers. On the other end are those people we judge to be seeking the opportunity to grow, mature, and become all they are capable of becoming.

The three continua we have described here can be presented as in Figure 3.1. If you choose some people you know fairly well and try to place them on these three continua, none of them will be at the extreme left or right in every case. In fact, just about every one of them, every time, will be closer to the middle. Additionally, most of them will be on the left of the continua in two cases and on the right side in the third case. For example, many people who are considered highly rational and calm (left side) are also seen as in control of their environment (right side) and more interested in self-actualization than in economic rewards (right side).

In any examination of individual behavior, therefore, we have to look at the *total person*. This requires an examination of the major components of individual behavior. The four major components that merit our attention are: values, perceptions, attitudes, and personality.

Values

A *value* is something that has worth or importance to an individual. As such, values help shape human behavior. Although many lists of values have been compiled, one of the shortest and yet most complete is that of Edward Spranger, who identified six values: theoretical, economic, aesthetic, social, political, and religious (Figure 3.2).

Different occupational groups tend to have different value profiles. For example, professors of biology tend to be highest in theoretical interests; business people have very high economic values; artists place great significance on aesthetic values; social workers have high social values; politicians have strong political values; and members of the clergy hold high religious values. However, to some degree, each of these values is present within and important to each one of us. We must remember that what may be important to the management is *not* necessarily important

A value is something that has worth or importance to an individual.

Figure 3.2
Spranger's value types

Theoretical.

The overriding interest of the theoretical person is the discovery of *truth*. In pursuing this goal the person often looks for identities and differences, trying to divest himself or herself of judgments regarding the beauty or utility of objects. The chief aim in life of this person is to systematize and order knowledge.

Economic.

The economic person is basically interested in what is *useful*. In addition to self-preservation, the person is concerned with the production of goods and services and the accumulation of wealth. The individual is thoroughly practical and conforms well to the prevailing stereotype of the American business person.

Aesthetic.

The aesthetic person sees highest value in *form* and *harmony*. While not necessarily an artist, the individual's chief interest is in the artistic episodes of life. For example, aesthetic people often like the beautiful insignia of pomp and power but oppose political activity that represses individual thought.

Social.

The highest value for the social person is *love* of people. This individual prizes other people as ends and is as a result kind, sympathetic, and unselfish. The social person regards love itself as the only suitable form of human relationship. This person's interests are very close to those of the religious person.

Political.

The political person is interested primarily in *power*. This individual need not be a politician. Since competition and struggle play a large part in all life, he or she will do well in any career or job in which a high power value is necessary for success, whether this be power over the people (as in the case of a top manager) or the environment (as in the case of an engineer who makes the final decision on how to build something).

Religious.

The highest value for the religious person is *unity*. This individual seeks to relate himself or herself to the embracing totality of the cosmos. For some there is an attempt to withdraw from active association with the outside world (as in the case of monks in a monastery); for others there is some self-denial and meditation coupled with a life of work among the local people who attend their church or subscribe to the same religious beliefs.

---

to the "rank and file." For this reason, values are of major importance in the study of human relations. This is clearly seen by an examination of modern employee values.

Modern employee values

Over the last two decades employee values have changed, and they are still in a state of flux. Much of this change has been indirectly explained in Chapter 2, which noted that motivators have greater impact on employee performance than hygiene factors. A recent study by researchers at the Opinion Research Corporation has found that over the last 25 years there has been a major shift in the attitudes and values of the American work force. The six major findings of the study were the following:

1. There is a consistent difference of opinion expressed by employees at many levels in the organization. We call this consistent difference, in which managers are usually more satisfied than are clerical and hourly employees, the "hierarchy gap." This gap is usually greatest between managers and hourly employees.

2. Most employees agree that their company is not as good a place to work as it once was.

3. Discontent among hourly and clerical employees seems to be growing. The distinctions that once clearly separated clerical and hourly employees are becoming blurred. Both groups value and expect to get intrinsic satisfaction from work. . . . all parts of the work force are beginning to overtly articulate their needs for achievement, recognition, and job challenge.

4. Most employees rate their pay favorably. However, hourly and clerical employees' satisfaction with pay does not offset either their high level of job dissatisfaction or their feeling that they are not treated with respect as individuals.

5. There is a downward trend in employees' ratings of the equity with which they are treated. In addition, expectations of advancement are the lowest they have ever been.

6. Employees increasingly expect their companies to do something about their problems and complaints; yet fewer than a fourth of the hourly and clerical employees surveyed rate their companies favorably on this issue.[1]

Changes in employee values.

These value changes can be attributed to many different factors. One is the affluence of America. Now that most people's basic needs are addressed, they are looking for ways to satisfy their high-level needs. A second is that individuals today are coming to believe that quality of life is just as important as is the acquisition of material things. The result, again, is an emphasis on the need for esteem and self-actualization satisfiers. When we examine individual behavior in the work place, it becomes obvious that the values of workers during the 1950s were quite different from those of the 1980s.

---

[1]M. R. Cooper, B. S. Morgan, P. M. Foley, and L. B. Kaplan, "Changing Employee Values: Deepening Discontent?" *Harvard Business Review*, January–February 1979, pp. 117–118.

Perception

Perception is a person's view of reality.

Perception is a person's view of reality, and it is affected by, among other things, the individual's values. For example, if the person is a member of a union, he or she may discount much of what management says about declining sales, decreased profit margins, and the need for the union and management to work as a team. Most of this talk may be regarded as an attempt by management to exploit the work force for its own gain. Conversely, many people in management admit that they have a hard time understanding the union's point of view, because they believe that the union is more interested in "ripping off" the company than in working for the overall good of both groups. This is an example of a common situation in which each person agrees with his or her own group's point of view but regards the other group's point of view as incorrect or biased. Human relationists call this *selective perception.* In order to understand why individuals perceive things differently, it is helpful to compare sensory reality and normative reality.

Sensory reality and normative reality

Sensory reality is physical reality.

Sensory reality is physical reality. A typewriter, an automobile, and a house are all physical objects that people tend to perceive accurately. However, sometimes physical items present perception problems. Before you read any further, examine the pictures in Figure 3.3 and answer the question accompanying each.

In Figure 3.3*A*, the two lines are the same length, although most people think that the lower line is longer than the upper one. This perceptual illusion is created by the two diagonal lines at the ends of each line, which make it seem stretched or compressed. In Figure 3.3*B*, the two lines running across the picture are horizontal, although most people think that the lines bend in at the end. This illusion is a result of the diagonal background lines, which seem to be bowing the center parts of the horizontal lines outward.

Normative reality is interpretive reality.

In Figure 3.3*C* we are moving away from sensory reality and toward **normative reality**, which is best defined as interpretive reality. In the first two pictures in Figure 3.3, there was a right answer, whether you saw it there or not. You can verify the answers by simply using a ruler to measure the lines or the distance between them. There is *more* than one right answer in Figure 3.3*C*, however, and what one person sees another may not. This is why we call it interpretive reality. Some people see a goblet in this picture; others see the facial profiles of twins, facing each other.

The picture in Figure 3.3*D* is deliberately ambiguous. Some people see a road, a rock, a tree and some surrounding terrain. Others see the face of a pirate. Still others see a rabbit. Look at Figure 3.4, in which the clear pictures of the pirate and the rabbit can be seen. Note that the am-

Figure 3.3

The perceptual processes (1. From Robert Leeper, "A Study of a Neglected Portion of the Field of Learning—the Development of Sensory Organization," *Pedagogical Seminary and Journal of Genetic Psychology*, **March 1935, p. 62. 2. From Edwin G. Boring, "A New Ambiguous Figure,"** *American Journal of Psychology*, **July 1930, p. 444. See also Robert Leeper (no. 1 above). Originally drawn by Cartoonist W. E. Hill and published in** *Puck*, **November 6, 1915.)**

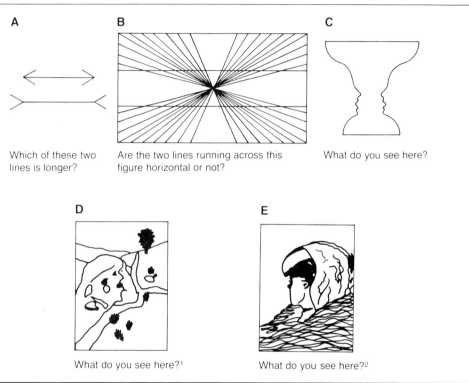

A

Which of these two lines is longer?

B

Are the two lines running across this figure horizontal or not?

C

What do you see here?

D

What do you see here?[1]

E

What do you see here?[2]

biguity is reduced if the artist puts more detail in one part of the picture than in the other.

Figure 3.3E is also a deliberately ambiguous picture. Some people see an old lady; some see a young lady. Figure 3.5 is a clear picture of both. Once again, the artist has reduced the ambiguity by putting in the necessary detail.

When we examine individual behavior and the impact of perception on that behavior, it is important to remember that people see what they either *want* to see or *are trained* to see. Therefore, in terms of human relations, the manager must try to understand the worker's perception of reality. Personnel willingly accept management's methods only when they perceive those methods to be in their best interests. Otherwise, they will resort to such perceptual pitfalls as selective perception, which we just examined, and stereotyping. For example, Harvey Lester, a

Figure 3.4
The pirate and the rabbit (From Robert Leeper, "A Study of a Neglected Portion of the Field of Learning—the Development of Sensory Organization," *Pedagogical Seminary and Journal of Genetic Psychology*, **March 1935, p. 62.)**

Pirate

Rabbit

Figure 3.5
The old woman and the young woman (From Robert Leeper, "A Study of a Neglected Portion of the Field of Learning—the Development of Sensory Organization," *Pedagogical Seminary and Journal of Genetic Psychology*, **March 1935, p. 62.)**

Old Woman

Young Woman

new employee, has been having trouble mastering his new job. His boss, Lois, tells him that if he does not improve she will have to let him go. Feeling that he is on the verge of being fired, Harvey quits. What Lois saw as a mild reprimand designed to improve output is interpreted as a threat resulting in a resignation. Each party interpreted the action differently.

Stereotyping

One of the most common perception problems is that of ***stereotyping***, which is generalizing a particular trait or behavior to all members of a given group. The manager who believes that no union can be trusted has a stereotyped view of unions. The worker who believes that management is always out to exploit the personnel also has a stereotyped belief.

Every one of us tries to stereotype people, whether it be in the job environment or in a social setting. We even have standard stereotypes for classes or nationalities. Read the following descriptions and try to identify the nationality described.

These people are loyal to family ties and always look after their younger brothers and sisters.

These people believe in fair play, are conservative, and keep a stiff upper lip.

These people are very scientific, industrious, and hard working.

These people love caviar, Bolshoi dancing, and music by Tchaikovsky.

These people love pasta, wine and, most of all, great opera.

Some typical stereotypes.

Most people say that the first description is that of the Chinese and the second is that of the English. The remaining three are German, Russian, and Italian. To some degree all these stereotypes are both accurate and inaccurate. For example, in regard to the first description, are not most people loyal to family ties? In regard to the second description, is Britain the *only* country in which fair play is important? And is Germany the *most* scientific and industrious of all nations? Research shows that most people of the world attribute these traits not to the Germans but to the Americans! The last two descriptions are also stereotypes, because they do not describe one group to the exclusion of all others.

In examining individual behavior, then, it is important to realize that most people employ stereotyping. It is an easy way to generalize about behavior. The effective manager, however, tries to evaluate each person as an individual and to remain aware of his or her own stereotypical beliefs so as to reduce their effect on his or her judgments.

Attitudes

Attitudes are a person's feelings about objects, activities, events, and other people. These feelings are usually learned over a period of time and are a major factor in determining individual behavior.

Components of attitudes

There are three basic components of attitudes: affective, cognitive, and conative. Each plays a major role in attitude formation.

The *affective component* is the emotional feeling that is attached to an attitude. It commonly refers to whether we like or dislike, love or hate, or are happy or sad about the attitude object.

The *cognitive component* refers to the beliefs a person has toward the object or event. Do you believe that your boss is out to get you,

The three components of attitudes.

that the union is self-serving, or that the company is more interested in profit than in people? Answers to such questions determine your attitude toward these objects.

The *conative component* is the behavior a person exhibits toward the attitude object. If you like your boss (have a positive attitude toward him or her), you will say nice things about the individual. If you enjoy your human relations course, you will show up for class and participate when asked to do so.

In the final analysis, attitudes are important because they lead to certain actions. If these attitudes are positive, the organization should benefit; if they are negative, the organization may not. For this reason, many organizations are interested in both measuring and monitoring the attitudes of their people.

Attitude measurement

One way of measuring attitudes is through the use of an *attitude questionnaire*. Figure 3.6 is an example of such an instrument.

Attitude questionnaires are important for several reasons. First, they reflect the attitudes current in the organization. Second, they provide a baseline against which to compare future attitude surveys. (Are attitudes improving or declining?) Third, they serve as a source of infor-

---

Figure 3.6
Attitude questionnaire (partial form)

Please fill out this questionnaire using the following numbers:
1 = Strongly agree
2 = Moderately agree
3 = Neither agree or disagree
4 = Moderately disagree
5 = Strongly disagree.
_____ Working conditions here are good.
_____ The pay is adequate.
_____ The fringe benefit program is better than in most other firms.
_____ My boss gives me credit and praise for a job well done.
_____ If I have a complaint to make, I feel free to talk to someone up the line.
_____ The management encourages suggestions for improvement.
_____ I feel I really belong in this organization.
_____ The people I work with and I all get along well together.
_____ Management is interested in the welfare of the workers.
_____ People who get promotions in this firm usually deserve them.
_____ My job is very interesting.
_____ My boss lives up to his/her promises.
_____ I know where I stand with my boss.
_____ My job seems to be leading to the kind of future I want.
_____ I am proud to work for this organization.

"*Come now, Mr. Hillman—everybody can't have a happy ending.*"

Drawing by Saxon; © 1982
The New Yorker Magazine, Inc.

Figure 3.7
Attitudes as an intervening variable

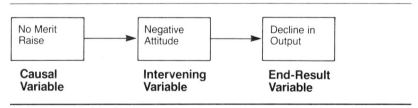

mation about what areas or issues the organization needs to pay greater attention to and where everything is all right.

In particular, the organization needs to realize that attitudes are an **intervening variable**. In order for an individual's attitude to decline, there must be some *cause*, such as a change in leadership style, a failure to get a merit raise, or the submission of a poor performance appraisal. This cause brings about a change in attitude which then results in a decline in output. We can diagram it as in Figure 3.7.

Attitudes are an intervening variable.

Conversely, if attitudes improve because the person is given a merit raise or is told how to obtain a merit raise in the future, his or her output increases.

Attitudes are internal. They cannot be seen; they can only be inferred through such end-result variables as output and can be measured by means of attitude surveys. Attention to attitudes, therefore, can be one of the keys to increasing productivity, because how a person feels about the organization will effect his or her output.

Personality

Personality defined.

Personality can be defined as a relatively stable set of characteristics and tendencies that determine similarities and differences between people. For example, some people are very outgoing while others tend to be introverted. Some are assertive while others are passive. Every individual has a different personality, which we can think of as a composite of all the person's behavioral components as reflected in how he or she acts.

Sometimes we try to generalize about an individual's overall personality by calling him or her aggressive, hostile, kind, easygoing, or warm. These adjectives are all designed to categorize the person in a word or two; although this may be an incomplete way of describing someone, we all tend to do it. Likewise, most of us look at the way a person walks, talks, and dresses in seeking clues to his or her personality.

Quite obviously, personality consists of *many* factors, making it very difficult to define the term. Psychologists, however, tend to accept certain ideas about personality:

Facts about personality.

1. **Personality is an organized whole; otherwise the individual would have no meaning.**
2. **Personality appears to be organized into patterns. These are to some degree observable and measurable.**
3. **Although there is a biological basis to personality, the specific development is a product of social and cultural environments.**
4. **Personality has superficial aspects, such as attitudes toward a team leader, and a deeper care, such as sentiments about authority, or the Protestant work ethic.**
5. **Personality involves both common and unique characteristics. Every person is different from every other person in some respects, while being similar in other respects.**[2]

Major forces affecting personality

What accounts for differences in personality? Four major forces can be cited as directly affecting personality development: heredity, culture, social class, and family relationships (Figure 3.8).

---

[2] James L. Gibson, John M. Ivancevich, and James H. Donnelly, Jr., *Organizations: Behavior, Structure, Processes*, 4th ed. (Dallas: Business Publications, Inc., 1982), pp. 56–57.

Figure 3.8
Major factors influencing personality

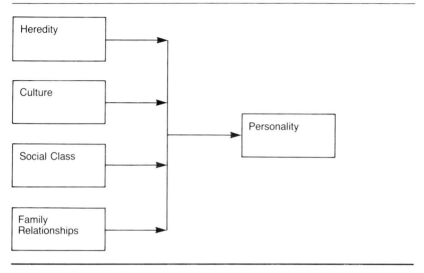

Heredity affects personality because people are born with certain physical characteristics. Intelligence, height, and facial features are all inherited. The person who is highly intelligent may be arrogant toward fellow students; the tall boy may be quiet because he feels awkward; the short boy may compensate for his size by being aggressive in his dealings with others.

Culture is important in that the values and beliefs of the society in which one is raised help determine how a person will act. A society that puts great value on money will be different from one in which leisure is emphasized over work. A society in which education is believed to be important will be substantially different from one in which education is frowned upon.

Social class helps shape personality because an individual's mores are heavily influenced by his or her neighborhood and community life. This social class also affects the individual's self-image, perception of others, and assumptions about authority, work, and money. A manager who wants to understand how people adjust to the demands of organizational life must consider these social class factors.

The four major factors that affect personality.

Family relationships influence personality by rewarding the person for certain behaviors and by not rewarding him or her for others. These actions help shape a pattern of behavior and serve as a basis for interpersonal relations outside the home.

Each of these four factors influences behavior, and the manager has little control over them. This is not to say that the superior cannot direct, channel, or reorient the individual's behavior. This can be done by using the motivational concepts we discussed in Chapter 2. However, unless the manager understands the bases for individual behavior, he or she will have great difficulty managing it.

Interpersonal behavior

Values, perceptions, attitudes, and personality are all important components of individual behavior. However, no one lives in a vacuum. People interact with other people. In fact, this is how we develop values, perceptions, attitudes, and, to a large degree, personality. Before finishing our discussion of individual behavior, therefore, we should examine this area of interpersonal behavior. We will do so by first studying the types of interpersonal needs people have and then looking at how the manager can interrelate with the employees on an interpersonal basis.

FIRO theory

FIRO helps examine individual needs.

One way of studying interpersonal relations is to examine an individual's need for such things as inclusion, control, and affection. Schutz's FIRO (Fundamental Interpersonal Relations Orientation) theory provides just such an approach for looking at these interpersonal interactions. At the heart of this theory is the assumption that all interpersonal behavior is aimed at satisfying one or more of these three interpersonal needs.[3]

The *inclusion need* is the need to establish and maintain a satisfactory relationship with people in regard to interaction and association. It represents the need to belong to a group, to associate with and to be accepted by others. This behavior often takes the form of joining a group or doing something to call attention to oneself, such as being the noisiest person in the classroom. As can be seen in Table 3.1, this interpersonal need can be either expressed or desired. In expressing an inclusion need, the person joins a group; in desiring inclusion, the individual undertakes attention-getting behavior because of a need to be included in the group. Finally, we should note that although some people have high expressed or desired needs to be included, others have low inclusion needs and *do not* want to be part of a group. In this case they do not initiate interaction with others. If they are loud or boisterous, it is to communicate to others that they do not wish to be included in any activities. This action is part of desired behavior (see Table 3.1), which is that behavior the individual wants others to initiate toward him or her.

The *control need* is the need to establish and maintain a satisfactory relationship with people in regard to power and authority. Control behavior refers to decision making and to the exercise of power. The interpersonal need can be either expressed or desired. If control need is

[3]William C. Schutz, *Interpersonal Underworld* (Palo Alto, California: Science and Behavior Books, 1967); *A Three-Dimensional Theory of Interpersonal Relations* (New York: Holt, Rinehart and Winston, 1958).

Table 3.1
FIRO—description of needs

Interpersonal Needs	Behavioral Expression	
	Expressed (Behavior you initiate or express to others)	**Desired** (Behavior you want others to initiate or express to you)
Inclusion needs	High: You want to initiate interaction with other people.	High: You need to be included by other people.
	Low: You do not want to initiate interaction with other people.	Low: You do not need to be included by other people.
Control needs	High: You need to control other people.	High: You want other people to control you.
	Low: You do not need to control other people.	Low: You do not want other people to control you.
Affection needs	High: You want to act close and personal to other people.	High: You want other people to act close and personal to you.
	Low: You do not want to act close and personal to other people.	Low: You do not want other people to act close and personal to you.

high, the person wants to control others (expressed) or to be controlled by them (desired). If control need is low, however, the person will want neither to control others nor to be controlled by them.

The ***affection need*** focuses on establishing and maintaining satisfactory relations with others in terms of love and friendship. A person with high expressed affection needs will want to act close and personal to others, but a person with high desired affection needs will want other people to act that way to him or her. Conversely, an individual with low affection needs will want neither to act close and personal to others nor to have others act that way to him or her.

To draw together these three needs into a meaningful composite, a simple analogy can be used. Consider a group of people who have rented a bus. The first issue to be resolved is that of inclusion: Who will ride the bus? The second issue is control. Who will drive the bus? The third issue is affection: Who will sit next to whom, and who will be in the immediately surrounding seats?

Schutz's FIRO theory is designed to help managers understand the interpersonal behaviors of their people (as well as themselves). In a manner of speaking, the theory assists the manager in determining why the subordinate is acting in a given manner. What expressed or implied needs does the individual have?

Transactional analysis

Another interpersonal approach that has gained popularity in recent years is transactional analysis. Although simple to comprehend, this method of analyzing and evaluating interpersonal communications is proving valuable to many organizational managers who want a better understanding of interpersonal behavior.

Transactional analysis (TA) involves the study of social transactions between people. At the heart of TA is a concern for three behavioral patterns known as *ego states*: child, parent, and adult.

Child ego state   Each of us has a little child within him or her. When in this state we are likely to sit, stand, walk, think, and feel as we did when we were children. Common facial expressions include pouting, broad grins, twinkling eyes, mischievous winks, and comic distortions. Voice tones are often loud, full of feeling, joyful, whining, or cute. Typical demeanors include playfulness, selfishness, intuitiveness, and creativity. When in the child state, we tend to be spontaneous, open, and happy. An example of a child ego state interaction is:

> **Fred: "I wish I could take off work tomorrow and play golf."**
>
> **Ernie: "Let's call in sick tomorrow and go over to the country club."**

Parent ego state   Parents serve as models for their children's behavior. When in this state we are likely to think, feel, and act as parents. These behaviors are sometimes supportive and sometimes critical. Common facial expressions include smiling, beaming, and winking or nodding (when being supportive), and resting hand on hips, pointing an accusing finger, and pounding the fist (when being critical). Voice tones reflect encouragement, warmth, and friendliness (when being supportive) and accusing, lecturing, and scolding (when being critical). Typical demeanors include teaching, coaching, and being protective (when being supportive), and being bossy, moralistic, and very proper (when being critical). An example of a supportive parent ego state transaction is:

> **Marie: "I told Nancy to go home and I'd cover for her."**
>
> **Gladys: "Poor thing; she hasn't felt well for a week."**

An example of a critical parent ego state transaction is:

> **Frank: "My secretary Nancy went home ill again today; she's so undependable."**
>
> **Bob: "What can you expect from women?"**

Adult ego state   The adult ego state deals objectively with reality. Problem solving and rational thinking are products of the adult ego state. This state is related not to age but to education and experience. When activated, the adult ego state enables a person to collect and organize information, predict the possible consequences of various actions, and make conscious decisions. By using the adult ego state, a person can help minimize regrettable actions and increase his or her potential for success. Common facial expressions indicate alertness, thoughtful attention, and self assurance. Voice tones are controlled, judicious, and confident.

Typical demeanors include listening, attentiveness, and concentration. An example of an adult ego state interaction is:

David: "What is the annual salary of this job?"

Patricia: "It starts at $15,000."

Types of transactions

These three ego states serve as a basis for analyzing interpersonal transactions. For our purposes, there are two types that merit consideration: complementary and crossed. A ***complementary transaction*** is one that progresses along expected lines. A ***crossed transaction*** is one that does not progress along expected lines. Figures 3.9 through 3.12 illus-

---

Figure 3.9
A complementary transaction

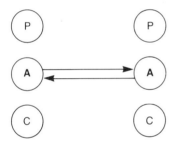

Bob: Where are those cost reports you want me to fill out?   **Boss:** Here they are in the big yellow envelope.

Figure 3.10
A complementary transaction

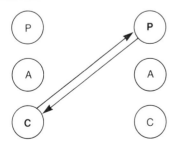

Bob: Boy, I'm beat. Those reports are time consuming.   **Boss:** I know what you mean. Go home now, you can finish up tomorrow.

Figure 3.11
A crossed transaction

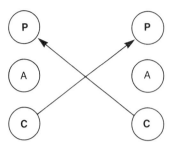

Mary: I feel sick.
Can I go home?

Boss: Oh, brother,
not again. You're
always feeling sick.

Figure 3.12
A crossed transaction

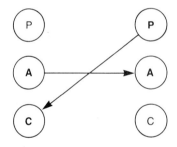

Mary: I'm sorry
I'm late. I was
delayed in another
meeting.

Boss: If you can't
get here on time,
Mary, send a sub-
stitute so the rest
of us aren't delayed.

trate two examples of each type. Note that in the complementary transactions the manager understands human relations and adopts the right
ego states. When the subordinate asks an adult question, the boss answers as an adult. When the subordinate adopts the child ego state and
talks to the manager as a parent, the boss responds as a parent addressing
a child.

If the manager does not choose the right ego state, a crossed transaction can occur, and interpersonal problems are likely. For this reason
the manager needs to understand transactional analysis and, where possible, to try to communicate with the personnel on an adult-to-adult
basis. Harris, one of the leading proponents of TA, offers the following
guidelines:

1. **Learn to recognize your child, its vulnerabilities, its fears, its principal methods of expressing these feelings.**
2. **Learn to recognize your parent, its admonitions, injunctions, fixed positions, and principal ways of expressing these admonitions, injunctions, and positions.**
3. **Be sensitive to the child in others, talk to that child, stroke that child, protect that child, and appreciate its need for creative expression. . . .**
4. **Count to ten, if necessary, in order to give the adult time to process the data coming into the computer, to sort out parent and child from reality.**[4]

TA guidelines.

Life positions

Another significant aspect of TA is the concept of life positions. Early in life individuals develop dominant ways of relating to others. These ways remain with the person, creating a life position, unless some major experience occurs to change it. So while the person may exhibit any of the four life positions we are about to describe, one will be dominant.

Life positions stem from two viewpoints: how a person views himself or herself and how the individual views others. There are two basic views, OK and not OK. These create four possible life positions:

I'm not OK–You're OK

I'm not OK–You're not OK

I'm OK–You're not OK

I'm OK–You're OK

These four positions are shown in Figure 3.13. The most desirable one and the one that involves the greatest likelihood of adult-to-adult transactions is the I'm OK—You're OK life position. This position reveals a healthy acceptance of oneself and of others. Through TA and other interpersonal approaches, one can learn to adopt this desirable life position.

Stroking

Stroking is a third key concept tied to TA. ***Stroking*** is "any act implying recognition of another's presence."[5] This applies to all types of recognition from a pat on the back (physical) to a kind word (psychological). If the stroke makes a person feel good, it is called a positive stroke; if it

---

[4] Thomas A. Harris, *I'm OK–You're OK: A Practical Guide to Transactional Analysis* (New York: Harper & Row, Publishers, 1966), pp. 95–96.

[5] Eric Berne, *Games People Play* (New York: Grove Press, Inc., 1964), p. 15.

Figure 3.13
Life positions

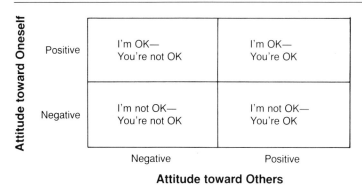

hurts the individual physically or psychologically, it is called a negative stroke.

Many people seek positive strokes. They want praise and recognition. However, when individuals feel guilty or have a poor self-image (they are "not OK" about themselves), they seek negative strokes. These strokes serve to restore balance in their mind, i.e., I deserved to be punished and I was.

The effective manager tries to show subordinates why they do not need to feel guilty. The manager urges them to adopt an I'm OK—You're OK lifestyle and gives them positive strokes for doing so.

Assertiveness training

Another way to develop improved interpersonal relations is with assertiveness training. The purpose of such training is to teach people appropriate ways of asserting themselves in work and social situations. The goals of the training are threefold:

The goals of the training are threefold.

1. the individual is taught how to determine personal feelings;
2. the person learns how to say what he or she wants;
3. the individual learns how to get what he or she wants.

Assertiveness training can be particularly helpful for those individuals who are bottling up too much inside themselves; they are becoming so uptight that psychologically they are going to explode. Before reading on, test how uptight *you* are.

How uptight are you?

The following descriptive statements are designed to measure how uptight you are. The interpretation of your quiz can be found at the end of the chapter. Circle the appropriate number (1–4) for each of the following statements. Then total your score.

	None or a little of the time	Some of the time	Good part of the time	Most or all of the time
1. I prefer things to be done my way.	1	2	(3)	4
2. I am critical of people who don't live up to my standards or expectations.	1	(2)	3	4
3. I stick to my principles, no matter what.	1	(2)	3	4
4. I am upset by changes in the environment or the behavior of people.	1	(2)	3	4
5. I am meticulous and fussy about my possessions.	1	2	(3)	4
6. I get upset if I don't finish a task.	(1)	2	(3)	4
7. I insist on full value for everything I purchase.	1	2	(3)	4
8. I like everything I do to be perfect.	1	2	(3)	4
9. I follow an exact routine for everyday tasks.	1	2	(3)	4
10. I do things precisely to the last detail.	1	2	3	(4)
11. I get tense when my day's schedule is upset.	1	(2)	3	4
12. I plan my time so that I won't be late.	1	2	(3)	4
13. It bothers me when my surroundings are not clean.	1	2	(3)	4
14. I make lists for my activities.	(1)	2	3	4
15. I think that I worry about minor aches and pains.	(1)	2	3	4
16. I like to be prepared for any emergency.	1	2	3	(4)
17. I am strict about fulfilling every one of my obligations.	1	2	3	(4)
18. I think that I expect worthy moral standards in others.	1	2	(3)	4
19. I am badly shaken when someone takes advantage of me.	1	(2)	3	4
20. I get upset when people do not replace things exactly as I left them.	1	2	3	(4)
21. I keep used or old things because they might still be useful.	1	2	3	(4)
22. I think that I am sexually inhibited.	(1)	2	3	4
23. I find myself working rather than relaxing.	1	2	(3)	4
24. I prefer being a private person.	1	2	(3)	4
25. I like to budget myself carefully and live on a cash basis.	1	2	(3)	4
Total score	3	10	36	20

Reprinted with permission of Barbara M. Weinel, Greenville Technical College, Greenville, South Carolina.

Passive, aggressive and assertive behavior. The term *assertiveness training* is something of a misnomer since the word *assertive* often conjures up thoughts of pushiness or belligerence. However, this is not what the term means. Actually, in assertiveness training the objective is to teach the individual how to make a clear statement of personal desires without being obnoxious or abusive. This can be made clear with an example. Consider the case of Mary Harrison, who has been asked to meet an incoming job applicant at the airport first thing in the morning, show the individual around the organization, make sure the person gets to all of his scheduled interviews, and see that he gets back to the airport on time for his departure flight. Mary does not want to take on this assignment because she is snowed under with work. There are three types of behavior available to her in responding to the situation: passive, aggressive, and assertive. Here is how each response would be used by Mary.

Passive: Mary is angry and really wants to tell her boss off. However, she grits her teeth, puts her work aside, and makes plans to get to the airport on time.

Aggressive: Mary tells her boss, "Hell, I'm not going to do that. I'm up to my nose in work. Get someone else who is not that important. I'm not going to be treated like this, so don't ask me to do it again."

Assertive: Mary says to her boss, "I appreciate your thinking of me, but I'm really snowed under with work. I don't have the time to do this. However, I don't think you'll have any trouble getting someone. There are a number of people in the department who have light work loads this week."

Notice that when using assertive behavior Mary employed an adult-to-adult TA transaction. She stood her ground without being rude or discourteous.

Becoming more assertive. How can an individual increase his or her assertiveness? Over the last decade many assertiveness-training programs have been offered by both organizations (for their own personnel) and professional consultants and trainers (for organizational personnel and the general public). While these various workshops employ different techniques for improving individual assertiveness, there are a series of basic steps that every participant should know. Phrased in the form of questions, the list includes the following:

1. Clarify the situation and focus on the issue. What is my goal? What exactly do I want to accomplish?

2. How will assertive behavior on my part help me accomplish my goal?

3. What would I usually do to avoid asserting myself in this situation?

4. Why would I want to give that up and assert myself instead?

Key questions for becoming more assertive.

5. What might be stopping me from asserting myself?
   a. Am I holding on to irrational beliefs? If so, what are they?

     b. How can I replace these irrational beliefs with rational ones?

     c. (For women only) Have I, as a woman, been taught to behave in ways that make it difficult for me to act assertively in the present situation? What ways? How can I overcome this?

     d. What are my rights in this situation? (State them clearly.) Do these rights justify turning my back on my conditioning?

6. Am I anxious about asserting myself? What techniques can I use to reduce my anxiety?

7. Have I done my homework? Do I have the information I need to go ahead and act?

8. Can I

     a. Let the other person know I hear and understand him/her?

     b. Let the other person know how I feel?

     c. Tell him/her what I want?[6]

Encounter groups

A third way in which to improve one's interpersonal skills is by attending an encounter group. During the last two decades, millions of people have participated in some form of encounter group in an effort to learn more about themselves in relation to others. Encounter groups take many forms including personal growth laboratories, marathon groups, interpersonal effectiveness laboratories, and Esalen groups. The most popular form of encounter group is the T–group, which will be the focus of our attention here. Before discussing how T–groups work, however, it is important to point out that there are a few consistent purposes desired by both encounter group participants and group leaders. Five of these are the following:

1. make participants more sensitive to how they are perceived by others and how their behavior affects others

2. help participants become more aware of their own feelings and how these feelings influence behavior

Objectives of encounter groups.

3. assist participants in achieving a deeper self-understanding including insights into their feelings, conflicts, defenses and effect on others

4. obtain information about the behavioral processes that help and hinder the effective functioning of groups

5. develop specific behavioral skills, such as how to effectively praise and criticize others, communicate with body language, and improve listening ability.

---

[6]Lynn Z. Bloom, Karen Coburn, and Joan Pearlman, *The New Assertive Woman* (New York: Dell Publishing, 1976), pp. 175–176.

How they work. Encounter groups, specifically T–groups consist of the group members and a leader. These groups are basically unstructured in that the leader provides no direction. Nor are there any agenda or rules. This often leads the participants to ask themselves questions, such as "What is going on here?" "Why isn't the leader providing direction?" "What are we supposed to be doing?" Gradually, however, they begin to focus attention on each other and what is happening to them. Finally, the focus turns inward and the members begin to analyze each other. Here is how a typical T–group discussion might go:

> **Group T.S. Leader: Okay, to get things started I would like everyone here to tell everyone else the kind of impression they made. Let's start and move clockwise beginning with Jill. Now, Jill, look Barry right in the eye and tell him what you think of him.**
>
> **Jill: Well, I've only just met Barry, but he strikes me as being a very serious person. Moving on around the table, George strikes me as being very nervous. I've noticed how in the early part of this T–group he did not know what was going on and seemed very upset. Frank is just the opposite. He seems to be very easygoing and un-concerned. Finally, Jane strikes me as wanting to be somewhere else. She is very uncomfortable in this T–group.**

As you can see, Jill's remarks were all directed toward describing her first impressions of the other members of the group. As the round-robin discussion continues, people in the group may start making comments about the way other people sit in their chairs, the clothes they wear, and their facial expressions. Then the discussion often refers to the opening and gets into personal attitudes ("Let me ask you, Jill: What makes you think I'm very uncomfortable?") or personal feelings ("Tell me George, how does all of this make you feel? Are you nervous, concerned, anxious? Would you like to be someone else?"). As the discussion continues, the members are given the opportunity to relate to others and to receive input regarding how they themselves are perceived.

How useful are these training groups? French and Bell offer the following comments:

The T–group is a powerful learning laboratory where individuals gain insights into the meaning and consequences of their own behaviors, the meaning and consequences of others' behaviors, and the dynamics and processes of group behavior. These insights are coupled with growth of skills in diagnosing and taking more effective interpersonal and group action. Thus the T–group can give to individuals the basic skills necessary for more competent action taking in the organization.[7]

However, it is equally important to point out some of the problems encountered with T–groups. For example, if some people in a group do not take well to criticism, the session can be not only frustrating but upsetting. They may feel that the other members are picking on them. Sec-

---

[7] Wendell L. French and Cecil H. Bell, Jr., *Organization Development*, 2nd ed. (Englewood Cliffs, N.J.: Prentice-Hall, Inc., 1978), p. 144.

ond, the leader may not be competent and effective. The person conducting the session must be skilled in the technique so that he or she stays out of the picture by not offering excessive direction (after all, it is supposed to be an unstructured group setting). At the same time, the leader must be knowledgeable enough to know when to enter the picture and prevent someone from being unduly hurt by the remarks of another person. If these guidelines are followed, T–group training can be very useful in acquainting the participants with small-group behavior and making them aware of how they are viewed by other people.

Specific guidelines must be followed.

Summary

Individuals are complex beings. Nevertheless, many descriptive clichés have been used in trying to sum them up in a word or two. In human relations, we need to be much more scientific in our analysis of individuals and to realize that people are a blend of many different types of behavior. For example, sometimes they are rational and at other times they are emotional; sometimes they are motivated by economic considerations and at other times they are self-actualizing. In order to more fully understand individual behavior, we examine four of the major components: values, perceptions, attitudes, and personality.

A *value* is something that has worth or importance to an individual. People have, in overall terms, six values: theoretical, economic, aesthetic, social, political, and religious. When examined in a job context, values can be studied in terms of worker satisfaction. The most recent research shows that while many nonmanagerial employees rate their pay favorably, they are dissatisfied with their chances of attaining achievement, recognition, job challenge, and other upper-level need satisfiers.

Perception is a person's view of reality. There are two types of perception: *sensory* (physical) and *normative* (interpretive). Normative perception is particularly important in the study of human relations, since people's interpretations of reality will influence their behavior. In particular, it can result in selective perception and stereotyping, perceptual problems that the effective manager tries to avoid.

Attitudes are a person's feelings about objects, activities, events, and other people. Attitudes have three basic components: (1) affective components, or emotional feelings, (2) cognitive components, or feelings the person has toward the object or event, and (3) conative components, or behavior exhibited toward the attitude object. It is common to find organizations using instruments such as questionnaires to measure these feelings in their employees because attitudes are often key variables affecting output.

Personality consists of a relatively stable set of characteristics and tendencies that determine both similarities and differences between one person and another. Some of the major forces affecting personality are heredity, culture, social class, and family relationships.

The manager should also be aware of the available approaches to understanding interpersonal behavior. After all, values, perceptions, attitudes, and, to a large degree, personality are developed through interpersonal relations. FIRO theory provides a way of examining behavior as a function of inclusion, control, and affection needs. Transactional analysis views interpersonal behavior in terms of ego states and kinds of transactions. Assertiveness training teaches people how to determine personal feelings, verbalize them, and get what they want without being abusive or obnoxious. Encounter groups are designed to make participants more sensitive to how they are perceived by others and how their behavior affects others.

Now that we have examined individual behavior, we turn our attention to group behavior, which is the focus of Chapter 4.

Key terms in the chapter

value	end-result variable
theoretical value	personality
economic value	FIRO
aesthetic value	interpersonal needs
social value	inclusion needs
political value	control needs
religious value	affection needs
perception	transactional analysis
sensory reality	child ego state
normative reality	parent ego state
stereotyping	adult ego state
attitudes	complementary transaction
affective component	crossed transaction
cognitive component	life positions
conative component	stroking
attitude questionnaire	assertiveness training
causal variable	encounter group
intervening variable	T-group

Review and study questions

1. Explain how the following continua of behavior help in describing people: rational–emotional, controlled by the environment–control of the environment, economic–self-actualizing.

2. What is meant by *value*? What types of values do people have? Describe some.

3. Are work values in America changing? Support your answer with examples.

4. What is meant by *perception*?

5. How does sensory reality differ from normative reality?

6. How does stereotyping cause human relations problems?

7. What is an *attitude*? What are the three basic components of attitudes? Describe each.

8. How can attitude measurement be of value to an organization? Explain.

9. What is meant by *personality*? What are some of the ideas that psychologists tend to accept about personality?

10. What major forces help account for personality differences? Describe each.

11. In what way can FIRO theory help the manager better understand interpersonal behavior? Include in your answer a discussion of the three interpersonal needs described by FIRO theory.

12. What is *transactional analysis*? What are the three basic ego states in TA?

13. How does a complementary transaction differ from a crossed transaction?

14. How can an understanding of TA be of value to the modern manager? Explain.

15. Of what value is assertiveness training to the modern manager? Would it have any value for subordinates? Explain.

16. How can encounter groups be of value to managers? Subordinates? What drawbacks are there in the use of these encounter groups? Be complete in your answer.

Interpretation of how uptight are you?

Scoring

25–45	Not compulsive or uptight.
46–55	Mildly uptight. Your compulsiveness is working for you, and you are successfully adaptive.
56–70	Moderately uptight. You are adaptive but uptightness has crept into your personality function, and you experience uncomfortable days of high tension.
71–100	Severely uptight. You are adaptive but quite uptight, insecure and driving hard. You have many days of nervous tension that should be eased off.

The closer you are to the rating of 100, the nearer you come to playing brinksmanship at the ragged edge that borders on exhaustion of your adaptive reserve and a slump into depression. One way of overcoming these problems is by following the suggestions offered in the section of the chapter where assertiveness training was discussed.

Joel's findings

As part of a major research undertaking in his corporation, Joel Gibson has spent the last three months collecting data on how the employees view their jobs. These findings have been compared to those obtained in a similar study 10 years ago and the profiles are quite different. Some of the major initial conclusions that Joel feels can be drawn from the profiles are the following:

1. Most women now are reporting that they work for the company because they want to pursue a career. Ten years ago, most of them said they worked to supplement family income.

2. Both men and women say that their jobs are symbols of self-worth and importance to them and rank job prestige ahead of money as a motivational factor. Ten years ago, job prestige ranked below money on their list of motivators.

3. Employees, in general, report that leisure and quality of work life are extremely important to them. Only 5 percent of married workers with families say they would be willing to work on Saturday and none say they would be willing to work on Sunday despite the higher rates of pay. Ten years ago, those willing to work on Saturday and Sunday were 37 percent and 14 percent, respectively, of the company work force.

4. Over one-half of the employees said they felt it was management's responsibility to include them in decisions that directly affected them, and they look forward to assuming the obligations that accompany this process. Ten years ago, over 75 percent of the respondents said that management should not include them in the process.

5. One-half of the employees say they work for the company because they like their jobs and those with whom they interact on a daily basis. The external rewards are important but the respondents say these rewards are a secondary issue.

Questions

1. In light of the discussion of values in the chapter and the material in this case, what conclusions can you draw regarding the importance of money to this company's work force?

2. What values have increased the most over the last decade? Put it in your own words.

3. How can an understanding of these values help management increase its effectiveness? Explain.

Case of personality

Frank Payne is a store manager for a southwest retail chain. He has been with the organization for five years, and his store's sales have been rated "low average" in comparison with sales of similar stores in locales with the same general population and per capita income. Frank's boss, Eloise Sutter, has been with the organization for 12 years. For five of those years, Eloise was a store manager, during which time her sales were the highest in the region, and she was rated as excellent by her employees.

Eloise believes that one of the most important characteristics of an effective store manager is a good personality. The individual has to like people, to be willing to listen to customer complaints without taking the matter personally, and to express a sincere interest in the well-being of the workers. To Eloise, Frank seems to lack all of these traits. He acts as if he has a chip on his shoulder, and Eloise is afraid that this type of personality is likely to lead to the loss of customer goodwill.

During her recent visit to Frank's store, Eloise watched him talk to a customer who wanted to return some merchandise. The woman insisted that the merchandise was damaged when she opened the package, and she wanted to exchange it for an undamaged item.

Frank refused to accept the return. "We don't sell damaged goods," he told the lady. "It must have been damaged after you took it from the store."

The customer was furious, and in a loud voice she began telling Frank what she thought of the store and its personnel. Many of the other customers in the store at the time heard the ruckus, and Eloise noticed that most of them left without buying anything.

When Frank resumed his discussion with Eloise, he explained that the woman had been wrong in saying that the merchandise was damaged and that the store should not be expected to take the loss. Eloise tried to help Frank see the customer's point of view, but she was unable to do so. She, thereupon, dropped the subject and turned to other business matters, including the decline in sales.

"Things haven't been going too well since you took over," she told Frank. "What seems to be wrong?"

Frank talked about some of the areas where he felt there were problems that needed to be straightened out. They all related to inventory control and the need for more motivated personnel. At no point during the conversation did Frank indicate that he might be causing any of the problems because of his personality or his leadership style.

Before leaving, Eloise walked around the store and talked to some of the employees. From her brief conversations with them she learned that they did not care much for Frank as a store manager. One of the workers referred to him as "uncaring," while another said he had "the personality of an army drill sergeant." Eloise decided that she would let Frank run the store for another three months but that if sales kept slipping she would have to replace him.

Questions

1. What type of personality would you expect to find in a successful store manager?

2. How might Frank's personality affect the attitudes of the workers? Explain.

3. Using what you know about transactional analysis, describe how you would advise Frank about being more effective. Do you think you would succeed? Explain.

Group
behavior

4

Goals of the chapter

Individuals may act on their own, but the perceptions, values, and attitudes that cause their behavior are often a result of group interaction. People are influenced by those around them. Therefore, we cannot adequately study human relations without considering group behavior. In this chapter we examine how people act within groups as well as how groups interact with each other.

The first goal of this chapter is to define the term *group* and to examine three of the most common types of groups. Then we answer the question: "Why do people join a group?" The second goal of this chapter is to study the major characteristics of groups, including roles, norms, status, and cohesiveness. The third goal is to look at decision making within groups. The fourth goal is to study intergroup behavior, noting some of the ways a group tries to gain power over other groups and how a manager can resolve intergroup conflict. The final goal is to examine the nature of committees and how these groups can be effectively employed in modern organizations.

When you have finished reading this chapter you should be able to:

1. define the term *group*
2. describe functional group, project group, and interest-friendship group
3. explain what is meant by the term *role* and discuss some common role-related problems
4. know how group norms determine the behavior of group members
5. define *status* and explain how status incongruency and status discrepancy constitute status problems
6. answer the question, "Are highly cohesive groups always high producing groups?"

7. list some of the benefits of group decision making vis-à-vis individual decision making

8. explain what is meant by the *risky-shift phenomenon*

9. cite the common symptoms of *group think* and some of the ways it can be prevented

10. discuss the major factors upon which high intergroup performance depends

11. list some of the ways in which groups try to gain power over other groups

12. describe some techniques managers can use to resolve intergroup conflict

13. relate the four guidelines for making committees more effective.

Definition of a group

What is a group? Unfortunately, there is no universally accepted definition of the term. However, there are three characteristics groups seem to have in common.

First, a group is a social unit of two or more members, all of whom engage, at some time or other, in *interaction* with each other. In work groups this interaction often occurs on a face-to-face basis, although some groups are geographically dispersed and interact through letters and telephone conversations.

Groups have three characteristics: interaction, dependence, and satisfaction.

Second, the members are all *dependent* on one another. In the pursuit of their objectives, each member realizes the need for the others. In a work setting, the individual is aware that the overall job cannot be done without assistance from the other people.

Third, the members of the groups receive some *satisfaction* from their mutual association. Otherwise they will drop out of the group. In a work setting, for example, they will ask for a transfer to another department or locale or will simply resign.

Now that we have examined the three major characteristics of a group, let us incorporate them into a meaningful definition. A ***group*** is a

A group defined.

social unit consisting of two or more interdependent, interactive individuals who are striving to attain common goals.

Types of groups

Many types of groups can be found in organizations. Most of them, however, can be classified as one of the following: functional group, project group, or interest-friendship group.

Individuals in functional groups perform the same tasks.

Functional group   A functional group is composed of individuals performing the same tasks. In a manufacturing firm, for example, it is common to find major functional groups or departments, such as marketing, production, and finance, and further breakdowns of the personnel within each group. In the marketing department, for example, there is often an advertising group and a personal selling group, and within the latter there are sales forces for product lines or geographic territories. In all these breakdowns, functional groups have been formed by the company for the purpose of promoting internal efficiency.

Project group   A project group consists of individuals from many different areas or backgrounds. The group's purpose is to attain its objective within predetermined time, cost, and quality limits, after which the group is disbanded and everyone goes back to his or her regular department. Project groups are often used in building spacecraft, skyscrapers, bridges, and ships. They have also been employed in designing new products and solving particularly complex problems. Whatever the objective, however, a project group draws personnel from many different areas of expertise and combines their talents in hopes of attaining the project goal.

A project group has members from many different backgrounds.

Interest-friendship group   An interest-friendship group is formed on the basis of common beliefs, concerns, or activities. On the job interest-friendship groups are sometimes found within departments, while in other instances they cut across departmental lines. For example, people who have been in an organization for a long time tend to have many contacts, and they often find it possible to ask friends in other departments to expedite a process or to put a high priority on a particular job.

Interest-friendship groups are formed on the basis of common beliefs, concerns, or activities.

These types of groups also function away from the job, as in the case of the three members of the accounting department and the three

Figure 4.1
Different types of groups

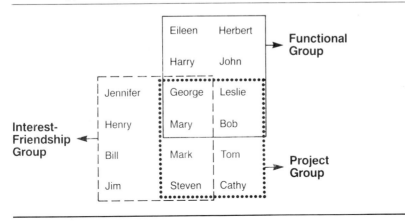

from production who are on the company bowling team. Their primary interest is to win the bowling league title. However, such friendships carry back to the job, and it is not uncommon to find people using their friendships to help attain job-related objectives.

Thus, it should be obvious that people are often members of two or more groups. Figure 4.1, for example, depicts three groups. Half the members of the functional group are members of the project group. Two of them are also members of the interest-friendship group. Such overlapping membership indicates that intragroup and intergroup behavior can be a very complex area, resulting in many kinds of behavioral problems. We examine some of these later in the chapter.

Why do people join groups?

People join groups for a number of reasons. Some of the most frequently cited are: satisfaction of needs, proximity, common activities, and similar interests.

Satisfaction of needs

As we noted in Chapter 2, people are motivated by various needs: physiological, safety, social, esteem, and self-actualization. The first of these is basically physical, while the last is primarily psychological. Between them are those needs that are satisfied through interpersonal relations, a blend of the physical and psychological. Without the physical presence of others, interpersonal relations cannot occur; and unless they do, the individual's psychological need to belong will not be satisfied.

People join groups to satisfy needs.

Yet individuals do not join groups for the sole purpose of interpersonal relations. Such socialization is also useful in helping them meet their needs. For example, people in groups feel secure (safety), and such social interaction also helps them feel important (esteem). Additionally, members of a group may be of use to each other by demonstrating shortcuts for doing their jobs, thereby enabling the individuals to increase their pay and satisfy physiological needs in the process. Finally, group members often help each other in self-actualizing by encouraging the development of competence. We can diagram these ideas as in Figure 4.2. Note that groups are primary in helping members meet their social or interpersonal needs. At the secondary level is safety and esteem need satisfaction. Finally, at the third level is physiological and self-actualization need satisfaction.

Proximity

People often form groups with those who work nearby.

People also join groups as a result of their proximity to the other members. For example, it is likely that members of a formal work group will also be members of an informal group because they are in close contact

Figure 4.2
Groups and need satisfaction

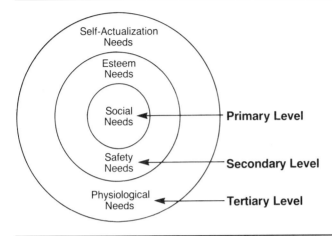

with each other on a daily basis. Conversely, if people work a great distance from each other, they are unlikely to be members of an informal work group, but they might associate with each other off the job if they live in the same neighborhood.

Activities

Still another reason people join a group is the activities they perform. For example, the foremen in a factory may not come into very close contact with each other on a daily basis, but they all perform the same activities at work. As a result, they tend to feel comradeship with one another. If nothing else, they share a job with similar responsibilities, challenges, and difficulties.

People join groups with those who do similar work.

Similar interests

People who have similar interests also tend to affiliate. All the top managers of the production department have similar interests (production efficiency and output) and are usually members of an informal as well as a formal group. Likewise, off the job, people belong to various clubs and associations related to their interests. Former military men join veterans' clubs, avid readers subscribe to book clubs, tennis enthusiasts join country clubs, and amateur painters or potters join local artists' associations.

We also know that when people confront similar dangers or problems, they group together. For example, students in a basic statistics class are usually very supportive of each other because of their anxieties

People with similar interests tend to aggregate.

about the difficulty of the subject. Also, research shows that when given a choice, people who are unhappy seek the companionship of others who are suffering the same misfortune. Thus, the truism "misery loves company" is scientifically supported. Workers who feel the organization is mistreating them tend to group together; so do managers who are trying to develop a new strategy for beating the competition. In each case, the group is held together by a common interest.

Characteristics of groups

All groups have certain characteristics. Some of the most important are roles, norms, status, and cohesiveness.

Roles

A role is an expected behavior.

A **role** is an expected behavior. In many organizations, job descriptions provide the initial basis for determining one's role. The individual can read this description and obtain a general idea of what he or she is supposed to be doing. Of course, the description does not cover everything, but it will give the person enough general information to begin doing the job.

Role ambiguity occurs when the job description is vague.

One of the most serious and most common role-related problems occurs when job duties are unclear either because the job description is vague or because no description has ever been written for the work. We call this *role ambiguity*, because what the individual is supposed to do is uncertain or vague. When this happens the individual is then forced to learn his or her responsibilities as he or she goes along. The further up the organizational hierarchy the job is, the more likely that the job description is, at best, incomplete and that role ambiguity occurs.

In role conflict two roles are mutually incompatible.

A second major role-related problem is *role conflict*. This occurs when an individual faces a situation in which he or she must assume *two roles*, but the performance of one *precludes* the performance of the other. For example, the company tells the supervisor to have all the workers fill out the new insurance benefit form and return it by 5 P.M. However, it is now 3:30 P.M., and the workers are extremely tired, having just moved some equipment from one end of the plant to the other. The supervisor would like to give them a break and then have them take it easy for the rest of the day. Clearly, the supervisor cannot play both roles: enforce the rules and be lenient.

Another illustration of role conflict is found in the case of the salesperson who is expected to meet a specific sales quota. Approaching the end of the sales year, the individual needs to close a big sale to meet this quota and has not called on one large firm. The person makes the sales pitch to this firm's purchasing manager, who indicates that the firm would like to place a very large order. However, the purchasing manager also observes that on such an order it is common for the salesperson to "kick back" 25 percent of the commission, a practice that is unethical and disagreeable to the salesperson. Here again we have role conflict. If the salesperson assumes the role desired by the purchasing manager, the sales quota can be met. If the salesperson refuses to go along with this scheme, the quota cannot be met. The individual cannot meet the sales quota and keep a clear conscience at the same time.

Managers must be aware of role ambiguity problems and must work with their people to identify and describe the objectives, authority, and responsibility associated with each person's position. In the case of role conflict, superiors have to be understanding and must realize that adherence to ethical practices is paramount. No firm can afford to engage in illegal business deals without suffering a severe backlash. The salesperson is right in rejecting the order and should apprise the boss of the situation. The superior should, in turn, praise the salesperson for rejecting the purchasing manager's offer and then should work most closely with the salesperson to help improve his or her sales quota. In this way the salesperson will not be under pressure to make a large sale at the last moment, and the role conflict will be eliminated.

Norms

Norms are behavioral rules of conduct adopted by group members. These norms indicate how each group member *ought* to act. Usually norms are few in number and relate only to those areas that have *significance* for the group. For example, a work group will often have norms related to output (how much you ought to do), participation (whether or not you should help out slower workers), and communication with management (what you should and should not say to the boss). It will not have norms related to where you should live, how you ought to raise your children, or what church you should attend.

Norms are behavioral rules of conduct.

Additionally, there are *degrees* of conformity. For example, you ought to turn out 480 pieces per day, plus or minus 20. There is thus an *acceptable range*, and those individuals who want to remain in good standing with the group will conform to it.

Overall, there are some conclusions that we can draw about individuals and their conformity to group norms.

1. Adults tend to be less conforming than children.

2. Women, because of our cultural values, tend to be more conforming than men.

3. Highly intelligent people tend to be less conforming than people of low intelligence.

4. If all other members agree on something, the remaining person is likely to go along with them.

5. If a person in the group disagrees with the others but receives support from one of them, the person is much less likely to conform.

The individual will take heart from the fact that some support has been forthcoming and will often cling tenaciously to his or her original position.

6. If a person does not understand what is going on, he or she is more likely to follow the direction of the group member who does seem to have a grasp of the situation.

Any individual who does not conform to at least the major norms of the group is denied membership. The person is not permitted to participate in group activities and, in some cases, is ostracized or is subjected to various forms of harrassment by the members.

The manager must be aware of group norms because they play a key role in determining what a group will and will not do. If the group's informal work norm, for example, is much lower than the quota set by the company, the group is likely to have low productivity. The manager's awareness of such informal norms, however, can serve as the basis for developing a change strategy, by which the manager can influence the group to increase its informal work norms. (These change strategies are explored further in Chapter 14.)

Status

Status is a term that refers to the relative ranking of an individual in an organization or group. Status can be achieved in a number of ways.

Status is the relative ranking of an individual or group.

In our society, a Rockefeller has status merely through being *born* into a rich, influential family. On the job, people can achieve status through the *position* they hold. For example, the president of the organization has more status than a vice president.

Other people achieve such status by the *job* they do. For example, in some firms the advertising manager has greater status than the purchasing manager.

A third way to achieve job status is through *personality*. An individual who gets along with others, is easy to work with, and is always ready to say a kind word is more likely to be given status by the other members of the organization than an individual with whom no one can work because he or she is unpleasant to others.

A fourth work status determinant is *job competence*. The better a person knows his or her job, the more likely it is that the person will be accorded status by members of the peer group. For example, in a group that values high productivity, those individuals who are the highest producers will be afforded the highest status.

Of course, to determine *exactly* how group status will be accorded we have to examine the specific situation. In some groups competence (what the person can do) is very important but in other groups job title (what position the person holds) is of greatest value in obtaining status. Additionally, if we were to move from one organization to another we

Figure 4.3
Changing status

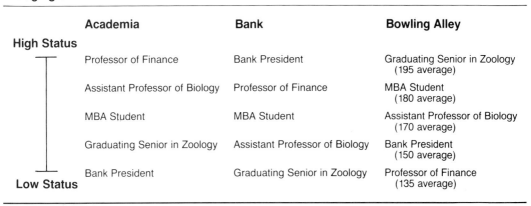

	Academia	Bank	Bowling Alley
High Status			
	Professor of Finance	Bank President	Graduating Senior in Zoology (195 average)
	Assistant Professor of Biology	Professor of Finance	MBA Student (180 average)
	MBA Student	MBA Student	Assistant Professor of Biology (170 average)
	Graduating Senior in Zoology	Assistant Professor of Biology	Bank President (150 average)
Low Status	Bank President	Graduating Senior in Zoology	Professor of Finance (135 average)

might well find different status determinants. This would be particularly obvious if we were to put six people, two professors, two bank executives, and two students into three different group settings. As seen in Figure 4.3, the status of these individuals will vary from one situation to the next. Yet if one were to give them scores, 1 point for first place through 6 points for sixth place, in all three group settings, one would find that the overall score per person is about the same. In short, they all have about the same *average* status across the three groups, but this status varies dramatically within the group. For example, in a university setting, the full professor has the highest status, followed by other faculty, and then students, and finally members of the group whose occupations are not academic. In a bank, the president has the highest status, followed by individuals knowledgeable in finance, students working for degrees in business (MBA), and then members of the group whose occupations do not relate to finance in any way. Finally, in a bowling alley, the status of each is accorded strictly on the basis of bowling skill.

In order to fully understand the importance of status within groups, it is important to realize that there can be status problems. The most serious is **status incongruency**, which occurs when there is a discrepancy between a person's supposed status and the way he or she is treated. For example, if all the vice presidents but one are given new desks, the one vice president with an old desk has a status problem because he or she lacks a *status symbol*. Other executives might not know how to interpret this event; many of them may think it is a sign that the vice president with the old desk is "on the way out."

A second status-related problem is **status discrepancy**, which occurs when people do things that do not fit with their status in their group. Union representatives who seem to be too friendly with company supervisors can threaten their status with the union members they serve. Man-

Status incongruency and status symbol are problems.

So is status discrepancy.

agers who eat lunch with their subordinates can also fall into this category. We can sum it up this way: Status is accorded to people for "acting properly," and any time people do things that do not fit into this category, they threaten their status.

Cohesiveness

Cohesiveness refers to the closeness or interpersonal attractions that exist among group members. If cohesion is high, members are motivated to remain in the group. If cohesion is low, members often leave the group.

However, cohesiveness does *not* guarantee high productivity. The individuals may all like each other very much and may also have an informal norm of low output; they have all agreed to do as little work as possible. Figure 4.4 provides an illustration. Note that Group X has the highest productivity. Everyone in this group is turning out more work than is required by the organization norm. In fact, all the high producers are in this group. Conversely, all the low producers are in Group Z. Their average is far below that of the other two groups. However, cohesiveness is very high. Everyone in the group is conforming to an informal work norm. Note how little each person's productivity deviates from this norm; this is why we can conclude that it is indeed an informal norm. Otherwise, there would be several high and low producers. For example, in Group X there is a greater variation between high and low producers, indicating less acceptance of a group norm. In Group Y the variation is even more significant. We can conclude that Group Z has the greatest cohesion and that Group Y has the least.

Group cohesiveness presents two major challenges to the manager. First, the individual needs to work closely with low-producing groups to motivate them to increase their productivity norms to the level established by the organization. Many of the ideas presented in Chapter 2 can be used in doing this.

Second, the manager has to protect the cohesiveness of the high-producing groups. Changes in the work or transfer of people into or out of the group can all negatively affect cohesion. One of the most famous cases of this has been provided by the coal mining industry in Great Britain, which introduced new technology and procedures into the mines after World War II Before the change, the miners had worked together in teams and there was high cohesion within these groups. However, the new technology disrupted these arrangements. Many of the small cohesive groups were reorganized into larger teams and some of the work previously done by the miners was now done by machine. The restructuring destroyed group cohesiveness, and the coal miners began to slow down their production. It became necessary for the companies to again reorganize some of their operations, this time, however, to better accommodate the miners.

Figure 4.4
Cohesion and productivity

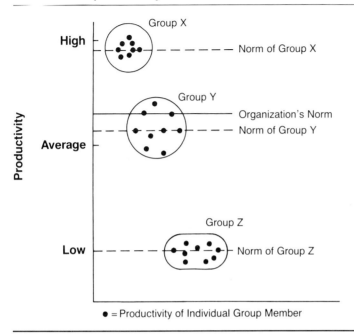

● = Productivity of Individual Group Member

Figure 4.5
Technology, people, and productivity

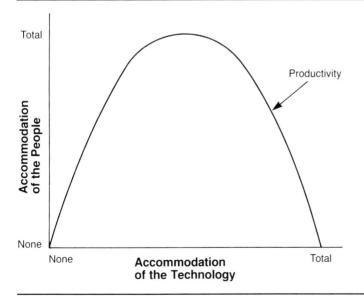

Quite obviously, every organization needs to consider both the technology and the people. If technology is overemphasized, cohesiveness declines and productivity falls. Conversely, if the people are accommodated at the expense of technology, the firm suffers in comparison with other companies that have adopted the latest technological breakthroughs. A balance is needed, as illustrated in Figure 4.5.

Intragroup behavior

Two major activities within groups are of primary interest to those studying human relations: decision making and communication. Decision making is of greater concern to us in this chapter, as we examine how groups get things done. In Chapter 5, in which we study informal groups, communication is discussed in depth.

Decision making

How are decisions made within groups? This is a difficult question to answer because it is multifaceted. However, we know some things about group decision making. Before examining these findings, read and fill out the questionnaire entitled, "Risk taking and you." Then read the interpretation at the end of the chapter. When you are done continue on to the next paragraph.

First, groups are often *more* effective than individuals in decision making. For example, when faced with the task of evaluating ambiguous situations, groups appear to be superior to individuals. They are also more effective in generating unique ideas or accurately recalling information. However, they are not as effective as individuals in solving problems that require long chains of decisions.[1]

Individuals are greater risk takers when acting in a group.

Second, individuals tend to take greater risks when they are in groups than when they are acting alone. This is known as the *risky-shift phenomenon.*[2] Behavioral scientists studying this phenomenon have used measures similar to the questionnaire that you answered in Figure 4.6. The individual is then placed in a group, which is asked the same questions. The people in groups tend to be greater risk takers. Why is this

---

[1] Bertram Schoner, Gerald L. Rose, and G. C. Hoyt, "Quality of Decisions: Individuals Versus Real and Synthetic Groups," *Journal of Applied Psychology*, August 1974, pp. 424–432.

[2] Dorwin Cartwright, "Risk Taking by Individuals and Groups: An Assessment of Research Employing Choice Dilemmas," *Journal of Personality and Social Psychology*, December 1971, pp. 361–378; Russell D. Clark III, "Group Induced Shift Toward Risk: A Critical Appraisal," *Psychological Bulletin*, October 1971, pp. 251–270; Dean G. Pruitt, "Choice Shifts in Group Discussion: An Introductory Review," *Journal of Personality and Social Psychology*, December 1971, pp. 339–360.

Figure 4.6
Risk taking and you

There are 10 situations presented below. In each case read the situation and then choose the lowest probability or odds that you would accept.

1. You have just learned that you have a serious heart ailment. If you choose not to have an operation, you can live another 10 years only. If you choose to have the operation, there is a chance that you will not survive the operation. Should you survive, however, you will have a normal life expectancy. Check the lowest probability of survival that you would consider acceptable:

   _____ 1 out of 10 _____ 3 out of 10 _____ 5 out of 10
   __✓__ 7 out of 10 _____ 9 out of 10 _____ You would not take the chance

2. You are playing chess against a much better player. Early in the game you notice that you have a chance for a quick win, providing your opponent does not see through your strategy. If he does, you are finished. Check the lowest probability you would consider acceptable for the risky play:

   _____ 1 out of 10 _____ 3 out of 10 __✓__ 5 out of 10
   _____ 7 out of 10 _____ 9 out of 10 _____ You would not take the chance

3. You have $5,000 in conservative stock holdings returning you 9 percent a year. You have learned from your cousin that she is in the process of selling stock in her new firm. If her company survives the next five years, your stock will quadruple in value. Check the lowest probability of survival that you would consider acceptable for investing the $5,000 in her company.

   _____ 1 out of 10 _____ 3 out of 10 _____ 5 out of 10
   _____ 7 out of 10 __✓__ 9 out of 10 _____ You would not take the chance

4. There are two colleges to which you are thinking about applying for admission. College A has a national reputation but also flunks out over 50 percent of all those admitted. College B has only a local reputation but the flunk-out rate is less than 2 percent. Check the lowest survival probability that you would accept in opting for College A.

   __✓__ 1 out of 10 _____ 3 out of 10 _____ 5 out of 10
   _____ 7 out of 10 _____ 9 out of 10 _____ You would not take the chance

5. You have a good steady job at a moderate rate of pay. Your best friend has offered you a job in his firm at a much higher rate of pay. However, his company is small and may not survive the next two years. Check the lowest probability of survival you would look for in this new firm.

   _____ 1 out of 10 _____ 3 out of 10 __✓__ 5 out of 10
   _____ 7 out of 10 _____ 9 out of 10 _____ You would not take the chance

6. You are thinking about getting married. Your spouse is a wonderful person but is also emotional and sometimes very hard to get along with. On the other hand this individual makes you happier than anyone you have ever met. Check the lowest probability of your marriage surviving, which you would accept before going ahead with the wedding.

   _____ 1 out of 10 _____ 3 out of 10 _____ 5 out of 10
   __✓__ 7 out of 10 _____ 9 out of 10 _____ You would not take the chance

7. You are the coach of a football team. You are going for the state title and are one point behind, having scored a touchdown just as the final gun went off. If you kick the extra point, you will have a tie. If you try a trick play, you can go for two points. What is the lowest probability of success with the trick play that you would accept?

   _____ 1 out of 10 _____ 3 out of 10 _____ 5 out of 10
   _____ 7 out of 10 _____ 9 out of 10 __✓__ You would not take the chance

8. You have saved $3,500 over the last two years and are considering buying a bond paying 13.5 percent annually. Your brother, an oil wildcatter, wants you to

Figure 4.6 (continued)

invest the money with him. If he is successful, you will double your money in one year. If he is not, you will lose it all. What is the lowest probability of success you would accept for investing with your brother?
_____ 1 out of 10 _____ 3 out of 10 __✓__ 5 out of 10
_____ 7 out of 10 _____ 9 out of 10 __✓__ You would not take the chance

9. You have the option of taking a steady job in the personnel department where your future with the firm is just about guaranteed. Or you can go with the advertising department. It will take five years of hard work before you know whether you will succeed in this department, but if you do your salary will be almost double that in the personnel department. If you fail, you will have to find another job elsewhere. What is the lowest probability of success in the advertising department that you would be willing to accept?
_____ 1 out of 10 _____ 3 out of 10 _____ 5 out of 10
_____ 7 out of 10 __✓__ 9 out of 10 _____ You would not take the chance

10. You can keep your current stateside job or take one in the Far East. If you stay here, you will receive moderate increases and promotions for the indefinite future. If you opt for the overseas assignment and do well, you will be a vice president within five years and will be one of the highest paid people in the firm. If you do not do well, you will be fired. What is the lowest probability of success in the overseas assignment that you would be willing to accept?
_____ 1 out of 10 _____ 3 out of 10 __✓__ 5 out of 10
_____ 7 out of 10 _____ 9 out of 10 __✓__ You would not take the chance

so? A list of some of the explanations offered for this phenomenon follows:

1. **If the decision proves to be wrong, the individual feels less guilt or concern because there were other people involved and responsibility is diffused among everyone.**

2. **In group discussions, risky people tend to be more influential than their conservative counterparts. As a result, the viewpoints of the former tend to win out.**

Behavioral explanations for the risky-shift phenomenon.

3. **Risk is a function of knowledge. The less someone knows about a given area or problem, the greater the risk he or she assumes in trying to remedy the situation. Since group thinking often leads to deeper consideration of, and greater familiarization with, the possible pros and cons of a particular course of action, the risk tends to be reduced. Thus a high risk decision for an individual can be a moderate risk for a group.**

4. **Risk taking is socially desirable in our culture. As a result, individuals in groups often choose a risk level that is equal to or greater than that risk which is acceptable to the average person.**[3]

We should note, however, that groups do *not* always encourage higher risk taking. Sometimes they motivate a manager to be even *more*

[3] Earl A. Cecil, Larry L. Cummings, and Jerome M. Chertkoff, "Group Composition and Choice Shift: Implications for Administration," *Academy of Management Journal*, September 1973, pp. 413–414.

Figure 4.7
Cost-per-unit curve

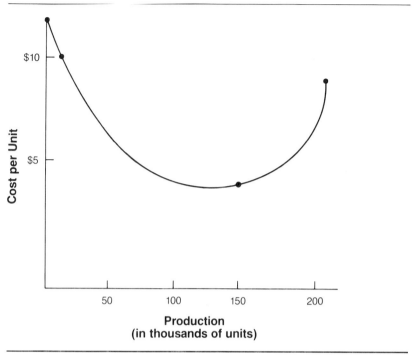

moderate in setting goals. For example, in many organizations it is common to find the head to the sales department encouraging the managers to strive for 20 percent higher sales. However, sometimes the individual manager's sales force reports that the market is not increasing and that at best a 10 percent rise in sales can be expected; the manager may then be influenced by the sales force to set a more realistic objective for the group. In short, group pressure, toward risky or more moderate goals, influences management behavior.

Additionally, it is important to remember that sometimes enlarging a particular objective is detrimental to the organization. Figure 4.7 is a graph of the cost-per-unit curve for production of an item by a large manufacturing corporation. The top management of the company was putting some pressure on the production manager and his staff to increase the yearly goal to 200,000 units this year. The production manager at first was planning to push for the increase, but his staff showed him the cost figures for the increase and predicted the effect of rising production costs on corporation profit. After listening to their arguments, the manager agreed to try to resist the pressure to increase the goal beyond 150,000 units, which was least expensive in terms of production costs. In turn, he was able to convince his superiors that the lower figure was a better goal.

Group think

One final question must be asked about decision making within groups. When are group-generated decisions *not* superior to individual decisions? The answer is: when group think comes into play.

Group think is social conformity to group ideas.

Group think refers to social conformity to group ideas.[4] It requires the individual to stop challenging the thinking of the group and go along with the consensus. Group think occurs when members of a decision-making body decide to avoid being too harsh in their judgments of the group's ideas. They adopt a "soft line" of criticism. Here is a description of some of the thinking that commonly accompanies this phenomenon:

1. The group's ideals are seen as humanitarian and as based on high-minded principles so there need be no concern about unethical behavior.

2. In order to be a member of the group, one has to avoid criticizing it and to help ensure cohesion by suppressing critical thoughts.

3. Amiability and esprit de corps among the members are very high, with the result that the members believe that other groups criticizing them are irrational.

The primary symptoms of group think include:

1. The group has the illusion, whether or not it is ever expressed, of invulnerability. It cannot be wrong.

2. Any warnings that the group's actions may be wrong are ignored or rationalized away.

3. If any member disagrees, there is pressure put on the person to express such doubts only within the group and to keep disagreement within acceptable bounds.

4. There is the illusion of unanimity among the members, especially in regard to the major areas of concern.

5. Individuals who are victims of group think often protect the leader and fellow members from adverse information that might shake the complacency they share.

Group think illustrates the serious consequences of a work team's becoming victim of its own group norms. Fortunately, managers can combat this phenomenon by following a handful of simple rules. First, the manager must encourage the open airing of objections and doubts. Second, one or more outsiders should be invited into the group to challenge the views of the members. Third, one member of the original group

---

[4] Much of the material in this section can be found in Irving Janice, "Group think," *Psychology Today*, November 1971, pp. 43–46; 74–76.

should be appointed to function as a lawyer who is challenging the testimony of the other members. Finally, after reaching a preliminary decision, the group should hold a "second chance" meeting at which every member expresses, as vividly as possible, all his or her doubts and the group thinks through the entire issue again before making a final decision.

Intergroup behavior

Intergroup behavior is interactions between or among two or more groups. Sometimes these groups are in the same department; sometimes they are in different departments. In any event, the groups, for some reason, have to coordinate their efforts to attain organizational goals. The purpose of intergroup behavior is to achieve high performance. However, sometimes power struggles develop between the groups, and conflict resolution is required.

Achieving high intergroup performance

High intergroup performance depends on a number of factors.

First, each group has to know what it is supposed to be doing. *Goals* must be clear. If Group A is charged with building Part A, Group B is responsible for constructing Part B, and Group C is supposed to assemble the two parts into a finished product, any delay by the first two groups will slow up Group C. Groups A and B both have to understand how to build the parts and to know how much output is required of them.

Second, there must be *cooperation* among all three groups, since a slow-up or bottleneck in *any* of them will result in a drop in production. Each group is a vital link in the production process.

Third, there must be *careful planning* of all interfaces between them, so that if one of the groups falls behind, the manager knows about it and can start correcting the problem before the situation gets out of control. One way this can be done is through daily monitoring of output. If production in any group falls off, the supervisor or department head is aware of it within 24 hours. Another way is to designate a liaison or coordinating manager, who works out any bottlenecks. For example, if Group A is falling behind because it has run out of raw materials, the coordinating manager checks with the purchasing department to see that the materials are rushed to the group. If some members of Group B stay home sick with the flu, the coordinating manager arranges for temporary replacements from other departments.

Clear goals, cooperation, and careful planning are needed.

Such planning and liaison work can do much to ensure high intergroup performance. However, this is not always enough. Sometimes the problem is that groups are squabbling with each other, a common occurrence when power struggles develop.

"They've always been such nice neighbors— friendly, quiet. Up until today, of course."

Drawing by Ziegler; © 1980
The New Yorker Magazine, Inc.

Power struggles

Power is influence over others; and although struggles for power can be detrimental to organizational efficiency, they are an inevitable part of intergroup behavior. Sooner or later one group will try to gain power over others by means of several behaviors.

Provide important services.

Providing services   One of the most common ways to gain power over other groups is to provide services for them that they either cannot or will not provide for themselves.

For example, many large and medium-sized businesses in industrial states are unionized. In order to deal with the union members, each company usually has an industrial relations department, which negotiates a contract with the union and works out the finer points of management-union prerogatives. What type of seniority system will there be to protect the rights of union members who have worked for the company for a long time? If some union people are laid off, in what order must they be rehired? What right of appeal does a member have if he or she is threatened with demotion or dismissal? Most departments look to the industrial relations department for help in resolving any problem related to these issues. As a result, in the area of labor-management issues, the industrial relations department holds power over the others.

Another example is the case of the personnel department that provides initial screening of prospective employees. Rather than having each department advertise job openings and interview all the candidates, many companies assign this task to the personnel department, where the large number of applicants is reduced to three or four. Then the department manager interviews these candidates and chooses one. Since most managers do not wish to spend the necessary time interviewing all the candidates, they relinquish some of this power to the personnel department.

Integrative importance

A second power struggle is directly related to the degree of integrative importance. If a group has an important integrative role in a process involving many groups, the other groups depend on it.

Play an important integrative role.

Consider the case of the manufacturing firm that produces a specialized power tool for industrial use. Figure 4.8 is a representation of the production process. There are five steps: manufacturing, assembly, painting, quality inspection, and packing. There are six major components to be manufactured. These are then sent to one of four assembly groups, each of which assembles an identical product. From here the products are forwarded to the painting groups, each of which is charged with painting 100 units a day. The products are then sent to the quality inspection group, which has a special machine that checks each for paint quality and determines that it works properly. If there is some failure in the product, the inspector identifies the problem, writes a ticket on it and, depending on what is wrong, sends it back to the assembly or painting group. If the product passes inspection, it is sent to the packing group, where it is carefully boxed and made ready for shipment. A close study of Figure 4.8 reveals that, of all the groups, quality inspection has the greatest integrative importance. There is only one such group and it performs a very important role. The group can either accept or reject the work of the other groups. Additionally, the other groups are larger in number or perform identical tasks. If one of these groups, such as assembly, is short of manpower because of illness, the other assembling groups can take up the slack. However, if the quality inspection people slow down, there is no one else to help them catch up, and the whole organization can be adversely affected. Therefore, because of its integrative importance, the quality inspection group has a degree of power over the others.

Budget allocation   A third common power struggle between groups is related to budget allocation. Most organizational groups, especially at the departmental level, would like to increase their budgets. Under favor-

Figure 4.8
Integrative importance of groups

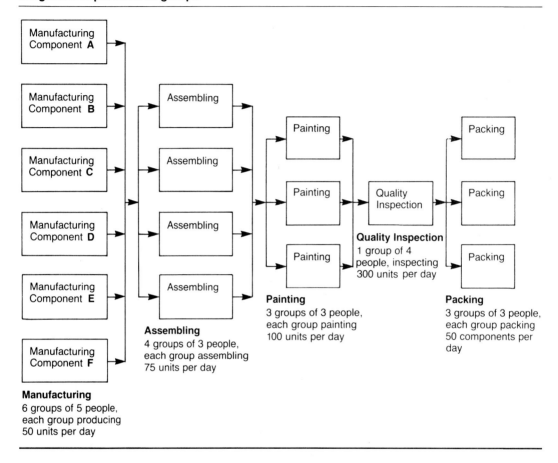

Manufacturing
6 groups of 5 people,
each group producing
50 units per day

Assembling
4 groups of 3 people,
each group assembling
75 units per day

Painting
3 groups of 3 people,
each group painting
100 units per day

Quality Inspection
1 group of 4
people, inspecting
300 units per day

Packing
3 groups of 3 people,
each group packing
50 components per
day

able economic conditions, when the average annual increase is 10 percent, they will fight for a 15 to 20 percent increase. If sales have not been good and budgets are being reduced by 10 percent, departmental groups will strive to maintain their original allocation.

Get a bigger budget allocation.

One of the most effective ways of succeeding in budget battles is to show top management that the department is doing a better job than most of the other departments. For example, the manufacturing group argues that its production costs have dropped and it is turning out more goods than ever before; if the group is given an increase in budget, more machines can be purchased and efficiency can be further improved. The marketing department produces statistics showing that sales per dollar of advertising are way up so its budget should be increased. Meanwhile the finance department opposes the manufacturing and marketing groups, arguing that the company is spending too much too fast and that it would be wiser to pay off some of the long-term debt, maintain a more liquid financial position, and add more finance personnel for control and evaluation purposes.

Quite obviously, each group has its own ax to grind, and a big increase in one group's budget can come only at the expense of the others. If the manufacturing group is given a 20 percent increase, the marketing and finance groups will feel slighted. If the large increase is given to marketing, the production and finance departments will be unhappy. If the finance department's argument convinces the top management to withhold increases, the other groups will be angry.

This group power struggle arises because of *goal conflict*. Each group must learn that its goal may not benefit other groups and that decisions must sometimes be made that appear to be detrimental to that group's welfare.

Conflict resolution

The astute manager is aware of these intergroup power struggles but also realizes that there are ways of eliminating or diminishing their negative effects. The individual works to accomplish this through what is called *conflict resolution*. There are a number of ways to resolve intergroup conflict. Four of the most common are: confrontation, collaboration, compromise, and altering the organizational structure.

Confrontation   Confrontation involves problem solving on a face-to-face basis. If the manager finds that several groups in the department are unable to get along and decides to use confrontation, the groups or their leaders are asked to meet to discuss their differences. Sometimes they are able to express their dissatisfaction with one another quickly and easily; sometimes it is a long process. In any event, there are some common complaints: "Those guys don't want to work with us. They're always doing something to slow up the flow of operations." "Whenever we're slow with our end of the work, those guys gripe, but if they're slow, they get angry if we say anything." "We don't know what the problem is with that group, but we just don't feel we can trust them, so we don't like working with them."

Confrontation involves face-to-face problem solving.

These standard responses are often the result of misunderstanding among the groups. By encouraging each group to express its objections, the manager can usually cultivate a feeling of harmony among them. Each group begins to see how the other groups view it and obtains better understanding of its own behavior. Then the groups are asked how they are going to increase their interaction with one another and what steps should be taken to insure that they do not slip back into their old habits.

This confrontation method is one of the most successful approaches to conflict resolution because it concentrates on solving the problem directly rather than trying to bypass it or to smooth over the issues.

Collaboration requires full cooperation of everyone.

Collaboration   Sometimes goals desired by two or more parties cannot be reached without the cooperation of those involved; this is when collaboration can be effective. Collaboration calls for all parties to work out their differences and to realize that without full cooperation all of them will fail. A common illustration is the case of the powerful union that wants a lucrative contract from a company on the verge of bankruptcy. It is obvious that if the union insists on its demands, the firm will go out of business. The only way to resolve the situation is for the union to take less money and to cooperate with the company in working to attain a more profitable position. When the company is stable, the union can resubmit its demands for a lucrative contract.

In compromise each party gives up something.

Compromise   *Compromise* occurs when each party gives up something and no one group is the clear "winner." Consider the case of the foreman who fires a worker for being late four days in a row. During the ensuing labor-management meeting required by the contract, the union argues that the offense has not justified such a harsh penalty. Both sides, the company and the union, then compromise on the situation: they agree that laying the worker off for five days (without pay) is sufficient punishment. Thus the worker has not been fired, but he has not escaped punishment for blatant infringement of the rules.

Reorganization can sometimes help.

Altering the organizational structure   If the manager finds that a particular group cannot get along with some of the other groups, he or she may decide to resolve the conflict by reorganizing the department structure. For example, using Figure 4.8 again, the manager finds that some of the members of the quality control group cannot get along with members of the other groups. He or she may simply remove the people by transferring them to other departments or work assignments and replacing them with more congenial workers. Or, if the manager finds that the assembling and painting departments resent the fact that their work can be sent back to them by quality control people, a supervisor may be appointed to make the final decision regarding what is to be returned as unacceptable. In this way the manager interposes someone between the antagonist (quality control) and the antagonized (assembly and painting groups). This type of organizational rearrangement has been found to be very effective in cases in which workers object to "taking orders" from other workers.

Committees

Another important type of group, commonly found in modern organizations, is the committee. There are two basic kinds of committees: ad hoc and standing. An ***ad hoc committee*** is formed for a particular reason, and when this objective has been accomplished, the group is disbanded. An example is a committee to review a new product offering before putting it on the market. A ***standing committee*** exists indefinitely. The most common example is the board of directors of a corporation.

There are a number of advantages to committees. Three of the most commonly cited include: (1) the opportunity for collective judgment, often producing a better decision than one person working alone, (2) the benefit it can provide in coordinating plans and transmitting information throughout the organization, and (3) the motivational value it creates among the members who often derive both enthusiasm and support for their decisions.

There are advantages.

On the other hand, there are disadvantages to committees. Three of the most commonly cited include: (1) they can be a big waste of time and money, (2) they are sometimes used for making decisions that can be best handled by an individual manager, and (3) when a deadlock is reached, the decision of the committee is sometimes a compromise that produces a truly inferior result.

And there are disadvantages as well.

Overall, however, the use of committees in modern organizations is growing. If they are employed properly, they can be very effective.

Using committees effectively

There are five basic guidelines that should be employed in using committees effectively. If these guidelines are followed, the committee can well be worth its cost in time and money.

The first guideline is to choose well-qualified individuals to serve on the committee. This choice must be directly tied to the objectives of the group. If the goal is to review production schedules, members should have a working knowledge of what these schedules are and how they are currently employed. If the goal is to formulate a more effective pay package, the members must know something about wage and salary administration.

Guidelines for effectiveness.

The second guideline is to have a specific agenda drawn up and delivered to each of the members prior to the meeting. This allows everyone to come prepared to discuss the issues, and, if any reading or preparatory work must be done, there is ample time to do it.

The third guideline is to have enough members to get the job done but not so many that they are continually getting in each other's way. The effective chairperson should encourage each individual to contribute ideas and opinions; however, if the committee is too large, this process will literally take up most of the time set aside for the meeting.

The fourth guideline is for the chairperson to keep the meeting heading toward its stated objective. From time to time the discussion will get off the main point. The chairperson must steer the group back on track.

These four guidelines cannot guarantee committee success. However, they have been found to improve committee performance markedly because they are designed to overcome specific common pitfalls.[5]

Summary

A group is a social unit consisting of two or more interdependent, interactive individuals who are striving to attain common goals. There are three types of groups: functional groups, project groups, and interest-friendship groups. Functional groups are composed of individuals performing the same tasks. Project groups consist of individuals from many different areas or backgrounds who are gathered together to carry out some task; when its task is completed the group is disbanded and its members return to their original departments. Interest-friendship groups are formed on the basis of common beliefs, concerns, or activities.

Why do people join groups? There are a number of reasons. Some of the most common are satisfaction of needs, proximity, activities, and similar interests.

Regardless of the reason for the group's formation, however, all groups have certain characteristics. These include roles, norms, status, and cohesiveness. A role is an expected behavior; it indicates what a person is supposed to do. Some of the most serious role-related problems include role ambiguity and role conflict. A norm is a behavioral rule of conduct that is adopted by group members. Norms dictate how each group member ought to act. The manager needs to be aware of group norms because they play a key role in determining what a group will and will not do. Status is the relative ranking of an individual in an organization or group. There are many ways of achieving job status, including position, the nature of the job, personality, and job competence. Two of the greatest job status-related problems with which the manager must be familiar are status incongruency and status discrepancy. Cohesiveness is the closeness of interpersonal attractions among group members. However, cohesiveness does not guarantee high productivity; a group can have high cohesion and low output. This situation occurs when the group members have all agreed to do as little work as possible.

The manager must also understand intragroup and intergroup behavior. Intragroup behavior consists of behavioral interactions within the group. Of primary interest in this chapter is decision making among the group members. Groups are often more effective than individuals in decision making, particularly when faced with estimating or

---

[5]For more on this topic see H. Kent Baker, "How to Make Meetings More Meaningful," *Management Review*, August 1978, pp. 45–47.

evaluating ambiguous situations, generating unique ideas, or accurately recalling information. Additionally, when making decisions in a group, individuals tend to be greater risk takers, a phenomenon known as the risky-shift. Furthermore, if groups are not careful they may become victims of group think, or social conformity to group ideas.

Intergroup behavior consists of behavioral interactions between or among groups. High intergroup performance can be achieved by making group goals clear, obtaining cooperation, and carefully planning all interfaces between the various groups. When such performance drops off, it is often a result of power struggles in which one group achieves or strives for some influence over the others. Some of the most common ways of gaining power are: providing services for other groups that they either cannot or will not provide for themselves; playing an important integrative role among the other groups; and defeating other groups in budgetary allocation battles. Some of the ways for resolving such conflicts include confrontation, collaboration, compromise, and altering the organizational structure.

The committee is another important type of group found in modern organizations. There are a number of advantages and disadvantages associated with the use of the committee. In order to obtain the greatest effectiveness from the use of such groups, however, four guidelines are important: well-qualified members, a specific agenda, a manageable group size, and a continual focus on the purpose of the meeting. If the group follows these guidelines, committee performance can be markedly improved.

Key terms in the chapter

group
functional group
project group
interest-friendship group
role
role ambiguity
role conflict
norms
status
status incongruency
status symbol

status discrepancy
cohesiveness
risky-shift phenomenon
group think
goal conflict
confrontation
collaboration
compromise
ad hoc committee
standing committee

Review and study questions

1. What are the three characteristics that all groups have in common? Identify them and give your definition of the term *group*.

2. How does a functional group differ from a project group? How do these differ from an interest-friendship group?

3. Why do people join groups? Cite at least three reasons.

4. What is meant by the term *role*? In what way are role ambiguity and role conflict role-related problems?

5. In what way do group norms determine how the members are going to act?

6. On the basis of the information provided in this chapter, what conclusions can be drawn about individuals and their conformity to group norms? Cite at least four.

7. What is meant by the term *status*? How do people achieve job status?

8. In what way is status incongruency a status-related problem? How about status discrepancy? In your answer, be sure to define each of these terms.

9. What is meant by the term *cohesiveness*? Are all high-producing groups highly cohesive? Do all low-producing groups have low cohesiveness?

10. Are groups more effective decision makers than individuals? Explain.

11. How does the risky-shift phenomenon help explain some of the decision making that goes on in groups?

12. What are some of the common symptoms that accompany group think? How can group think be prevented?

13. High intergroup performance depends on a number of factors. What are three of the major ones?

14. What are some of the ways groups try to gain power over other groups? Cite and explain at least two.

15. How can a manager go about resolving intergroup conflict? Give some examples.

16. Of what value are committees? What are four guidelines chairpeople should follow in effectively managing committees?

Analysis of risk taking and you

Each answer has a value, depending on the probability you choose. In every situation where you opted for a probability of 1 out of 10, your score is 1. This same logic applies to answers of 3, 5, 7, and 9. If you chose not to take the risk, your score for that situation is 10. Using this scoring key enter your scores below and add up the total.

Situation	Score
1	7
2	5
3	9
4	7
5	5
6	7
7	10
8	10
9	9
10	10
Total	___

High scores indicate unwillingness to take risks; low scores reveal a high risk propensity. Based on those who have taken this test, the interpretation of scores is:

Low risk taker — 70 or more
Moderate risk taker — 31–69
High risk taker — 30 or less

Now go back to the test and answer each situation from the standpoint of an advisor to someone else who is being confronted with these situations. Then add up your score before continuing on to the next paragraph.

Was your new score lower than your previous one? For most people it is. They are greater risk takers when in a group or giving advice to others than they are when making decisions that affect them personally.

The new supervisor

When Gary Paterson was put in charge of the small-products assembly department, output was at an all-time low. Bob Willard, the retiring supervisor, had been in charge of the department for the last 10 years, during which time the output had slowly declined. When Bob had first taken over the department, the average worker was assembling 200 units a day but the company norm was 225. During his decade as supervisor, the firm introduced some technological advances, and the norm was raised to 250 units per day. However, the average output declined to 193.

The management's time-and-motion studies showed that the figure of 250 units was well within the ability of the average worker, and the manual dexterity tests given to members of the department revealed that each was physically capable of attaining this objective. Bob, however, explained the situation in terms of changing values. "People are different today," he said. "They no longer want to work hard. They've lost the old work ethic, especially our young people, and that's who works in the assembly department. Why, the average age there has declined from 29 to 23 in the last 8 years. I don't know. I guess lower output is just something we're going to have to learn to live with."

These remarks had Gary very worried. He wondered how he might keep the output from declining even more. After serious thought, he decided to call the department together and talk to everyone as soon as he took over. During this talk he emphasized three points to the assembled workers. First, he told them that he wanted them to continue working in their present groups. Since the members of all eight groups knew one another very well, he said, there was no sense breaking up satisfied work teams. However, if someone did want to change to another work group, he promised to help him or her do so, although it would require a mutual exchange of personnel with the other group. Second, he urged them all to come talk with him if they had any problems. Third, he asked their assistance in boosting output to 225 units per person per day.

During the next three months, Gary was asked to make a few changes in group composition. He also resolved several job-related technical problems. Overall, however, he found the groups to be congenial and fun to supervise. In addition, output began to move up slowly. At the end of 90 days, the average daily output was 219 units.

One of the women in the department, when asked why production was up, said, "We like this new supervisor. He's a good guy. He talks to us, helps us solve problems, and doesn't keep emphasizing output. He lets us work at our own pace. It's such a change from when Bob Willard was here."

Questions

1. Is group cohesion in the small-products assembly department high or low? Has cohesion changed since Gary took over?
2. Have group production norms changed since Gary took over? Explain your answer.
3. What role do the workers want the supervisor to assume? How did Bob err in this regard? What is Gary doing right?

Something's got to be done

A large southern corporation has recently run into a problem with its sales force. For the last five years, the firm provided its salespeople with automobiles. However, the corporate comptroller found that it would be less expensive to ask everyone to use his or her own car and to be reimbursed by the firm. The reimbursement rate is currently 23 cents per mile.

At first the salespeople all agreed, believing that it cost less than 23 cents a mile to operate a personal car so there would be a financial incentive involved. However, in the last 60 days the firm has found that the salespeople want to go back to the company car system. Their biggest complaint is that the company is taking three to four months to reimburse them.

The comptroller has checked with the accounting department, which informed him that reimbursement is a low-priority item. After the corporation pays its suppliers and personnel, attention is directed to reimbursement vouchers. The comptroller has told the head of the accounting department that this practice must be changed and that bills must be paid on a "first come, first served" basis.

Unfortunately, this rule has not yet been put into practice. One of the salespeople explained, "Accounting has a lot of power over the other departments around here. If we want bills paid, we have to rely on them. However, there is nothing we can do to retaliate, so they treat us badly. If you ask me, accounting is power crazy. Something's got to be done."

Questions

1. In what way does the accounting department have power over the other departments? Explain.
2. Why has the accounting department not responded to the directive from the comptroller?
3. If you were called in to handle this problem, what form of conflict resolution would you use? Explain.

The informal organization

5

Goals of the chapter

In Chapters 3 and 4 we examined individual behavior and group behavior. To complete our discussion of the social system, we now study the informal organization, which engages in both individual and group behavior.

The first goal of this chapter is to examine the nature of the informal organization. How does it differ from the formal organization? The second goal is to study the communication patterns that exist within informal organizations, with particular emphasis on grapevines and grapevine activity. The third goal is to examine the benefits associated with the informal organization. The fourth goal is to review some of the drawbacks of the informal organization. The fifth goal is to look at some of the ways the manager can deal with the informal organization.

When you have finished reading this chapter you should be able to:

1. compare and contrast the formal and informal organizations
2. describe the difference between authority and power and explain which is of greatest importance in the informal organization
3. discuss some of the behavioral controls used by members of the informal organization to ensure compliance with its norms
4. explain how the informal communication network functions
5. list some of the conditions under which people are most likely to be grapevine-active
6. identify the primary benefits associated with the informal organization
7. outline the greatest disadvantages associated with the informal organization
8. cite some of the ways in which a manager can deal with the informal organization.

129

Nature of the informal organization

The informal organization plays a significant role in the dynamics of human behavior at work. As a result, no discussion of human relations would be complete without consideration of this area. In this part of the chapter, we examine the nature of the informal organization by pointing out how it differs from the formal organization. In particular we direct our attention to four major areas: (1) interpersonal relations, (2) informal leadership, (3) behavioral control, and (4) dependency. Before reading on, however, take the informal organization quiz and obtain a preliminary evaluation of both your use and understanding of this organization.

Interpersonal relations

In the formal organization, relationships between people are clearly defined. For example, all the members of an assembly group are charged with assembling 30 units an hour and placing the completed items on a large table. Everyone is supposed to be doing the same job and turning out an identical number of items. Most organizations, however, do not work this way.

Over time, workers begin to form friendships with one another. This in turn results in their going beyond their job descriptions and carrying out activities that are more to their liking. Consider the case of the assembly group we mentioned previously. Although each person is supposed to be working independently of the others, we know that in every group there are slow workers and fast workers. Additionally, some of these workers are so well liked that their peers help them with their work. Conversely, some will be disliked and will be ignored by their fellow workers.

Figure 5.1 is an illustration of the degree of assistance that some members of a work group give to others. Note that Jeff is helping two of his coworkers but is not receiving any help in return. This indicates that Jeff is probably a very fast worker. Chuck receives assistance from four of his fellow workers, so Chuck is not a fast worker. However, the other members of the group like him and are therefore willing to assist him in assembling the units. Barbara and Ed help each other. Joe receives help from Barbara but does not reciprocate. Finally, Larry neither receives help from anyone nor does he give any.

A sociogram shows intragroup social relationships.

Figure 5.1 is an illustration of a ***sociogram***, a schematic drawing that shows the social relationships that exist between members of a group. In this case the relationship is being measured in terms of who helps whom. Sociograms provide interesting insights to informal group behavior, because they help pinpoint those members who are most popular, those who do all the work, those who get help from others, and those with whom no one interacts.

The informal organization: an initial appraisal

The following 15 statements are designed to measure your understanding and use of the informal organization. Assume you are a manager and answer each statement from that viewpoint. An interpretation of your answers is provided at the end of the chapter.

	True	False
1. I always work through formal channels.	___	___
2. I don't care how my people get things done as long as they get them done.	___	___
3. Everyone should have a job description and stick to it exclusively.	___	___
4. If I can get things done faster, I cut across formal channels and use whatever means necessary.	___	___
5. All rules and procedures are made to be obeyed.	___	___
6. I use the informal organization to both give and get information.	___	___
7. I discourage grapevine activity.	___	___
8. Almost all of the grapevine communications are inaccurate.	___	___
9. The grapevine can be influenced by management.	___	___
10. The grapevine is inevitable.	___	___
11. Workers will form into informal groups regardless of what the organization does.	___	___
12. The grapevine's basic objective is to undermine management's efforts.	___	___
13. Most informal communiques are passed to others on a purely random basis.	___	___
14. The goals of the informal organization are almost always in conflict with those of the formal organization.	___	___
15. Just about all grapevine messages are started by individuals with an ax to grind.	___	___

Figure 5.1
Who helps whom?

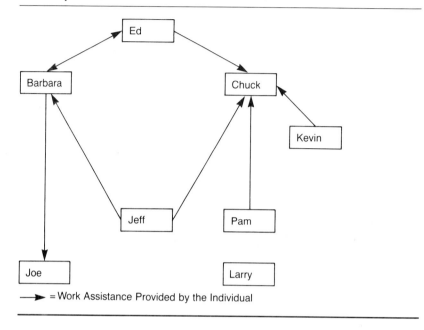

→ = Work Assistance Provided by the Individual

Informal leadership

In the formal organization a leader is designated by the management, while in an informal organization the leader is chosen by the members of the group. If the formal leader does a good job, he or she is often promoted away from the department. If the informal leader does a good job, he or she maintains that position, but if he or she does a poor job, someone else will be chosen who can help the group meet its objectives.

Authority is the right to command.

Power is the ability to influence.

When we compare formal and informal leaders, therefore, we can see that the formal leader has authority and the informal leader has power. **Authority** is the right to command, and it is given by the superior to the subordinate. **Power** is the ability to influence, persuade, or move another person to one's own point of view. The informal leader uses his or her power in two ways: (1) to achieve informal group objectives, such as persuading the foreman that since the workers are doing the best they can there is no need to crack down any harder, and (2) to maintain his or her position of leadership in the group.

What makes these concepts of authority and power in the formal and informal organizations so interesting is that the person who has the authority may *not* always have the power. We can illustrate this with Figures 5.2 and 5.3, which represent the organization of a fictional depart-

Figure 5.2
Formal authority

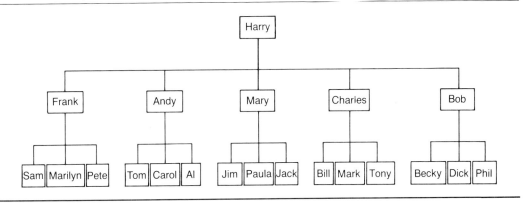

Figure 5.3
Informal power

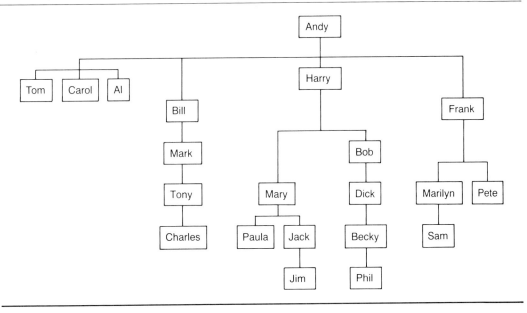

ment. In both illustrations, the closer a name is to the top of the figure, the more power the individual has in the department. Figure 5.2 shows the formal organization chart. Note that Harry is in charge of five subordinates, and each of them has three subordinates. Figure 5.3 shows the informal organization. Here we see quite a difference. For example, although Harry is the designated leader, Andy is the person with the real power. For some reason, Harry listens to Andy and goes along with whatever he says. One common explanation for such an arrangement is that Harry is new on the job, and Andy has been around for a long time and is the informal group leader. Realizing that he must rely heavily on Andy's help, Harry defers to him on most matters.

There are other interesting facts revealed by the informal organization chart. For example, Andy's three subordinates have more power than the other 12 subordinates. (Look how high up in the informal power structure they are located.) Also, although Mary and Bob are equal in authority (see Figure 5.2), Bob has more power than Mary. Moreover, Charles is supposed to be in charge of Bill, Mark, and Tony, but a close look at Figure 5.3 shows that Bill is giving the orders in the group and Charles has the *least* amount of power. Finally, although all the subordinates are supposed to be equal, some are more equal than others. A look at Bob's subordinates, Becky, Dick, and Phil, shows that Dick has the greatest power and Phil has the least.

Some people like to define the formal organization as the one the company creates and the informal organization as the one the people themselves re-create. Certainly there is a give-and-take between the needs of the organization and those of its personnel. A commercial firm, for example, is most interested in attaining economic goals such as profit and return on investment. The people in the organization are most concerned with getting good pay, adequate fringe benefits, and satisfying work. The company needs to make the workers see its point of view, and they must persuade the top management to understand theirs (Figure 5.4).

Satisficing behavior leads to satisfactory payoffs.

Who usually wins this conflict between organizational goals and individual-group goals? Usually, neither side emerges totally victorious. Each side takes less than it deems ideal, but neither accepts anything less than it regards as minimal. In human relations terms, we say that each side engages in *satisficing behavior* by agreeing to accept adequate or satisfactory payoffs from the other. Let us take an illustration. The company announces that beginning Monday all workers must clock in. The news is not well received by the informal organization, which decides to work around the rule if possible. One way of doing so is to have the group member who arrives first clock everyone else in and to rotate the assignment at the end of the day by having everyone take turns clocking out all the group members. In this manner, the company's rules are obeyed and the group finds a way to live with them.

Another illustration of satisficing behavior occurs in the case of the company that offers its people a three percent increase in salary and a three percent increase in fringe benefits. This offer is ideal for management, because if the union accepts it, the company will be able to surpass its goals of a 15 percent return on investment. The union, meanwhile, counters with a demand of nine percent for both salary and benefits. The two then compromise on five percent. Each side gets less than it wanted originally, but both can live with the contract because it provides them with satisfactory output or results that are "good enough."

Figure 5.4
Organizational goals and individual-group goals

The Organization Goals	The Individual-Group Goals
● Good profit	● Good pay
● High return on investment	● Job security
● Adequate worker efficiency	● Adequate fringe benefits
● High quality goods and services	● Challenging work
● Strong competitive posture	● A chance to achieve
● Low tardiness and absenteeism	● Work satisfaction
● Low turnover	

Behavioral control

When people in the formal organization do something right, they are given rewards; when they do something wrong, they are punished. If Barry reduces overhead in his department by five percent, he may be placed on a list of "up-and-coming" young executives. On the other hand, if departmental overhead increases dramatically and he is unable to control it, he may be labeled as incompetent and may lose the chance of ever being promoted.

In the informal organization, also, rewards and punishments are dispensed to the members. These, however, usually take the form of giving or denying need fulfillment. If Paula conforms to group norms, she is included in group activities and provided with social interaction. If she violates group norms or refuses to act "properly," she is ostracized and may even be subjected to pressure and ridicule and made to look foolish in the eyes of the other members. In Figure 5.1, a sociogram illustrated who in a department was helping whom; Larry neither helped anyone else nor was helped by them. From this we can conclude that he is not a member of the informal group, since one of the most common informal norms is that of assisting one's peers.

Dependency

Despite the strength of the informal group leader, the formal leader has a greater capacity for rewarding and punishing the personnel. The formal leader can give both physical and psychological rewards to those who obey organizational directives and do things well. Because the informal leader can give only psychological rewards, not everyone conforms to informal group norms. Some people resist because they believe there is more to be gained by *not* joining the informal group, and not even the most extreme form of ostracism budges them. This was clearly seen a number of years ago in the case of the West Point cadet who was accused

Figure 5.5
Informal organization structure

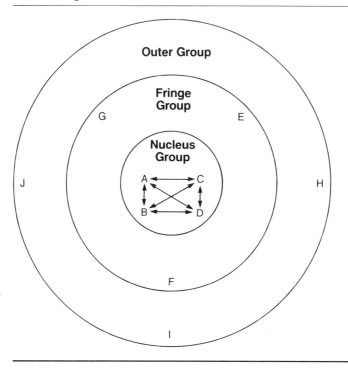

of cheating, judged guilty by his peer review board (made up of other cadets), and told to resign his commission. However, the man was not found guilty by those in authority and was allowed to stay at the academy. Because he refused to abide by the decision of his peers, none of them talked to him or interacted with him for the remainder of his stay at West Point. Despite such pressures, the cadet remained at the academy and graduated with his class.

The nucleus group contains full-fledged members of the informal organization.

Those individuals who agree with the informal group's norms, however, strive for membership and depend on the group for social interaction and support. As a result, we have three subgroups in an informal organization structure; these are illustrated in Figure 5.5. First is the ***nucleus group***, which consists of full-fledged members of the informal organization. The arrows between their names signify that each member interacts with all the others. Second is the ***fringe group***, consisting of those seeking admission to the informal organization. These people are often new members of the work force who are being screened for membership by the nucleus group. Finally, there is the ***outer group***, consisting of individuals who have been rejected for membership. These people have failed to measure up to the requirements set for admission to the

The fringe group members are seeking admission.

The outer group members have been rejected.

group. Numerous reasons can be cited for this failure: doing too much work, doing too little work, having an unpleasant personality, and "squealing" to a supervisor about a member of the nucleus group.

Informal communication

One of the most interesting behavioral aspects of the informal organization is its communication pattern. Commonly referred to as the ***grapevine***, this communication network is used to carry information between members of the informal organization. In this section, we examine the pattern of grapevine communication and four of the most likely causes of this activity.

The grapevine is the informal communication network.

How the grapevine works

The grapevine arises from social interaction and tends to be an *oral*, as opposed to written, form of communication. Bud in engineering can send a message through the interdepartmental mail asking Doris in accounting if she is going to the party on Friday. However, it is more likely that Bud will either call and ask Doris or wait until they meet later in the day.

Much of the information carried by the grapevine deals with matters that are of current interest to the personnel. The introduction of new work procedures in the metals department, the details of an accident in Plant 2, and the installation of a new computerized accounting system in the comptroller's offices are the kinds of topics commonly discussed via the grapevine. As you can see, these topics are sometimes of interest to people in many departments, so the number of individuals on a grapevine can be extremely large. This is particularly true when the message is viewed with concern or fear. For example, when the personnel throughout the firm learn about the introduction of new work procedures in the metals department, they may see this as the beginning of an efficiency move by management. If this does prove to be the case, the various departments have been forewarned and each will have already taken action to ensure that its own efficiency is already as high as can be expected. Meanwhile, if the message proves to be total fabrication and no new work procedures have been introduced, grapevine activity related to this topic will cease. Since grapevine members begin checking on the truth of a rumor almost immediately, one of these two actions will be initiated very shortly.

Grapevine networks   Many people believe that the grapevine consists of a long chain of people with each individual passing the message to the next person in the chain. The type of communication network, known as the *single strand*, is illustrated in Figure 5.6; it is the *least* frequently used.

Figure 5.6
Informal communication networks

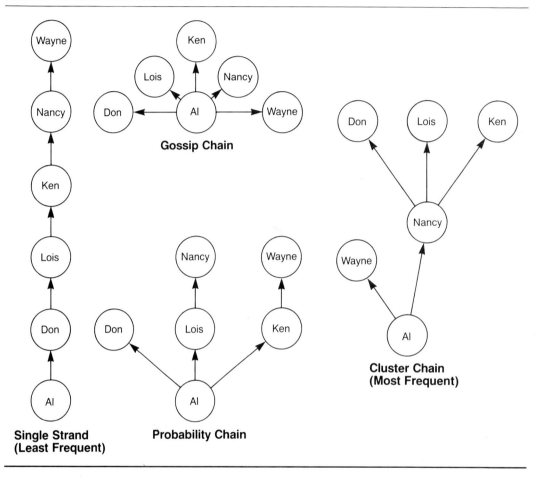

Another way in which informal messages can be communicated is by one person telling all the others. This is called the *gossip chain* (Figure 5.6). While more commonly used than the single strand, the gossip chain is also one of the less frequently used grapevine networks.

A third way in which information is passed through the grapevine is on a *random basis*. One person arbitrarily tells another, who goes on and tells one or two others (Figure 5.6). This is known as the *probability chain*, and of the three we have discussed, it is the most widely used.

However, the *most common* grapevine network of all is known as the *cluster chain*. It works this way: one person tells two or three people who in turn either keep the information to themselves or pass it on to

The most common grapevine network is the cluster chain.

two or three other people. As a result, we have one individual passing the message to a cluster of people, and those who pass it on also tell it to another cluster. In Figure 5.6, for example, Al tells the message to Wayne and Nancy. Wayne keeps it to himself, while Nancy passes it on to Don, Lois, and Ken. Al and Nancy are the links with their respective clusters.

Carrying this idea a step further, we can conclude that if 100 people learn of a particular happening, such as the firing of a top manager, it is very likely that the word was spread by only 15 or 20 people. These individuals are known as *liaison* people, because they serve as the links between those who have the information and those who do not. Commenting on the predominance of the cluster chain, Davis has reported that in one company he investigated, a quality control problem had occurred and 68 percent of the executives knew about it. However, only 20 percent of them had spread the information. In another firm he studied, 81 percent of the executives knew that a top manager planned to resign, but only 11 percent had passed the news to the others.[1]

Liaison people are very *selective* in the way they communicate. There are some people to whom they pass information and others whom they bypass. For example, Ed Anderson has just learned that he is to be promoted to vice president of international operations. However, the formal announcement will not be made for 10 days. Ed is very anxious to tell someone but he has to be selective in leaking the news, for he does not want to tell anyone who will circulate the story back to top management for fear they might reverse the promotion decision. Ed chooses his best friend, Bob James, to tell about the impending promotion. Bob is delighted and, realizing the confidential nature of the communique, passes the information to other people who he *knows* will treat the matter confidentially. Ten days later the formal announcement is made, and to most people in the organization, it comes as a surprise. Furthermore, even those who knew of the promotion through the grapevine are careful not to let on. If any one of them does indicate prior knowledge, he or she will be bypassed by future grapevine messages.

Bypassing people, however, is *not* always a sign of distrust or unreliability. The grapevine bypasses those who are not supposed to get a particular message. For example, in one company the president planned a party for 25 top executives. The grapevine learned about the party but did not know for sure which executives were on the list. As a result, only those they thought would be invited were told about the party by informal communicators. As it turned out, 23 executives learned of the upcoming announcement, and of these 22 were *actually* on the list. The cluster chain is indeed a selective communication network.

---

[1] Keith Davis, *Human Behavior at Work: Organizational Behavior*, 6th ed. (New York: McGraw-Hill Book Company, 1981), p. 339.

Grapevine activity Some people tend to be very active on the grapevine and others are fairly inactive. However, given the proper situation and motivation, just about anyone will be "grapevine-active." In fact, research reveals that there is little difference between the activities of men and of women on the grapevine. If people feel they have cause to be grapevine-active, they will be. Let us discuss four of the most likely causes of grapevine activity.

When people lack information they tend to be grapevine-active.

First, if people lack information about a situation, they try to fill in these gaps via informal channels. Sometimes these efforts lead to distortion of facts or fabrication of rumors. For example, not long ago a senior executive was informed by the company president that his office was to be refurbished. He was to be given a new desk, bookcases, furniture, and a very expensive rug. This was a reward for the successful advertising program he had developed for one of the firm's new product lines. As soon as the man's office was torn up, the grapevine began to hum. Before the afternoon was over, rumor had it that the executive had been fired and that his office was being made ready for a new advertising manager. Also, the personnel associated with the manufacture and sale of the new product line all became very concerned, fearing that the next step would be a reduction in their own work force.

The same is true when there is insecurity in a situation.

Second, people are active on the grapevine when there is insecurity in a situation. Continuing our illustration above, the first thing that people associated with the new product did was contact the sales manager to ask if there were any truth to the rumor. The manager informed them that sales for the product were running 37 percent ahead of projections. After putting these facts together with those about the work being done in the senior executive's office, the workers realized that he was being rewarded for the product's success. They then passed this information back through the grapevine, and informal communications related to this development ceased. There was nothing more to talk about.

Or when people have a personal interest in the situation.

Third, there is grapevine activity whenever people have a personal interest in a situation. For example, if Mary and her boss get into an argument over the monthly cost control report, Mary's friends will tend to be grapevine-active. Likewise, if the management decides to lay off 15 salespeople, the rest of the sales force will be interested in the situation because they have a stake in what is going on. People want to share among themselves any information about what is happening in the part of the world that is important to them.

Or when they have new information.

Fourth, people are most active on the grapevine when they have information that is recent rather than stale. Research shows that the greatest spread of information occurs immediately after it is known. When most people learn the news, grapevine activity slows down.[2]

---

[2] For more on grapevine activity see Roy Rowan, "Where Did that Rumor Come From?" *Fortune*, August 13, 1979, pp. 130–137.

Benefits of the informal organization

Every organization has an informal structure. By definition, then, there must be some very important benefits to be derived from its existence, otherwise it would cease to function. One of the most obvious reasons for an informal organization is that most of the personnel, both workers and managers, like it, want it, use it, and benefit from it! In this section we examine five major benefits to be derived from the informal organization: (1) getting things done, (2) lightening managerial work loads, (3) providing job satisfaction, (4) serving as a safety valve for employee's emotions, and (5) providing feedback to the manager.

Getting things done ✓

One of the primary benefits of the informal organization is that it supplements the formal organization in getting things done. Howard, a supervisor in the components assembly department, needs some help in securing parts from an outside supplier. The company's purchasing department is dragging its feet on the matter. Howard's friend Claire is the comptroller's secretary and a cousin of Greg, who is in charge of purchasing. Howard calls Claire and tells her his problem. Claire contacts Greg, who calls in Eddie, one of his assistants. Their discussion might go something like this:

The informal organization can help get things done.

> "**How come Howard down in the manufacturing section is having trouble getting parts from outside suppliers?**"
>
> "**Is he calling to complain again?**"
>
> "**No, I got the message from someone else in the firm. Apparently this order is jeopardizing the production schedule. What is its current status?**"
>
> "**Well it's sitting on my desk, but I wanted to get some of my other paperwork cleared up before sending the order to the supplier.**"
>
> "**Forget about sending it. Call it in this afternoon and tell them we need those parts by tomorrow.**"
>
> "**Okay, I'll get on it right now.**"

Later in the afternoon, Howard gets a call from Eddie telling him that the parts are on the way, and they arrive the next morning.

We can diagram this flow of communication as in Figure 5.7. Note that Howard used the authority of the purchasing manager to help him get the needed parts. However, he worked through the informal organization in contacting Claire, and she used the network in reaching Greg. Without the informal organization everyone would go "through channels" and it would take a lot longer to accomplish anything. Many of the organization's best workers would leave, and those who remained would simply stop putting out extra effort. After all, who wants to spend all his or her time fighting organization red tape?

Figure 5.7
The informal organization in action

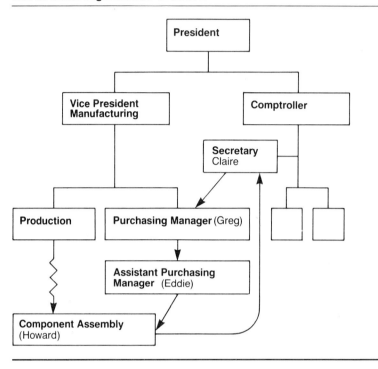

✓Lightening managerial workloads

It can lighten the manager's workload.

Another benefit of the informal organization is to lighten managerial work loads. When managers realize that the informal organization is on their side, they are more likely to delegate authority and to rely on their subordinates to get things done. This results in looser, more generalized control and often creates a feeling of trust among the workers, who respond by showing the manager that they are indeed reliable. The outcome is higher productivity.

✓Providing job satisfaction

It can bring about job satisfaction.

An accompanying benefit is *job satisfaction*, a term that relates to the favorableness or unfavorableness with which the personnel view their work. This topic is discussed in greater depth later, but let us briefly examine a few of its aspects here. Satisfaction is a relative matter in that whether people are satisfied or dissatisfied is determined by how well their expectations fit with what they are given. If Tony has been led to believe that the company stresses imagination and creativity and finds himself instead saddled with rules and procedures, he will be dissatisfied. Conversely, if Dick expects his new job to pay well but to be boring, and to his surprise finds the work both interesting and challenging, he will be very satisfied.

Job satisfaction is also related to absenteeism, turnover, and productivity. The higher the satisfaction, the lower the likelihood of both absenteeism and turnover and the higher the likelihood of productivity.[3] When personnel find the work satisfying, they derive a sense of meaningfulness and tend to remain on the job. Much of this satisfaction is related to the social environment in which the work is done. Thus the informal organization helps create a *climate* conducive to high productivity.

Serving as a safety valve

The grapevine also functions as a safety valve for employees' emotions. It lets the workers blow off steam and release some of their job pressures. When a person is angry over something, he or she needs some release for the frustration and resentment. This is where the informal organization plays a role. For example, if Don and his boss were to have an argument and he were to tell the boss where to get off, he could be fired. Instead, Don complains to his fellow workers. By sharing his problem with other employees, Don is able to release much of his pent-up anger in a way that does *not* threaten his job. Also, after he talks about the issue for a while, it is likely to appear minor and he can turn his attention back to doing his job.

It can serve as a safety valve for employee emotions.

Providing feedback

Perhaps the greatest overall benefit of the informal organization is that of providing the manager with feedback. The grapevine, in particular, reflects how the workers feel about the company, the managers, and the work. By tapping the communication flow, the manager can learn what is going on. If a manager makes a bad decision or does not know how to supervise the subordinates properly, this information will eventually be carried back to the *boss*. What better way to protect one's job than by learning of problems through the grapevine and working to correct them before the boss asks, "What's this I hear about you having trouble with . . . ?"

And provide the manager with feedback.

[3] For more information about this issue see Benjamin Schneider and Robert A. Snyder, "Some Relationships between Job Satisfaction and Organizational Climate," *Journal of Applied Psychology*, June 1975, pp. 318–328; Ray Wild, "Job Needs, Job Satisfaction, and Job Behavior of Women Manual Workers," *Journal of Applied Psychology*, April 1970, pp. 152–162.

Drawbacks of the informal organization

Despite its potential benefits, the informal organization has drawbacks. The most common include: (1) resistance to change, (2) goal conflict, (3) conformity problems, and (4) rumor.

Resistance to change

One of the greatest drawbacks of the informal organization is its resistance to change. Quite often the organization systematically ignores or only partially carries out directives related to such changes as new work procedures or rules. The overriding philosophy of many informal organizations is "Live and let live." They do not want the status quo changed.

The informal organization sometimes fights change.

Of course, change is inevitable. Technological innovations, plant redesign, and competitive developments in the external environment all require the organization to adapt operations to meet these conditions. If an innovative press is developed that will reduce current printing costs by 33 percent, a printing company has to buy it. However, part of this cost savings may be a result of manpower reduction. This is why the informal organization will fight the change. It does not want any of its members to be fired. Nor, as noted about group cohesion in Chapter 4, does the informal organization approve of any people being reassigned. If the company breaks up a cohesive group, productivity may drop off (see Figure 4.5).

Another reason the informal organization resists change is that work standards or quotas are often increased. In many cases, change generates new job demands; in *all* cases, it brings about higher efficiency (or at least attempts to achieve efficiency). For example, if a company establishes new work procedures, it is usually because a faster way of doing the job has been discovered. If work assignments are changed, it is because the firm has found a way to get more output with the same number of people. The informal organization resists such efficiency moves for three reasons. First, as mentioned, the people like the status quo and believe that any change will disrupt their pleasant work environment. Second, if they conform and do more work, the management may believe that it can introduce change any time it wants, and it may begin regarding the people as mere factors of production who need not be consulted in advance about changes. By resisting, the informal organization insures that management keeps the human element in mind when introducing change. Third, many members of the informal organization believe that it is unfair of management to introduce efficiency measures and keep all the profit for the company. If the people are going to do more work, they should be paid more money. Keep in mind, however, that this is not always a fair argument. If the firm buys a new machine for $500,000, the cost savings may allow it to pay for the machine and keep costs at a competitive level but may not increase profits. Of course, not being privy to such financial data, the informal organization may simply assume that changes in the work environment always increase profit.

Goal conflict

Goal conflict occurs whenever someone is asked to pursue two objectives that work against each other. For example, Joe wants to be a member of the informal organization but also wants to meet the work quota assigned by management. The informal organization quota is only 80 percent of the company quota. Clearly, Joe cannot be totally loyal to both.

It can lead to goal conflict.

As we discover later in this chapter, the management must carefully cultivate mutual interests with informal groups so as to integrate the goals of both. This is not an area where the firm will ever achieve perfect harmony, since there will always be some differences between the formal and informal organizations, but the management must strive to reduce the differences to an "acceptable" level.

Conformity

Closely related to goal conflict is the problem of conformity. Group norms and sanctions are used in persuading members to accept informal goals. Sometimes these norms and sanctions are so strong that individuals feel compelled to go along with the group in spite of their own inclinations. More likely, however, the informal organization becomes so much a part of the employees' work lives that they are unaware of its presence. As a result, they conform without consciously weighing the pros and cons of such action; even if their conformity were pointed out to them, they would be unwilling to deviate from these informal norms.

It can result in conformity.

Rumor

Rumor is considered the most undesirable feature of the informal organization. Many people believe that the word is synonymous for the total product of the grapevine, but this is not so. Rumor is the unverified or untrue part of grapevine information. Communication theorists often define rumor as a product of interest and ambiguity.[4]

It can cause rumors.

Rumor = Interest × Ambiguity

The logic behind this equation is quite simple. First, there can be no rumor unless the issue is of interest to someone. You undoubtedly have

---

[4]See, for example, Gordon W. Allport and Leo Postman, *The Psychology of Rumor* (New York: Holt, Rinehart and Winston, Inc., 1974), p. 33.

never heard a rumor about the impact of the ice age on the existence of the penguin. However, you may have passed on a rumor about the type of examination given by a math professor in whose class you were currently registered. Second, if all the facts about a situation are known, there is no cause for rumor. If the professor told you that the final exam would come from the last 10 chapters of the book, ambiguity would be much less than if the questions were to be drawn from all 20 chapters and all class discussion. Ambiguity would be further reduced if the professor gave out a list of 50 equations from which the 25 exam problems would be drawn exclusively. Ambiguity could never be totally eliminated (which 25 equations?), but it would be reduced.

Rumor is both maintained and magnified through the use of selective filtering and elaboration. *Selective filtering* involves the screening of rumor so that part of the story is maintained and the rest is discarded. Usually, the part that is kept is the part that is of greatest interest to the person repeating the rumor. This is then *elaborated* upon: details are added and are rearranged to fit the individual's point of view.

Let us take an example:

Marie Anderson, Bob Fairchild, and Harvey Mayoral are in Professor Brilliant's math class. Marie has a 93 (A) average, Bob an 83 (B) average, and Harvey a 73 (C) average. The professor has announced to the class that they have a choice about taking the final examination. Anyone who does not take the examination will receive a final grade one letter below the grade average he or she has earned on the other tests. Anyone who takes the examination and scores at least 50 points will receive a final grade equal to the grade average he or she has earned on the other tests. Anyone who takes the examination and scores higher will receive a final grade correspondingly higher than the grade average he or she has earned on the other tests.

Harvey does not want a D in the course, so he goes to Professor Brilliant to get some more information on the structure of the exam. The professor tells him that there will be five problems, each worth 20 points. One problem will be similar to those done in class in the past three weeks, two are similar to those done in laboratory sections with the teaching assistant in the last three weeks, one will be drawn from the problems at the end of the last six chapters of the text, and one problem will come from the last six chapters in the student study guide. Harvey has not bought the student study guide, nor has he done any of the problems at the end of the chapters. However, he has been to class and to lab, and he feels he can brush up on that material without too much work.

When Bob asks him what the professor said about the exam, Harvey answers, "Most of the material will come from lecture and, most importantly, lab, with a little attention to the text problems and study guide assignments." Bob has bought neither the text nor the study guide. He has been sharing his girlfriend's text, but they split up last week. He has only his class and lab notes, and he doubts whether these will get him through. He therefore decides to skip the final and take a C.

When Marie asks him about the makeup of the exam, Bob says, "Harvey told me that just about all of it is going to come from the text

and study guide and almost nothing from lecture and lab." Marie, who has been doing all the assignments, spends most of her time working on text and study guide problems. She gets a perfect grade on the two exam problems drawn from the text and study guide. Because she has merely perused her class and laboratory notes, she cannot do the other problems. She earns only 53 points on the final exam and just manages to keep her A.

After the test scores have been posted, Marie remarks to Bob, "Boy, did Professor Brilliant cross us up! The exam wasn't anything like he said it would be."

Harvey, hearing her, disagrees. "No, that's not so, Marie. The exam was exactly what Professor Brilliant promised. I got a 73 on the exam and kept my C."

What happened in the transfer of information from Harvey to Bob to Marie? Harvey and Bob filtered and elaborated on the message to suit their own study habits and in the process created a rumor. Harvey had the lecture and lab notes; this was his strong suit. He, therefore, filtered out much of the reference to the text and study guide material before giving Bob his interpretation of the professor's message. This led Bob to bypass the exam. Why did Bob tell Marie that the exam would be drawn most heavily from the text and study guide? Because Bob *wanted* to believe that. It provided the basis for his deciding not to take the exam. Remember, he was unprepared for questions taken from the text and the study guide. All he had was the class and lab notes. Therefore, he did not actually lie to Marie, he simply told her what he believed. And this is how rumors get started, with each person passing on his or her *own* interpretation of a message.

Dealing with the informal organization

In dealing with the informal organization, the manager must undertake two major tasks: (1) recognize the inevitability of the informal network, and (2) attempt to influence its direction so that the goals of both the formal and informal organizations are in harmony.

Recognize its inevitability

Some managers believe that the disadvantages of the informal organization more than outweigh the benefits. As a result, they try to develop means of "stamping it out." However, this approach is never really successful. Using the grapevine as a representative segment of the informal organization, Davis has offered the following explanation of its inevitability:

. . . In a sense, the grapevine is a human birthright, because whenever people congregate into groups, the grapevine is sure to develop. It may use smoke signals, jungle tom-toms, taps on the prison wall, ordinary

The grapevine cannot be eliminated.

Miss Johnson, I have a message of great importance for all employees. Please connect me with the grapevine.

Published by AMACOM, division of American Management Association. Cartoon by Henry Martin. Copyright 1975. Reprinted by permission of Henry R. Martin.

conversation, or some other method, but it will always be there. Organizations cannot "fire" the grapevine because they did not hire it. It is simply there.[5]

Because the informal organization is inevitable, the manager must develop methods for influencing it.

Influence its direction

One of the most direct ways for a manager to influence the informal organization is by tapping its grapevine, learning what is being communicated, and countering any negative rumors by getting the organization's

---

[5] Davis, *op. cit.*, pp. 337–338.

message into the channel. This can be done by learning who the liaison people in the informal network are and using them as a point of entry.

Of course, if the manager begins feeding rumors or half-truths back into the grapevine, the liaison people will either modify the message or simply refuse to carry another organization message. The manager cannot fight rumor with rumor. He or she must determine whether the information in the grapevine is accurate or not, and when it is inaccurate, must substitute correct information.

Do managers really use the grapevine to influence the informal organization? Research shows that they do. Knippen studied the grapevine in a large grocery store and found that although employees knew only 42 percent of the grapevine information, managers knew about 70 percent. Furthermore, while the managers accounted for only a small percentage of the 170 employees, they initiated almost 50 percent of the grapevine information. On the average, each manager told eight other people, while the typical employee told four. The managers were not waiting to see what information the employees were passing through the grapevine. Rather, they were using this informal channel to get their own messages across.[6]

The manager should seek to influence it.

The purpose of these management-initiated messages should be to smooth the way for more cooperation between the formal and informal organizations. The manager's objective should be to create conditions that help align the goals of both groups. When this is accomplished, the manager will find that resistance to change is minimized, rumors are reduced, and overall organizational cooperation is achieved.

Summary

The informal organization plays a significant role in the dynamics of behavior at work. Comparison with the formal organization shows that the two organizations differ in terms of interpersonal relations, leadership, behavioral control, and dependency. One of the informal organization's most interesting behavioral aspects, however, is its communication network. Commonly referred to as the *grapevine*, this communication network is used to carry information between members of the informal organization. Four common types of grapevine network are the single strand, gossip chain, probability chain, and cluster chain. The cluster chain, which involves the selective transmission of messages, is the most common.

Some people tend to be very active on the grapevine, but others are fairly inactive. However, given the proper situation and motivation, just about everyone will be grapevine-active. Research reveals that

---

[6]Jay Knippen, "Grapevine Communication: Management Employees," *Journal of Business Research*, January 1974, pp. 47–58.

some of the most likely causes for such activity are lack of knowledge about a situation, insecurity, personal interest in a situation, and the possession of recent information.

Some of the commonly cited benefits of the informal organization are: getting things done, lightening managerial workloads, providing job satisfaction, serving as a safety valve for employee emotions, and providing feedback to the manager. Despite such benefits, however, there are some major disadvantages to the informal organization: resistance to change, goal conflict, conformity, and rumor.

In any event, the informal organization is inevitable. It cannot be stamped out, so the manager will do well to understand its presence and, if possible, to influence its direction so that the goals of both the formal and informal organizations are brought into harmony. Some of the most effective ways of doing this include tapping the grapevine to learn what is going on, countering rumor with fact, and creating conditions that help align the goals of both groups. If this can be accomplished, the manager will find that resistance to change is minimized, rumors are reduced, and overall organizational cooperation is achieved.

Key terms in the chapter

sociogram
authority
power
satisficing behavior
nucleus group
fringe group
outer group
grapevine
single strand

gossip chain
probability chain
cluster chain
goal conflict
conformity
rumor
selective filtering
elaboration

Review and study questions

1. One of the ways in which the informal organization differs from the formal organization is that of interpersonal relations. What is meant by this statement?

2. How does the formal leader differ from the informal leader?

3. In what way is authority different from power? Which is of greater importance in the informal organization?

4. What is meant by *satisficing behavior*? Give an illustration.

5. What are some of the behavioral controls used by members of the informal organization to ensure compliance with its norms?

6. In the informal organization structure, how does the nucleus group

differ from the fringe group? How does the fringe group differ from the outer group?

7. How does each of the following grapevine networks function: single strand, gossip chain, probability chain, cluster chain? Explain.

8. In your own words, when are people most likely to be grapevine-active? Give at least three illustrations.

9. In what way does the informal organization help in getting things done?

10. One of the most commonly cited benefits of the informal organization is that it helps lighten managerial workloads. How does it help do this?

11. Does the informal organization help create job satisfaction? Explain.

12. One of the biggest complaints about the informal organization is that it tends to resist change. Is this true? Defend your answer.

13. What is rumor? In what way does rumor depend upon interest and ambiguity? What roles are played by selective filtering and elaboration?

14. How should the manager deal with the informal organization? Make your answer complete.

Interpretation of the informal organization: an initial appraisal

This quiz consists of two parts. Questions 1–7 measure your use of the informal organization. Questions 8–15 measure how much you really know about the informal organization.

Do you use the informal organization? The following key is for scoring your answers to Questions 1–7. For each answer you have that agrees with this key, give yourself a point.

1. False	5. False
2. True	6. True
3. False	7. False
4. True	

The higher your score, the greater the likelihood that you use the formal one. However, if you have a score of 6 or 7, you have to be careful that you are not simply ignoring the formal structure. An extremely high score can indicate total disregard for organizational policies and procedures, but only you can determine this. Most effective managers have a score of at least 5 on this part of the quiz.

What do you know about the grapevine? Questions 8–15 are designed to measure your knowledge of the informal organization. For each answer you have that agrees with this key, give yourself a point.

8. False	**12.** False
9. True	**13.** False
10. True	**14.** False
11. True	**15.** False

If you currently know a great deal about the informal organization, your score here will be in the 6–8 range. In any event, as you read the material in this chapter you will learn the logic behind each of the above answers.

It's only a rumor

Karl Childs can hardly believe it. This is his fifth month as plant manager and virtually every week something has gone wrong. Two weeks ago during a short thunderstorm one of the managers tripped on the sidewalk just outside the main office and Karl had to insist that the safety department put a rubber mat outside the door to provide some traction for people walking on that wet pavement. Thank heavens it wasn't a visitor to the plant or a lawsuit would have ensued!

Then last week the comptroller's office showed up to investigate inventory shortages in the warehouse. Karl felt as if the audit team thought he had stolen the missing inventory.

Today, he learned through the grapevine that the union was concerned about the new machinery being installed in some of the departments. The central office approved the purchase of this machinery over eight months ago, but it has taken until now to get the order filled. The machinery represents the latest technological advances in the industry and will really boost productivity. This should mean increased profits for the firm, and according to the incentive plan in the union contract, an average bonus of about 3.2 percent for all the plant employees.

The grapevine, however, is passing a message that says the machinery will result in a cutback of about 10 percent of the work force in those departments where the equipment is being installed. A clause in the contract giving management this right lends some credibility to the rumor.

Karl has told his people that there will be no reduction in the work force. However, he is sure that the union has either not received the message or is choosing not to believe it. He is certain that once the machinery is installed and no one is laid off the rumor will die. However, he is wondering whether he should continue to ignore the rumor or take some immediate action to squelch it before it goes any farther. He has received both suggestions from his people and is unsure which course of action is better.

Questions

1. How do rumors like the one in this case get started? Explain.
2. What options are available to Karl in dealing with the problem?
3. What would you recommend that Karl do? Explain.

A call from a friend

It is company practice in the Bellante Insurance Company to hire secretarial summer help. At the end of the summer, a few of the part-time people are hired to replace the regular personnel who retire or quit, and the rest are let go. Last summer Jennifer McDermott finished a year of secretarial school and, being unable to find any full-time employment, took a job with the Bellante Company. During the summer her work was more than adequate, and she was praised a number of times by her boss. However, no offer of full-time employment was extended, and as the summer drew to a close she began looking around for another job. There was an advertisement for a secretarial job in the Sunday paper that particularly interested her, although it offered $50 a month less than what Bellante paid for full-time work.

The following Monday, Jennifer decided that if she did not hear anything about full-time employment at Bellante by Wednesday morning, she would call the other firm and set up an appointment for Friday. She did so. Then, on Wednesday afternoon, her boss called her in and said that the company was going to make her an offer the following week. Since she had already set up an appointment with the other firm, however, she decided to keep it. After the interview, she was offered a full-time job. Jennifer promised to give her answer by Monday. "If you like, you can start working for us on Monday," the personnel manager told her. Jennifer said she would think it over.

On Saturday afternoon, Jennifer received a call from one of her friends at Bellante. "Has Bellante offered you a job?" Jennifer said that she heard they were going to, but she was unsure of either the salary or the requirements. Her friend then told her that the opening that the manager had told Jennifer about was at a branch office across town. Since Jennifer did not have a car, it would take her almost two hours to get there. She therefore decided to accept the job offer from the other company.

On Monday, she called the Bellante manager to tell him that she had already taken a full-time job. When he asked her why, she said that she did not have a car and could not travel the distance to the branch office in less than two hours. The manager was amazed that Jennifer knew so much about the job he had not yet offered her. However, even though he questioned her very closely, she was unwilling to tell him how she had obtained the information.

Questions

1. What does this case show about the grapevine and its selective communication system?

2. If you were the manager, would you attempt to find out who told Jennifer that the vacancy was in the branch office or would you let the matter drop?

3. In this case, was the grapevine of value to the informal organization? The formal organization? How can the manager avoid being second-guessed by the grapevine in the future? Explain.

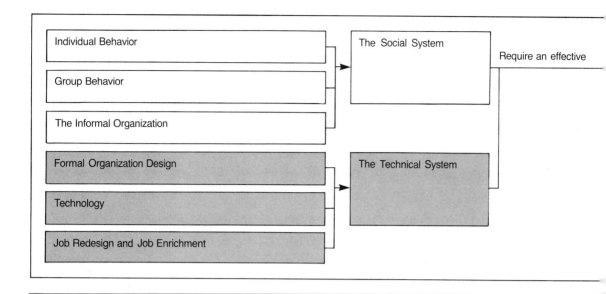

The
technical system

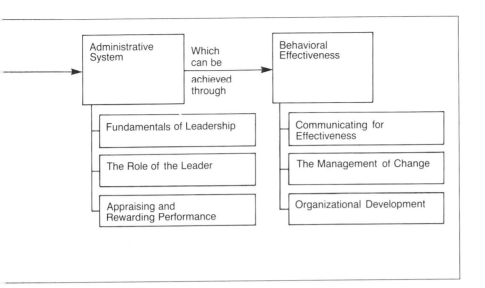

The overall objective of this part of the book is to study the technical system of organizations. In Part III we examine individual behavior and group behavior, which occur within a prescribed organizational framework or structure commonly referred to as the *technical system*. The primary focus of attention in the technical system is the organization structure. However, modern human relationists are interested in more than just the structure itself. They also want to know the particular factors of organization design, including technology, and the ways in which jobs can be redesigned to be more rewarding for the personnel and more efficient for the organization. Thus, the technical system has three major components that warrant our attention: (1) the formal organization design, (2) the impact of technology on people at work, and (3) job redesign and job enrichment.

In Chapter 6, we study formal organization design. Our primary interest is to examine how organization structures are put together. We begin by looking at some of the principles of universal design and the characteristics of the ideal bureaucracy. Then our attention switches to contingency organization design and explores why no two organization structures are identical. The heart of the chapter is given to an examination of the four major organization design factors: job descriptions, departmentalization, span of control, and decentralization and delegation of authority. In addition we study important contingency design factors, including the size of the organization, the dynamics of the environment, and the type of technology being used by the organization.

Having examined basic and contingency organization design, we then focus our attention on one of the most important structural variables of all—technology. In Chapter 7, we examine technology and its impact on people at work. This relationship, often referred to as the *sociotechnical system*, is important for modern human relations because it forces the manager to pay increased attention to the technical–human interface in modern organizations, an interface that is of major importance because of the great acceleration in the evolution of technology in the last 50 years. In the first part of Chapter 7, we trace the evolution of technology from the handicraft era to the era of cybernated technology and note the impact of knowledge on technological growth. Then we identify and describe the four major characteristics of a post-industrial society, discuss the effect of technology on work values, and describe how technology can lead to alienation. Finally, we explain how technological advances can engender fear of replacement by machine and outline some of the ways in which effective planning can result in an integration of technology and the organizational personnel. At this point attention is given to industrial democracy and participative management.

In Chapter 8, we study how modern organizations deal with the challenge of technology and its dysfunctional effects. One of the ways of doing so is to redesign jobs and enrich them with psychological motivators, and the overall goal of the chapter is to study how this can be done. We explain what job design is and explore some of the ways in which jobs can be redesigned, including job rotation, job enlargement, and job enrichment. Then we describe core job dimensions and illustrate how selected enrichment principles can be used to fulfill these dimensions. In the last part of the chapter we explain the value of quality circles and Theory Z in meeting the sociotechnical challenge, cite some illustrations of job enrichment in action, and describe some of the current challenges in job design.

When you have finished reading this part of the book you should have a solid understanding of the technical system. In particular, you should: know how organizations design their structures and the roles that are played by both universal design principles and contingency design principles, be aware of the impact of technology on the organizational personnel and the ways in which such technology can lead to alienation, be able to explain how technology can bring about fear of job replacement, and be capable of outlining some of the ways in which effective planning can bring about the needed integration of technology and organizational personnel. Additionally, you should know what is meant by job redesign, how organizations redesign jobs, and what the important job core dimensions and job enrichment principles are that play such a key role in job redesign. Most importantly, you will be aware of the all-important personnel–organizational structure interface and how modern human relations managers try to integrate the needs of both groups in attaining overall efficiency.

Formal organization design

6

Goals of the chapter

The formal organization is designed by the management. Tools of this organization include job descriptions, written policies, organization charts, and the delegation of formal authority. The first goal of this chapter is to study how an organization is formally structured by examining the concepts of universal design theory. Most organizations use these concepts as a point of departure in organizing their operations. The second goal of the chapter is to point out how contingency organization design modifies these universal guidelines. The third goal is to study the four major organization design factors: job descriptions, departmentalization, span of control, and decentralization and delegation of authority. The final goal is to review other important design factors that have become the focal point of interest in recent years, including organization size, dynamism of the environment, and production technology. Throughout the entire discussion, we shall study the ways in which modern enterprises adapt formal organization design principles to accommodate the personnel. Effective organization design is as much a matter of human relations as it is organizational principles. When you have finished reading this chapter, you should be able to:

1. describe universal design theory
2. identify the characteristics of an ideal bureaucracy
3. explain what is meant by *contingency organization design* and list some contingency design principles
4. cite the importance of job descriptions in the organizing process
5. identify and describe the major forms of departmentalization
6. define *span of control* and describe its impact on organization design
7. list some of the major factors determining a manager's span of control

8. define *line authority*, *staff authority*, and *functional authority*

9. explain the reasons behind line-staff conflict and ways to reduce such conflict to a minimum

10. describe the acceptance theory of authority and its importance for the manager

11. note some of the benefits and drawbacks associated with centralization and decentralization of authority

12. explain the effects of size of the organization, dynamics of the environment, and production technology on organization design.

Universal design theory

No two formal organization structures look exactly alike. However, all of them rely on some basic design concepts, which are then modified to meet the specific requirements of the organization. Early (classical) theorists believed in the concept of a *universal design theory*, composed of a series of principles that could be used in organizing an enterprise. Some of these principles were:

Principles of universal design theory.

1. *Division of labor*—Work specialization will bring about maximum efficiency.

2. *Parity of authority and responsibility*—When work is delegated, the person given responsibility for a job must have the authority to get the work done.

3. *Unity of command*—Everyone should have one and only one boss.

4. *Unity of management*—There should be one manager and one plan for all operations having the same objective.

5. *Span of control*—There is an optimum number of subordinates that a superior can effectively manage (usually three to six).

Many modern organizations rely upon these principles in organizing their operations. However, the principles are used as guidelines and not as rules. Most organizations would not hesitate to break one of these rules if they believe doing so would be more effective. Additionally, if an organization were to adhere rigidly to any series of organizing principles, the result might well be a bureaucracy in which everything was done by the book and the outcome might be a mass of red tape, inefficiency, and lack of concern for the people in the structure. A brief look at bureaucracy should make this clear.

Bureaucracy

The term *bureaucracy* usually brings to mind a giant organization replete with rules, policies, procedures, and a distinct lack of concern for the personnel. Max Weber, most famous for his analysis of these structures, identified the following characteristics of the *ideal* bureaucracy:

1. a clear-cut division of labor resulting in a host of specialized experts in each position.
2. a hierarchy of offices with each lower one being controlled and supervised by the one immediately above it.
3. a consistent system of abstract rules and standards which assure uniformity in the performance of all duties and the coordination of various tasks.
4. a spirit of formalistic impersonality in which officials carry out the duties of their office.
5. employment based on technical qualifications and protected from arbitrary dismissal.[1]

Characteristics of the ideal bureaucracy.

A close analysis of these characteristics reveals both advantages and limitations. On the positive side, the ideal bureaucracy is scientifically designed and laid out. Its rules and standards assure uniformity of action, and the impersonality of the officials ensures that they will not reward or punish people on the basis of personal likes or dislikes. Everything is tied to job performance and obedience to the rules.

On the negative side, the organization encourages mediocrity. Everyone is supposed to do things in a uniform manner. This means that if a cost control report is due in five days, you submit it on the fifth day, neither early nor late. Additionally, you do not work too fast; you do not work too hard; you do not volunteer for extra assignments; you do not try to excel. Arnold Toynbee, the renowned historian, described civil service bureaucracy in this way:

In the world of civil service plunging into action is the archcrime. When you sight an objective you must not head straight for it. You must consult a thousand colleagues who have a right to file objections in the names of a hundred other government departments that are all great powers, and you must not feel frustrated or guilty when you find yourself bogged down. The civil servant's duty is not to achieve desirable results; it is to follow the correct procedure.[2]

The motto of the bureaucrat is: "Never take the initiative."

In most cases the advantages of the ideal bureaucracy are outweighed by its disadvantages. Failing to address the human needs of the personnel, this organization design cannot accommodate the brilliant executive, the daring advertising manager, the creative engineer, or any above-average person. Over time, these people leave the bureaucracy to work for a competing company whose organization accommodates their needs. Two alternatives are then available to the bureaucracy: it may eventually be driven out of existence by the more effective competition, or it can modify the rigidity of its design. The latter is most commonly chosen, in which case the organization develops a *modified* bureaucratic design.

---

[1] Peter M. Blau, *Bureaucracy in Modern Society* (New York: Random House, Inc., 1956), pp. 28–33.
[2] In *Management's Mission in a New Society*, ed. Dan H. Fenn, Jr. (New York: McGraw-Hill Book Company, 1959), p. 7.

Most large businesses are modified bureaucracies. They alter the basic ideas set forth by Weber and the universal design theorists to meet the needs of the specific situation. This has led to the emergence of contingency organization design.

Contingency organization design

Contingency organization design is based on the principle that the organization structure accommodates the specific needs of the situation. For example, instead of ruling that everyone should have one and only one boss, we would examine a particular job to see if there are times when the person filling it might be more effective if he or she had two or more bosses. While the unity of command principle is still widely practiced in many organizations, it has been successfully violated. For example, in the construction of skyscrapers, aircraft, and aerospace vehicles, unity of command is abandoned and efficiency is increased.

How does the manager know when to follow one of the universal design principles and when to modify it? By experience. What worked well the last time? If he or she has no personal experience with a particular issue, the manager can consult with colleagues, review current management literature, or, if these approaches fail, use his or her best judgement. In any event, the manager will begin to compile a list of contingency organization design principles, many of which are human relations in orientation, that relate how to handle specific situations. Advocates of this approach believe strongly in the formulation of "if—then" propositions.

Contingency organization design principles and human relations

Here are five illustrations of contingency organization design applied to common situations.

If the organization is in a highly competitive environment, *then* it must decentralize authority to the operating level so that people there can make swift, on-the-spot decisions.

"If—then" contingency design principles.

If a manager is unable to adequately control all the subordinates, *then* this number must be reduced.

If capable subordinates have a desire for more authority and responsibility, *then* the manager should delegate it.

If the size of the organization increases, *then* the manager should consider the implementation of rules and policies so as to more effectively manage this larger number of personnel.

If a decision involves a lot of money, *then* it ought to be made by top management; *if* a decision involves a small amount of money, *then* it ought to be made by lower-level management.

These design principles are important in the study of human relations because they illustrate how a concern for the structure can be blended with a concern for the personnel. In each of the above stated principles, organization design concepts were modified to address the human element. Universal design theory and its bureaucratic emphasis has given way to a modern contingency approach in which a balance is being struck between the need for design efficiency and for human relations effectiveness.

The principles are human relations in orientation.

Major organization design factors

Now we study major factors in formal organization design with particular emphasis on how they are used in modern organizations and why an understanding of them is important to the study of human relations. In each case, we first examine the basic factor and then discuss how it is modified in practice. For example, after looking at job definitions and how they are important to efficiency, we investigate how organizations attempt to modify or redesign jobs to make them more interesting and rewarding. Likewise, we examine the issue of authority to determine where the manager gets his or her authority and then look at why astute managers never give orders that will not be obeyed. In short, every organizing factor has to be modified to meet the situation. The formal organization cannot be structured according to a master blueprint the way a high-rise building can; it must be flexible and responsive to environmental considerations.

There are four major organization design factors that are used by virtually every organization: (1) job descriptions, (2) departmentalization, (3) span of control, and (4) decentralization and delegation of authority.

Job descriptions and human relations

In a well-run organization, all the employees know what they are supposed to be doing, to whom they report, and who reports to them. This knowledge is generally conveyed to each person in the form of a *job description*. Figure 6.1 contains some illustrations of job descriptions.

Quite often these descriptions are written in such a way as to promote *division of labor*. For example, secretaries are charged with typing and taking dictation; sales managers are responsible for working with the salespeople in setting quotas and motivating the sales force to meet these objectives; unit managers are accountable for the overall profit performances of their units. The first of these three jobs is the most technical and can be defined in much more specific terms than the last, which tends to be more open-ended. In any case, a job description limits the individual's range of activities.

Is the idea of task specialization an effective organizing principle? It depends. We know from research, for example, that many organizations reach new levels of efficiency through job specialization. However, there

---

Figure 6.1

Illustrations of job definitions

Personnel Officer in a Large State Agency

Performs responsible administrative work managing personnel activities of a large state agency or institution. Work involves responsibility for the planning and administration of a personnel program that includes recruitment, examination, selection, evaluation, appointment, promotion, transfer, and recommended change of status of agency employees, and a system of communication for disseminating necessary information to workers. Works under general supervision, exercising initiative and independent judgment in the performance of assigned tasks.

Flight Attendant for a Commercial Airline[1]

Performs or assists in the performance of all enroute cabin service to passengers or ground cabin service to delayed or cancelled passengers in a resourceful and gracious manner. Works in an environment subject to various climatic conditions, changing locales, variable hours and working conditions, dry air, moderate noise levels, dim lighting, confined spaces, and continuous and frequent contact with others. Provides passengers with appropriate safety information, insures compliance with government and company regulations, provides leadership, direction and assistance to passengers during emergencies, including aircraft evacuation, assists passengers with baggage and garments, answers passenger inquiries, deals with disorderly passengers and unusual incidents (bomb threats, hijacking, delays, etc.), and serves food and beverages.

Stenographer-Clerk in an Insurance Firm[2]

Under direct supervision, takes and transcribes moderately difficult dictation from one or more individuals, performs a variety of clerical duties, and usually carries out a regularly assigned, specific clerical task related to the functions of the unit. Performs miscellaneous typing and related duties as assigned.

---

[1] Courtesy of Eastern Airlines.
[2] Richard M. Hodgetts, *Introduction to Business*, 2nd ed. (Reading, Mass.: Addison-Wesley Publishing, 1981), p. 204.

is an *optimum* degree of specialization in most jobs, and *overspecialization* can result in lower output, attitudes, and productivity. This idea is illustrated in Figure 6.2.

In many organizations, the optimal balance is attained through a human relations concept known as *job design*. The work is restructured to blend the needs of the organization with those of the person doing the work. Since we examine job design in great depth in Chapter 8, let us defer detailed discussion here and simply set forth some of the common characteristics of carefully designed jobs:

General characteristics of well-designed jobs.

1. **Is sufficiently difficult so as to be challenging.**
2. **Is sufficiently diverse so as to be interesting.**
3. **Provides for constructive interaction with other workers.**
4. **Work cycle is sufficiently long so that the work is not repetitive or monotonous.**
5. **Scope is large enough that the worker can feel he or she makes a meaningful contribution to the product or service.**

Figure 6.2
Relationship between specialization and efficiency: a typical illustration

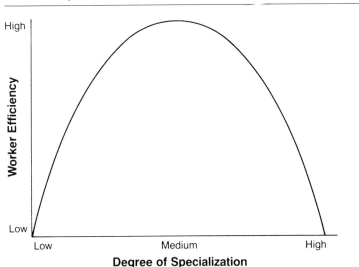

6. **Provides for regular and frequent feedback regarding how well one is doing.**
7. **Allows considerable self-control over one's work.**[3]

So while job descriptions and division of labor are important organizational concepts, in modern enterprises they are modified to accommodate the needs and desires of the personnel. Taken in the extreme, job descriptions could make the worker a mere adjunct of the machine. The worker would be told when, what, and how to function. When modified in human relations terms, the job descriptions help explain the job and how it is to be done, but do not shackle or constrain the worker's ability to function effectively.

Departmentalization

Departmentalization is a term applied to the process of grouping employees into units on an organization-wide basis. Sometimes the basis for departmentalization remains the same for all levels of the hierarchy, and at other times it differs from level to level.

---

[3]Raymond A. Katzell and Daniel Yankelovich, *Work, Productivity and Job Satisfaction: An Evaluation of Policy-Related Research* (New York: The Psychological Corporation, 1975), pp. 184–185.

Figure 6.3
Functional departmentalization (partial organization chart)

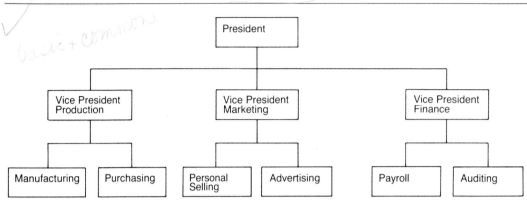

Types of departmentalization   One of the most common bases for departmentalization is function. Personnel are grouped into departments on the basis of the jobs they perform. Figure 6.3 is an illustration of *functional departmentalization*. Note that there are three major functional departments: production, marketing, and finance. Within each of these are two derivative functional departments: manufacturing and purchasing in the production department, personal selling and advertising in the marketing department, and payroll and auditing in the finance department. In each instance the personnel are being organized on the basis of function or job.

This form of departmentalization is the most popular because it is usually quite easy to organize the personnel this way. The only question that must be asked is: what does this individual do? A salesperson is assigned to the personal selling department, a machinist is put in manufacturing, and a payroll clerk works in the payroll department.

Some by product.

Many of the large firms with which most of us are familiar, including General Motors, General Electric, and RCA, are organized by product. As organizations grow in size they tend to abandon a functional structure at the top and substitute a *product departmentalization* arrangement (Figure 6.4). The firm still needs production, marketing, and finance departments, but these are now located within the specific product area. The result is the formation of a *profit center*, which often is operated like an independent business. The vice president of Product A is held accountable for sales, growth, and profit of this product line. The same is true for the vice presidents of Products B and C.

Some geographically.

As organizations grow even larger and expand operations to more areas they often use *geographic departmentalization*, the grouping of

Figure 6.4
Product departmentalization (partial organization chart)

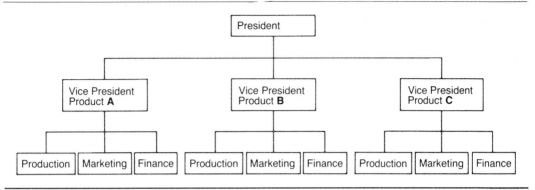

Figure 6.5
Geographic departmentalization (partial organization chart)

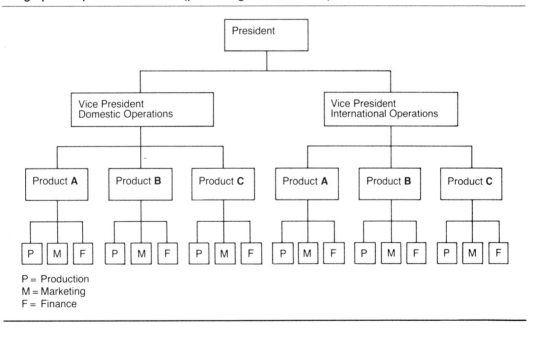

P = Production
M = Marketing
F = Finance

people and activities on the basis of location. Figure 6.5 is an illustration; note a manufacturing firm with three product lines has expanded into international operations.

Departmentalization and human relations   An organization uses departmentalization to achieve internal efficiency. Part of this efficiency is a result of employee satisfaction.

The functional departmentalization arrangement helps create satisfaction by grouping together those people performing similar activities. As we saw in Chapter 4, most people enjoy interacting with others who have similar interests, tastes, and preferences. A feeling of togetherness is created. Thus, a functional organization structure can provide employee satisfaction.

The advantages of each departmentalization form should be understood.

A product departmentalization arrangement can also promote esprit de corps. The personnel are members of a profit center and have the authority to run the unit as they see fit. This organization design encourages initiative and hard work and is often a source of satisfaction for its members. As one top executive in a product organization put it, "Our product line was the firm's biggest profit item last year, and each of us draws a sense of accomplishment from this."

A geographic departmentalization arrangement offers similar psychological rewards. The personnel often watch the performance indications of their geographic locale, such as sales for the region or the store, to see how well they are doing in comparison with the other regions or stores. By organizing geographically, a company can often achieve higher efficiency.

Span of control

Span of control is the number of subordinates reporting to a superior.

Span of control refers to the number of subordinates who report to a specific superior. Classical organization theorists believed that narrow spans (3 to 6 subordinates) were superior to wide ones (7 to 10 or more). By definition, this line of thinking encourages *tall* structures, as in Figure 6.6, as opposed to *flat* structures, as in Figure 6.7. Note that with a span of control of 2 it takes 6 hierarchical levels to organize 63 people (Figure 6.6), whereas a span of 8 needs 3 levels to organize 73 people (Figure 6.7).

For years, organizational theorists have argued the relative merits of tall and flat structures. So far, no research has shown conclusively that one is always superior to the other; however, there are times when one offers better results than the other. For example, Porter and Lawler have reported that in companies with less than 5,000 employees the flat structure tends to provide greater job satisfaction but in larger companies the tall structure brings about higher job satisfaction.[4] It also appears that upper-level managers experience greater satisfaction in tall structures and lower-level managers are more satisfied in flat structures.[5]

[4] Lyman W. Porter and Edward E. Lawler, III, "The Effect of 'Tall' Versus 'Flat' Organization Structure on Managerial Job Satisfaction," *Personnel Psychology*, Summer 1964, pp. 135–148.
[5] Chris J. Berger and L. L. Cummings, "Organization Structure, Attitudes and Behavior: Where Are We Now?" *Academy of Management Proceedings*, 1975, pp. 176–178.

Figure 6.6
Tall organization structure (span of 2)

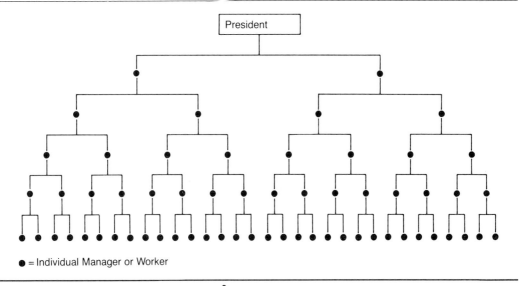

● = Individual Manager or Worker

Figure 6.7
Flat organization structure (span of 8)

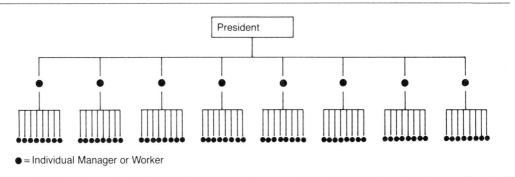

● = Individual Manager or Worker

The human relations element Figure 6.8 presents some of the major factors that influence spans of control on a more *individualized* or human relations basis. Work experience, job difficulty, and managerial style are all important determinants of span of control. However, this list is not all-inclusive; there are far too many factors for us to consider here. For example, technology seems to have an impact on span of control. Firms in industries with a high level or a low level of technology usually have narrow spans of control, whereas firms in industries with a middle level of technology tend to have wide spans of control. If all the subordi-

---

Figure 6.8
Some major factors determining span of control

Narrow Span	Wide Span
Subordinates have less than 5 years of job experience.	Subordinates have 10 or more years of job experience.
Subordinates have no assistants.	Subordinates have assistants of their own.
Subordinates are supervised exclusively by the superior.	Subordinates are supervised in part by others.
Subordinates all carry out different functions.	Subordinates all carry out similar functions.
Organization is large.	Organization is small.
Work is nonroutine.	Work is routine.
Worker error will prove to be a costly mistake.	Worker error will not prove very costly.
Coordination among the subordinates is of major importance.	Coordination among the subordinates is not of major importance.
Manager wants close control of subordinates.	Manager prefers loose control of subordinates.
Manager is located high up the organization.	Manager is located in the middle to lower levels of the hierarchy.

---

nates work in one location, the most effective span of control tends to be wider than if they are divided among three or four locations. Drawing together all the evidence currently available, however, we can make the following generalizations:

1. **the optimal span of control in most situations is in the range of 5 to 10.**
2. **in determining the ideal span, consideration of the costs associated with both wide and narrow spans must be studied.**
3. **in establishing a span for a specific situation, factors such as the desirability of group solidarity, the need for job satisfaction, the amount of control required, the nature of the work, the stability of the environment, and the extent of assistance to the manager have to be taken into consideration.**[6]

By adhering to such guidelines, the organization addresses the issue of optimum spans and attempts to find the right span for each manager and situation. In so doing, the enterprise also addresses the human relations side of span of control: how one balances organizational efficiency (lowest possible costs, greatest possible productivity and profit) with personnel needs and desires (autonomy, decision-making authority, and a chance to be creative).

---

[6]John B. Miner, *The Management Process: Theory, Research, and Practice*, 2nd ed. (New York: MacMillan Publishing Company, 1978), p. 291.

Decentralization and delegation of authority

In recent years more and more firms have begun decentralizing decision making, pushing responsibility for decisions further down the line toward the operating level. How does one know if an organization is basically centralized or decentralized? This question can be answered by looking at such criteria as: (1) whether a large or small number of decisions are made lower down the management hierarchy, (2) whether these decisions are important ones or just minor issues, and (3) how much checking is being made on the decisions by higher management. If a large number of decisions are being made, many of them are important, and there is a minimum of checking, the organization is *decentralized*. If the reverse is true, the organization is centralized.

Criteria for measuring decentralization.

Delegation, meanwhile, involves the distribution of work to subordinates. If the manager gets the people actively involved in carrying out departmental assignments, there will be a great deal of delegation. We know, however, that many managers tend to delegate only minor matters and to keep most of the work for themselves. In so doing they fail to develop the real potential of their subordinates and may overwork themselves in the process.

Delegation involves distribution of work to subordinates.

Is decentralization better than centralization? Should a manager always delegate as much work as possible? Before answering these questions, we need to examine the *types* of authority that can be decentralized and delegated and to understand why people are willing to obey the orders of those in authority.

Types of authority   In all, there are three types of authority: (1) line authority, (2) staff authority, and (3) functional authority.

Line authority.   Line authority is *direct* authority and is evident when a superior gives orders to a subordinate. The military is a classic illustration. The general gives orders to the colonel, who gives orders to the major, on down to the corporal who gives orders to the private. Likewise, in a business setting, orders flow down the line from superior to subordinate.

Line authority is direct authority.

Staff authority.   Staff authority is *auxiliary* authority. It is supportive in nature. Individuals with staff authority assist, advise, recommend, and facilitate organizational activities. In a business setting, the company lawyer commonly has staff authority and recommends courses of action to the manager. For example, the company lawyer often counsels the chief executive officer and provides legal advice on company matters ranging from advertising claims in an ad campaign to the proper way of firing someone who has been caught stealing from the firm.

Staff authority is auxiliary authority.

Figure 6.9
Line-Staff conflict

Line Managers	**Staff Specialists**
Are interested in what is going to happen in the short run.	Are interested in what is going to happen in the long run.
Want simple, easy-to-use solutions.	Like to provide sophisticated difficult-to-implement solutions.
Are action-oriented; they want to solve the problem *now*.	Are thought-oriented; they want to examine the problem in depth and solve it *later*.
Do not always know the right questions to ask in obtaining help.	Have a lot of answers, so they spend their time looking for questions.
Like to solve problems on the basis of experience, intuition and "gut feeling"; quantitative, theoretical, or complex recommendations make them nervous.	Like to solve problems using the latest and most sophisticated techniques; regard solutions made "off the top of the head" as inferior.

Line-Staff conflict.   Many firms have found, to their dismay, that while those with staff authority can provide line managers with valuable assistance, there is always the chance of line-staff conflict. Often, line people are middle-aged, have earned their position through years of experience with the company, and are intimately familiar with the work being done by their subordinates. They are charged with making final decisions on matters related to their area. Often, staff people are young, have education rather than experience, and are full of ideas about how to improve efficiency. Line managers sometimes feel that staff people lack practical experience, and since they have the ultimate authority for decisions, line managers are reluctant to accept advice without first giving it serious thought. After all, if an error is made, the line manager is responsible! Staff managers regard the line managers as conservative, behind the times, and unwilling to consider new ideas. They feel that the line managers should let them investigate problems, analyze alternatives, and come up with recommendations, which the line should immediately implement. Figure 6.9 lists other characteristics of line managers and staff managers that lead to disagreement.

Given these contrasting attitudes, every organization needs to develop communication between line managers and staff managers so that the full value of staff expertise can be obtained. Some suggestions are:

1. Line managers must realize that staff managers are there to assist them in getting things done. They should be encouraged to draw upon this expertise when they have a problem.

2. Staff managers must realize that their job is to recommend and ad-

*"What do you mean, I don't communicate?
Didn't you read the memo I left you at breakfast?"*

From the *Wall Street Journal*, permission Cartoon Features Syndicate.

vise but not to give orders. The line manager is the final judge of what will be done. The staff manager must "sell, not tell."

3. Line managers should explain their plans and ideas to the staff personnel, rather than keep them in the dark. A good staff specialist cannot help anyone unless he or she knows what is going on and what problems need attention.

4. Staff specialists should follow the principle of **completed staff work**, which states that when a solution or recommendation is presented to the line manager, the latter can either approve or disapprove of it. All details must have been worked out by the staff prior to presentation.

Ways of resolving line-staff conflict.

Suggestions such as these ensure better use of staff specialists while reducing line-staff conflict, which is a common human relations problem.

Functional authority. *Functional authority* is authority in a department other than one's own. An individual or department is often given functional authority over a specific process that is performed by individuals in other departments. For example, the finance department is charged with controlling expenditures and revenues. Therefore, the vice president of finance often has the functional authority to request weekly sales

Functional authority is authority in a department other than one's own.

data from the marketing department. The legal department often has the functional authority to review all new advertising campaigns to screen them for illegal or unethical practices or to make certain the company does not make any claims that are false or cannot be substantiated.

Functional authority allows for intraorganizational efficiency. However, there are problems associated with its use. One of the most common is that of power-grabbing. Another is undermining a manager's authority in his or her own department. In order to prevent such problems, several guidelines are commonly used:

1. Functional authority is given only to those who can provide a specific expertise or who need it to improve organizational efficiency.

Guidelines in using functional authority.

2. Functional authority is limited to telling people how they are to do something (provide the data on this special form) and when it is to be done; it seldom involves where, what, or who, in order not to seriously undermine their manager's authority.

3. Functional authority should be described in writing so that everyone knows who has this authority and what areas it covers.

4. No one should be given functional authority in another department without that department manager's being apprised of the decision.

5. When this authority is used the manager of the department should be kept informed about what is being requested of his or her personnel. To do otherwise is to bypass (and often undermine) his or her authority in the department.

If these guidelines are followed, human relations problems associated with the use of functional authority can be reduced and organizational efficiency can be enhanced.

Formal authority and worker acceptance   The manager in the formal organization has authority, which is defined as the right to command. This authority flows from the top down, with each manager receiving his or her authority from the respective superior.

Let us take an example. Jane is the store manager in a large retail chain. She has been charged with improving return on investment and profit, and after studying the store's operations very carefully, she has concluded that far too many people are coming in late, leaving early, and abandoning their work stations to walk around the store and talk to their friends in other departments. Jane has decided to counter this inefficiency by sending a written memo to the department managers telling them to fire anyone who comes late or leaves early. A week later Barney is caught clocking out his friend Phil, who has gone home an hour before. The department manager fires both men, and Jane backs up the decision. Where does the department manager get the right to fire the two workers? It comes from the store manager. Where does she get the right? From

Figure 6.10
Flow of formal authority

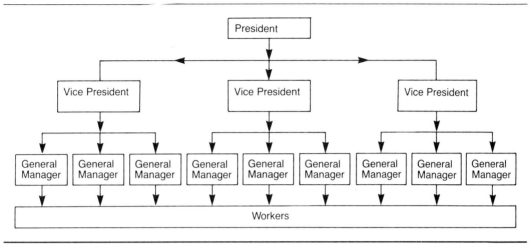

her boss, and so on up the line until we reach the company president, who receives his or her authority from the board of directors, who represent the owners of the firm. The owners, quite obviously, have the right to run the organization as they see fit, provided that no laws are broken. Formal authority flows down the line from superior to subordinate, as illustrated in Figure 6.10.

However, formal authority does not account for the total process. For example, Jane backs up the manager but the union decides to fight the decision and calls for a walkout. What will happen? It is possible that the top management will decide to compromise by allowing Jane to lay off the two workers for a week but not fire them. In this case, Jane's authority will have been limited by a higher decision. Why might the top management decide to modify her decision? Several reasons can be cited: union pressure and the possibility of losing a great deal of money if the store were to remain on strike for an extended period.

Our example of management intervention introduces one of the major rules for effective managers: never give an order that will not be obeyed. In this case the union may be so strong that it can force the top management to override the store manager's decision. When we discuss formal authority, therefore, we must also examine the role of the order takers. Will they obey? Are they likely to fight the order? Can we enforce sanctions (such as firing them) that will force them to comply or will reduce the likelihood that some of the other workers will fight our decision?

To answer these questions we must consider the *acceptance theory of authority*. This theory, formulated by Chester Barnard, holds that peo-

People will obey orders only if four conditions exist.

ple will obey orders only if four conditions exist. First, the person must understand what he or she is being asked to do. Second, at that time the person must believe the order is not inconsistent with the purpose of the organization. Third, the person must believe that the order is compatible with his or her own interests. Fourth, the person must be able to mentally and physically comply with the order.[7] If one or more of these conditions is not met, the person will refuse to obey.

Of course, if workers sat around all day deciding whether or not they were going to follow orders, management would literally be at their mercy. However, it does not work that way. Quite often, as Barnard noted, it is possible to secure the consent and cooperation of subordinates.

First, the four conditions necessary for acceptance are generally present, so the person usually accepts the communication as authoritative. Second, each individual has . . . a "zone of indifference." Orders falling within this zone are accepted without question. The others either fall on the neutral line or are conceived of as clearly unacceptable. The indifference zone tells the story, and it will be either wide or narrow, depending upon the inducements being accorded the individual and the sacrifices the worker is making on behalf of the organization. The effective executive assures that all individuals feel they are receiving more from the organization than they are giving. This widens the indifference zone, and the subordinates agreeably accept most orders. Third, one person's refusal to obey will affect the efficiency of the organization. It will also threaten the other members. When this happens, co-workers will often pressure the individual to comply, and the result is a general stability within the organization.[8]

Decentralization and delegation: contingency views

Having now discussed the types of authority a manager can have and the importance of the worker accepting this authority, let us return to our question about how much decentralization and delegation of authority is optimum.

Decentralization Should every organization decentralize to as great a degree as possible? The answer is no. In past years firms like DuPont, General Motors, Standard Oil of New Jersey, and Sears, Roebuck and Company have decentralized. Some students of management have been quick to cite them, claiming that if the big successful organizations are decentralizing, every other company should also. However, decentralization is not an overwhelming trend. Many firms in industries such as copper, nickel, aluminum, and steel have tended to remain basically

---

[7] Chester I. Barnard, *The Functions of the Executive* (Cambridge, Mass.: Harvard University Press, 1938), p. 73.

[8] Richard M. Hodgetts, *Management: Theory, Process and Practice*, 3rd ed. (Hinsdale, Ill.: Dryden Press, 1982), p. 36.

Table 6.1

Centralization or decentralization?

	Centralization	**Decentralization**
Benefits	Assures uniformity of standards and policies among the organization units. Permits the use of outstanding talent in managers by the whole organization rather than a single unit. Ensures uniform decisions. Helps eliminate duplication of effort and activity.	Reduces the total responsibility to more manageable units. Encourages more involvement of the personnel in the decision-making process. Shortens lines of communication. Brings decision making closer to those affected by the decision. Disperses power and authority among many people.
Drawbacks	Makes great demands on a few managers instead of spreading responsibility. Forces top managers to possess a broad view, which may be beyond their ability. Gives vast amounts of authority and power to a few people. Reduces a sense of participation for all but a few.	Allows a lack of uniformity of standards and policies among organizational units. Necessitates making of decisions without capable managers, who may be unavailable or unwilling to participate. Can create coordination problems among the various organizational units. Can lead to interunit rivalry, which can interfere with the organization's overall effectiveness. Requires training programs, which can be time consuming and costly.

centralized (International Nickel, Alcoa, Bethlehem Steel, and Jones & Laughlin). The decision to decentralize depends on size and environmental changes. Firms that are in highly competitive environments or have been diversifying are much more likely to decentralize than those that are in stable environments and are not increasing their operations through merger or acquisition. Table 6.1 compares some of the benefits and drawbacks associated with centralization and decentralization. Some contingency questions, however, must be asked before a decision about decentralization is made. They include:

1. *How much coordination will be needed between units or individuals?* The more coordination required the greater the need for centralization. If only limited coordination is needed, decentralization is possible.

Questions for deciding whether to remain centralized or to decentralize.

2. *Where can planning be accomplished best?* If planning must be performed by individuals possessing a broad overview of the entire organization, centralization will be needed. If, however, planning can be oriented to local, more specialized functions and duties, decentralization will be best.

3. *Are rigid controls necessary?* If strict performance standards are essential, centralization will be preferable; if not, decentralization is more likely to be possible.

4. *Are the individuals who will be a part of the decentralized unit capable of self-direction, self-motivation, and self-control?* The more capable subordinates are of handling authority, the more authority they can be given.

5. *Are the individuals who will be part of the decentralized unit willing to assume the self-generating responsibilities of decentralization?* The attitude of the affected individuals must be favorable toward receiving more authority if the change is to be successful.

6. *Will initiative and morale be significantly improved by decentralization?* Decentralization typically improves the initiative and morale of the affected (decentralized) unit, but what will be the effect on other levels? Ideally, the response to decentralization will be favorable from all quarters; however, this is not always the case.

Delegation.   Some managers are reluctant to delegate authority, and some subordinates are afraid to accept it. Figure 6.11 provides some reasons for both of these occurrences. Research reveals that regardless of job descriptions or company directives, subordinates who want to exercise authority will either encourage their boss to delegate it to them or will simply take it upon themselves to do the tasks. Similarly, subordinates who do not want authority to be delegated to them will simply

---

Figure 6.11

Why delegation does not take place

The boss is reluctant because he or she:	The subordinate is reluctant because he or she:
Feels he or she can do better personally.	Would rather ask the boss than do it personally.
Is unable to instruct the subordinates.	Is afraid of harsh criticism.
Lacks confidence in the subordinates.	Lacks self-confidence.
Has inadequate control warnings.	Does not have the necessary resources.
Dislikes taking a chance.	Has inadequate positive incentives for accepting the work.

Adapted from William H. Newman, E. Kirby Warren, and Jerome Schnee, *The Process of Management*, 5th ed. (Englewood Cliffs, N.J.: Prentice-Hall, 1982), p. 227.

refuse to accept it. In the final analysis, however, the problem rests with the manager.

Formal delegation may be less important to the final outcome than the individual tendencies of managers to make their own decision or defer to superiors. Clearly many managers are unwilling to take the risk of making decisions and being held accountable. They claim that their freedom of action is restricted, when in fact they merely do not want to accept responsibility for their own decisions. It seems apparent from . . . research that if delegation is to prove effective, managers must be found or developed who can accept delegation and make decisions in accordance with the requirements of this . . . role.[9]

How can you be more effective in delegating? Some of the most helpful human relations guidelines are the following:

1. Make sure the people to whom you delegate are able to do the job.

2. Give these individuals all of the relevant information you have about the task to be accomplished.

3. Clearly spell out to them the results that you expect.

4. Make sure they understand the standards and guidelines that will be used to measure their performance.

5. Monitor their progress through meetings, personal inspections, and status reports so you know what is going on.

6. Establish controls that will alert you to any problems they are having.

7. If there is a need for you to get involved, do so. Do not wait until the situation is out of control. Remember, you have only delegated authority not abdicated responsibility!

How well do you personally do as a delegator? In answering this question, take the quiz to see how effective you are as a delegator.

Other important factors

The four factors we have just examined (job descriptions, departmentalization, span of control, and decentralization and delegation of authority) were of great interest to universal design theorists. However, there are other important factors to which they gave little attention; only with recent interest in contingency organization design and human relations have these become a focal point. Three of the most important are: (1) size of the organization, (2) dynamism of the environment, and (3) production technology.

---

[9]Miner, *The Management Process: Theory, Research, and Practice*, pp. 278–279.

How effective are you as a delegator?

The following questions are designed to measure how well you delegate. If you are a manager, answer the questions from that point of view. If you are not a manager, use your personal insights to help identify how you would respond to each if you were put in a managerial position.

	Yes	No
1. Do you make sure your people get all of the information they need to carry out delegated assignments?	_____	_____
2. Do you ensure that your people are trained to handle tasks before you delegate the work to them?	_____	_____
3. If your people make decisions that you think you can handle better, do you overrule them?	_____	_____
4. Do you use subordinate mistakes to weed out incompetents and serve as a lesson to others to shape up or ship out?	_____	_____
5. If a subordinate makes a decision and it proves to be wrong, do you assume a portion of the responsibility yourself because final accountability rests with you (as opposed to letting this person take the entire blame)?	_____	_____
6. When someone comes to you asking for help with a decision, do you make the decision rather than spend time helping them work it out?	_____	_____
7. Do you define the limits of delegated authority so your people know the authority they have and do not have?	_____	_____
8. Do you trust your people enough to let them handle any situations on their own?	_____	_____
9. If your people do make mistakes, do you use them to find out what went wrong and how they can be prevented in the future (as opposed to punishing them for the error)?	_____	_____
10. Have you a follow-up system for evaluating how well things are going without having to continuously look over your subordinates' shoulders?	_____	_____

Size of the organization

Size is an important variable, because small organizations or departments require a different type of structure from that of large ones if maximum efficiency is to be achieved. In fact, behaviorists argue the disadvantages of bureaucracy, but as organizations get larger and larger, the most successful are those that become more and more formally structured. Child has commented on this development.

Large organizations tend to be much more formalized.

> **Much as critics may decry bureaucracy, we found that in each industry the more profitable and faster-growing companies were those that had developed this type of organization in fuller measure with their growth in size above the 2,000-or-so employee mark. At the other end of the scale, among small firms of about 100 employees, the better performers generally managed with very little formal organization. The larger the company, the higher the correlation between more bureaucracy and superior performance.**[10]

However, these findings must not be construed to mean that every organization automatically becomes more bureaucratic in design as it grows in size. Much of this trend toward formalization is determined by the number of people in the local area. If an organization doubles in size but the number of people in each department or geographic unit remains the same, there will be far less formalization than if they are all located under one roof. Furthermore, as Miner has noted, "taking all considerations into account, the evidence argues strongly for an approach to departmentation that produces relatively small units."[11]

Dynamics of the environment

Another important factor affecting organization structure is the dynamics of the environment. Is the organization operating in a stable or turbulent setting? The most significant research in this area has been conducted by Burns and Stalker.[12] They investigated 20 industrial firms in Great Britain for the purpose of determining the impact of the technological and market environment on, among other things, organization structure. They arrayed the firms according to the environment in which each operated, from the most stable to the least predictable. They found that organizations operating in a stable environment made great use of organization charts, job descriptions, rules, policies, and standing plans. Conversely, those operating in a very dynamic environment had no organization charts, job descriptions, or standing plans. The former was highly structured; the latter was very flexible.

The dynamics of the environment will affect the structure.

---

[10] John Child, "What Determines Organization Performance? The Universals vs. the It-All-Depends," *Organizational Dynamics*, Summer 1974, p. 13.

[11] Miner, *The Management Process: Theory, Research, and Practice*, p. 306.

[12] T. Burns and G. M. Stalker, *The Management of Innovation* (London: Tavistock Publications, 1961).

Table 6.2

A comparison of mechanistic and organic structures

Some Key Dimensions	Mechanistic Structure	Organic Structure
General nature	calm	turbulent
Predictability	certain	uncertain
Technology	stable	dynamic
General nature of the work	routine, repetitive	nonroutine, varied
Goal-setting process	from the top down	participatory
Time perspective	short run	long run
Motivation	emphasis on extrinsic rewards	emphasis on intrinsic rewards
Overall values	efficiency, security	effectiveness, risk taking
Interpersonal relationships	formal	informal
Authority	based on job title	based on job knowledge

Figure 6.12

A mechanistic-organic continuum

Mechanistic ——————————————— Organic

They gave the name *mechanistic* to the first group and the name *organic* to the second (Table 6.2 compares some of the key dimensions of both). This particular construct can be placed on a continuum as in Figure 6.12. As the environment becomes more and more dynamic, an organization begins moving away from a mechanistic design and toward an organic design if it wants to remain competitive. Changing market conditions will force it to respond in order to survive. Thus, we are much more likely to find bureaucracies operating successfully in stable than in dynamic environments, although the role of human relations is important in all types of environments.

Production technology

So will the production technology.

A great deal of research has been conducted on the relationship between production technology and organization design. Woodward, in particular, has proved that the most effective form of organization tends to vary with the type of production technology being used.[13] Drawing upon research gathered from 100 firms, she found that their technology fell into 1 of the 3 categories:

1. *Unit and small-batch production*—used by firms making one-of-a-kind items or a small number of units produced to customer specifications.

---

[13] Joan Woodward, *Industrial Organization: Theory and Practice* (London: Oxford University Press, 1965).

Figure 6.13
Woodward's findings on technology and organization structure

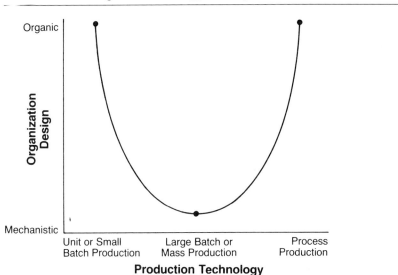

2. *Mass and large-batch production*—used by companies producing a larger quantity of goods as in the case of assembly-line operations.

3. *Process production*—used in producing a continuous flow of a product, as in an oil refinery or a nylon plant.

Woodward discovered a "U-shaped" relationship between production technology and the type of organization structure used by successful firms in each technological class. The most successful unit and process firms employed organic designs, while their counterparts in mass production relied on mechanistic structures (Figure 6.13). From a human relations standpoint, we can see that as production technology continues to increase, there is a continual movement away from mechanistic and toward people-oriented, organic designs.

Summary

Formal organizations rely on universal design principles as a point of departure in organizing their structures. In practice, these principles are modified and extended by contingency design factors.

One of the primary factors is the job description, which outlines the work to be done. The major challenge in using job descriptions is that of determining the optimum degree of specialization required for the job.

Departmentalization is a term applied to the process of grouping employees into units on an organization-wide basis. Sometimes this basis remains the same for all levels of the hierarchy, but at other times it differs from level to level. Three of the most common bases are functional, product, and geographic.

Span of control refers to the number of subordinates who report to a specific superior. Classical organization theorists believed that narrow spans were superior to wide ones. However, research reveals that the optimum span depends on the situation. The major criteria used in determining this optimum include: the manager's experience, the size of the organization, the difficulty of the work being done by the subordinates, and the need for close control.

Decentralization involves the pushing of decisions further down the line toward the operating level. Delegation entails the distribution of work to the subordinates. The types of authority that can be decentralized and delegated include line authority, staff authority, and functional authority. In using authority the manager must be aware of the acceptance theory, for in the final analysis the manager has authority only if the subordinates accept the orders.

Numerous arguments can be cited for both decentralization and delegation of authority. What the manager needs to do is weigh the benefits and drawbacks associated with each.

In addition to these four major factors of organization design, three others have been the focus of attention in recent years. One is the size of the organization. As the number of people in a local area increases, it is common to find the organization moving toward more formalization. A second is the dynamics of the environment; as it increases, mechanistic structures commonly give way to organic ones. A third is production technology; as it increases, there is a trend away from mechanistic structures and toward human-oriented, organic designs. This impact of technology on organizational personnel will be examined in greater depth in the next chapter.

Key terms in the chapter

universal design theory
division of labor
parity of authority and
responsibility
unity of command
unity of management
span of control
bureaucracy
contingency organization design

job description
functional departmentalization
product departmentalization
geographic departmentalization
flat structure
tall structure
decentralization of authority
delegation of authority
line authority

staff authority
completed staff work
functional authority

acceptance theory of authority
mechanistic structure
organic structure

Review and study questions

1. What is universal design theory? List some universal principles of organizing.

2. How does an ideal bureaucracy function? Identify some of its characteristics.

3. Advocates of the contingency organization design approach believe strongly in the formulation of "if—then" propositions. What is meant by this statement?

4. How important are job descriptions to formal organization design? Explain your answer.

5. Of all the types of departmentalization, which is most commonly used? How does one go about organizing the personnel with this type of departmentalization?

6. How does functional departmentalization differ from product departmentalization? How does functional departmentalization differ from geographic departmentalization? Explain.

7. How does span of control affect whether an organization will have a tall or a flat structure? How can a manager go about determining the optimal span of control? Explain.

8. What is decentralization? What is delegation of authority?

9. In all, there are three types of authority: line, staff, and functional. What kind of authority does each give to the manager?

10. What are some of the reasons for line-staff conflict? How can these be prevented or minimized? Explain.

11. How valuable is the acceptance theory of authority to the practicing manager? Defend your answer.

12. What are some of the factors that determine whether an organization would be decentralized? What are the factors that influence whether a manager should or should not delegate a lot of authority to the subordinates? What are some useful guidelines the manager should follow in delegating work to subordinates?

13. How does the size of the organization affect organization design?

14. What impact does the dynamics of the environment have on organization design?

15. Does production technology have an effect on organization design? Explain.

Interpretation of how effective are you as a delegator?

Give yourself one point for each of the following answers.

1. Yes	**6.** No
2. Yes	**7.** Yes
3. No	**8.** Yes
4. No	**9.** Yes
5. Yes	**10.** Yes

A good score is eight or above; an excellent score is nine or above. If you failed to get the right answer for any of the questions, go back and read the questions again. By examining the logic and reasoning behind the statement, you can develop the most effective philosophy for delegating authority.

Stay where you are

A West Coast manufacturer of radios and electronic components has been so successful over the last five years that it is thinking of expanding operations. A market research study, conducted by the company's people, has revealed a growing market in the field of calculators. In particular, the study forecasts a sales growth of 500 percent over the next seven years for hand-held calculators currently retailing for $9.95 to $19.95.

The manufacturing firm believes it has the technical expertise to produce these calculators. Before making the final decision, however, the company brought in a consulting firm to review the proposed expansion and offer its recommendations. A month ago the consulting firm submitted its report. While confirming the accuracy of the company's sales forecast, the consulting firm offered the following advice:

We do not recommend that you expand your operations into the small, hand-held calculator business. There are several reasons supporting this recommendation. First, you are currently in a stable environment. All your radios are sold directly to a large national retailer, and all your component work is done under a subcontracting agreement. Before the beginning of the year you can estimate with 95 percent accuracy what your annual sales are going to be. Second, you lack knowledge about how to market products. If you go into the calculator business, you are opting for a very dynamic environment. Technology is continually changing, and Japanese firms currently dominate the market. You would have to reorganize to be prepared to compete with these well-entrenched firms. We advise you to stay in your current market and forget about expanding into the calculator business.

Questions

1. What type of organization structure do you think the company has currently, mechanistic or organic? Explain.

2. If the company decides to move into the hand-held calculator business, what changes would you expect to see in its organization design?

3. Do you agree or disagree with the recommendations of the consultants? Explain.

A matter of authority

Gary Bridges is the administrator of a private Midwestern hospital. Gary's college training in administration and his 10 years of experience in a number of Southern hospitals enabled him to land this job six months ago. It is the largest health-care institution in a 100-mile radius.

Much of Gary's day is spent handling work-related problems and trying to keep the hospital running within budget. Initially, the union was very helpful to Gary, but last week something happened to strain this relationship.

An orderly was caught taking some supplies home and was fired by her supervisor. The union appealed the firing, arguing that the penalty was too stiff. They asked Gary to overrule the supervisor and reinstate the orderly after a three-week layoff. Gary is reluctant to do this because it would undermine the supervisor's authority in her department. However, the union has informed him that if he does not agree there is a very good chance they will walk out.

The head of the accounting department has told Gary that the financial effect of a walkout on the hospital would be severe. The institution would lose money for at least six months and perhaps the entire year. Gary is at a loss about what to do, and he must decide in three days.

Questions

1. What type of authority does the supervisor have over her subordinate? Can Gary override her decision and comply with the union request?

2. What does this case illustrate about formal authority and Barnard's acceptance theory?

3. What do you think Gary should do? Why?

Technology and people at work

7

Goals of the chapter

There are many factors to which the organization must respond. One of the most important is that of technology, for as technology increases the organization finds itself bombarded with change. The relationship of technology to people at work is known as ***sociotechnical systems***, and modern managers are finding that they must give increased attention to this technical–human interface. In particular, today's workers report that they are dissatisfied with formal organization designs that fail to take into account their personal needs. In many cases, the result is alienation, as reflected in feelings such as powerlessness, isolation, and self-estrangement.

The goal of this chapter is to examine technology and its effect on the organizational personnel. First, we trace the evolution of technology from the handicraft era to the cybernated technology stage. Then we examine the impact of knowledge on technology and review some of the reasons why the modern technological engine is moving at an ever faster clip. Next we look at the post-industrial society and identify the four major characteristics that differentiate it from earlier societies. Then we study technology and its effect on people at work, with primary attention to work values, alienation, and the replacement of personnel by technology. The last part of the chapter is devoted to identifying some of the ways in which the technical–human interface can be resolved.

When you have finished reading this chapter you should be able to:

1. trace the evolution of technology from the handicraft era to the cybernated technology stage
2. describe the impact of knowledge on technological growth
3. identify and describe the four major characteristics of a post-industrial society

4. discuss the effect of technology on work values

5. describe how technology can lead to alienation

6. explain how technology can bring about fear of replacement by machine

7. discuss how industrial democracy and participative management can bring about an integration of technology and the organizational personnel.

The evolution of technology

One of the most dramatic events of the twentieth century has been the dynamic development of technology. Today people are traveling faster than ever before, residing in houses made of material that was unavailable 25 years ago, using home appliances and tools that make their lives more enjoyable, and, thanks to medical technology, living longer than ever. However, technology has had its price. Many people are now living at a very fast rate, being subjected to what Alvin Toffler has called *future shock*—the effect of enduring too much change in too short a time.[1] How has our society arrived at this advanced state of technology? We attempt to answer this question by examining the eras of technological development through which mankind in general and the United States in particular have progressed.

Handicraft era

The handicraft era was characterized by self-sufficiency.

The first phase of technological development was the *handicraft era*. During this period people made things by hand. They built their own houses, made their own clothes, and developed their own medicines and herbs to combat illness. In short, they were self-sufficient. The only specialists during this era were carpenters, cobblers, and tailors, who provided the local population with their services and in turn received goods or money with which to buy food, clothing, and shelter. However, these craftsmen were to be found only in larger towns where their services were required. In outlying areas such as farm communities, for example, there was little need for a tailor or a cobbler, although a blacksmith might be able to eke out a living. In any event, there was a minimum of specialization. Almost everyone was a jack-of-all-trades.

If mankind was to progress, however, it was necessary for people to specialize, for with specialization comes increases in productivity and output. Many individuals welcomed such advances because they saw the chance to obtain cheaper and more abundant goods and services.

---

[1] Alvin Toffler, *Future Shock* (New York: Bantam Books, 1971).

Before examining the next era, we should note one important point. In the handicraft era, people were self-reliant, autonomous, and able to see the fruits of their labors. They could associate with their work. If a farmer was too sick on Monday to work, he saw an untilled field on Tuesday; if he plowed the field on Tuesday, he could see his progress on Wednesday. The individual was in command of the job, and things were done (or not done) because of his efforts. At the end of a long day a person could feel a sense of accomplishment. As industrialism entered the picture, however, much of this sense of self-worth and individual initiative declined, because people began to realize that they were no longer the most important factor of production. Machines had replaced them. As will be seen in the next chapter, there is now a trend toward redesigning work so that it again has some of the characteristics it possessed during the handicraft era: challenge, autonomy, a chance to use a variety of skills, and the opportunity to do meaningful work.

Mechanization era

In the mechanization era, machine labor replaced man labor.[2] One of the most significant developments of this era was job specialization, by which workers were assigned a limited number of tasks that were to be repeated over and over again. One of the earliest examples was reported by Adam Smith in his famous book, *The Wealth of Nations* (1776). Commenting on job specialization, or *division of labor* as it is often called, as it was applied to the manufacture of pins, he wrote:

The mechanization era saw the use of machine labor.

> A workman not educated to this business . . . nor acquainted with the use of machinery employed in it . . . could scarcely, perhaps, with his utmost industry, make one pin in a day, and certainly could not make twenty. But, in the way in which this business is now carried on not only the whole work is a peculiar trade, but it is divided into a number of branches, of which the greater part are likewise peculiar trades. One man draws out the wire, another straightens it, a third cuts it, a fourth points it, a fifth grinds it at the top for receiving the head; to make the head requires two or three distinct operations; to put it on, is a peculiar business, to whiten the pins is another; it is even a trade by itself to put them into the paper, and the important business of making a pin is, in this manner, divided into about eighteen distinct operations, which, in some manufactories, are all performed by distinct hands.[3]

With this method of job specialization, Smith found, a group of workers could make about 12 pounds of pins in a day. This tremendous increase in output could be traced directly to: (1) the increase in dexterity of each worker, (2) saving time that was formerly lost as the worker switched from one job (drawing the wire) to another (straightening it),

---

[2] Daniel A. Wren, *The Evolution of Management Thought*, 2nd ed. (New York: The Ronald Press, 1979), pp. 44–46.

[3] Adam Smith, *The Wealth of Nations* (New York: The Modern Library, 1937), pp. 4–5.

and (3) the invention of new machines that enabled one employee to do the work of many.

During this period mankind began to harness energy and use it to drive machinery; the spinning jenny and the power loom are illustrations. There was thus an increase of mechanization on two fronts: the workers and the machines. Each was seen as a complement to the other, and between them productivity increased dramatically. The age of mechanization was upon us.

Mechanistic technology

Mechanistic technology represented a further increase in the use of machines and job simplification. Eli Whitney, best known for his invention of the cotton gin, introduced standardized interchangeable parts in his production plant and was soon turning out muskets and clocks in greater quantities and at lower cost than ever before. A century later this basic idea was further extended through the development of the modern assembly line, such as that used by Henry Ford in building his Model T. Now the pace of technology was increasing and the role of the worker was diminishing. The number of tasks the person had to perform was decreasing and the amount of skill required was also declining. The employer no longer hired John Jones because of his experience and skill; he simply hired a person who could perform certain simple functions on a product coming down the assembly line. If the individual did the job poorly, could not keep up with the pace of the line, or simply did not like the work and decided to quit, a replacement could be easily obtained.

Mechanistic technology brought the assembly line.

Automated technology

In many organizations, *automated technology* has replaced mechanistic technology. Automated technology involves the linking together and integrating of assembly-line machines in such a fashion that many functions are performed automatically without human involvement. Some people have contended that this development represents the beginning of a second industrial revolution. Modern auto assembly lines are an excellent illustration.

Automated technology modernized the assembly line.

Cybernated technology

At present, a fifth stage, *cybernated technology*, is emerging. The term *cybernetics* refers to automatic control; today, by means of cybernated technology, machines are running and controlling other machines. A classic example is provided by modern computers which can monitor the temperature throughout a plant or building and order the heating and air conditioning units to turn off or on as needed. This form of environmental control is helping reduce energy costs through industry.

With cybernated technology machines run other machines.

"Lighter, smaller, competitive, fuel-efficient . . . I think Research and Development may have done it again!"

R & D, knowledge, and technology

How has mankind been able to accomplish such tremendous break-throughs in technology? One way is through the billions of dollars annually invested in research and development (R & D). Total R & D expenditures in the United States are now more than $250 billion annually. These funds are bringing about the development of all sorts of new products. The results can be seen in any large retail store—more goods than ever before. And it does not stop here. Thanks to research breakthroughs, we have supersonic transport, telecommunication satellites, and computers for medical research. In short, at work or at home, the employee is surrounded by technological innovation. Furthermore, there is no going back. Technology is speeding up, and the modern organization is being forced to accommodate many breakthroughs. What is the basic cause of this accelerative technological thrust? The answer is found in *knowledge*, technology's fuel.

There have been tremendous advances in science.

Every year more and more people receive college degrees. The number of highly educated people in the population is increasing. Many of these graduates have studied physical sciences, and organizations employ them to discover new ideas that can be marketed to the general public.

On the basis of our discussion so far in this chapter, we can draw three conclusions:

1. There have been some tremendous technological breakthroughs over the past century.

2. More money is being spent on R & D every year.

3. A well-educated, highly intelligent segment of our society is seeking still further technological advances. Relying upon just this information we could postulate that such advances will be coming faster and faster; research shows that this is indeed what has been happening over the past century.

Knowledge is technological fuel

The rate at which information has been gathered has been spiraling upward for 10,000 years. The first great breakthrough occurred with the invention of writing. The next great leap forward did not occur until the invention of movable type by Gutenberg in the fifteenth century. Prior to this period, Europe was producing about 1,000 book titles per year, and it was taking about 100 years to turn out a library of 100,000 titles. In the 550 years since Gutenberg's accomplishment, a tremendous acceleration has occurred: by 1950 Europe was producing 120,000 titles per year. What had once taken a century now required only 10 months. Today the world's output of books is more than 2,000 titles per day.

Naturally, every book will not lead to a technological breakthrough, but the accelerative curve in book publication crudely parallels the rate at which mankind discovers new knowledge. Advances in science support this statement. For example, before the movable type press, only 11 chemical elements were known and it had been 200 years since the last one, arsenic, had been discovered. The twelfth element was discovered while Gutenberg was working on his invention. Over the next 550 years, over 70 additional elements have been discovered, and since 1900 scientists have been isolating new elements at the rate of 1 every 3 years.

Much of this advance must be attributed to the fact that 90 percent of all the scientists who ever lived are now alive and new discoveries are being made every day. In fact, what has been learned in the last 30 years is greater than all the knowledge mankind had gathered up to 1950. Commenting on the relationship between technology and knowledge, Toffler has said,

If technology . . . is to be regarded as a great engine, a mighty accelerator, then knowledge must be regarded as its fuel. And thus we come to the crux of the accelerative process in society, for the engine is being fed a richer and richer fuel every day.[1]

The technological engine

Much of the new information that is being gathered through research and development is not directly usable, at least for the moment. However, so much research is being done that the percentage that can be applied re-

[1] Toffler, *Future Shock*, p. 30.

sults in massive technological change. Let us consider the area of transportation. In 6000 B.C., the fastest form of travel was the camel caravan, which averaged 8 miles per hour. By 1600 B.C., mankind was able to move at roughly 20 miles per hour, thanks to the chariot. The late 1880s saw the emergence of an advanced steam engine capable of attaining 100 miles per hour. From this point on the pace accelerated dramatically. It took but 58 years for researchers to quadruple the steam engine speed, so that in 1938 aircraft were flying at 400 miles per hour. By 1960, rocket planes were approaching 4,000 miles per hour, and astronauts were orbiting the earth at 18,000 miles per hour. Technology has enabled us to go faster and faster.

In addition, scientific discoveries are being brought to fruition at a faster rate. For example, in 1836 a machine was invented that mowed, threshed, tied straw into sheaves, and poured grain into sacks. The machine was based on technology that even then was 20 years old, but it was not until 1930 that such a combine was actually marketed. The first English patent for a typewriter was issued in 1714, but it took 150 years for typewriters to be commercially available. Today such delays between idea and application are almost unthinkable. It is not that we are more eager or less lazy than our ancestors, but we have, with the passage of time, invented all sorts of social devices to hasten the process. Thus, we find that the time between the first and second stages of the innovative cycle—between idea and application—has been cut radically. Frank Lynn, for example, in studying 20 major innovations including frozen foods, antibiotics, integrated circuits, and synthetic leather, found that since the beginning of this century more than 60 percent has been slashed from the average time needed for a major scientific discovery to be translated into a useful technological form. Today a vast and growing research and development industry is consciously working to reduce the lag still more.[5]

In addition, the number of consumer goods is increasing so rapidly that the time between introduction and decline is getting smaller. Cheaper, better-quality, or more useful goods are being produced. To a large degree, technology is creating a disposable product society. In the process, the United States has found itself entering a *post-industrial society*, in which changes in the external environment are bringing about a whole different set of internal values. Technology is changing America in general and employees in particular.

Post-Industrial society

In the past 30 years the United States has progressed from an industrial society to a post-industrial society. This transition has involved four major changes: (1) a service-oriented work force, (2) dynamic increase in

[5] *Ibid.,* pp. 27–28.

number of professional and technical workers, (3) increase in importance of technology, and (4) planning and controlling of technological growth.

Service-Oriented work force

Over half of all U.S. workers are in service jobs.

Unlike the work force in other countries, the majority of the U.S. work force is no longer engaged in manufacturing or agriculture; it is engaged in services. Workers in transportation, utilities, trade, finance, insurance, real estate, services, and government now constitute approximately two-thirds of the total work force. The remaining one third are in agriculture, forestry, fisheries, mining, construction, and manufacturing. In order to release such a large number of people from manufacturing and maintain our production output, we had to have made great technological advances. The result, quite obviously, has been a dramatic change in the work environment.

Dynamic increase in number of professional and technological workers

There has been a tremendous growth in professional and technical jobs.

Another characteristic of post-industrialism is the dynamic growth in numbers of workers in professional and technical occupations. In particular, the number of white-collar and service workers is increasing in numbers while that of blue-collar and farm workers is declining. The percentage of white-collar workers in the labor force is approximately 65 percent, while the number of blue-collar workers stands at about 35 percent.

Increase in the importance of theoretical knowledge

Theoretical knowledge is very important.

A third characteristic of a post-industrial society is an increase in the importance of theoretical knowledge. Industrial societies are interested in the practical side of things. They concentrate on what works and ignore the rest. A post-industrial society, however, is concerned with more than just this short-run, heavily pragmatic view. For example, in hospitals today a great deal of research is being done. Medical institutions are collecting all sorts of data on their patients: from what ailment is the person suffering? How old is the patient? What is the patient's height, weight, age, sex, and religion? Is there any variable to which the problem can be traced, and if so, can we make any generalization about how people with this ailment might be cured? In many cases the data are analyzed, but no answer is found. Nevertheless, medical personnel keep this information stored in a computer. They do not need to find any short-run value for it. Perhaps in a few years they will have enough data from which to postulate a theory regarding the causes and cures for the ailment. The same is

Table 7.1
Human, social, and organizational evolution

Era	Prevailing Ethic	Process or Mechanism	Human Needs	Predominant Goals
Handicraft Era	Individualism Craftsmanship	Family Guilds Entrepreneurism	Physiological Safety/Security Belonging Esteem	Human survival Personal identity Independence

Mechanization and assembly-line eras	Individualism
	Competition
	Mass production
	Supremacy of the
	    organization
		Job simplification
		Scientific
		    management
		Bureaucracy
			Physiological
			Safety/Security
			Belonging
				Human survival
				Organizational
				    efficiency
				Profit

Post-industrial era	Collaboration
	Industrial
	    democracy
	Individual-
	    organizational
	    congruency
		Automation
		Job enrichment
		Adhocracy
		Human resources
		    management
			Physiological
			Safety/Security
			Belonging
			Esteem
			Self-actualization
				Adaptability
				Optimization of
				    human and
				    organizational
				    objectives
				Institutional
				    interdependency

true in many other areas, from physics and chemistry to psychology and sociology. The purpose of this theoretical knowledge is to serve as a base for projecting and planning for the future. A post-industrial society is more future-oriented than its predecessors. (See Table 7.1 for a more detailed comparison of these societies or eras.)

Planning and controlling of technological growth

The fourth and final characteristic of post-industrial society is an attempt to plan and control technological growth. When we examine the first three characteristics of a post-industrial society, we realize that it is an environment totally different from anything we have yet seen. It is a society in which highly educated people work in "think jobs" and in which a tremendous amount of money is spent each year on research and development, with much of the new knowledge being stored for future use. What will the year 2000 look like? The prospect scares many people and helps account for the fact that planning and control have now become important considerations. Without giving attention to monitoring our technological environment and deciding how we want it to grow, mankind faces a truly uncertain future. Toffler recognizes the challenge.

There are attempts to plan and control technological growth.

Our first and most pressing need, therefore, before we can begin to gently guide our evolutionary destiny, before we can build a humane future, is to halt the runaway acceleration that is subjecting multitudes

Your job and you

This quiz is designed to examine the relationship you have with your job. How comfortable do you feel doing your work? What role is played by technology? After you read each statement, try to be as candid as possible in your answer. Interpretations are provided at the end of the chapter.

	Highly Disagree	Disagree	Indifferent	Agree	Highly Agree
1. While you have certain things you have to do every work day or work week, you set the pace at which you work; management simply judges you on whether or not you have reached your over-all objectives.		✓			
2. Basically, you do the same thing day after day, and the work is downright dull.				✓	
3. Your job is mentally challenging; it requires rigorous thought.		✓			
4. Your job is meaningless; anyone could do it and, to be quite frank, you are embarrassed when someone asks you what you do for a living.		✓			
5. On your job, you feel extremely tense and anxious, even though you may not know why.		✓			
6. There is virtually no chance for you to socialize on your job.		✓			
7. No matter how fast you work, there is always more to do; you can never get finished.		✓			
8. Your work environment is a very comfortable, enjoyable place; it is relaxing and encourages high productivity.				✓	

	Highly Disagree	Disagree	Indifferent	Agree	Highly Agree
9. Your job requires a variety of skills, and people in the organization admit that it takes real talent to do what you do.		✓			
10. Face it, on your job you are a small cog in a big machine; if you cannot master the latest technology, the organization will find someone who can.				✓	

to the threat of future shock while, at the very same moment, intensifying all the problems they must deal with—war, ecological incursions, racism, the obscene contrast between rich and poor, the revolt of the young, and the rise of a potentially deadly mass of irrationalism.[6]

As the external environment changes, the environment within organizations alters as well. Technology permeates the organization's boundaries, affecting not only the structure (as we saw from Woodward's research, reported in Chapter 6) but the personnel as well.

Technology and people at work

Technology has an effect on people at work for two reasons. First, technology is causing a change in people's values, which they bring to the work place with them. Second, technology is leading to changes in the work environment. In analyzing this people–work environment–technology interface, we should consider five areas: (1) technology and work values, (2) alienation in the work place, (3) the fear of replacement by machine, (4) how workers feel about their jobs, and (5) the quality of work life issue. Before doing so, however, take the quiz on your job and you.

Technology and work values

Technology carries the connotation of efficiency. For example, new machines are brought into the work place because they will do the job faster than either the workers or the old machines can. This emphasis on effi-

---

[6] *Ibid.*, p. 486.

ciency may have been one of the central themes of industrialism, but as we noted in our discussion of post-industrial societies, efficiency no longer occupies a central position.

The result is a discerning employee who believes that many of the organization's rules are outmoded and that its philosophy needs to be completely revised. One writer described typical young employees this way:

> They tend to see themselves as basically rejecting the Calvinist Work Ethic, as being more honest, more open to new ideas and experimentation, more concerned with beauty, more interested in world events, more self-centered, more optimistic about the future, and less impressed with formal authority.
>
> The other kinds of changes they would like to see in society are: more participation in decisions that affect them, less emphasis on material things, more acceptance of other people's peculiarities, more emphasis on work being meaningful in its own right, and more freedom to do their own thing providing it doesn't hurt anybody.[7]

Technology can affect values.

Most organizations would disagree with these ideas, believing that they would be detrimental to the enterprise at large.

First came the profit-maximizing era.

Without addressing this thesis directly, let us note that management in the United States has witnessed three managerial phases. First, there was the era of *profit maximizing*, in which all decisions were directed toward making the greatest amount of money possible. Self-interest and the free market system were used in determining the most efficient allocation of resources. Underlying these basic values was a philosophy of hard work, competition, and the belief that the workers were merely factors of production. Some organizations today, especially small business firms, seem still to adhere to this model.

Followed by trusteeship management.

During the Depression and the post-World War II period, many organizations made a transition to *trusteeship management*. In many cases, the owners were no longer the managers, and the organization became much more interested in its interface with society at large. Some of the values of trusteeship management are: consideration of employee needs for security, belonging, and recognition (the middle portions of Maslow's need hierarchy), a belief that the employee has rights to be respected, recognition of the importance of trading off profit for social good, and a decline in the support of the maxim of survival of the fittest. Most organizations still operate within the confines of this management philosophy.

And quality-of-life management.

The most recent system to emerge is known as *quality-of-life management*. Continuing the trend established by the trusteeship management era, organizations operating with this philosophy believe that people must be managed more humanistically than ever before; profit is to be considered more as a means to an end than as an end itself; and there must be trade-off between profit and responsibility to society and

---

[7] Eugene Koprowski, "The Generation Gap, From Both Sides Now," *Management of Personnel Quarterly*, Winter 1969, p. 4.

Figure 7.1
Some underlying reasons for value changes among young people

They Were:	So They:
Raised in affluence	Take technological conveniences for granted
Physically more mature	Resent being treated as children
Raised on TV	Expect immediate action
	Have been exposed to masses of information
	Are aware of incongruities in society
	Respond to action rather than words
	Have been exposed to violence
Raised on protest	Are aware of injustice, poverty, and discrimination
	Have no live heroes

the workers. The values adhered to by these organizations include: emphasis on cooperation between management and personnel, and redesign of work life so that it meets some of the demands the workers bring to the workplace (job redesign is examined in great depth in Chapter 8). While there is an emerging interest in this philosophy of work, quality-of-life management has not yet been widely accepted by American managers. We should note, however, that while most managers are operating in the trusteeship management stage, most of the incoming, young workers are demanding a philosophy much closer to that of quality-of-life management. (See Figure 7.1.) In short, the values of the organization and the personnel are growing farther and farther apart. The impact of technology in people's daily lives is encouraging them to seek a higher quality of life, but the impact of technology within the organization is being used to promote the trusteeship management philosophy. There appears to be clash between the effects of technology on the personnel and on the organization!

Technology and alienation

Of all the behavioral implications of technology, the most important seems to be that of alienation. This concept incorporates: (1) powerlessness, (2) meaninglessness, (3) normlessness, (4) isolation, and (5) self-estrangement.

Powerlessness. Many workers feel they are at the mercy of technology. Workers on the assembly line, for example, remain at their stations and the work comes to them. If the line is moving very fast, they have to work faster to accommodate it. Sometimes the speed of the line is so rapid that no one can keep up. In order to avoid getting in trouble, many workers come in early and begin building a backlog of stock for when they get behind. One management researcher worked on an assembly

Technology can cause powerlessness.

line for four months to study the quality of work life there. His first job consisted of installing stabilizer bars, which give the car stability in cornering. Try as he might, he was unable to install the bar in the allotted 75–80 seconds. Yet this was the time established for the job by engineering. Feeling powerless in his efforts to keep up, he complained to the foreman.

> **After I had complained to the foreman about the difficulty of the job, and after other workers had also complained to both the foreman and the union committeeman, the company clocked the job. When the time study was completed, the company seemed surprised to discover what we had known all along—that the job required 150% of the time the engineers had allotted to it. No wonder I was always behind! The company then removed some of the tasks from the job, which made it slightly easier. The job was still difficult, however, and required building stock ahead of time each day.[8]**

Meaninglessness. Many employees are unable to determine what they are doing or why they are doing it. Individuals who put a bolt on a widget, assemble two minor parts of a major system, or test a component that will be placed in a giant machine feel no relationship with the finished product. Technology helps create this meaninglessness through its emphasis on job specialization, as in assembly-line work.

It can lead to meaninglessness.

How do workers adapt to these conditions? Some simply fail to show up for work. It is not uncommon to find assembly plants with manpower shortages when the hunting season opens. Those who do show up for work often spend a large percentage of their work day playing mental games (doing multiplication tables in their mind) or daydreaming.

> **Counting cars was one conscious method I used to pass the time; other methods came unconsciously. One time I realized I was doing my job to the rhythm of an aria from an opera I had heard the last weekend. Another time I found myself a thousand miles away, driving an imaginary automobile down a highway I had not been on in years. How many chassis went by during my mental lapses—and whether I even did my job—I don't know and never found out.[9]**

Normlessness. Human behavior is no longer guided by the norms of society; instead, technology sets the rules. People begin responding to the needs of the equipment and machines rather than to their personal needs. Additionally, when people are beset by the rapid pace of technology, their values begin to change. A type of impermanence is emerging, in which people's relationships to things and to one another are being altered. Consider, for example, the fact that advancing technology is lowering manufacturing costs so greatly that it is often cheaper to replace

It can bring about normlessness.

[8]John J. Runcie, "By Day I Make the Cars," *Harvard Business Review*, May–June 1980, pp. 107–108.
[9]*Ibid.*, p. 109.

something than to fix it. Additionally, new and better things are coming out all the time—televisions, washers, dryers, and refrigerators. If one of these appliances gives us a significant amount of trouble, we trade it in or throw it out to make room for a new one. Our relationships with things we own are changing. The same holds for our relationship with people. More and more Americans are changing their places of residence each year.

In seventy major United States cities, for example, including New York, average residence in one place is less than four years. Contrast this with the lifelong residence in one place characteristic of the rural village. Moreover, residential relocation is critical in determining the duration of many other place relationships, so that when an individual terminates his relationship with a home, he usually also terminates his relationship with all kinds of "satellite" places in the neighborhood. He changes his supermarket, gas station, bus stop and barber shop, thus cutting short a series of other place relationships along with the home relationship. Across the board, therefore, we not only experience more places in the course of a lifetime, but, on average, maintain our link with each place for a shorter and shorter interval.

Thus we begin to see more clearly how the accelerative thrust in society affects the individual. For this telescoping of man's relationships with place precisely parallels the truncation of this relationship with things. In both cases, the individual is forced to make and break his ties more rapidly. In both cases, the level of transience rises. In both cases, he experiences a quickening of the pace of life.[10]

What norms, or rules of conduct, should govern one's relationship to the surrounding physical and human environment? The answer is becoming more and more uncertain. As technology continues to increase, the response is more often, "I don't know." A state of normlessness is being created.

Isolation.   The individual becomes detached from society. People who find the clamor and pace of big-city life to be too much are now leaving with their families to seek isolation in the countryside. Others are going farther and setting up communes far from civilization that offer their members a chance for a relaxed, slower-paced way of life. On the job people cannot run away from technology. If only to keep up with the competition, it is a part of their work life. Here, then, the individual is locked in, forced to cope with technology. However, there is still isolation in many cases, for the person is often confined to one locale, as in the case of a worker on an auto assembly line who must remain at a particular place on the line for the entire work day; a computer operator who has to stay near the machine, checking on jobs being run, and remaining alert for any machine malfunctions; or a press operator who is confined to the general area of the printing press, constantly observing the speed

It can cause isolation.

---

[10] Toffler, *Future Shock*, pp. 93–94.

and feed of the paper and being prepared to adjust or stop the machine should something go awry. All these people are isolated within a given area and, depending on the specific situation, isolated from other workers. At best, the technology allows them to interact only with those in their immediate vicinity; at worst, the demands of the job sometimes stop them from associating with anyone for extended periods of the work day.

Self-Estrangement.   The worker can no longer find intrinsic satisfaction in what he or she is doing. The work becomes merely a means to earn a living. There is no fun or challenge associated with it. If another job offered more money, he or she would quit. Technology creates self-estrangement by reducing the scope and importance of the work itself. As we saw in Chapter 2 when we discussed Herzberg's two-factor theory, the things people liked best about their jobs were related to the work itself: they were intrinsic motivators, such as achievement, responsibility, and the possibility of growth. Technology eliminates many of these. Faunce has summed up much of what we have said about technology and alienation:

*It can result in
self-estrangement.*

> **The most persistent indictment of industrial society is that it has resulted in the alienation of industrial man. Loneliness in the midst of urban agglomeration; loss of social anchorage in mass society; the absence of a predictable life trajectory in an era of unprecedented social change; and the powerlessness of man within the complex social, economic, and political systems he has created are common themes in the social criticism of the industrial way of life.**[11]

Of course, not all workers suffer the negative effects of technology. Research reveals that some employees seem to experience little alienation. This is particularly true, to use Woodward's classification scheme, among workers in small-batch technology firms and process-production companies. Those in mass-production industries, however, do suffer alienation. Figure 7.2 shows that there is a curvilinear relationship between technology and alienation.[12] After conducting a review of the literature in this area, Luthans has reported:

> **Blauner studied four diverse technological situations—a print shop, a textile mill, an automobile assembly line and a highly automated chemical plant. He found that alienation was a direct function of the type of technology in operation. For example, in the automobile assembly line, alienation of the workers was widespread. On the other hand, in the chemical plant, which operated on a continuous-process form of technology, alienation was noticeably absent. The reasons given**

[11] William A. Faunce, *Problems of an Industrial Society* (New York: McGraw-Hill Book Company, 1968), p. 84.

[12] See: Michael Fullan, "Industrial Technology and Worker Integration in the Organization," *American Sociological Review*, December 1970, pp. 1028–1039; and Jon M. Shepard, *Automation and Alienation: A Study of Office and Factory Workers* (Cambridge, Mass.: The MIT Press, 1971).

Figure 7.2
Technology and alienation

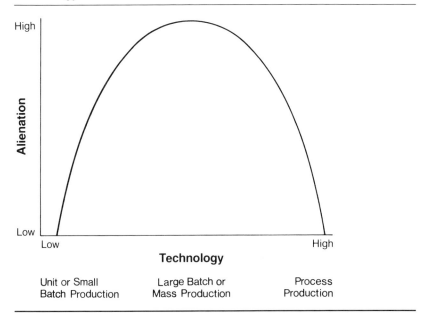

were that on the assembly line the workers were powerless and suffered from self-estrangement, whereas in the chemical plant the workers had meaningful jobs in which they had a great deal of responsibility and control. Thus, there is little doubt that technology has an effect on the alienation of workers, but it appears to be highly selective in nature.[13]

Fear of replacement by machine

Another problem created by technology is the workers' fears that they will be replaced by machines. This fear is typical among people who are not highly skilled or who are performing paperwork functions, such as checking forms, filling out structured reports, or entering data in accounting ledgers. All of them could possibly be replaced by a computer—and sometimes they are. Consider, for example, the insurance company that computerized most of its routine, paper-processing tasks. Realizing that their jobs could be threatened by such a move, the workers sought to delay implementation of the machine while seeking transfers to other departments. The management assured the workers that all efforts would be made to find work in other units for any displaced per-

Technology can cause fear of replacement.

---

[13] Fred Luthans, *Organizational Behavior*, 2nd ed. (New York: McGraw-Hill Book Company, 1977), pp. 91–92.

sons, and within the first month of the machine's installation, 30 percent of the personnel were transferred to other units. However, this merely served to increase the anxiety among the remaining members, who believed that there were fewer jobs available in the company for them.

As one of them said, "You mark my words. There just aren't enough jobs in the company to absorb everyone. So it's just a matter of time before the company announces that it will be laying off some of us." The statement seemed to reflect the sentiments of the other members because at about this time the management noticed a decline in cooperation from these people. Both the managers and the systems engineers who were revising the work schedules found many of the workers unwilling to answer questions about their work assignments or providing only minimal information. In fact, one manager described the workers as "downright hostile." Another said, "They think they're going to be fired, so they're doing everything they can to screw us up."

As a result it took three weeks longer than anticipated to get everything straightened out and transferred to the computer. Meanwhile, what about the personnel? Well, true to their fears, 20 per cent of the original department was laid off.[14]

Situations like this are typical in many organizations in which machines can be used in place of workers. The United States Post Office is another illustration. Years ago, a mail clerk stood before a bank of labeled pigeonholes called cells and quickly sorted the envelopes according to neighborhood, post-office branch, and even carrier route. At top speed, most could sort around 30 letters a minute or 1,800 an hour. If they were talking to one another, the rate would be slightly lower. Today much of this has changed. In many post offices around the country, the clerks no longer talk to one another, nor do they have control over the pace of their work. Now they sit with earphones clamped over their heads listening to prescribed radio programs, many of which play rock music that shuts out the noise around them and builds a psychological tempo that encourages them to sort the mail faster. In addition, there is a letter sorting machine that puts envelopes before them at the rate of 60 per minute or 3,600 an hour. In the second that the envelope is before the mail sorter, he or she taps a key, which assigns the envelope to one of the cubbyholes along a conveyor belt. In the old days, a good worker could sort mail into 77 different cells. The machine is not only twice as fast but more accurate as well.

How workers feel about their jobs

Despite the feelings of alienation which many workers find in their jobs, the effect of technology can be lived with. In fact, most workers report that there are many things they like about their job.

---

[14] Richard M. Hodgetts, *Management: Theory, Process and Practice* (Philadelphia: W. B. Saunders Co., 1975), pp. 417–418.

Table 7.2
How workers feel about life in the plant

	Yes	No	Uncertain
Do you have to take a day off every once in a while?	54.3%	43.3%	2.4%
Is absenteeism a big problem in the plant?	86.1	9.1	4.8
Do you ever drink at lunchtime?	40.4	59.6	——
Have you ever gotten high while working on the line?	32.7	66.3	——
Have you seen others in the plant get high while working on the line?	50.9	49.1	——
Do you think it's not important how much you know but who you know that counts?	78.4	12.0	9.6
Does your supervisor treat everyone fairly?	43.8	48.1	8.2
Would the company be better off without a union?	2.9	88.0	9.1

*These are only some of the attitudinal questions used in the larger research project. In the questionnaire, attitudes were measured on a five-point scale rather than on the three-point scale shown here, and the percentages represent only those workers who actually answered each question.

Note: Several of the statements presented to the workers have been edited into question form for this article, but the substance remains the same.

Reprinted by permission of the Harvard Business Review. Exhibit from "By Days I Make the Cars" by John F. Runcie (May–June 1980). Copyright © 1980 by the president and fellows of Harvard College; all rights reserved.

One of the primary advantages is pay and benefits. A typical response to the question how long do you intend to work for this company is "until I retire." Many workers believe that given their education and training they could not do as well in another organization.

They like the pay and benefits.

A second advantage is, despite their feelings of alienation, that the organization is a good place to work. For example, Runcie surveyed over 200 assembly-line workers and found that many of them had enough seniority to transfer to easier jobs in the plant. However, they did not want to do so. They liked their current jobs regardless of the problems that went along with them.

On the other hand there are problems. As seen in Table 7.2, workers in one plant had some particular gripes including the need to take a day off, feelings that the supervisor did not treat everyone fairly, and the belief that who you knew was more important than how much you knew.

But not supervisory favoritism.

The quality of work life issue

A more important sociotechnical issue is the quality of work life (QWL). Modern employees who work in large batch or mass production technology have the highest reported levels of alienation (see Figure 7.2). However, these workers also seem at a loss in determining what can be done. Runcie reports that "Workers see only a few places where changes

... would be effective."[15] Examples include better manufactured parts that meet all design specifications and more objective (no favoritism) supervision.

They distrust QWL committees.

Additionally, when management and workers have formed QWL committees, there has not been very active support from the employees. Many workers distrust these types of joint committees, believing that, in the long run, the only change will be to speed up the assembly line. A number of managers also feel that these committees are of no real value. The result is a stereotyped view of the workers.

> **The technology of the assembly line fosters the idea that the people should be like the products rolling off the line. All the workers should think the same, act the same, do the same things. When a person comes along who does not play by the rules and wants simply to be seen as an individual, the members of the system react to bring the person back to the norm. But no one person totally fits the mold. Everyone is different and people can only adapt so far. Maybe how they are treated has to change. Some supervisors, union officials, and workers realize this—but sadly, not enough do.[16]**

What then is the answer in dealing with sociotechnical problems? One part of the solution is the use of job enrichment and other redesign techniques discussed in the next chapter. Another part of the answer must be found in the industrial environment itself. In many European countries industrial democracy is used. In the United States participative management is more prevalent. Both offer possibilities for meeting the sociotechnological challenge.

Meeting the sociotechnical challenge

The dysfunctional effects of technology can be traced, in large part, to the fears it creates among the personnel. Human relations management requires that the employees' interests be both considered and protected by management. The workers need to feel confident that in the long run they will gain from technology. In other words, there must be a supportive climate between the personnel and the management. If this climate can be created, the workers will be more receptive to the changes being thrust upon them by technology. Two alternatives to attaining this objective are industrial democracy and participative management.

Industrial democracy and participative management

Industrial democracy is legally sanctioned.

The two major trends in management–worker relations over the last 25 years are those of industrial democracy and participative management. Both involve shared decision making between the workers and manage-

---

[15]*Ibid.*, p. 111.
[16]*Ibid.*, p. 115.

ment. However, despite their similarity of intent, there are fundamental differences in their methods. Industrial democracy is a formal, and usually legally sanctioned, arrangement of worker representation in the form of committees, councils, and boards at various levels of decision making. Participative management, on the other hand, is an informal style of face-to-face leadership in which management and workers share decision making in the work place. It is sometimes called *shop-floor democracy*. Some countries of the world make more use of one than the other.

Participative management is informal in nature.

Germany   In Germany, for example, companies with more than 500 workers have supervisory boards that set company policy. These boards are two-thirds shareholder representatives and one-third worker representatives. Firms with more than 2,000 employees have 50 percent representation on these boards. By law, industrial democracy is a way of life in Germany.

Scandinavia   In the Scandinavian countries—Norway, Sweden, and Denmark—there are also statutory requirements regarding worker representation on governing boards. For example, for almost 40 years Sweden has required that companies with more than 50 employees have work councils with representatives from management and labor which meet regularly to solve problems and exchange information.

Industrial democracy is prevalent.

However, Scandinavians also lead the way in terms of shop-floor democracy. In some of their factories autonomous work groups have been introduced. These groups have autonomy and decision-making discretion which allow them to determine for themselves how to do their jobs. Their range of authority often extends from the receipt of orders to progress control and final inspection.

As is participative management.

Britain   The United Kingdom and Ireland are the only countries in the European community that do not have statutory requirements for information dissemination, consultation, or worker representation on boards. However, this appears to be changing. Current legislative efforts are likely to require that firms with more than 500 people discuss all major proposals affecting the workers with their trade union representatives. The government also believes that employees should have a right of representation on the boards of their companies. Some organizations are already moving to meet these recommendations. For example, the post office has expanded its board of directors from 7 to 19. Seven of the representatives are from management, seven are from trade union members, two are independents chosen from a list submitted by the government minister responsible for the post office, two are members who represent the consumers' interests, and the last is a chief executive from the management side.

Industrial democracy is increasing.

Not all organizations are waiting for government-determined industrial democracy. Some are opting for their own version of participatory management.

Certainly, Chrysler (UK) Ltd. seems to be an example of an attempt to make participative management and industrial democracy walk hand-in-hand. In 1976 the company encouraged trade union representatives to sit in on management discussions, allowing them to participate in management decisions where they wish. . . . At the plant level, employees have been involved in discussions involving production, health, and safety at work, as well as the company's future. Worker participation even extended to two seats on the Board of Directors. . . . worker morale has improved and the company's labor relations have been drastically transformed.[17]

The United States In the United States participative management and industrial democracy have both developed. The former, if only because of the American traditions of individualism and democracy, always has been very popular. However, industrial democracy is also gaining in importance.

Participative management is popular.

In the early 1970s General Foods opened a pet-food plant in Topeka, Kansas, and designed the facilities so that things could be run with a minimum of supervision. The workers took over many of the traditional management tasks including interviewing job applicants, assigning jobs, and deciding pay raises. The result was that commitment and satisfaction among the workers dramatically increased.

Yet, industrial democracy is also quite present in the United States. By the early 1920s paternalistic firms had elected bodies of worker representatives, who had some input regarding management decisions. More recently companies like the Eaton Corporation have begun employing the concept. Overall, however, industrial democracy has not made the inroads in the United States that it has in Europe. Yet the concept has important value in helping management meet the sociotechnical challenge.

Matching the approach and the situation

Should organizations use greater participative management, more industrial democracy, or a combination of the two? The answer will depend on both the country and the specific situation. For example, research reveals that Americans tend to like a participative approach much more than do other cultures. Table 7.3 shows that over 50 percent of the American subordinates in a major research study reported satisfaction in decision-making situations with a participative supervisor. Additionally, this research study reported that Americans, more than any other group, felt they profited from self-planning.

Several reasons can be offered for this. Sense of accomplishment may be greater when executing one's own plan rather than the assigned plan.

17 Bernard M. Bass and V. J. Shackleton, "Industrial Democracy and Participative Management: A Case For a Synthesis," *Academy of Management Review*, October 1979, p. 395.

Table 7.3

Reported satisfaction of subordinates following decision making with participative superiors

Number	Culture	Percent of Subordinates Most Satisfied in Decision-Making Meetings with Participative Supervisor
65	Dutch-Flemish	64.7
50	Nordic:	56.4
	Danish, Norwegian, Swedish, Austrian, West German, German-Swiss	
202	Anglo-Americans:	53.1
	British-Northern Irish, American, Australian	
179	Latin:	52.6
	Brazilian, Columbian, French, Italian, Spanish, French-Swiss, Walloon	
28	Japanese	50.0
37	Indian	29.4

Adapted from Wayne F. Cascio, "Functional Specialization, Culture, and Preference for Participative Management," *Personnel Psychology*, Winter 1974, p. 599.
Reprinted with permission.

There may be more commitment to see the validity of a plan by executing it successfully and more confidence that it can be done. Understanding of the plan is likely to be greater. Human resources may be better utilized. There may be a perception of more flexibility and more room for modification and initiative to make improvements in an assigned plan. There are likely to be fewer communication problems and consequent errors and distortions in pursuing instructions. Finally, competitive feelings aroused between planners and those who must execute the plans are avoided because planners and doers are the same persons.[18]

American firms doing business in the states are likely to find a participative management approach of great value in meeting the socio-technical challenge. In overseas countries, industrial democracy must be heavily relied upon. However, this is not an either-or situation. America has exported participative management to the world and is now beginning to import some of the industrial democracy practices from abroad. The result is an emerging mutual support between participative management and industrial democracy. The eventual key to whether this support will continue rests in the degree to which participative management brings about self-planning in the organization. As Bass and Shackleton have noted, "Self-planning is the key to the complementarity of participative management and industrial democracy."[19] As technology advances the worker will have to take over more and more of the industrial process.

---

[18] *Ibid.*, pp. 397–398.
[19] *Ibid.*, p. 400.

Table 7.4

Issues that can be dealt with best by industrial democracy, participative management or both

Issues	Industrial Democracy	Participative Management	Reason
Pay benefits	Yes	No	Principles of equity, company finances, need to avoid maximizing self-interest.
Job satisfaction	No	Yes	Participative management will directly improve.
Career development	Yes	Yes	Broad policies need to be set at higher levels, but career planning is best as self-planning.
Working conditions: sociotechnical issues	Yes	Yes	Plant-wide problems and community affairs are best dealt with by council and staff. On the other hand, changes may be instituted and implemented best through participation in the decision process at the local level.
Job security	Yes	Yes	Market conditions and finance of the firm as a whole require organization-wide attention. Yet some commitment to strategies, such as sharing reductions in hours, can be best accomplished at local levels via participative endeavor.

Bernard M. Bass and V. J. Shackleton. "Industrial Democracy and Participative Management: A Case for Synthesis," *Academy of Management Review*, October 1979, p. 401. Reprinted with permission.

The two approaches can help meet the sociotechnical challenge.

Can industrial democracy and participative management help organizations deal with sociotechnical issues? Researchers, in particular, argue that it can do this and more. As seen in Table 7.4, the development of both areas can be helpful in dealing with a large range of modern industrial problems from sociotechnical issues to pay and benefits, job satisfaction, career development and/or job security.

The primary way in which the sociotechnical challenge is being met currently is through the use of job enrichment and job design. These topics are the focus of our attention in the next chapter.

Summary

Technology has gone through five stages. The first was the handicraft era, in which people made things by hand. Next came the mechanization era, characterized by machine labor replacing man labor. This was followed by the mechanistic technology stage, as seen in the case of the early auto assembly lines. Next came automated technology, in which assembly-line machines were linked together in such a way that many functions were performed automatically. At present a fifth stage, cybernated technology, is emerging, in which machines are running and controlling other machines.

These technological breakthroughs have been possible because large amounts of money are being spent annually on R & D and because more and more members of our society are attaining higher levels of education. When these R & D funds and highly educated people are brought together, the result is an accelerative thrust from which more and more goods and services can be produced at an ever-increasing rate. At the same time, the United States has entered the stage of post-industrialism, which is characterized by: (1) a service-oriented work force, (2) a dynamic increase in number of professional and technical workers, (3) an increase in the importance of theoretical knowledge, and (4) planning and controlling of technological growth.

In the work place, technology has some specific effects on the personnel. First, the values they bring to the work place are changing, because technology is affecting their daily lives. People now reject the work ethic, are less impressed with formal authority, and demand more participation in decisions that affect them. Within the organization, technology is leading to a more structured environment that rejects these basic values. This results in a clash between the types of values promoted by technology in the external environment and those developed by it in the internal (work) environment.

Technology is causing alienation in the work place. This alienation is taking a number of different forms, including powerlessness, meaninglessness, normlessness, isolation, and self-estrangement.

Additionally, technology is causing some workers to fear they will be replaced by machines. This is particularly true among those who are not highly skilled or who are performing paperwork functions that can be handled by computers.

Despite these feelings, many workers find life in a modern factory quite livable. In particular, they like the pay and benefits and, to a large extent, seem unclear as to how the quality of work life can be improved.

One way in which the sociotechnical problem is being addressed is through participative management practices. A second way, which seems to be gaining in favor, is the use of industrial democracy. In the next chapter we address job enrichment and job design, the two most popular methods for meeting the sociotechnical challenge.

Key terms in the chapter

sociotechnical systems
future shock
handicraft era
mechanized technology
mechanistic technology
automated technology
cybernated technology
post-industrial society
profit-maximizing management

trusteeship management
quality-of-life management
powerlessness
meaninglessness
normlessness
isolation
self-estrangement
industrial management
participative management

Interpretation of your job and you

This quiz is designed to measure the effect that the technological surroundings of your job have on you. Keeping in mind that there are five possible responses to each statement, here is the way to score each:

	Highly Disagree	Disagree	Indifferent	Agree	Highly Agree
1.	-2	-1	0	1	2
2.	2	1	0	-1	-2
3.	-2	-1	0	1	2
4.	2	1	0	-1	-2
5.	2	1	0	-1	-2
6.	2	1	0	-1	-2
7.	2	1	0	-1	-2
8.	-2	-1	0	1	2
9.	-2	-1	0	1	2
10.	2	1	0	-1	-2

If you have a positive score, the impact of technology and stress on your job is not at all negative. In fact, you are doing quite well in beating the dysfunctional effects of technology and stress. A score of 4 or better is a very good sign. Conversely, a score of -4 or less indicates that technology and job-created stress is getting to you. A score of -7 or less is a sign that you should consider switching jobs.

Review and study questions

1. What was the basic characteristic of the handicraft era? What was the basic characteristic of the mechanization era? Explain.

2. How does mechanistic technology differ from automated technology? How does automated technology differ from cybernated technology?

3. Alvin Toffler has said, "If technology is to be regarded as a great engine, a mighty accelerator, then knowledge must be regarded as its fuel. And thus we come to the crux of the accelerative process in society, for the engine is being fed a richer and richer fuel every day." What is meant by this statement?

4. What are the four characteristics of a post-industrial society? Describe each.

5. How did the prevailing ethic change as mankind progressed from the handicraft era, to the mechanization and assembly-line eras, to the post-industrial era? Explain.

6. Which needs, in Maslow's need hierarchy, are considered to be most important in the handicraft era? The mechanization and assembly-line eras? The post-industrial era?

7. How have the predominant goals of mankind changed as it progressed through the handicraft era, to the mechanization and assembly-line eras, to the post-industrial era? Explain.

8. What is meant by the terms *profit-maximization management*, *trusteeship management*, and *quality-of-life management*?

9. The impact of technology on people's daily lives is encouraging them to seek a higher quality of life, but the impact of technology within the organization is being used to promote the trusteeship management philosophy. What is meant by this statement?

10. How can technology cause powerlessness, meaninglessness, normlessness, isolation, and self-estrangement? Discuss each condition separately.

11. Refer to Woodward's classification scheme in Chapter 6. What effect, in terms of that scheme, does technology have on alienation?

12. How does technology lead personnel to fear replacement by machines? Explain.

13. The major step the modern organization must take in integrating technology and people is to determine the effect that technology is likely to have and to develop a plan for reducing its dysfunctional effects. What is meant by this statement?

14. What role can be played by industrial democracy and participative management? Explain.

The old versus the new

Sue Ryan was a secretary at Wilshire Community College for three years. During this time she received three salary raises and was now at the top of her salary range.

Sue enjoyed working at Wilshire because the work was not extremely demanding, and she liked the interaction with both the faculty and her fellow workers. However, one day she realized that if she remained at the college she would never increase her salary more than five to seven percent a year. This dismayed Sue, because she had just bought a new car and had been hoping to vacation in Europe with some school friends next year. With her current salary, she could afford the car but not the trip.

Then she learned that a new factory had opened in town. The plant was owned and managed by a national corporation, which had decided to assemble some of its consumer products in the area. According to a newspaper ad she read, the starting salary for assemblers was 25 percent higher than her current salary, and there was a guaranteed cost-of-living raise.

Sue decided to find out more about the job. She went to the company's personnel office, talked to someone about the job qualifications, and learned that in addition to what she knew already, there was also a very good medical and pension plan—far better than what was in effect at the community college. After giving the matter serious thought, Sue decided to quit her secretary's job and go to work for the assembly plant.

For the first four weeks things went quite well. Sue was so busy trying to master her job and keep up with the speed of the line that she had little time to think about anything else. At night she was so tired that she went right home and fell into bed. However, as she began to gain control of the job and to learn some of the shortcuts, Sue realized that her job was quite different from the one she had at the college. For one thing, there was no one working very close to her. The nearest person was 35 feet away, and because of the machine noise, Sue had to almost shout if she wanted to talk to the woman. In addition, the line was moving so fast that Sue really did not have time for any extended talking. It was all she could do to keep up.

As the next few months passed Sue began to reevaluate her decision. She realized that while the assembly line job certainly paid well, it was not very enjoyable work. In fact, she disliked it. As a result, at the end of the fourth month, she called her former boss at Wilshire and asked if she could return to the community college. He told her she could, and two weeks later Sue resigned her job at the assembly plant. As she went into the personnel department to pick up her paycheck and sign some termination papers, she noticed that she was not alone. Seven other women were also terminating their employment that day. On the way out she heard one of the personnel people saying into the phone, "I don't know what the problem is over here, but we've got a turnover rate of almost 40 percent and we haven't been operating six months yet."

Questions

1. What did Sue dislike about her assembly line job? Incorporate into your answer a discussion of alienation.

2. What particular features of her old job do you think enticed Sue to return to the community college?

3. How can the assembly plant deal with the problem of high turnover? Explain.

Let's keep it a secret

Nordington Sheet & Tube is a medium-sized manufacturing corporation located in the Midwest. Last year the company's comptroller reported to the president that the firm's machinery required more maintenance than ever before. Given the facts that the machines were greatly depreciated for income tax purposes and that the government was offering a tax credit for the purchase of new capital equipment, the comptroller suggested that now might be a good time to replace some of this machinery.

In particular, the comptroller recommended that they sell almost 25 percent of the current machinery and replace it with the most modern equipment available. The purchase price was over $20 million, but with reduced maintenance costs, tax credit savings, and rapid depreciation in addition to the increase in productivity, the company could recoup its total investment in less than five years. Moreover, the new machinery would require the same number of personnel to operate as before, so the company need have no concern about a labor–management rift over layoffs. The idea sounded fine to the president and the board of directors and they ordered the comptroller to purchase the machines.

The first step the comptroller took was to meet with the vice president of production and tell him the good news. Then the two sat down to discuss how to decide what types of machines would be best. They spent the next month calling machine manufacturers to have their representatives visit the plant, look at the old equipment, and present recommendations and prices for new equipment.

The workers themselves were not involved in this process. In fact, they really did not know what was going on when they saw the first manufacturer's representative come through the plant with the production vice president. After several more representatives showed up, however, one of the workers decided to ask the next one what he was doing at Nordington. Once they were out of earshot of the vice president, the representative told the worker, "The company's buying new equipment to replace some of this old stuff. I'm here to take a look at some of these machines and then see if we have something that would do a better job. It's sure going to be a lot different around here once you get these new machines in."

The worker did not ask any more questions. Later in the day, he told his fellow workers what the representative had said. This immediately caused great concern among the machinists. Some of them thought that the representative was wrong, but the majority reasoned that he would not have been there if he hadn't been asked to tell the firm about more modern equipment. The workers became concerned that there would be a mass layoff once the new machines were installed. After taking a vote, they sent a group of three representatives to talk to the vice president. The vice president told them, "Yes, we are getting new machines, but this will have no effect on employment. We're going to need just as many people afterwards as we do now."

The workers apparently did not believe the vice president. Within two weeks, 15 percent of the department had quit and another 10 percent were actively looking for employment with other firms in the area. Upon learning of this development, the company president sent the production vice president a memo ordering him to have a meeting with the entire department in order to tell the workers the company's machine purchase plans and answer any questions they might have. "This information should have been communicated to them months ago," the president wrote. "I only hope it's not too late to save the situation."

Questions

1. What is the basic concern of the workers? Why are some of them quitting?
2. How could this problem have been prevented? Explain.
3. In complying with the president's memo, how should the vice president handle the situation? Make your answer thorough and detailed.

Job redesign
and job enrichment

8

Goals of the chapter

How can modern organizations deal with the challenge of technology and the dysfunctional effects it creates? One of the primary ways is to redesign jobs and enrich them with psychological motivators, such as increased autonomy, feedback, and task variety. In this chapter we study how this can be done.

The first goal of this chapter is to examine the current status of work in America and the need for an improved quality of work life (QWL). The second goal is to examine the nature of job redesign and some of the most commonly used job redesign techniques. The third goal is to study core job dimensions and job enrichment principles employed in redesign programs. The fourth goal is to look at some successful job enrichment programs. The fifth goal is to examine some of the current challenges in job redesign.

When you have finished reading this chapter you should be able to:

1. identify the four alternatives available to management for dealing with the problem of boring jobs
2. explain what job design is all about
3. tell how job rotation, job traction, job enlargement, and job enrichment work
4. describe the five core job dimensions and illustrate selected enrichment principles that help create these dimensions
5. cite some illustrations of job enrichment in action
6. describe some of the current challenges in job design.

Work in America

Many workers today admit that they are bored with their jobs. They feel no challenge or desire to do a particularly good job. There is no excitement in their work-lives.

What can management do about this? There are four alternatives available:

There are numerous ways to deal with boring jobs.

1. The organization can do nothing.

2. The management can offer the workers more money for accepting these dull, repetitive, uninteresting jobs.

3. The organization can try to replace the workers with machines by automating many of the jobs.

4. The company can redesign the work so that it has meaning for the employees.

The most important of these alternatives in the study of human relations is the last.

There is a need to give workers more of a challenge, more of a whole task, more opportunity to use advanced skills, more opportunity for growth, and more chance to contribute their ideas. The classical design of jobs was to construct them according to the technological imperative, that is, to design them according to the needs of technology and give little attention to other criteria. The new approach is to provide a careful balance of the human imperative and the technical imperative. *Jobs are required to fit people as well as technology.* **This is a new set of values and a new way of thinking that focuses on QWL.**[1]

Much of what we discuss in this chapter relates to lower-level jobs. The reason is quite simple—most of the dull, repetitive jobs are located at the bottom of the hierarchy. Of course, middle-level and top-level managers also quit their jobs because they can find no meaning in them. However, their number is quite small in contrast to that of their counterparts further down in the organization. How can lower-level jobs be made more meaningful? One of the primary ways is to redesign the work itself.

The nature of job redesign

Job redesign refers to any activities involving work changes with the purpose of increasing the quality of the worker's job experience or improving the worker's productivity.[2] Under this term can be included such

---

[1] Keith Davis, *Human Behavior at Work: Organizational Behavior*, 6th ed. (New York: McGraw-Hill Book Company, 1981), p. 287.

[2] J. Richard Hackman and J. Lloyd Suttle, eds., *Improving Life at Work* (Santa Monica, Calif.: Goodyear Publishing Company, 1977), p. 98.

commonly used job redesign techniques as job rotation, job traction, job enlargement, and job enrichment.

Job redesign is a unique way of improving organizational efficiency. This is true for four reasons.

First, job redesign alters the basic relationship between the worker and the job, which has long been a human relations problem. The scientific managers tried to deal with the problem by blending the physical requirements of the work with the physical characteristics of the workers, and screening out those who did not measure up. When behavioral scientists entered industry, they attempted to refine this process by improving the selection and training of the workers. As with the scientific managers, however, the concentration of effort was still on the people doing the job. The work was treated as a fixed commodity that could not be altered. Job redesign breaks with this tradition and is based on the assumption that the work itself can be a powerful influence on employee motivation, satisfaction, and productivity.

Moreover, after jobs are changed, it usually is difficult for workers to slip back into old ways. The old ways simply are inappropriate for the new tasks, and the structure of those tasks reinforces the changes that have taken place. Thus, one need not worry much about the kind of backsliding that occurs so often after training or attitude modification activities, especially those that occur off-site. The task-based stimuli that influence the worker's behavior are very much on-site, every hour of every day. And once those stimuli are changed, behavior is likely to stay changed—at least until the job is again redesigned.[3]

Second, job redesign does not attempt to change attitudes first (such as inducing workers to care about work results in a zero-defects program) but believes that positive attitudes will follow if the job is redesigned properly. Initial attention is given to determining how the job ought to be done. Once this is worked out, the individual doing the work will be forced to change his or her old behavior and hopefully will like the new arrangement so much that attitude toward the job will then be positive.

Job redesign is a unique way of improving organizational efficiency.

Third, job redesign helps individuals regain the opportunity to experience the kick that comes from doing a job well. There is more here than just satisfaction; there is a sense of competence and self-worth in which people feel themselves stretching and growing as human beings.

Fourth, sometimes when an organization redesigns jobs and solves people-work problems, other opportunities for initiating organizational change are presented. For example, technical problems are likely to develop when jobs are changed, offering management the opportunity to smooth and refine the entire work system. Interpersonal issues are also likely to arise, often between supervisors and subordinates, providing the organization a chance to do developmental work aimed at improving the social and supervisory aspects of the work system.

---

[3]*Ibid.*, p. 102.

In any event, job redesign is a very important tool, for it provides a basis for developing and utilizing the organization's resources. In the next section we examine three job redesign techniques commonly used in this process.

Job redesign techniques

While numerous techniques can be employed in job redesign, three of the most popular are: (1) job rotation, (2) job enlargement, and (3) job enrichment.

Job rotation

In job rotation the worker moves from one job to another.

Job rotation involves moving a worker from one job to another for the purpose of reducing boredom. For example, six workers are charged with assembling, soldering, testing, painting, and packaging a piece of sophisticated machinery. As seen in Figure 8.1, the first person assembles Components A, B, and C; the second assembles D, E, and F; and each of the other workers performs a specific function on the unit. The arrows in

Figure 8.1
Job rotation

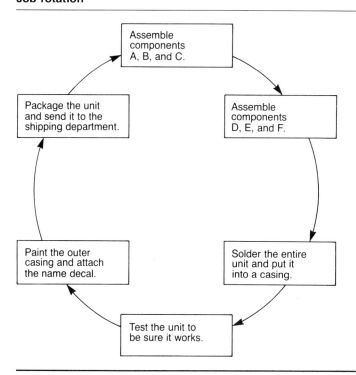

"How was the vacation, Cartwell?"

Drawing by Harry Schwalb, *Changing Times*, September 1978.

the figure illustrate how job rotation works. Each person moves to the task, immediately following the one he or she has been doing. The person assembling Components A, B, and C now assembles Components D, E, and F; the worker soldering the unit and putting it into a casing now tests the unit to be sure it works; the individual packaging the unit now moves to assembling Components A, B, and C. Continually moving all the workers in this manner can often keep them more interested in their work than if they each did the same thing day after day. Another benefit of job rotation is the perspective it provides the individual as to how his or her activity fits into the overall work flow. A third benefit is that the individual's identification with the final output increases. All these benefits can help increase work motivation.

Job enlargement

Job enlargement involves giving the worker more to do. Usually this new work is similar to what the person has done before. For example, if Joe is wiring, Ralph is soldering, and Mary is testing the product, the three of them may have their jobs enlarged by allowing each to perform all three functions. One of the ways in which this job redesign can result in efficiency is through the time saved by not having to pass the product from one person to the next. Additionally, there is the psychological reward associated with completing a unit as opposed to performing just

Job enlargement gives the worker more to do.

one small task on a large product. Some researchers have reported that the main advantages of job enlargement appear to be increased job satisfaction and improved quality.[4]

Job enrichment

Job enrichment, a technique that is more behaviorally sophisticated than job enlargement, attempts to build psychological motivators, as described by Herzberg's two-factor theory, into the job. In particular, job enrichment programs attempt to give the worker more authority in planning the work and controlling the pace and procedures used in doing the job.

Industrial research reveals that a number of firms have had success with job enrichment, including American Telephone and Telegraph (AT&T), General Foods, and Travelers Insurance. At AT&T, for example, employees who were handling insurance correspondence with stockholders were chosen for a job enrichment program. Using a test group and a control group, the researchers enriched the jobs of the test group by permitting them to sign their own names to the letters they prepared, encouraging them to become experts in the kinds of problems that appealed to them, holding them accountable for the quality of their work, and providing them with expert assistance in carrying out these duties. After six months, the group's quality, attitudes, and productivity had increased, and their tardiness, absenteeism, and work costs had declined. The control group's performance on these factors, meanwhile, had remained the same.[5]

Core job dimensions

Why do redesign techniques such as the three discussed in the previous section often lead to increases in productivity and higher satisfaction among the personnel? The answer rests not only in the physical changes that take place in the work environment, but also in the psychological changes that take place within the employees. In particular, it has been found that certain dimensions can be built into the work that will bring about higher output, lower absenteeism, higher quality, and greater internal work motivation. Research reveals that there are five *core job dimensions* that are extremely useful in enriching jobs: (1) skill variety, (2) task identity, (3) task significance, (4) autonomy, and (5) feedback.[6]

---

[4] Alan C. Filley, Robert J. House, and Steven Kerr, *Managerial Process and Organizational Behavior*, 2nd ed. (Glenview, Ill.: Scott, Foresman and Company, 1976), p. 345.

[5] Robert N. Ford, *Motivation through the Work Itself* (New York: American Management Association, 1969), pp. 20–44.

[6] J. Richard Hackman and Greg R. Oldham, "Development of the Job Diagnostic Survey," *Journal of Applied Psychology*, April 1975, pp. 159–170.

Skill variety

Skill variety is the degree to which a job requires the completion of different activities, all of which involve varying talents and capabilities. The two most common types of skills are motor skills and intellectual skills. Motor skills help one with "doing" tasks, and intellectual skills are used with "thinking" tasks. If a job can draw on both, it will provide greater variety than if only one of them is needed.

Two common types of skills are motor and intellectual.

Bob Williams is a salesman for a large machine manufacturer. The machine he sells is very complex and requires a technical sales pitch. Advertising is also very important in gaining customer attention and arousing initial interest. The typical sales strategy is to mail an advertising brochure to potential customers and then follow up by sending in a salesperson to those who express interest.

Bob had been the company's number one salesman for three years and had been thinking about quitting because the challenge of selling was losing its excitement. He started to feel that the requisite technical sales presentation did not allow him to exercise his creativity. He decided to stay on, however, after the vice president of sales asked him to help write the advertising brochure.

"We need some input from you regarding how to make the initial pitch to the customer," the vice president told him. "You know how these people think; we'd like to put your ideas into the brochure." Delighted with the chance to do some "think" work, Bob dropped his plans to leave the company.

Task identity

Task identity involves the degree to which the job requires completion of a whole or identifiable piece of work. The more an individual does on the job, the more likely he or she will identify with the task. Assembly-line employees who put a bolt on a car or weld part of the structure have little task identity. Those who complete a major part of the car (working as a member of a group) have much greater task identity.

Completion of an identifiable piece of work increases task identity.

Jane Copeland is an assembler-packer for a consumer goods manufacturer. A year ago Jane used to assemble two parts of a seven-part consumer product. Then, thanks to a job redesign program, she was given all seven parts to assemble as well as the responsibility of packaging the product. The result—in Jane's group there was a 90 percent decline in absenteeism and turnover and a seven percent increase in output.

Task significance

Task significance is the degree to which a job has a substantial impact on the lives or work of other people. When employees are able to see how the work they do influences others, they tend to be more motivated to do a good job.

A job with substantial impact on others has high task significance.

Alice Bodelyn is a manuscript editor for a college textbook publishing firm. Generally, Alice is assigned two manuscripts at the same

time and for the next two to three months she reads the material, edits it for grammar, makes style and substance recommendations, and then sends it back to the respective author in batches of three to four chapters for the author's comments. As the edited manuscript reaches completion, Alice discusses the content of the book with a member of the design department, who will work up a cover for the text. Finally, the author visits the publishing house, meets Alice and the cover designer, and spends a few days with them and the marketing people who are putting together the advertising campaign.

Alice has been a manuscript editor for four years and she has received a personally autographed copy of each book from its author. When asked what she likes best about her work, she says, "I feel an integral part of an important team. When I look at the finished book I see part of myself in it."

Autonomy

Autonomy provides the worker with work freedom.

Autonomy is the degree to which the job provides the worker freedom, independence, and discretion in scheduling the work and determining how to carry it out. As people begin to plan and execute their assignments without having to rely on others for direction and instructions, they develop feelings of strong personal responsibilities for job success and job failure and are motivated to do the best possible job.

Dick Jackson is a life insurance agent for a large company based in New York. Dick usually begins his work day at 10 A.M., calling on one or two prospective customers and taking a third to lunch. Then he returns to the office to answer correspondence and prepare material for people he will be meeting later in the day. From 4 P.M. to 6 P.M., Dick talks to customers in the office, and three days a week he works evenings. Last year Dick was again a member of the million dollar club, having sold $1.92 million of life insurance.

This past week the district manager asked Dick if he would like to leave his current job and become an office manager. "What for?" asked Dick. "I've got freedom in my current job. Who wants to be tied down to a nine-to-five office schedule?"

Feedback

Feedback tells the worker how well he or she is doing.

Feedback is the degree to which the work required by the job results in the individual's receiving direct, clear information about the effectiveness of his or her performance. Feedback allows people to monitor their own work rather than depend on someone else to do it for them.

Group A is charged with wiring the panels for a complex telecommunications satellite. If the wiring of these panels is done incorrectly, it could result in a malfunction of the entire system during or after launching into earth orbit. To prevent such an occurrence, there are a few simple tests that can be conducted on the panels. Owing to the complexity of the wiring, however, it is not uncommon for each panel to have three or four incorrectly placed wires. When this occurs, errors are caught by the test group and are noted on an error chart. The panel is then returned to Group A for partial rewiring.

Group A has recently protested this procedure, claiming that it is virtually impossible to wire a panel correctly on the first try. There are bound to be a few errors, and the group is embarrassed when a panel is sent back by the test group. The members of Group A have asked management to redesign their work and incorporate testing as one of their functions while, of course, maintaining a small test group to make a final check of the panel. The company agreed, and over the last four weeks none of the 40 panels sent to the test group has been returned. "Once we know there's an error," said a member of Group A, "we can correct it before sending it on. This type of feedback, from our own group, reduces tension and helps us to do a better job."

Motivating potential score

Researchers have used the five core job dimensions described in this section to develop a *motivating potential score* formula:

$$\text{Motivation potential score (MPS)} = \left[\frac{\text{Skill variety} + \text{Task identity} + \text{Task significance}}{3} \right] \times \text{Autonomy} \times \text{Feedback}$$

Although we do not need to get into the mathematics of the formula, one overriding conclusion can be drawn from it. If the organization wants to redesign jobs so that the employees are motivated, it must build in autonomy, feedback, and at least one of the three remaining dimensions. This last statement becomes clear when we see that if there is no autonomy or no feedback, the MPS will be zero, since these two dimensions are multiplicative. Likewise, if all the three other dimensions are zero, the MPS will be zero.

Testing of these job core characteristics has provided some breakthroughs in job design. In particular, researchers have found that if these dimensions are present, individuals with high growth needs will be more motivated, productive, and satisfied than if they work on tasks without these dimensions.

Job profile charts

In addition, it is possible to construct job profile charts so that enrichment programs can more effectively be designed. For example, in Figure 8.2, Job 1 is low on skill variety, task identity, and task significance. Job 2 is low on task significance, autonomy, and feedback. Job 3 is low on skill variety, task significance, and feedback. The first question the organization must answer is: can the particular job be enriched; i.e., can Job 1 be redesigned so that it has greater skill variety, task identity, and task significance? If the answer is yes, then the people charged with the redesign program know where to begin. If the answer is no, the employees must be made to realize that there is nothing that can be done to restructure the job.

A job profile chart helps identify core job dimensions.

Figure 8.2
Profile chart of core job dimensions for three jobs

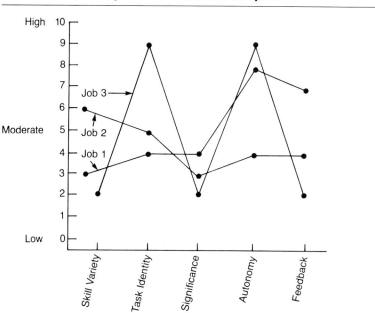

Before our discussion of this point closes, one thing should be made very clear: some jobs cannot be enriched. There may be no way of increasing the task significance of a dishwasher's job. Nor can American auto-assembly lines, under present conditions, provide a person with skill variety. In some cases the individual must conform to the work pattern because the work pattern cannot be altered.

How much of these core dimensions can you find in your own job? One way of answering this question is to analyze your work views systematically with the help of the short quiz on how you view your work.

Job enrichment principles

There are many ways of enriching jobs so as to provide more meaningful work. In this section, we examine five job enrichment principles: (1) formation of natural work units, (2) establishment of worker-client relationships, (3) combining of tasks, (4) vertical loading, and (5) opening of feedback channels. We study how each principle can be used in redesigning work. Figure 8.3 illustrates how each principle is tied to one or more of the core job dimensions.

How you view your work

The quiz is designed to provide insights into how you view your work. If you do not currently work full time, refer to your last full-time job in answering the questions. If you have not had a full-time job, think of one you would like to have (be reasonable in your choice), and use it throughout the quiz. Interpretations are provided at the end of the chapter.

I. Read the following job-related questions very carefully and decide how accurate each is in describing your job. Then answer each using the following scale:

1. None
2. Very little
3. A little
4. A moderate amount

5. Some
6. Quite a bit
7. A lot

1. To what degree does your job allow you to do a whole series of different things, employing a variety of skills and talents in the process? _____

2. To what degree does your job allow you to complete a whole piece of work in contrast to just a small part of an overall piece of work? _____

3. How much significance or importance does your job have? _____

4. How much freedom do you have to do your job your own way? _____

5. To what degree does the job itself provide feedback on how well you are doing? _____

6. To what degree do your boss or fellow workers let you know how well you are doing? _____

II. Determine how accurate each of the following statements are in describing your job. Use the following scale to record your answer:

1. Highly inaccurate
2. Mostly inaccurate
3. Slightly inaccurate
4. Uncertain

5. Slightly accurate
6. Mostly accurate
7. Highly accurate

1. Your job is simple and repetitive. _____

2. Your boss and coworkers never give you feedback on your work progress. _____

3. Your job provides you no chance to use personal initiative or judgment in carrying out tasks. _____

4. Your job is not really very significant or important. _____

5. Your job provides independence and freedom in doing the work your way. ____

6. Your job provides the chance to completely finish pieces of work that you begin. ____

7. How well you do your work really affects a lot of other people. ____

8. Just by the way the work is designed, you have many opportunities to evaluate how well you are doing. ____

9. Your job calls for you to use a lot of complex and/or high-level skills. ____

10. Superiors often let you know how well you are doing your job. ____

11. Your work is set up in such a way that you do not have the chance to do an entire piece of work from beginning to end. ____

12. Your job provides few clues regarding how well you are performing your tasks. ____

Formation of natural work units

Natural work units give a worker some job ownership.

In many organizations, the workers all contribute to providing a product or service but do not have any basis for identifying with the work. A secretary in the typing pool types all the correspondence and reports assigned by the supervisor of the pool. On a given day there may be letters from five or six departmental managers as well as part of a speech for the vice president of personnel. After a while, all the work blurs together and the secretary identifies with none of it. He or she is simply a producer of typed material. This analogy holds for a person on an auto-assembly line who is installing upholstery. One car looks like another. The job has no real meaning.

One way of enriching jobs such as these is through the formation of *natural work units*, in which the employee obtains some ownership of the work. For example, responsibility for all the work requested by a single department or person could be assigned to one typist. Instead of typing one part of a large report, the typist now types it all. Over time, the person begins to identify with the task and to see how the material is of value to those who receive the finished product. The formation of natural work units contributes to two core job dimensions: task identity and task significance (see Figure 8.3).

Figure 8.3

Example of the relationship between selected job enrichment principles and core job dimensions

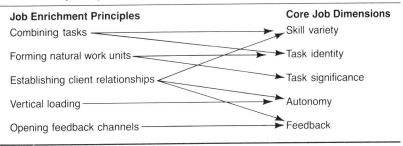

Job Enrichment Principles	Core Job Dimensions
Combining tasks	Skill variety
Forming natural work units	Task identity
Establishing client relationships	Task significance
Vertical loading	Autonomy
Opening feedback channels	Feedback

Establishment of worker-client relationships

Workers seldom come in contact with the ultimate user of their product or service. If such a relationship can be established, however, job commitment and motivation will usually be enhanced. There are three steps in the *establishment of worker-client relationships*: (1) identify the client, (2) determine the most direct contact possible between the worker and the client, and (3) set up a system by which the client can evaluate the quality of the product or service and convey the judgments directly to the worker.

Establishing worker-client relationships can contribute to three core job dimensions: skill variety, autonomy, and feedback. Skill variety increases because the worker has the chance to exercise interpersonal skills in both managing and maintaining the client relationship. Autonomy increases because the person is given responsibility for deciding how to manage the client relationship. Feedback increases because the worker has the opportunity to receive both praise and criticism for his or her output.

Worker-client relationships contribute to skill variety, autonomy, and feedback.

Combining of tasks

The principle of **combining tasks** is based on the assumption that higher work motivation can result when a series of simple tasks are combined to form a new and larger work module. For example, a few years ago a Corning Glass Works plant redesigned the job of assembling laboratory hot plates by combining a number of tasks that had been separate. The redesigned job called for each operator to assemble an entire hot plate. Costs declined and motivation increased as a result of the redesign effort. The combining of tasks contributes to two core job dimensions:

Combining of tasks can increase motivation.

skill variety and task identity. The enlarged job requires a greater variety of skill, and as the individual begins turning out finished products, task identity increases. The assembler can see the unit taking shape as the various pieces are affixed and soldered.

Vertical loading

Vertical loading occurs when the gap between the "doing" and "controlling" aspects of the job are reduced. In particular, responsibilities that formerly were reserved for management are now delegated to the employee as part of the job. Some ways of vertically loading a job include the following:

- **Give the worker the responsibility for deciding work methods and for advising or helping to train less experienced workers;**
- **Provide increased freedom to the worker including decisions about when to start and stop work, when to take breaks, and how to assign work priorities;**
- **Encourage the workers to do their own troubleshooting and manage work crises rather than immediately calling for a supervisor;**
- **Provide workers with increased knowledge of the financial aspects of the job and the organization, and increased control over budgetary matters that affect their work.**[7]

When a job is vertically loaded, autonomy increases and workers begin feeling personal responsibility and accountability for the outcome of their efforts.

Opening of feedback channels

In most jobs there are ways of *opening feedback channels* so each worker can monitor his or her own performance. One way, discussed already, is to establish direct worker-client relationships by which the individual can learn what the client likes and dislikes about the product or service being provided. Another is to place as much control as possible in the hands of the worker. For example, rather than having quality checks performed by people in the quality assurance department, let the worker do the checking. Such a move ensures immediate feedback and allows the individual to exercise self-control. Placing quality-control functions in the hands of workers can result in higher quantity and quality of output. This principle helps overcome one of the main human relations problems—failure to tell people how well they are doing.

Tradition and established procedure in many organizations dictate that records about performance be kept by a supervisor and transmitted up (not down) the organizational hierarchy. Sometimes supervisors

---

[7] Hackman and Suttle, *Improving Life at Work*, pp. 138–139.

even check the work and correct any errors themselves. The worker who made the error never knows it occurred and is therefore denied the very information that could enhance both internal work motivation and the technical adequacy of his performance. In many cases, it is possible to provide standard summaries of performance records directly to the workers. This would give the employees personally and regularly the data they need to improve their effectiveness.[8]

Job enrichment in action

There have been a number of successful applications of the job enrichment concepts we discuss in this chapter. Perhaps the best known is that by Volvo, the Swedish car manufacturer. Job enrichment has also been effective in many other organizations, ranging from manufacturing firms to insurance companies. Let us examine three cases of job enrichment in action as well as address the two currently most popular job enrichment concepts from Japan: quality circles and Theory Z.

Volvo

In the early 1970s, Volvo built a new auto assembly plant in Kalmar, Sweden. Instead of having the work come to the people, however, the management decided to construct an assembly line in which the people went to the work. The company felt that people would do a better job if it was the product that stood while the personnel did the moving. Additionally, the management believed that people want to have social contact on the job, and on the typical assembly line this is not possible because the employees are physically isolated from one another. If the work were patterned according to the people, the Volvo management believed, the employees could act in cooperation, have more time to discuss work-related problems, and decide among themselves how best to organize their jobs. This new approach was to be based on stimulation rather than restriction.

The design for Kalmar incorporated pleasant, quiet surroundings, arranged for group working, with each group having its own individual rest and meeting areas. The work itself is organized so that each group is responsible for a particular, identifiable portion of the car—electrical systems, interiors, doors, and so on. Individual cars are built up on self-propelling "carriers" that run around the factory following a movable conductive tape on the floor. Computers normally direct the carriers, but manual controls can override the taped route. If someone notices a scratch in the paint on a car, he or she can immediately turn the carrier back to the painting station. Under computer control again, the car will return later to the production process wherever it left off.

Each work group has its own buffer areas for incoming and out-

---

[8] *Ibid.*, pp. 139–140.

going carriers so it can pace itself as it wishes and organize the work in-side its own area so its members work individually or in subgroups to suit themselves. Most of the employees have chosen to learn more than one small job; the individual increase in skills also gives the team itself added flexibility.[9]

In addition, each team does its own inspection. After a car passes three work group stations, it goes through a special inspection station where people with special training test it. If there are any persistent or recurring problems, a computer-based system flashes the results to the proper group station, informing them of the particular problem and reviewing how they solved it the last time.

Volvo has had good success with job enrichment.

This design employs many of the ideas we discussed in this chapter, including the five core job dimensions, and Volvo has reported success with its approach. In fact, since the success with the Kalmar plant, the company has introduced this job design program in four other plants. In addition, a recent survey among the unionized employees at Kalmar reports that almost all of them are in favor of the new working patterns. Figure 8.4 lists findings and suggestions that resulted from the Volvo program.

Sherwin Williams

Sherwin Williams is a well-known paint manufacturer. One of the primary success ingredients in the paint industry is low-cost production. After conducting preliminary analysis, Sherwin Williams reached the conclusion that a well-designed work layout coupled with the use of autonomous work groups could bring about increased plant productivity. The company decided to try out its ideas.[10]

The plant chosen for the project is in Richmond, Kentucky, and was designed to manufacture and package auto paint. Each color requires a different formula and, since there are many paints being produced, the process calls for sophisticated technology and skilled operators. The company decided to run the plant with work teams that would carry out their jobs in an unsupervised environment. A technician, for example, was to have total responsibility for a batch of paint from inception to final storage prior to shipment.

Autonomous work groups were formed.

Industrial engineers and a sociotechnical systems consultant designed the plant. Layout followed the actual flow of the product through the manufacturing cycle, and the work space was kept open to allow for interaction and communication among team members. Each autonomous work group was assigned a complete task, and each team member

---

[9] Pehr G. Gyllenhammar, "How Volvo Adapts Work to People," *Harvard Business Review*, July–August 1977, p. 107.

[10] Ernesto J. Poza and M. Lynne Markus, "Success Story: The Team Approach to Work Restructuring," *Organizational Dynamics*, Winter 1980, pp. 3–25.

Figure 8.4
Job design guidelines from Volvo

1. Each unit should be free to develop individually without interference or detailed control from headquarters.
2. A positive management attitude toward change is a prerequisite for positive results.
3. Positive achievements seem related to the extent that managers understand that the change process will, sooner or later, affect several organizational levels.
4. Problems can be encountered if change is formalized and targets, minutes, and figures are requested too early.
5. Progress seems to be fastest when a factory or company starts by forming a joint management and union steering committee to look at its own problems.
6. The fastest way to get ideas flowing is to set up discussion groups of less than 25 people in each working area.
7. A new plant, product, or machine provides an opportunity to think about new working patterns.
8. An investment in one new facility or work group area often results in spontaneous changes in related facilities or groups.
9. Most factories have a number of tasks that need not be done on assembly lines. Once a few have been found, others will reveal themselves.
10. So that change suggestions will emerge from inside, changes of work organization must be integrated with a structure of employee consultation.

Reprinted by permission of the *Harvard Business Review*. Exhibit from "How Volvo Adapts Work to People" by Pehr G. Gyllenhammer (July/August 1977). Copyright © 1977 by the president and fellows of Harvard College; all rights reserved.

learned all of the jobs the group performed. In this way job rotation within the team was possible. The results were impressive.

1. The original estimate of work force size was 200, but the facility was able to operate with 160 employees.
2. While the average absenteeism rate at Sherwin Williams plants was 6.7 percent, for autonomous work team members it was 2.5 percent.

   The results were impressive.

3. The cost per gallon of paint in this facility was 45 percent lower than in other plants manufacturing auto paint, and productivity was 30 percent higher.
4. The facility produced the highest quality paint manufactured by the firm with 94 percent of production rated excellent as compared to a 75 percent all-plant average.
5. Paint which failed to meet product specifications decreased by 25 percent; paint returned from customers declined by 75 percent; and product availability reached a record high.
6. During the entire period in which the plant was under study, 1,108 days of operation, there were no lost-time accidents.

Using autonomous work groups effectively: six useful guidelines

There are a number of important guidelines which should be followed if autonomous work groups are to be used effectively. Robert DuBrin, a well-known management expert, has suggested the following:

1. In order to properly house a team operation, an organization must be redesigned thoroughly and a systems point of view maintained.
2. Attention has to be paid to the design and layout of the physical setting; i.e., building space must allow for the product flow and for the interaction of people necessary to perform teamwork.
3. It is usually necessary to create a relatively flat organization structure where team members are in control of a significant amount of their work.
4. Autonomous work groups are the most effective when the status barriers between management and employees are broken down, because this permits the establishment of an atmosphere of trust and open communication.
5. Only employees who show pride in their work and enjoy working in cooperative effort with others should be chosen for such a group; self-nomination or asking for volunteers for the autonomous work groups will decrease selection error.
6. The management should be prepared to transfer employees who do not make it as team members or team leaders to more traditional jobs; some people are not suited to team arrangements even though they might volunteer themselves for such assignments.

Andrew DuBrin, *Contemporary Applied Management* (Plano, Texas: Business Publications, Inc., 1982), p. 114.

The Sherwin Williams experiment was successful because the firm carefully designed the facilities and the work. It also drew upon a high quality work force to form the teams. These are two major prerequisites for successful autonomous work groups. Other prerequisites are presented in using autonomous work groups effectively.

A major insurance firm

Another example of job redesign bringing about increased work productivity has been reported by Champagne.[11] In this case the job enrichment program was implemented in the keypunch department of a major insurance company. The program is particularly useful in understanding the value of job redesign because in this case there were two groups: test and control.

A job enrichment workshop was held.

After making an analysis of how the keypunch workers functioned in this firm, the job redesign experts put the workers through a three-day workshop on what job enrichment is all about. During this time the researcher tried to get the keypunch operator actively involved in the redesign program. By the time the workshop ended, a total of 73 possible

---

[11] Paul J. Champagne, "Explaining Job Enrichment," *Supervisory Management*, November 1979, pp. 24–34.

Figure 8.5
Percentage change in volume of completed work

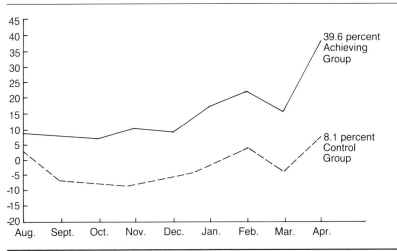

Paul J. Champagne, "Explaining Job Enrichment," *Supervisory Management*, November 1979, p. 29. © 1979 by AMACOM, a division of American Management Associations. Reprinted by permission.

job-change items had been introduced by the group members. After examining the feasibility of each item, 25 changes were targeted for implementation. The four most important were to be these:

1. Keypunch operators would become responsible for their own work. Included in their enriched jobs would be responsibility for scheduling and for meeting these schedules.

   Objectives were established.

2. Operators would correct obvious coding errors. If they knew the information being given to them was wrong, they had the authority to change it appropriately.

3. Each operator would correct his or her own errors. The workers could redo incorrectly punched cards.

4. Operators would deal directly with clients. Before the job redesign program, work from unidentified sources was given to them in one-hour batches. After the program, the operators had their own customers with full responsibility for these clients' jobs.[12]

The results of this program were more favorable than even management had anticipated. Figure 8.5 shows the increase in the average num-

Output increased.

[12] *Ibid.*, p. 28.

Figure 8.6
Reaction to job enrichment program

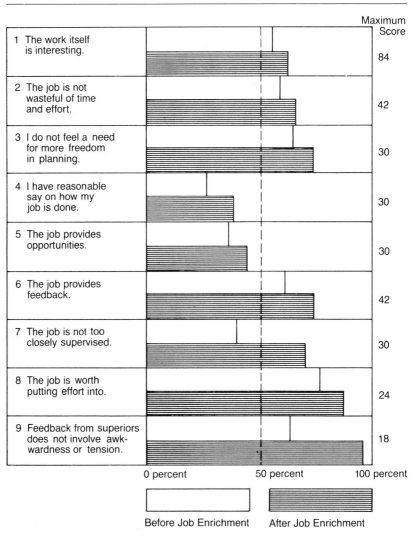

Paul J. Champagne, "Explaining Job Enrichment," *Supervisory Management*,
November 1979, p. 30. © 1979 by AMACOM, a division of American Management
Associations. Reprinted by permission.

ber of computer cards keypunched and verified per hour. While the
control group increased its output by 8.1 percent, the test group's output
rose by 39.6 percent.

Another important change was in job attitudes. Attitude surveys
were administered both before and after the job enrichment program. As
seen in Figure 8.6, nine categories of job attitudes were measured. In

*So did job
attitudes.*

every case the attitudes were greater after the program than before. Two of the largest changes were in terms of decreased close supervision (number seven in the table) and improved feedback from superiors (number nine in the table).

A third positive change was reported in terms of quality of work. Before the job enrichment program, 40 percent of those in the test group (called the high achieving group) were rated as outstanding keypunch operators. After the program this increased to 55 percent. Also the number of poor operators declined from 10 percent of the group to 5 percent. At the same time the number of errors per 100 dropped from 4 percent to 1.53 percent and for two months toward the end of the study this collective rate was below 1 percent.

A fourth positive change was reported in terms of absenteeism. Before the study, the test group had an average absenteeism rate of 10 days per person per year. The control group's average was 8.5 days annually. At the end of the program, absenteeism in the achieving group declined to just over 7 days, while the control group's absenteeism rate rose to just over 11 days. These figures represent an improvement of 24 percent for the achieving group and a decline of 29 percent for the control group.

While absenteeism declined.

This study is particularly valuable in understanding the impact of job enrichment in dealing with sociotechnical problems because the redesign focused heavily on such job dimensions as feedback, autonomy, task identity, and task significance. By changing the job dimensions, the firm was able to achieve increased productivity.

Quality circles

In the past five years individuals and organizations interested in job enrichment have begun expanding their focus beyond job dimensions and into such areas as *quality circles*. Today the quality circle concept is extremely popular in American industry. Some of the best-known firms currently employing the concept include General Electric, Honeywell, and Lockheed. However, it is the Japanese that actually popularized quality circles.

The objective of a quality circle is to increase quality, improve productivity, and/or raise morale—all at a relatively low cost. While some circles have slightly different approaches, most work the same way. The circle consists of five to ten well-trained employees, whose work is related in some way, and a team leader or foreman. The circle's task is to study production or service problems that fall within their scope of work. In most cases the circle will undertake a project that can be handled within a three to six month time frame. During this time, the group will meet for an hour or two each week to study a problem that the members have identified. Typical examples include production bottlenecks, quality control problems, improperly designed parts, and inadequate service procedures. Circle members then suggest steps that should be undertaken to correct the problems. If these steps can be taken by the

The focus is on problem solving.

members of the circle, they implement their own suggestions. If the problem is more comprehensive in nature, the members often confine their actions to recommendations. In any event, a solution is eventually identified and implemented. Commenting on their use in Japan, Ouchi, who has gained an international reputation for his study of Japanese management, has noted that:

> **The underlying messages are many . . . . Perhaps the first message . . . is that a firm can realize the full potential of its employees only if it both invests in their training and then shares with them the power to influence decisions. Without training, the invitation to participate in decision making will lead only to frustration and conflict. Without a sharing of decision-making power, an investment in training will be both frustrating and wasteful. That . . . firm that hopes to learn from the Japanese example need only do that which the Japanese have done. Just as they have studied the United States industrial system and have blended together the best aspects of both, so we must do the same.**[13]

A number of American firms are heeding Ouchi's advice. For example, Honeywell, the giant electronics and computer firm, currently has 150 quality circles throughout its North American operations. In most cases, the circles are made up of a half-dozen assembly workers and a team leader who meet every two weeks to examine productivity problems. In the process, the members also find that the increase in autonomy is beneficial to the quality of work life, and tardiness and average absenteeism has gone down while efficiency has risen.[14]

Lockheed, another high technology firm, has also had positive results with quality circles. In the first two years, with only 15 circles in operation, the firm reported saving over $2.8 million. In one operation alone the company reduced rejects from 25 to 30 per 1,000 hours to less than 6 per 1,000 hours. Furthermore, of those employees who participated in the study, 97 percent indicated a strong preference to continue with the program.[15]

Of course, the quality circle concept is not a panacea for organizations facing sociotechnical problems. However, if used properly, it can be extremely useful in helping to meet this challenge. Some of the most important human relations ideas which must be kept in mind include the following:

1. Quality control circles are a method of employee development as well as a means for improving organizational output and efficiency. If the development side is ignored, the efficiency side will suffer.

---

[13] William G. Ouchi, *Theory Z: How American Business Can Meet the Japanese Challenge* (Reading, Mass.: Addison-Wesley Publishing Company, 1981), p. 268.

[14] Mike Michaelson, "The Decline of American Productivity," *Success Unlimited*, October 1980, p. 28.

[15] Ed Yager, "Examining the Quality Control Circle," *Personnel Journal*, October 1979, p. 684.

2. Membership in a quality circle should be voluntary. No one ought to be forced to join a quality circle; this can negatively affect the person's contribution to the group.

3. Participants should all be fully trained. This training should be not only technical but also provide the individuals with insights regarding conference techniques and/or group dynamics so they will know how to work more effectively in groups.

4. Quality circles are group efforts not individual efforts. Showing off and competition must be minimized and cooperation and interdependent behavior must be encouraged.

5. The quality circle's project should be related to the members' actual job responsibilities. In this way the members are working to improve the quality of their own jobs, something in which they ought to have a high interest.

Quality circle guidelines.

6. The quality circle program should help employees see the relationship between their work and the quality of the goods or service being generated by their efforts. This quality and improvement awareness development should be used to further commit the members to quality.

7. If there is a quality control department in the organization, the relationship between the department and the quality control circle should be clarified before the circle begins its job. This will prevent intergroup fights and squabbling. The best way usually is for the circle to complement the quality control department.

8. If the organization is just starting the quality control concept, a pilot study is in order. Then, if the circle produces results and wins acceptance of the managers and employees alike, use can be expanded.

9. Management should use the suggestions set forth by the quality control circle. If none of the recommendations are adopted, the circle will lose effectiveness, and both membership and morale in the circle will drop off.

10. Management must be willing to grant recognition for all ideas that are set forth by the circle. If this is not done, the program is likely to backfire.[16]

Theory Z: beyond job enrichment

No discussion of job enrichment would be complete without some consideration of Japanese management practices. Today it seems that many American firms are looking at the way the Japanese manage and asking

---

[16] The ideas in this section can be found in: *ibid.*, pp. 684, 708; and DuBrin, *Contemporary Applied Management*, pp. 120–122.

the question: what can we learn from them? One of the most detailed responses to this question has been provided by Ouchi in his best selling book, *Theory Z: How American Business Can Meet the Japanese Challenge*. Ouchi presents and describes the seven dimensions that characterize Japanese management. These dimensions have helped Japanese firms become more competitive in the world market and, in many instances, successfully compete against American companies. Before examining these dimensions, it should be noted that while they have helped Japanese companies deal with the challenges confronting them, there is no proof that these same approaches would work in America. On the other hand, Japanese management experts like Ouchi do believe that a modified Japanese approach can work well in the United States. These seven dimensions are discussed below along with a consideration of the American model of Theory Z.[17]

Lifetime employment   In large Japanese firms individuals are virtually guaranteed a lifetime of employment. This policy relieves managers of the pressure to obtain an immediate return from the individual and permits long-term training and development programs. The employees also adopt a long-term view of career development and are more willing to operate within the bounds of organizational norms.

Consensual decision making   Unlike in the United States, in Japan a decision is not implemented until all affected parties have considered the problem, offered their views, and indicated their support for the final decision. This process is slow in arriving at a decision, but implementation is rapid and effective due to the prior agreement of those involved.

Collective responsibility   Since responsibility for the success or failure of a project is borne collectively by all who are involved, the process eliminates the ability to judge performance and confer awards on the basis of individual contribution. It also leads to performance through peer pressure and creates a high degree of cohesiveness within the group.

The Japanese model has seven major dimensions.

Slow evaluation and promotion   Japanese firms follow a practice of slow evaluation and promotion. The evaluation frequently involves a number of supervisors who are familiar with all aspects of the individual's performance. This process prevents a rapid rise to the top by the bright young star, but it also reduces errors in selecting those who enter the ranks of top management.

[17] Ouchi, *Theory Z: How American Business Can Meet the Japanese Challenge*.

Informal control   Control of activities within Japanese firms is very informal and unstructured. The basic assumption in the firm is that when an individual fully understands the philosophy of the organization, he or she will make the appropriate decision without the need for formal guidelines and controls. While this approach is not set down in writing, the theory is communicated through a common culture shared by key managers and, to some extent, all other employees.

Nonspecialized career paths   The Japanese train their employees in all aspects of the business. This policy improves communication between departments, leads to loyalty to the company rather than the profession, and decreases the likelihood that someone will quit and move to another firm. Since the person is trained for one company specifically, much of the individual's knowledge is of limited value to anyone else.

Wholistic concern   Japanese organizations pay close attention to their people, both off and on the job. This approach is cultural to Japan. Many years ago when industrialization began to flourish, parents were reluctant to allow their children to come to the large cities to work in factories and industrial establishments unless they could be sure that the children would be taken care of. As a result, the owners built dormitories, provided healthy food, and ensured that the children would receive the moral, intellectual, physical, and domestic training that would prepare them for life. Today Japanese firms use this wholistic concern to create a work environment that nurtures high morale and team spirit among employees.

The American model   Can American firms follow the Japanese example in meeting sociotechnical challenges? Ouchi believes it is possible via a modified American approach, which he calls Theory Z, that combines some features of Japanese firms with some from American firms. In particular he recommends consideration of lifetime employment, consensual decision making, slower evaluation and promotion, informal control, a moderately specialized career path, and wholistic concern. This modified approach incorporates five of the features of Japanese management along with one half-way step (career paths). Can it be done? Can American businesses emulate the Japanese model and be successful? Some firms are looking into the value of using Theory Z including General Motors, Ford, Chrysler, Hewlett-Packard, General Electric, Westinghouse, IBM, Texas Instruments, Honeywell, Lockheed, Fairchild Camera and Instrument, and Brunswick, to name a dozen. The great challenge will be getting people to go along with the changes. On the positive side, however, if it will take a change toward Theory Z management to survive, businesses are likely to make the transition. In any event, American business in the 1980s can certainly profit from studying Japanese management practices, if not outrightly adopting them.

Theory Z is a modified approach for American firms.

Current challenges in job design

Job design is a very important issue in human relations. After all, design-ing work so that the employees achieve a sense of task identity and task significance and are provided with skill variety, autonomy, and feedback stimulates motivation. Much of what we have discussed in this chapter has been directed toward this end. However, there are some current job design challenges of which the modern manager should be aware.

First, we need to learn more about the theory and practice of job design. It is not a preassembled innovation that can be simply plugged into an organization and forgotten. Considerable skill and sophistication is needed to design, install, and maintain such programs successfully.

Second, better ways have to be found to diffuse job redesign throughout the organization. For example, Walton studied eight organi-zations in which successful job design projects had been conducted.[18] In only one of them did he find that significant diffusion took place. Quite obviously, strategies for facilitating job design innovations throughout the organization must be devised.

However, there are still job enrichment problems to be solved.

Third, more attention has to be given to improving the jobs of lower-level managers. These jobs are often poorly designed with limited autonomy and feedback. Additionally, lower-level managers tend to be caught in the middle. They are too high in the hierarchy to associate with the rank and file and too far down to be accepted by the other managers. They also have problems when their subordinates' jobs are redesigned and theirs are not. More decision making and special tasks traditionally reserved for management are given to the workers, and the job of the manager becomes less meaningful. If work redesign is to be diffused throughout the organization, the jobs of those lower-level managers must be improved.

Fourth, the role of labor unions in initiating and executing job re-design programs has to be expanded and elaborated. The position of many organized labor representatives is one of suspicion. They do not understand the value of job redesign and are concerned that manage-ment will use it to increase work output or exploit the employees in some other way. In Europe, union–management cooperation is common; in fact, unions often take the initiative in suggesting work redesign. At present in this country, little is known regarding how best to achieve union participation in such activities. Clearly, research in this area is needed.

In sum, the challenge facing unions, management and behavioral scientists in articulating and elaborating the role of unions in work re-design activities is a substantial one. But it is also a challenge that is worthy of considerable effort on the part of those who care about im-proving the quality of life in organizations. For without the active in-

[18] R. E. Walton, "The Diffusion of New Work Structures: Explaining Why Success Didn't Take," *Organizational Dynamics*, Winter 1975, pp. 3–22.

volvement of organized labor, it is doubtful that work redesign can ever evolve into a strategy for change that actively *develops*—not just utilizes—human resources in organizations.[19]

Summary

Many workers are bored with their work, feeling no challenge or desire to do a particularly good job. What can management do about this? There are various alternatives available, but the most practical is that of redesigning the work so that it has meaning for the employees. There are a number of ways of doing so: job rotation, job enlargement, and job enrichment. The last is the most commonly employed approach.

How does one go about enriching jobs? Some of the latest research reveals that five core job dimensions are extremely useful in this process: skill variety, task identity, task significance, autonomy, and feedback. Researchers have used these five core job dimensions to develop a motivating potential score with which to evaluate a job. The formula shows that in order to redesign jobs so that the employees are motivated, the work must have autonomy, feedback, and at least one of the other three core job dimensions. The common job enrichment principles that can be used in obtaining these dimensions include formation of natural work units, establishment of worker-client relationships, combining of tasks, vertical loading, and opening of feedback channels.

A number of successful applications of job enrichment are discussed in this chapter, including those at Volvo, Sherwin Williams, and a national insurance company. Attention was also focused on how Japanese firms meet the sociotechnical challenge. In the last part of the chapter, current challenges in job design were examined. Two of the most important include improving the jobs of lower-level managers and stimulating labor unions to initiate and support redesign programs.

Key terms in the chapter

job redesign
job rotation
job enlargement
job enrichment
core job dimensions
skill variety
task identity
task significance

autonomy
feedback
motivating potential score
job profile chart
vertical loading
quality circle
Theory Z

---

[19] Hackman and Suttle, *Improving Life at Work*, p. 162.

Review and study questions

1. What are the four alternatives available to management in dealing with the problem of boring jobs? Explain.

2. How is job redesign a unique way of improving organizational efficiency?

3. Explain how each of the following job redesign techniques works: job rotation, job enlargement, and job enrichment.

4. In your own words, what is meant by each of the following core job dimensions: skill variety, task identity, task significance, autonomy, and feedback?

5. How have researchers used the five core job dimensions described in this chapter to develop a motivating potential score formula? Be sure to incorporate a discussion of the formula in your answer.

6. How can a profile chart be constructed from the core job dimensions? Give an illustration.

7. Define each of the following job enrichment principles: formation of natural work units, establishment of worker-client relationships, combining of tasks, vertical loading, opening of feedback channels. How does each work?

8. Which of the core job dimensions does each of the job enrichment principles (discussed in the answer to the preceding question) help fulfill? Explain, using a figure or drawing to relate each principle to its respective core job dimension(s).

9. What are the six commonly accepted guidelines for job redesign programs? Explain each.

10. How has Volvo used job enrichment to redesign its assembly line at Kalmar, Sweden?

11. How has the Sherwin Williams company successfully employed autonomous work groups?

12. Have there been any successful applications of job redesign in insurance firms? Cite one and explain how it worked.

13. How do quality circles work? Of what value are they in helping meet the sociotechnical challenge?

14. What is Theory Z all about? Does it have any benefits for American business firms? Explain.

15. What are the current challenges in job redesign? Describe them.

Interpretation of how you view your work

This quiz is designed to measure the five dimensions discussed in the chapter. (Feedback has more questions associated with it because information on feedback from both the job itself and the personnel in the organization were obtained.) Here is how to get your score for each dimension: (a) take all six of your answers to Part I and enter them in the appropriate place on the answer sheet; (b) take your answers in Part II for each of these numbers: 1, 2, 3, 4, 11 and 12 and subtract each one from 8 before entering the result in the appropriate place below; and (c) take your answers in Part II for numbers 5, 6, 7, 8, 9 and 10, and enter them in the appropriate place. As you can see, the answers from Part II that have an asterisk were handled with reverse scoring; a low answer received a high score and vice versa.

Skill variety	Task identity	Task significance
I. 1. _____	I. 2. _____	I. 3. _____
II. 1.* _____	II. 6. _____	II. 4.* _____
9. _____	11.* _____	7. _____
	Feedback	Feedback
Autonomy	(from the job)	(from others)
I. 4. _____	I. 5. _____	I. 6. _____
II. 3.* _____	II. 8. _____	II. 2.* _____
5. _____	12.* _____	10. _____

The largest total you can have for any of the above job dimensions is 21 and the smallest is three. Divide all of your answers by three to determine your average score per job dimension. Average scores tend to be in the range of 4.5–6.0. If you score lower than 4.5, your job is low on this particular job dimension; if you score higher than 6, your job is high on this particular job dimension. If you do not like your current job, you can likely determine why if you examine work from the standpoint of these job dimensions. The reverse is also true; if you like your current job, you should be able to determine why from your totals.

A terrific new job

Nate Henderson is very pleased with his new job. He received his Ph.D. in marketing three months ago and has taken a position with a large Southern state university.

Prior to finishing the degree, Nate worked for a junior college, where he taught five courses a semester. A typical fall schedule called for two sections of Accounting I, two sections of Introduction to Business, and one section of Salesmanship. During the spring semester Nate usually taught two sections of Accounting I, two sections of Principles of Marketing, and one section of Introduction to Management. Usually, Nate arrived at the office by 8:30 A.M., and his first class started by 9 A.M. By 4 P.M. he was finished, and he would leave around 4:30 P.M. The college required Nate to be on campus from 9 A.M. to 4 P.M. every weekday, as well as to attend some Saturday meetings (usually one a month) related to administrative and scholastic matters. In addition, he had 40 advisees, whom he counseled on class scheduling and other school-related issues.

What a difference it is at the state university! Nate teaches only three classes now, a graduate course in marketing and two sections of Basic Marketing. Aside from the time when he is scheduled to teach, his work week is virtually his own. The first class begins at 10:30 A.M. on Monday, Wednesday, and Friday and the second at 11:30 A.M. on these days. Wednesday afternoon from 2 to 5 P.M. he conducts his graduate course.

Except for counseling 10 students who are directly assigned to him and attending monthly faculty and department meetings, Nate is free. This free time, his department chairperson has explained, is to be devoted to writing and research. The department expects Nate to write two referred articles in his first two years if he hopes to have his contract renewed for two more years. Two referred articles would represent quite an achievement for any faculty member, but Nate feels he can do it. In fact, had he realized how really enjoyable university teaching was, Nate would have hurried to finish his Ph.D. earlier, instead of procrastinating and spending three years at the junior college.

Questions

1. Compare and contrast Nate's junior college job with his current one according to job skills, task variety, task significance, autonomy, and feedback.
2. Why does Nate like his present teaching job better than his previous one?
3. If you were president of the junior college, how could you redesign faculty jobs so as to enrich them? Explain.

The new advertising manager

Mary Eddington had been the assistant advertising manager for a Midwestern retail chain for seven years before she finally decided to move on. She accepted an offer from a national toy manufacturing company to succeed the retiring head of advertising.

The toy company's sales had been increasing at an annual rate of 12 percent, but the president believed that with a new advertising campaign things would really get off the ground. "All we need," he told Mary, "is a more creative approach, one that will appeal to kids. After all, they're the ones for whom the parents buy the toy. Up to now we've lacked that something that makes our ads really effective. I'd like you to develop a whole new approach."

After giving the matter serious thought, Mary hit upon a plan. First, she contacted a number of private schools and offered them free toys for their nursery and kindergarten classes. The toys she chose were manufactured by both Mary's company and the competition. Then she and her advertising staff visited with the teachers and students to find out what the children liked about the toys, which ones they played with, and which ones they did not care for. Next, they ran an ad effectiveness program to determine what parents and children liked and remembered about their ads and those of the competition. Finally, Mary took her staff to the plant and let them watch the way the toys were made.

All this took four months, after which she assembled her staff in a conference room. "Since I've arrived," she told them, "we have been trying to identify and understand our customer as well as learn about how the toys are made. By this time you should know a great deal about what we're trying to do in this company and how we go about it. Now I want you to think about how we can change our advertising so that it really appeals to our market."

The result was an ad campaign that boosted sales over 35 percent. In addition, the company received an award for having one of the outstanding ads of the year.

When the president asked Mary how she did it, she replied that it was all a matter of getting the personnel involved. "I knew they had the talent," she said, "so it was just a matter of getting them enthusiastic about the job. By talking to the people who buy the toys as well as those who manufacture them, they started to realize how important their work is and how much others count on them. This motivated them to do an even better job."

Questions

1. Was Mary attempting to enlarge or enrich the jobs of her advertising staff? Explain.

2. What core job dimensions are now present in the advertising people's work?

3. Which job enrichment principles did Mary use in motivating the advertising personnel? Explain.

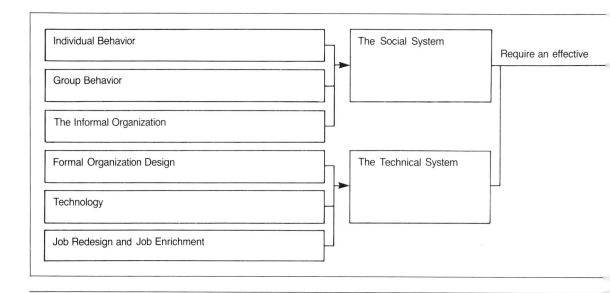

The administrative system

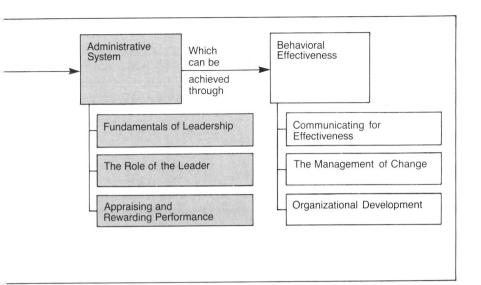

IV

The overall objective of Part IV is to study the *administrative* system of organizations. In Parts II and III we examined the social and technical systems of organizations, noting the role of both individuals and structure in the work place. This interaction of people and structure can have dysfunctional results, unless there is an effective administrative system to handle the situation. This system can be defined in one word—leadership. In this part of the book we study leadership: what it is, how it works, and the importance of systematically appraising and rewarding job performance.

In Chapter 9 we start by studying the fundamentals of leadership. We define the term *leadership*, present some of the leadership characteristics found in effective managers, and describe some of the personal qualities that appear to be related to managerial effectiveness, including superior intelligence, emotional maturity, motivation drive, problem-solving skills, managerial skills, and leadership skills. Then we introduce and explain what is meant by Theory X and Theory Y and discuss the importance of the immaturity–maturity theory to the study of leadership. Next, we examine the two major dimensions of leadership, concern for people and concern for work, and explain one of the most popular contingency models of leadership, giving primary emphasis to the type of leader who is most effective in each situation. Finally, we consider the value of another theory of management, the path-goal theory, in the study of human relations.

Having examined the fundamentals of leadership, we then turn to the leader's role in the organization. What do effective leaders do? In Chapter 10 we discuss the leader's "linking pin" function, explain what is meant by the term *teamwork*, and identify the three key factors necessary to develop teamwork. Then we turn our attention to

251

the leader's role as a counselor and review the kinds of counseling often given by managers. Next we define the term *power*, explain the various types of leader power, and note which are used most widely by effective managers and which are not. In the final part of the chapter we explain the importance of time management to the effective leader and identify important steps for managing time well. Finally, we discuss how the manager should deal with stress.

Then, in Chapter 11, we study how a leader appraises and rewards performance. We begin by discussing the performance appraisal cycle and explaining some of the currently popular evaluation methods, including graphic rating scales, the paired comparison method, assessment centers, behaviorally anchored rating scales, and management by objectives. Then we describe the major problems associated with performance appraisal. Next we outline the most common intrinsic and extrinsic rewards, discuss the role of equity in performance appraisal, and examine the link between performance and rewards. Finally, we identify the discipline used when performance is inadequate and explain how the "red-hot stove rule" can be used in effectively employing discipline.

When you have finished reading this part of the book you should have a solid understanding of the administrative system in modern organizations. In particular, you should know the definition of leadership, the role the leader must attempt to play in the organization, and the various ways in which performance can be measured, rewards can be given, and discipline can be carried out.

Fundamentals
of leadership

9

Goals of the chapter

The goals of this chapter are to examine the nature of leadership, to study leadership behavior, and to investigate two of the most famous contingency leadership models. In the first part of the chapter we review some of the leadership and personal characteristics effective leaders often possess and examine the assumptions that many leaders hold regarding the nature of organizational personnel. Then we look at various styles of leadership: authoritarian, paternalistic, participative, and laissez-faire. Finally, we examine contingency leadership with particular attention to Fiedler's contingency model and the path-goal theory of leadership.

When you have finished reading this chapter you should be able to:

1. define *leadership*

2. list leadership characteristics found in effective managers

3. describe some personal characteristics that appear to be related to managerial effectiveness, including superior intelligence, emotional maturity, motivation drive, problem-solving skills, managerial skills, and leadership skills

4. compare and contrast Theory X and Theory Y

5. discuss the importance of the immaturity–maturity theory to the study of leadership

6. describe the two major dimensions of leadership, concern for people and concern for work

7. explain Fiedler's contingency model, giving primary emphasis to the type of leader most effective in each situation

8. discuss the value of the path-goal theory of leadership to the study of human relations.

253

The nature of leadership

*Leadership
involves
influencing people.*

Leadership is the process of influencing people to direct their efforts toward the achievement of some particular goal(s). Some managers are highly effective, but most are, at best, only moderately successful. What accounts for this difference? Some people believe the answer rests in **leadership characteristics**, such as drive, originality, and tolerance of stress, which, they say, are universal among successful leaders. If you have these qualities, you will do well in leading others; if you lack them, you will be ineffective in the leadership role.

Others argue in favor of **personal characteristics**, such as superior mental ability, emotional maturity, and problem-solving skills. They claim there is no universal list of leadership characteristics, so we must turn to personal characteristics that interact with one another to produce the desired outcomes. Only through an awareness of how these characteristics influence managerial effectiveness can we truly understand the nature of leadership. To begin our study of this subject, we examine both approaches, leadership characteristics and personal characteristics, and then address the importance of managerial assumptions regarding the nature of organizational personnel.

Leadership characteristics

Recent leadership studies have pointed out the importance of environmental influences on leadership effectiveness. However, published research indicates that, regardless of the situation, certain characteristics favor success in the leadership role.

From 1920 to 1950 the study of leadership characteristics, known as **trait theory**, sought to isolate those factors that contribute to leader effectiveness. This approach assumed that attributes such as initiative, social dominance, and persistence were the primary factors in leadership success and failure. Unfortunately, the research studies conducted during this period failed to produce a universal list of traits. Additionally, in most cases, no consideration was given to the possibility that different situations might require different characteristics, or that a specific situation might demand so little of the leader or might be so unfavorable that leadership characteristics would be of little, if any, value. Despite the arguments for situational leadership, however, Ralph Stogdill, one of the leading authorities in the field, concluded that a selected group of characteristics do, in fact, differentiate leaders from followers, effective from ineffective leaders, and high-echelon from low-echelon leaders.

> **The leader is characterized by a strong drive for responsibility and task completion, vigor and persistence in pursuit of goals, venturesomeness and originality in problem-solving, drive to exercise initiative in social situations, self-confidence and a sense of personal identity, willingness to accept consequences of decision and action, readiness to absorb interpersonal stress, willingness to tolerate frustration and delay,**

ability to influence other persons' behavior, and capacity to structure social interaction systems to the purpose at hand.[1]

The greatest problem with trait theory, however, is that no common list has been forthcoming. Some traits appear important, but their value is situationally determined. A leader with a capacity to structure social interaction systems may do well when directing subordinates with a high need for social interaction but poorly if the subordinates or the situation does not allow for such interaction. For example, assembly-line work is not designed for manager-subordinate interaction, so the ability to initiate or structure such relationships is of little value to the foreman. As a result, leadership effectiveness appears to be situational in nature. This finding has led many researchers to turn their attention to personal characteristics of effective leaders.

With trait theory, no common list of leadership characteristics has been discovered.

Personal characteristics

Many personal characteristics appear to be related to managerial effectiveness, but an exhaustive list is beyond our current needs. We will examine six major personal characteristics that significantly contribute to leadership effectiveness. They are: superior intelligence, emotional maturity, motivation drive, problem-solving skills, managerial skills, and leadership skills.

Superior intelligence   Research reveals that effective managers tend to have superior intelligence.[2] By this we mean that there is a minimum level of mental ability below which we are unlikely to find successful leaders. Conversely, there may well be a ceiling above which we are again unlikely to find effective leaders. Williams, for example, reports that psychological assessments he conducted over a 15-year period suggest that:

IQs from about 120 to 135 are the ideal range for managerial success. This ranges from the 91st to the 99th centiles of the general population on the best adult intelligence test. . . . Individuals with IQs from 115–119 are acceptable in some managerial positions but seldom in top companies with strong competition for promotion. Managers with IQs below 115 are at a distinct disadvantage when competing with other managers, except at the first-line supervisory level. Those with unusually high IQs (say, over 135) sometimes become undesirably theoretical and/or become bored with the routine that exists in many line positions.[3]

There seems to be an ideal IQ range.

[1] Ralph Stogdill, *Handbook of Leadership* (New York: The Free Press, 1974), p. 81.

[2] Glen Grimsley and Hilton Jarrett, "The Relation of Managerial Achievement to Test Measures Obtained in the Employment Situation: Methodology and Results," *Personnel Psychology*, Spring 1973, pp. 31–48.

[3] J. Clifton Williams, *Human Behavior in Organizations*, 2nd ed. (Cincinnati: South-Western Publishing Co., 1982), pp. 413–414.

Keep in mind, however, that intelligence is a relative matter. Some geniuses are excellent leaders, while some people with IQs (intelligence quotients) in the 120–135 range lack the personality to manage effectively. Additionally, one can have a superior intellect and be in the wrong job. For example, a person with high verbal skills and abstract reasoning ability and low quantitative ability might do poorly in an accounting firm or a bank, and an individual with low verbal skills and high quantitative abilities might be a total failure as a personnel manager. Yet both have high IQs and their mental abilities are comparable.

Leaders are self-confident and calm.

Emotional maturity   Successful leaders are *emotionally mature*. They are self-confident and capable of directing their subordinates in a calm, conscientious manner. If a subordinate makes a mistake, the effective leader tries to use the experience as an opportunity to teach and counsel the person so as to prevent recurrence of the problem. The leader realizes that little is to be gained from bawling out the subordinate (except maybe to embarrass the latter in front of his or her peers), especially if the person really wanted to do the job right.

Effective leaders also have a sense of purpose and meaning in life. They know who they are, where they are going, and how they are going to get there. They are practical and decisive and have confidence in their own abilities. Additionally, the goals they set for themselves are often challenging as well as realistic.

Finally, because they are emotionally mature, successful leaders are neither ulcer-prone nor workaholics. They know how to deal with stress, to delegate work that is either minor in importance or is best handled by someone more technically skilled, and to handle the challenges of the job without resorting to alcohol or drugs. Because they know and understand themselves, they are able to cope with the demands of both their business and personal lives. For example, the divorce rate among successful leaders is no greater than that in the general population.

They have high drive.

Motivation drive   Effective leaders have high *motivation drive*. In particular, they seem most motivated by the opportunity to achieve the chance for power or control over a situation and by the need to self-actualize.[4] Additionally, as we noted in our discussion of money in Chapter 2, they are motivated by increased personal income, because it is a sign of how well they are doing. Effective leaders often measure their progress in quantitative terms: how much money they are making; how many promotions they have had; how many subordinates they control. If we were to compare highly successful, moderately successful, and unsuc-

[4] See, for example: David C. McClelland and David H. Burnham, "Power is the Great Motivator," *Harvard Business Review*, March–April 1976, pp. 100–110.

Figure 9.1
Leadership success and need drive

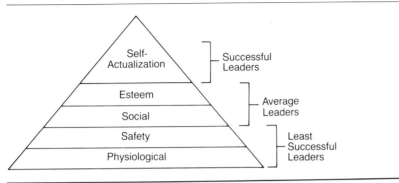

"Heard a rumor that you've lowered your standards."

Drawing by Charles E. Vadum, *Changing Times*, December 1981.

cessful leaders in terms of need motivation we could assign each to specific levels of Maslow's need hierarchy, as in Figure 9.1.

Additionally, we know from research that successful leaders tend to have subordinates who are also interested in fulfillment of self-actualization and esteem needs. Average leaders have followers who are most concerned with esteem and social needs. The least successful leaders have subordinates who are most interested in safety and physiological needs. In short, successful leaders tend to attract a particular type of subordinate, as do the average and least successful leaders, and these subordinates have need drives similar to those of their superiors.[5] In large measure, highly motivated leaders attract or develop highly motivated subordinates.

Problem-solving skills Effective leaders also possess *problem-solving skills*. They see a problem as both a challenge and an opportunity to prove their managerial abilities. As such, these skills are closely related to high motivation drives, for without such motivation leaders might be unwilling to assume the risk that comes with problem-solving. These individuals also have a great deal of self-confidence. Conversely, average leaders and, especially, ineffective leaders tend to shun problem-solving because they either are unprepared to deal with the issues or have learned through experience that they are not up to the task.

They are problem-solvers.

Managerial skills Effective leaders, especially at the upper levels of the hierarchy, have *managerial skills*. These skills are of three types, technical, human, and administrative:

Technical skills: The knowledge of how things work. This is very important for lower-level managers such as foremen.

Human skills: The knowledge of how to deal with people. This is very important for middle-level managers who must lead other managers. Without a solid understanding of such behavioral areas as interpersonal communication, motivation, counseling, and directing, middle-level managers would be ineffective in leading their subordinates.

They possess administrative skills.

Administrative skills: The knowledge of how all parts of the organization or department fit together. This skill covers many activities, from formulating organizational objectives, policies, and procedures, to developing techniques for handling office work flow, to coordinating a host of seemingly unrelated functions that enable the enterprise to operate as an integrated unit.

As shown in Figure 9.2, the leader's place in the hierarchy determines the degree of managerial skill he or she must have. As managers prove their effectiveness and begin moving up the ranks, they need to learn more about human and, in particular, administrative skills. Some will develop great administrative proficiency and continue their upward climb; others will find they are unable to develop the requisite degree of administrative skill and will remain where they are. In the final analysis, administrative skill makes the difference between leaders who will head the organization and leaders who must be content to manage at the intermediate and lower levels.

---

[5]Jay Hall, "To Achieve or Not: The Manager's Choice," *California Management Review,* Summer 1976, pp. 5–18.

Figure 9.2
Skills needed at different hierarchical levels

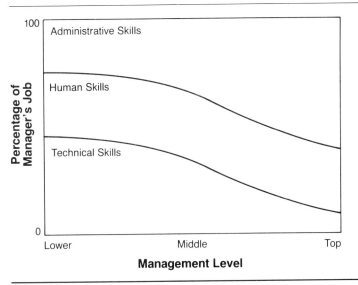

Leadership skills   Although what leadership style is effective depends on the situation, some personal characteristics seem to contribute to the *leadership skills* of managers. Some are task-related, while others are more social in nature. The task-related characteristics of effective leaders, as isolated by Stogdill, include initiative, need to excel or achieve, task orientation, drive for responsibility, and responsibility in pursuit of objectives. Some of the social characteristics of effective leaders are administrative ability, interpersonal skills, tact and diplomacy, ability to enlist cooperation, popularity, social participation, cooperativeness, and attractiveness.[6]

They tend to have certain leadership skills.

The nature of organizational personnel

Leadership characteristics and personal characteristics provide insights regarding who leaders are. However, it is also important to understand why leaders act as they do. Part of this explanation can be found in the opinions leaders have about their people. Are the subordinates content with satisfying lower-level needs or do they strive also for esteem and

---

[6]Stogdill, *Handbook of Leadership*, pp. 80–81.

self-actualization fulfillment? How important is money to them? As managers begin to answer these questions, they express their assumptions about the nature of the organization's personnel. One of the finest summaries of such managerial assumptions has been provided by Douglas McGregor. He called these assumptions Theory X and Theory Y.[7]

Theory X   Theory X assumptions hold that people are basically lazy and that in order to get them to work, it is often necessary to use coercion and threats of punishment. McGregor summarized the assumptions this way:

Theory X assumptions.

1. **People, by their very nature, dislike work and will avoid it when possible.**
2. **They have little ambition, tend to shun responsibility, and like to be directed.**
3. **Above all else, they want security.**
4. **In order to get them to attain organizational objectives it is necessary to use coercion, control, and threats of punishment.[8]**

From this summary of their attitudes, we can arrive at two conclusions regarding Theory X managers. First, they like to control their subordinates because they feel such control is in the best interests of both the organization and its personnel. Second, they believe that people work to satisfy their lower-level needs (security above all else) and that upper-level need satisfaction is not very important. Additionally, since lower-level needs are satisfied with physical rewards, such as money, job security, and good working conditions, Theory X managers will withhold these rewards if the workers do not comply with organizational directives.

Quite obviously this management thinking does not provide for those workers who dislike close control or who desire satisfaction of upper-level needs. All management can offer the workers is more physiological and safety rewards. If the workers balk at this, management will resort to punishment, a reaction that accords with the fourth Theory X tenet listed above.

The use of punishment seems to be a logical method of solving the issue; either the workers do the job or management will get tough. However, the problem rests on the fact that management mistakes causes for effects, the result being a self-fulfilling prophecy. Believing punishment is a necessary tool for effective management, the company introduces it the minute the workers start offering resistance, with mental notes, "See, it's like we said. You have to get tough with these people if you want any performance." Yet it is management's fault that the workers are discontent in the first place.[9]

---

[7] Douglas McGregor, *The Human Side of Enterprise* (New York: McGraw-Hill Book Company, 1960).

[8] *Ibid.*, pp. 33–34.

[9] Richard M. Hodgetts, *Management: Theory, Process and Practice*, 3rd ed. (Hinsdale, Ill.: Dryden Press, 1982), p. 321.

Why, then, do many managers have trouble motivating their subordinates? The answer rests in the erroneous assumptions they have about the nature of the organizational personnel. Believing that they need to treat their people like children, providing low-level need satisfaction rewards if the work is done well, and withholding these benefits if the work is done poorly, the managers use a "carrot-and-stick" theory of motivation. This approach may be useful in getting a donkey to pull a cart, but it is seldom effective in motivating people. A more realistic set of assumptions are those described in Theory Y.

Theory Y   Modern behavioral research has provided the basis for formulating assumptions for a new theory of management, which McGregor called Theory Y. Its assumptions are:

1. **The expenditure of physical and mental effort in work is as natural to people as is resting or playing.**
2. **External control and the threats of punishment are not the only ways of getting people to work toward organizational objectives. If people are committed to objectives, they will exercise self-direction and self-control.**
3. **Commitment to objectives is determined by the rewards associated with their achievement.**
4. **Under proper conditions, the average human being learns not only to accept but to seek responsibility.**
5. **The capacity to exercise a relatively high degree of imagination, ingenuity and creativity in the solution of organizational problems is widely distributed throughout the population.**
6. **Under conditions of modern industrial life, the intellectual potentialities of the average human being are only partially utilized.**[10]

Theory Y assumptions

As you can see, Theory Y presents a much more dynamic view of the organizational personnel. They are now seen as interested in both lower-level and upper-level need satisfaction and as having untapped potential. This theory urges management to reevaluate its thinking and to begin focusing attention on ways of enabling the personnel to attain their upper-level needs. Motivation is viewed as a problem that must be solved by management. No longer can the leader hide behind Theory X assumptions, claiming that workers are by nature lazy and unmotivated.

Before continuing, however, we should answer one very important question: is a Theory Y manager always superior to a Theory X manager? Although we have presented Theory Y as a modern, superior view of the workers, it is not without its critics. Some of them point out that Theory Y can be dangerous in that it allows too much freedom to the workers, many of whom not only need but want close direction and control. Additionally, Theory Y assumes that people want to satisfy their needs while on the job. However, many satisfy their needs off the job, as in the case of

---

[10]McGregor, *The Human Side of Enterprise*, pp. 47–48.

workers who want a shorter work week so they will have more leisure time.

Therefore, to put these two theories in perspective, we must acknowledge that some people respond better to Theory X management than to Theory Y management. However, many managers tend to underrate the workers, subscribing much more heavily to Theory X than to Theory Y. Chris Argyris has made this very clear with his immaturity–maturity theory.

Immaturity–maturity theory   While at Yale University, Argyris made an examination of industrial organizations for the purpose of determining the effect that management practices had on individual behavior. According to his theory, seven changes take place in an individual's personality as he or she matures. First, the individual moves from a passive state as an infant to an active state as an adult. Second, as an infant, the individual depends heavily on others for assistance, but as he or she matures there is an increasing degree of independence. Third, an infant is capable of behaving in only a few ways, but with maturity this capability increases dramatically. Fourth, an infant has casual, shallow interests, but as the individual grows older, he or she becomes capable of developing deeper, stronger interests. Fifth, an infant's time perspective is very short and encompasses only the present; as the child matures, however, this perspective increases to include both the past and the future. Sixth, an infant is subordinate to everyone, but with maturity the individual achieves an equal or superior position. Seventh, a child lacks an awareness of "self," but the mature individual is aware of and is able to control the "self" (Table 9.1).

The individual's personality changes as he or she matures.

Argyris contends that the healthy personality is one that develops along the continuum from immaturity to maturity. However, many organizations are not geared for mature people. Organizational rules, policies, and procedures are all designed to keep the personnel passive, dependent, and subordinate. They are supposed to respond to management's needs, follow orders, and accomplish organizational objectives. In so doing, they become an extension of the organization's physical assets and are often treated more like things of production than like people. This has led Argyris to report:

> **An analysis of the basic properties of relatively mature human beings and formal organization leads to the conclusion that there is an inherent incongruency between the self-actualization of the two. This basic incongruency creates a situation of conflict, frustration, and failure for the participants.**[11]

---

[11] Chris Argyris, *Personality and Organization: The Conflict between the System and the Individual* (New York: Harper & Row Publishers, Inc., 1957), p. 175.

Table 9.1
Immaturity–maturity development

Immaturity		Maturity
Passivity	→	Activity
Dependence	→	Independence
Capable of behaving in a few ways	→	Capable of behaving in many ways
Casual, shallow interests	→	Deep, strong interests
Current time perspective	→	Past, present, and future time perspective
Subordinate position	→	Equal or superior position
Lack of awareness of "self"	→	Awareness and control of "self"

The state that Argyris is referring to as *immature* is the same state that is promoted and nurtured by Theory X management, yet this style of management does not have to be tolerated. Organizations can encourage mature behavior from their people. Argyris, himself, has reported a case in which the president of a company asked him how to motivate the company workers more effectively. The two men visited a company production plant where 12 women were assembling a product similar to a radio. The group also had a foreman, an inspector, and a packer.

Professor Argyris suggested a one-year experiment in which each of the women would assemble the total product herself. The president agreed, and over the ensuing months, production under the new method was closely monitored. During the first month, production dropped 70 percent. The next three weeks saw a continual down slide as workers' morale declined. However, by the eighth week production began to rise. By the end of the fifteenth week output was at an all-time high, error and waste costs had decreased 94 percent, and complaints had dropped 96 percent. By employing a Theory Y-oriented leadership style, the management was able to improve overall performance. How, exactly, does one employ Theory X or Theory Y on the job? This question can be answered best with an examination of leadership behavior. Before doing so, however, examine your own basic beliefs about people by answering the short quiz on your assumptions about people.

Leadership behavior

Leadership behavior is the way leaders actually carry out their jobs. There are four styles of leadership behavior: authoritarian, paternalistic, participative, and laissez-faire. On a continuum, they range from high concern for work and people to general lack of concern for the work and the personnel. Depending on the situation, any one of these styles can be ideal.

Your assumptions about people

Read the following 10 pairs of statements. In each case, show the relative strength of your beliefs on assigning a weight from 0 to 10 to each statement. The points assigned to each pair *must* total ten points. If you totally agree with one statement and totally disagree with the other, give the first one a 10 and the second a zero. If you like both statements equally, give each 5 points. The interpretation of your answers is provided at the end of the chapter.

1. Most employees are fairly creative but often times do not have the chance to employ this ingenuity on the job. ___8___ (a)

   Most workers are not creative at all, but then again the job does not lend itself to creativity so nothing is lost. ___2___ (b)

2. If you give people enough money, this will greatly offset their desire for interesting, challenging, and/or meaningful work. ___3___ (c)

   If you give people interesting, challenging, and/or meaningful work, they are less likely to complain about money and fringe benefits. ___7___ (d)

3. Workers who are allowed to set their own goals and standards of performance tend to set them higher than management would. ___6___ (e)

   Workers who are allowed to set their own goals and standards of performance tend to set them lower than management would. ___4___ (f)

4. People want freedom to do work the way they believe is right. ___9___ (g)

   People want to be told what to do; freedom actually makes them nervous. ___1___ (h)

5. The better an individual knows his or her job, the more likely it is that the person will work only hard enough to produce the minimum amount acceptable to management. ___2___ (i)

   The better an individual knows his or her job, the more likely it is that the person will find satisfaction in the work and try to produce at least as much as the average worker in the organization. ___8___ (j)

6. Most workers in a modern organization are not up to the intellectual challenge presented by their jobs. ___3___ (k)

Most workers in a modern organization have more than sufficient intellectual potential to do their jobs. ___7___ (l)

7. Most people dislike work, and if given the chance, they will goof off. ___1___ (m)

Most people like work, especially if it is interesting and challenging. ___7___ (n)

8. Most employees work best under loose control. ___9___ (o)

Most employees work best under close control. ___1___ (p)

9. Above all else, workers want job security. ___1___ (q)

While workers want job security, it is only one of many things they want, and it does not rank first on all lists. ___9___ (r)

10. It increases a supervisor's prestige when he or she admits that a subordinate was right and he or she was wrong. ___10___ (s)

A manager is entitled to more respect than a subordinate, and it weakens the former's prestige to admit that a subordinate was right and he or she was wrong. ___0___ (t)

Authoritarian leadership

Authoritarian leaders tend to be heavily work-centered, with much emphasis given to task accomplishment and little to the human element. Such leaders fit the classical model of management in which the workers are viewed as factors of production.

These individuals can be very useful in certain situations. For example, when a crisis occurs and the organization needs a "get-tough" leader, the authoritarian manager is often ideal. Attention should be focused on objectives, efficiency, profit, and other task-related activities, and this is just to the manager's liking.

Unfortunately, there are not that many instances where an authoritarian manager is superior to all others, although there are a fairly large number of such managers in industry today. These people have authoritarian personalities, often developed because their parents were also authoritarian. They were taught early in life to be submissive toward superior authority and, in turn, have used this parental model to dominate those who hold positions subordinate to theirs. As a result they tend to be "yes men" when talking to their bosses and to demand the same type of behavior from their own personnel.

Authoritarian leaders are work-centered.

Paternalistic leadership

Paternalistic leaders are heavily work-centered but, unlike authoritarian leaders, have some consideration for the personnel. They tend to look after their people the way a father does his family. Their basic philosophy, far out of step with the needs of most employees, is "work hard and I'll take care of you." This style of management was prevalent in the late nineteenth century, when some businesses went so far as to provide the workers with lodging, medical services, a company store, and even churches for religious worship. The Pullman Corporation, famous for the Pullman railroad sleeping car, was such a company, and like other firms that built company towns, it eventually found the workers fighting its paternalism. We know from human relations studies that people do not want to be treated like children or to feel they are owned by the company.

When practiced by leaders, paternalistic management is similar to what, in Chapter 1, we called System 2: the leader expects the subordinates to do as they are told, accomplish assigned objectives, and rely on him or her to see that equitable rewards are forthcoming. The paternalistic leader is similar to the authoritarian in a demand for blind obedience and an intolerance of questions such as, "Why am I being assigned this job? How will this work help my career? What can I expect from the company over the next five years?" Such questions are seen as indicating a lack of confidence in the leader, something the paternalistic manager will not tolerate.

Many managers in this country are paternalistic leaders, who believe their subordinates want someone to look after them and provide job security, cost-of-living raises, insurance programs, retirement plans, and other extrinsic rewards. Actually, these leaders are confusing management with manipulation. In terms of Theory X and Y, they are *soft Theory X managers.* They do not believe people are totally lazy or security-oriented, but they do feel workers have a tendency toward acting this way. By playing the role of the parent, these leaders believe they can get the most productivity out of their people. Unfortunately for them, most workers resent this type of leadership, although there are some who like it. Employees who have been smothered with affection and security by their parents often welcome a boss who acts the same way. They now have a surrogate parent who takes care of them when they are on the job. However, these people are exceptions to the rule; most workers dislike paternalism.

Participative leadership

Participative leaders have a high concern for both people and work. They are best represented by System 3 and System 4 management, which we described in Chapter 1. These leaders encourage their subordinates to play an active role in operating the enterprise, but they reserve the right to make the final decision on important matters. In short, they delegate authority but do not abdicate in favor of subordinate rule. Some management experts have contended that no manager can perform effectively over an extended period of time without some degree of employee participation. This is certainly true of U.S. managers, for it is an accepted norm in this country that workers have a voice in what goes on.

One way in which this is commonly done is through delegating authority to the lowest possible organizational level. A second way is through encouraging feedback from the subordinates. While an authoritarian manager is busy telling the personnel what to do, the participative leader is getting information on what is going well and what is going poorly. From this feedback, the manager is able to decide what should be done next. No leader can be truly effective without the support of the subordinates, and feedback is a key indication of such support. Finally, participative leaders discuss objectives with their people and then give them the opportunity to attain these objectives. This is in contrast to authoritarian leaders who keep objectives to themselves, distrust their subordinates, delegate very little, and try to do too many things themselves. The participative manager builds esprit de corps by sharing objectives and providing the chance for subordinates to fulfill their esteem and self-actualization needs. The personnel, in turn, like this approach and work harder for the leader.

This pattern of leadership behavior has been well explained by Graen and his associates, who have popularized the *vertical dyad linkage theory*. A *vertical dyad* is the relationship between a leader and an individual subordinate. The basic premise of the theory is that leaders typically establish a special relationship with a small number of trusted subordinates, who make up the "in group." Among these individuals there is a great deal of mutual trust and support, and together they constitute an effective team. The greater the number of subordinates in this group, the greater the potential for increased teamwork and productivity. Moreover, when managers have effective systems of this nature, their subordinates are also likely to have such systems, since subordinates often copy the style used by their boss. When this happens, there develops a pattern of participative leadership behavior from the top of the organization to the bottom.[12]

Laissez-faire leadership

Laissez-faire is a French term meaning noninterference. As we move across the continuum from authoritarian to participative leadership, the subordinates begin playing an increasingly larger role. If a leader continues this transition, however, he or she will come very close to abdicat-

Laissez-faire means noninterference.

---

[12] For an excellent discussion of reciprocal influence processes in leadership, see Gary A. Yukl, *Leadership in Organizations* (Englewood Cliffs, New Jersey: Prentice-Hall, Inc., 1981), Chapter 2.

Figure 9.3
Leader–subordinate interactions

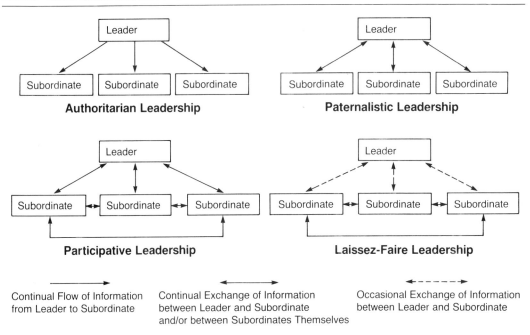

Continual Flow of Information from Leader to Subordinate

Continual Exchange of Information between Leader and Subordinate and/or between Subordinates Themselves

Occasional Exchange of Information between Leader and Subordinate

ing the leadership position. We can diagram the comparisons between leadership behaviors we have discussed, as in Figure 9.3. Note that the subordinates in the laissez-faire leadership diagram are interacting with one another to get the work done. The leader is only checking in on occasion to see how things are going.

Are there some subordinates for whom this style is effective? Yes, although they are not very common. University professors are an example. Very seldom does the department chairperson check up on the professor to see if the individual is having any problems, meeting classes on time, or conducting appropriate research activities. The chairperson usually meets with the professor prior to the beginning of the academic year to discuss objectives and assignments and relies on him or her to fulfill these obligations by the end of the school year. This approach works for highly skilled professionals in any area. The office manager of a research and development laboratory leaves the scientists alone to get their work done. Only occasionally does the manager check in to see that everything is running smoothly. In a business setting, some managers employ a laissez-faire style with their outstanding copywriters and design people, and a board of directors uses it with a president who has led the company into a new period of prosperity. In each case, the subordinates play a tre-

On average, participative leadership is most effective.

mendous role in running the show. Keep in mind, however, that although this style can work effectively with some people, it does not work well with most. On average, the participative style tends to be most effective.

Leadership dimensions

Each of the four leadership styles we have just examined contains some degrees of concern for work and for people. These two dimensions—concern for work and concern for people—have been found to be *independent* dimensions. This means, for example, that someone can be high in one of the dimensions without having to be low in the other. As a result, there are four basic leadership behaviors:

High concern for work, high concern for people.

High concern for work, low concern for people.

Low concern for work, high concern for people.

Low concern for work, low concern for people.

Four independent dimensions.

Figure 9.4 is a leadership grid incorporating these behaviors.

Keeping in mind that any one of these can be an effective leadership style, depending on the situation, let us examine some specific examples of each style and place them in the grid in Figure 9.5. First, let us take the foreman on an assembly line. The foreman is charged with seeing

Any leadership style can be effective.

Figure 9.4
A leadership grid

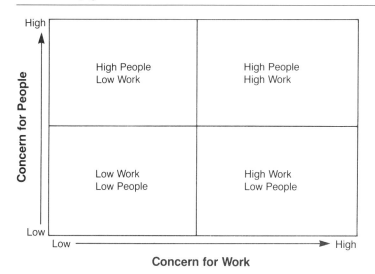

Figure 9.5
Contingency leadership styles applied to a leadership grid

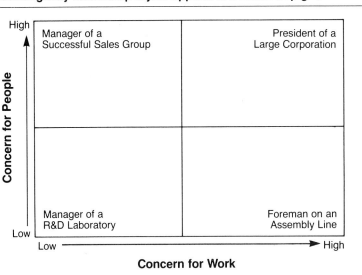

Concern for Work

that the workers keep up with the line. The most effective style for such a person is usually one that stresses high concern for work (for this is where the emphasis is needed) but low concern for people. (After all, what can a foreman do for them since the whole operation is automated?)

Conversely, the manager of a successful sales group has little need to be concerned with a work emphasis. The people are doing the job; sales are very high. The leader can therefore concentrate attention on praising the salespeople and encouraging them to keep up the good work. The individual needs a style with high concern for people and low concern for work.

The president of a large corporation, meanwhile, has to have high concerns for work and for people. The individual must be concerned with long-range planning, budgets, and programs and must be friendly, approachable, and willing to look out for the personal welfare of all the employees.

Finally, in the lower left corner of Figure 9.5 is the manager of a research and development lab. This individual has highly competent personnel, so there is no need to be concerned with production. These workers are self-motivated. Likewise, there is no need for the manager to praise them for a job well done, because they are skilled scientists who receive intrinsic satisfaction when they are praised by their peers. Such praise from their boss, however, means very little to them, since the manager of such a laboratory is usually not a scientist and so would be less able to value their work. As a result, the most effective style for the leader is low concerns for both people and work. The manager should be prepared to help them if called upon, but for the most part he or she should stay out of the way.

We should keep one thing in mind about this discussion. The examples we have used in Figure 9.5 are all presented to conform to one of the four leadership dimension combinations. However, we are not saying that every foreman on an assembly line should have high concern for work and low concern for people or that every president of a large company ought to have high concerns for both work and people. It all depends on the situation. In an effort to more fully understand leadership, many researchers have turned to an investigation of contingency leadership models. This represents the latest development of leadership theory, and every student of human relations should be familiar with it.

Contingency leadership models

Today we are in a *contingency* phase of leadership study. The human relations manager must adapt his or her style to meet the situation. Drawing upon our discussion of leadership and personal characteristics, we now address the question, "What specific style of leadership is best in which type of situation?" To answer this question, we need to match the styles with the environmental demands. In this section, we examine two contingency approaches: (1) Fiedler's contingency model and (2) the path-goal theory of leadership.

Fiedler's contingency model

The best-known contingency model of leadership effectiveness was developed by Fred Fiedler and his associates.[13] This model represents a significant departure from earlier trait and behavioral leadership models because Fiedler contends that group performance is contingent on both the motivational system of the leader and the degree to which the leader can control and influence the situation. In Fiedler's view, there is a difference between leader behavior and leadership style. *Leader behavior* is the specific acts in which a leader engages while coordinating and directing the work group. For example, the individual can praise the followers, make useful suggestions to them, and show consideration for their welfare. *Leadership style* refers to the underlying needs that motivate the leader's behavior, i.e., the personal needs he or she is attempting to satisfy. Fiedler has found that while a leader's behavior or action changes to meet the situation, his or her basic needs remain constant. In order to

It is the best-known contingency model.

[13] Fred E. Fiedler, *A Theory of Leadership Effectiveness* (New York: McGraw-Hill Book Company, 1967).

Figure 9.6
Least preferred coworker scale

Pleasant	__:__:__:__:__:__:__:__ 8 7 6 5 4 3 2 1	Unpleasant
Unfriendly	__:__:__:__:__:__:__:__ 1 2 3 4 5 6 7 8	Friendly
Accepting	__:__:__:__:__:__:__:__ 8 7 6 5 4 3 2 1	Rejecting
Frustrating	__:__:__:__:__:__:__:__ 1 2 3 4 5 6 7 8	Helpful
Enthusiastic	__:__:__:__:__:__:__:__ 8 7 6 5 4 3 2 1	Unenthusiastic
Tense	__:__:__:__:__:__:__:__ 1 2 3 4 5 6 7 8	Relaxed
Close	__:__:__:__:__:__:__:__ 8 7 6 5 4 3 2 1	Distant
Cold	__:__:__:__:__:__:__:__ 1 2 3 4 5 6 7 8	Warm
Cooperative	__:__:__:__:__:__:__:__ 8 7 6 5 4 3 2 1	Uncooperative
Hostile	__:__:__:__:__:__:__:__ 1 2 3 4 5 6 7 8	Supportive
Interesting	__:__:__:__:__:__:__:__ 8 7 6 5 4 3 2 1	Boring
Quarrelsome	__:__:__:__:__:__:__:__ 1 2 3 4 5 6 7 8	Harmonious
Self-Assured	__:__:__:__:__:__:__:__ 8 7 6 5 4 3 2 1	Hesitant
Inefficient	__:__:__:__:__:__:__:__ 1 2 3 4 5 6 7 8	Efficient
Cheerful	__:__:__:__:__:__:__:__ 8 7 6 5 4 3 2 1	Gloomy
Guarded	__:__:__:__:__:__:__:__ 1 2 3 4 5 6 7 8	Open

Adapted from Fred E. Fiedler and Martin M. Chemers, *Leadership and Effective Management* (Glenview, Ill.: Scott, Foresman and Compnay, 1974), p. 75.

classify leadership styles, then, Fiedler and his colleagues developed the least-preferred coworker scale.

The LPC asks, "With whom can you work least well?"

Least-preferred coworker scale   The least-preferred coworker (LPC) scale uses a questionnaire that asks the leader to describe the person with whom he or she can work least well (Figure 9.6). From the responses, an LPC score is obtained by adding the item scores. This score reveals the individual's emotional reaction to people with whom he or she cannot work well.

Fiedler found that the leader with the high LPC score describes a least-preferred coworker in favorable terms. The individual tends to be relationship-oriented and obtains great satisfaction from establishing close personal relations with the group members.

Conversely, the leader with a low LPC score describes his or her least preferred coworker in unfavorable terms. The individual tends to be task-oriented and obtains much satisfaction from the successful completion of tasks, even if it comes at the risk of poor interpersonal relations with the workers.

Situational variables   In addition to administering the LPC test to each individual, Fiedler sought to determine the major situational variables that could be used to classify group situations. He discovered three:

Leader-member relations are very important. The leader who is trusted by the subordinates can often influence group performance regardless of his or her position power. Conversely, the leader who is distrusted by the members must often rely solely on position power to get things done.

Leader-member relations are important.

Task structure is the degree to which the leader's job is programmed or specified in step-by-step fashion. If the job is highly structured, the leader knows exactly what is to be done, and if there are any problems, the organization can back the leader up. If the job is highly unstructured, there is no one right solution to the problem, and the leader will have to rely on personal relationships in getting the group to do things his or her way.

So is the degree of task structure.

Leader position power is the authority vested in the leader's position. For example, the president has more power than the vice president, and the division head has more power than the unit manager.

And the leader's position power.

Fiedler's findings   Fiedler then brought together the LPC scores (which identified leadership style) with the situational variables to find what leadership style works best in each situation.

Figure 9.7 illustrates all the variables in the model. At the bottom of the graph are the eight possible combinations of situational variables (leader-member relations, task structure, and leader position power). Note that in Situation 1, on the left, things are very favorable for the leader; leader-member relations are good, the task is highly structured, and leader position power is strong. Meanwhile in Situation 8, on the right, things are very unfavorable for the leader. Leader-member relations are poor, the task is unstructured, and the leader's position power is weak. As we move across the continuum from the first to the eighth situation, things get progressively worse for the leader.

The task-centered leader is best in very favorable or unfavorable situations.

What type of individual does best in each of these eight situations? As can be seen from the model, a task-oriented leader does best in very favorable situations (1, 2, and 3) or very unfavorable situations (7 and 8), and the relationship-oriented leader does best in the moderately favor-

The relationship-centered leader is best in moderately favorable or unfavorable situations.

Figure 9.7
Identifying the effective leader

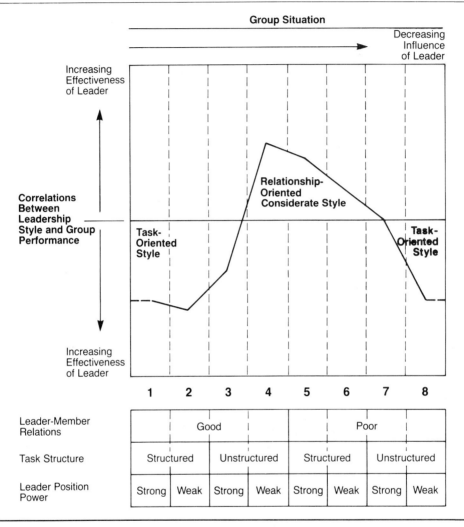

Fred Fiedler, "Style or Circumstance: The Leadership Enigma," *Psychology Today*, March 1969, p. 42. Reprinted with permission.

able and moderately unfavorable situations (4, 5, and 6). Fiedler explained it this way:

> **The results show that a task-oriented leader performs best in situations at both extremes—those in which he has a great deal of influence and power, and also in situations where he has no influence and power over the group members.**

> **Relationship-oriented leaders tend to perform best in mixed situa-**

tions where they have only moderate influence over the group. A number of subsequent studies by us and others have confirmed these findings.

The results show that we cannot talk about simply good leaders or poor leaders. A leader who is effective in one situation may or may not be effective in another. Therefore, we must specify the situations in which a leader performs well or badly.[14]

Fiedler's theory and human relations   Fiedler's theory offers several important alternatives for improving human relations. First, the organization as well as the leader is responsible for the latter's success, since a leader can be effective or ineffective depending on the situation. Many personnel psychologists and managers tend to view the executive's position as fixed and to turn their attention to changing the person's basic leadership style. However, this is the wrong approach. In order to change a leader's style one has to alter his or her personality. This can take from one to several years; a few lectures or some brief but intensive training will not do it.

What then should be done? The answer is: develop training programs that provide a leader with the opportunity to learn in which situations he or she can perform well and in which failure is likely.

Develop training programs for leaders.

Second, engineer the job to fit the leader. This recommendation is based on the fact that it is a lot easier to change the leader's work environment than his or her personality. Any one of the three situational variables can be altered. For example, the leader's position power could be improved by giving him or her a higher rank, or it can be reduced by forcing the leader to consult with the subordinates rather than make unilateral decisions. Likewise, the leader's task can be made more explicit or can be changed to be more vague. Finally, leader-member relations can be altered. The group can be made more homogeneous or more interdisciplinary, or the leader can be reassigned to a group that gets along well or one that is continually engaged in squabbling.

Engineer the job to fit the leader.

Applying these recommendations to Figure 9.7, we can move the leader back and forth on the grid depending on our objectives. For example, a task-centered manager operating in Situation 5 will not be very effective. A relationship-centered leader would do better. However, if we can do something to change leader-member relations from poor to good, we will have moved the leader to Situation 1. (You can verify this by comparing the three major variables for Situations 1 and 5 and noting what happens when the leader-member relations are changed.) Likewise, a relationship-oriented manager operating under the conditions in Situation 8 will be ineffective. However, the person would do quite well in Situation 4. This can be arranged by simply working to improve the leader-member relations from poor to good. (Again, you can prove this

---

[14] Fred Fiedler, "Style or Circumstance: The Leadership Enigma," *Psychology Today*, March 1969, p. 42.

by comparing the three major variables for Situations 8 and 4 and noting what happens when the leader-member relations are changed.) If the leader were aware of his or her strengths and weaknesses, the individual could try to change the group situation to match his or her leadership style.

However, we must remember that good leadership performance depends as much upon the organization as it does the leader. This means that we must learn not only to train men to be leaders, but how to build organizations in which specific types of leaders can perform well.

In view of the increasing scarcity of competent executives, it is to an organization's advantage to design jobs to fit leaders instead of attempting merely to fit a leader to the job.[15]

Path-goal theory of leadership

Path-goal leadership theory draws heavily on expectancy motivation theory and high concerns for both people and work. The theory has been proposed by Robert House and has been expanded and refined by him and others over the last decade.[16] The theory can be summarized as follows:

1. The leader can improve subordinate motivation by making the rewards for performance more attractive. By giving the people raises, promotions, and recognition, the leader can increase the subordinates' valence (preference) for goal achievement.

2. If the workers' assignments are poorly defined, the leader can increase motivation by providing structure in the form of helpful supervision, subordinate training, and goal clarification. Reducing the ambiguity of the job makes it easier for the subordinate to pursue the goals. Expectancy (the likelihood of attaining this first-level outcome) should increase.

   If we take these two steps together, we can see that in the first, valence is increased, and in the second expectancy is increased. Recall the expectancy theory: Motivational force = Valence × Expectancy. It is obvious that path-goal theory is designed to increase worker motivation.

3. If the work of the subordinates is already greatly structured, as in the case of assembly-line workers or machinists, the leader should refrain from introducing any more structure. Such actions will be

Tenets of path-goal theory.

---

[15] *Ibid.*, p. 43.

[16] Robert J. House, "A Path-Goal Theory of Leader Effectiveness," *Administrative Science Quarterly*, September 1971, pp. 321–338; and Robert J. House and Terence R. Mitchell, "Path-Goal Theory of Leadership," *Journal of Contemporary Business*, Autumn 1974, pp. 81–97.

viewed as unnecessary and overly directive. Instead of worrying about the work, the leader should now spend more time being concerned with the personal needs of the people by giving them attention, praise, and support.

At present there is some research support for the path-goal approach to leadership,[17] although it does appear that more work needs to be done in both expanding and refining the original theory.[18] One reason is that in some unstructured situations subordinates react negatively to attempts by the leader to clarify goals and reduce ambiguity. The employees would rather handle the situation themselves. On the other hand, there is fairly strong evidence to support the path-goal theory proposition that increasing consideration for subordinates whose work is already highly structured will increase their job satisfaction.

For human relations study, path-goal theory provides three important benefits. First, it helps integrate expectancy theory and contingency leadership. Second, it reemphasizes the importance of high leader concerns for both the work and the people. Third, it encourages the leader to analyze the situation in determining the right degree of each—concern for structure and concern for people—that will be required.

Summary

Leadership is the process of influencing people to direct their efforts toward the achievement of particular goal(s). What makes a leader effective? Some people believe the answer rests in leadership characteristics such as drive, originality, and the tolerance of stress. The greatest problem with this trait theory approach, however, is that it does not take the situation into account. A leadership style that is effective in one situation may not be effective in another.

In an effort to address the situational nature of leadership, many

---

[17] Robert J. House and G. Dessler, "The Path-Goal Theory of Leadership: Some Post Hoc and A Priori Tests," in J. G. Hunt and L. L. Larson, eds., *Contingency Approaches to Leadership* (Carbondale, Ill.: Southern Illinois University Press, 1974), pp. 29–55; and H. P. Sims, Jr. and A. D. Szilagyi, "Leader Structure and Subordinate Satisfaction for Two Hospital Administrative Levels: A Path Analysis Approach," *Journal of Applied Psychology*, April 1975, pp. 194–197.

[18] John E. Stinson and Thomas W. Johnson, "The Path-Goal Theory of Leadership: A Partial Test and Suggested Refinement," *Academy of Management Journal*, June 1975, pp. 242–252; Andrew D. Szilagyi and Henry P. Sims, Jr., "An Exploration of the Path-Goal Theory of Leadership in a Health Care Environment," *Academy of Management Journal*, December 1974, pp. 622–634; H. Kirk Downey, John E. Sheridan, and John W. Slocum, Jr., "Analysis of Relationships among Leader Behavior, Subordinate Job Performance and Satisfaction: A Path-Goal Approach," *Academy of Management Journal*, June 1975, pp. 253–262; and Charles Greene, "Questions of Causation in the Path-Goal Theory of Leadership," *Academy of Management Journal*, March 1979, pp. 22–41.

people have turned to personal characteristics. Some of the most commonly cited personal characteristics of leaders include superior intelligence, emotional maturity, motivation drive, problem-solving skills, managerial skills, and leadership skills. The degree and importance of each is situationally determined. For example, some situations require the leader to rely heavily on human skills, but others demand administrative skills.

In order to lead personnel effectively, it is also necessary to form some opinions about them. Some managers are adherents of the Theory X philosophy, which holds that people are basically lazy and that in order to get them to work, it is often necessary to use coercion and threats of punishment. Other managers support Theory Y, which holds that people are interested in both lower-level and upper-level need satisfaction, have untapped potential, and, if given the right rewards, exercise self-direction and self-control in attaining organizational objectives.

Many organizations keep the people in a state of immaturity. This has led Argyris to conclude that there is a basic incongruence between the needs of the healthy personality and the demands of the average organization. Yet this does not have to be the case. Experiments in job design, for example, have illustrated that people who are given increased responsibility and the chance for upper-level needs satisfaction often produce far more than they have in the past.

Leadership styles also vary. Some situations require authoritarian leadership behavior, but others call for a paternalistic leader; some are best handled with a participative leadership style, and others require a laissez-faire manager. Each of the four styles can be described in terms of two dimensions: concern for work and concern for people. Every leader exercises some degree of each, and since they are independent dimensions, the individual can be high in one without having to be low in the other. The person can be high in both or, for that matter, low in both.

Today, we are in a contingency phase of leadership study. The best-known contingency model is that of Fred Fiedler, who has found that task-centered leaders do best in very favorable or very unfavorable situations and relationship-oriented leaders are most effective in situations that are moderately favorable or moderately unfavorable. He recommends matching the leader to the situation rather than trying to change the individual's personality to fit the job.

The path-goal theory of leadership draws heavily on expectancy motivation theory and leader concern for both people and work. In essence the theory holds that: (1) the leader can improve subordinate motivation by making the rewards for performance more attractive, (2) if work assignments are poorly defined, the leader can increase motivation by providing structure in the form of helpful supervision, subordinate training, and goal clarification, and (3) if the work is already greatly structured, the leader should concentrate on the personal needs of the individuals by giving them attention, praise, and support. At present, some research supports the path-goal approach to leadership, but more work needs to be done to expand and refine the theory.

Key terms in the chapter

leadership
leadership characteristics
personal characteristics
technical skills
human skills
administrative skills
Theory X
Theory Y
immaturity–maturity theory
authoritarian leadership
paternalistic leadership

participative leadership
vertical dyad linkage theory
laissez-faire leadership
leadership dimensions
Fiedler's contingency model
least-preferred coworker scale
leader-member relations
task structure
leader position power
path–goal theory of leadership

Review and study questions

1. What is meant by *leadership*? Put it in your own words.
2. How do leadership characteristics differ from personal characteristics? Explain.
3. Are there any leadership characteristics that appear to account for success in the leadership role? What are they?
4. Do effective leaders have superior intelligence? Are there intelligence ranges within which we are likely to find successful leaders?
5. Successful leaders are emotionally mature. What does this statement mean?
6. In terms of need drive, how do successful leaders differ from average leaders? From least successful leaders?
7. What are the three types of managerial skills every leader must have? Explain.
8. What are the basic assumptions of Theory X? How accurate are they?
9. What are the basic assumptions of Theory Y? How accurate are they?
10. Is a Theory Y manager always superior to a Theory X manager? Explain.
11. According to Argyris, what are the seven states through which an individual progresses as he or she matures?

12. Many organizations are not geared for mature people. What does this statement mean?

13. How does authoritarian leadership behavior differ from paternalistic leadership behavior?

14. How does participative leadership behavior differ from laissez-faire leadership behavior?

15. Of the four leadership behaviors described in this chapter, which is the most effective? Why?

16. The two leadership dimensions—concern for work and concern for people—have been found to be independent dimensions. What does this statement mean?

17. What type of leader would do best in a situation requiring high concern for work, low concern for people? High concern for both? Low concern for both? Explain your answers.

18. What are the three major situational variables in Fiedler's contingency theory? Describe each.

19. According to Fiedler, what type of leader is most effective in which kind of situation? Be complete in your answer.

20. In what way is Fiedler's theory useful in the study of human relations?

21. In your own words, what is the path-goal theory of leadership all about? How can an understanding of this theory contribute to one's knowledge of human relations? Explain.

Interpretation of your assumptions about people

This test measures your tendency to support Theory X and Theory Y beliefs. In getting your scores for each, fill in the answer sheet below and then plot a graph by placing a dot at the point where your Theory X and Theory Y scores intersect.

Theory X Score		Theory Y Score	
2	(b)	8	(a)
3	(c)	7	(d)
4	(f)	6	(e)
1	(h)	9	(g)
2	(i)	8	(j)
3	(k)	7	(l)
1	(m)	9	(n)
1	(p)	9	(o)
1	(q)	9	(r)
0	(t)	10	(s)
18		82	

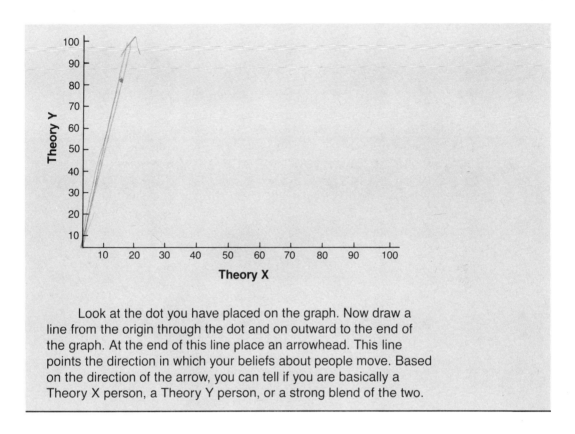

Look at the dot you have placed on the graph. Now draw a line from the origin through the dot and on outward to the end of the graph. At the end of this line place an arrowhead. This line points the direction in which your beliefs about people move. Based on the direction of the arrow, you can tell if you are basically a Theory X person, a Theory Y person, or a strong blend of the two.

One more time?

David Mooney was brought into the Farling Company to straighten things out. David had worked for a competitor, Butler Company, for 18 months, and during that time its profits had risen each year. Before his takeover, however, Butler had lost money for seven years in a row, each year slightly more than the last. Within six months, David had the firm in the profit column, and at the end of the fifth quarter, earnings were at an all-time high.

The board of directors at Farling was impressed with David's performance at Butler and believed he could bring them out of their tailspin. Farling had been losing money for 18 months, and the board thought it was time to get a new president.

David visited the firm, talked to the board and the management team, and decided to accept the job. Within three years he had purchased new equipment, fired 20 percent of the work force, refused to hire new personnel to replace workers who quit or retired, and trimmed the management force by 15 percent. He also instituted cost-cutting procedures, put in time clocks, had time-and-motion studies done, and demanded that everyone carry their own weight.

During the first three years at the helm, David had dramatic success. However, after its earnings and profits increased to record levels, Farling's performance started to slip, and by the end of the fourth year, things were beginning to look bleak again. The board hired a management consulting team to study the situation, and the team concluded that David had an effective style for turning around a company that was in trouble. However, once things were under control, he was the wrong person to head the firm. They advised that David should be replaced. Some members of the board agreed with these recommendations, but others were reluctant to replace David. "Maybe," they said, "he can turn it around again."

Questions

1. Refer to Figure 9.7 in the text and identify David's leadership style.
2. Why was David effective in turning around the company? Explain.
3. Should David be replaced? Defend your answer.

Paternalism? No thanks

Joan Charlson and Robert Ewing were classmates in high school. After graduation Joan went to work as a cashier for a bank, while Robert got a job in an insurance company. Both organizations offered their employees free tuition at the college of their choice. The only restrictions were that no more than two courses could be taken per term and that the employee had to have a grade of B or better to qualify for reimbursement. In addition, both firms had excellent employee benefit programs, including free dental care and retirement after 20 years at one half the average of one's salary over the five years before retirement.

Joan was surprised at the high degree of paternalism exercised by the bank at large and by her boss. He was always looking after his people, making sure everything was going all right, and keeping track of what everyone was doing. While Joan initially liked this approach, she soon tired of it. She felt there was not enough freedom to exercise her own judgment. As a result, she asked for a transfer to another department. However, things there were basically the same. Although this upset her, Joan stayed with the bank. She took three courses every semester (paying for the third one herself) and every summer, so that at the end of four years, she finished her bachelor's degree in accounting and began looking for another job.

While reading the "help wanted" columns, Joan noticed that Robert's company was hiring new accountants. She called Robert and the two of them had lunch. During the meal Joan asked Robert how he liked the insurance firm. He painted a glowing picture. In particular, he told Joan about the benefit program and leadership behavior of the managers. However, it seemed to Joan that Robert's firm was very much like her own. What particularly disturbed Joan was Robert's comment that he was in no hurry to finish his degree because raises and salary promotions were tied most heavily to time on the job and not to educational requirements or personal drive.

After interviewing with a half-dozen companies, Joan took a job with a large accounting firm. She told her dad, "This company doesn't baby you. It's perform or get out. I'm going to be on my own, and I like that. I don't need extensive benefit programs, I need the chance to succeed on my own. My new boss is a real participative management type. He tells me what needs to be done and relies on me to do it. I'm going to like working for this new firm."

Questions

1. Contrast the leadership behaviors of Joan's old boss and her new boss.
2. Is it possible that both bosses are effective in their jobs? Explain.
3. Drawing upon the path-goal theory of leadership, explain the type of boss for whom Joan would like to work. Be complete in your answer.

The role of the leader

10

Goals of the chapter

In Chapter 9 we examined the fundamentals of leadership; in particular, we studied the nature of leadership, leadership behavior, and contingency leadership styles. Now we want to turn to the role of the leader by answering the question, "what do effective leaders do on a day-to-day basis?" Although there are many tasks the leader must perform, six are of primary importance: representing and supporting the subordinates, developing teamwork, counseling wisely, using power properly, managing time well, and managing stress well. The goal of this chapter is to examine these tasks, beginning with leader-member related activities and then moving to tasks that tend to be performed by the leader alone.

When you have finished reading this chapter you should understand the role of the leader and should be able to:

1. discuss the leader's linking pin function
2. explain what is meant by *teamwork*
3. describe the three key factors necessary to the development of teamwork
4. tell why employees need counseling and cite the kinds of counseling often given by managers
5. define *power* and explain what the various types of power are
6. explain the three ways of managing time and tell how effective leaders manage their time well
7. discuss how the manager should deal with stress.

Represent and support the subordinates

One of the primary roles of the leader is to represent the subordinates to his or her boss. The leader must be the interface between the work group and higher management. At the same time, he or she must be personally supportive of the group members.

Linking pin function

Leaders are like linking pins.

One way of looking at leaders is as *linking pins* that represent or connect their group in the hierarchy to the one directly above it. Made famous by Rensis Likert, the idea is depicted in Figure 10.1.[1] Note that the lowest-level managers, the supervisors, are links between each of their three subordinates and their own group managers. In turn, the group manager represents the three supervisors to the department manager. This idea, if continued up the line, would result in an integrated organization. If this linking pin connection is weak, however, effectiveness will suffer. Likert has stated:

> **The linking pin function . . . will be performed well in an organization when each work group at all the different hierarchical levels above the nonsupervisory level is functioning effectively as a group and when every member of each group is performing his functions and roles well. Whenever an individual member of one of these groups fails in his leadership and membership roles . . . the group or groups under him will not be linked into the organization effectively and will fail in the performance of their tasks. When an entire work group ceases to function effectively as a group, the activities and performance of all the work groups below such a group will be correspondingly adversely affected.[2]**

Supportive behavior

The leader must be supportive.

In addition to representing them to the upper management, the effective leader must strive to remove roadblocks, define tasks, and motivate the subordinates toward goal attainment. This may require further training of the workers, purchase of new equipment, or more efficient scheduling of material delivery.

In any event, the basis of supportive behavior is trying to understand employee needs. What kinds of support are required for the workers to do a better job? Often the answer is found in *social exchange*

---

[1] Rensis Likert, *New Patterns of Management* (New York: McGraw-Hill Book Company, 1961), pp. 113–115.
[2] *Ibid.*, p. 114.

Figure 10.1
The linking pin function

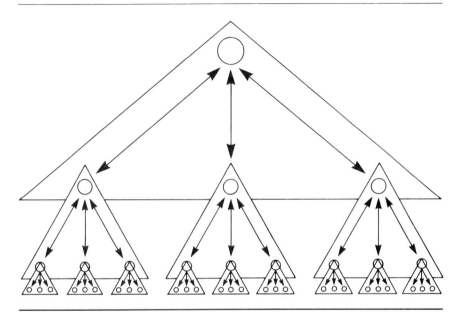

theory. If the leader wants something from the subordinates, he or she must be willing to give something in turn. The effective leader knows the value of supportive role behavior.

Develop teamwork

A second important role of the leader is to develop *teamwork*. Davis has cited some of the prerequisites for teamwork.

> **A group is able to work together as a team only after all the people in the group know the roles of all the others with whom they will be interacting. All members also must be reasonably qualified to perform their jobs and want to cooperate. When this level of understanding is reached, members can act immediately as a team based upon the requirements of that situation, without waiting for someone to give an order. In other words, team members respond voluntarily to the job and take appropriate actions to further teamwork goals.**[3]

Figure 10.2 is an illustration of teamwork in action. In Part A, the formal hierarchy, each manager leads four subordinates; Part B illustrates

---

[3] Keith Davis, *Human Behavior At Work: Organizational Behavior*, 6th ed. (New York: McGraw-Hill Book Company, 1981), p. 261.

Figure 10.2
Organizational teamwork

A. The Formal Organization

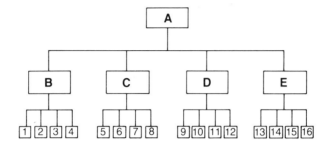

B. Teamwork in the Formal Organization

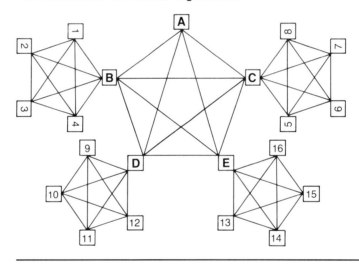

the coordination as it actually operates. Each leader is coordinating the activities of the subordinates via teamwork. Whenever a leader is placed in charge of an operating team for which each person in the group must contribute some effort toward goal attainment, teamwork is necessary. Consider the following example:

At the Harrison Company the unit monthly cost control report must be completed by the fifth business day of the following month. The data for this report cannot be collected before the second business day of the new month because it takes a half-day for the accounting people to send the data to the computer department and another half-day for the material to be analyzed and fed back to the various units. In addition to the computer print-out, other data must be collected by the unit personnel, but each unit must make its own collection.

In Unit 2 the manager and four assistants all work together to get the report done in one morning. First, Barney, the manager, fills in as much of the report as he can from the information he already has. Dave and Joan analyze the computer print-out, glean the necessary information, make additional calculations where needed, and pass the information to Barney. Meanwhile, Steve and Jenny make phone calls and visit with other departments to gather the rest of the data. They, too, pass the results to Barney.

Drawing upon all the information, Barney works up a rough draft of the report and gives copies to each of the four subordinates. All then meet for 30 minutes and review what is in the paper. If there are any problems or errors, they are spotted by the group and corrections are made. Once everything is in order, Barney gives the report to his secretary for final typing. The secretary carries the report to the division manager's office.

During the last year Barney's unit has submitted its report first each month, and it has never been sent back because of errors or incompleteness.

As you can see, Barney's unit has teamwork. Everyone pulls together. This is in contrast to Ralph's group, Unit 4, which has never been on time with its report. The division manager recently sent his subordinate to check on the reason for the tardiness. This is the subordinate's report:

Ralph waits until the day the report is due before taking any action. Then he fills in as much of the report as he can and has his secretary make some telephone calls or visit the other departments to gather the rest of the information. The problem here is that the secretary really does not know what information to ask for, so she accepts whatever she is given. This is why many of Ralph's numbers do not seem to make sense when they are analyzed at the division level. If the secretary is out sick or has some other pressing jobs, she generally puts off typing the report for a day or two.

The few times Ralph asked his people for some help, he met resistance from them. They apparently feel that the unit's monthly cost control report is not within their area of responsibility and they resent being asked to help out. When they do help with the report, their work is sloppy. Three of them really do not know how to fill out the report, and the other person does not seem to care. There is no teamwork in the unit. If Ralph does not do the job, it does not get done.

What accounts for the success of the first manager and the lack of success of the second? The answer rests with teamwork. Barney understands the key factors in developing teamwork, but Ralph does not.

Key factors in developing teamwork

There are three key factors in the development of teamwork: the leader, the subordinates, and the environment (Figure 10.3). They are interdependent. For example, if the leader cannot get along with the subordinates, the group members do not like the leader, or the environment is not conducive to effective teamwork, overall group efficiency suffers.

Figure 10.3
Teamwork determinants

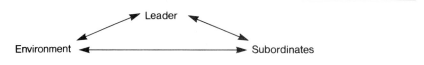

The leader   The leader must build an environment in which team-work can happen. Research shows that between the leader and the sub-ordinates there must be trust, cooperation, and compatibility. Some lead-ers have the training, experience, and personality that allow them to build teamwork among their people almost immediately. Others require more time because the subordinates are reluctant to trust them, the work environment is not conducive to teamwork, or they lack the personal characteristics needed to create the right environment.[4]

The subordinates   No matter how hard the leader tries to develop teamwork, the subordinates have a key role to play in this effort. If the norms of the group restrict output, the leader is starting out in a weak position. If there has been bitter union-management conflict over a re-cently negotiated contract, the leader may find no basis for developing effective teamwork. If the leader is paternalistic but the subordinates want a participative leader, there will be teamwork problems. Finally, if some of the group members do not get along with one another, there will be mini-mum cooperation between them. This will reduce group teamwork.

The environment   Most teamwork problems are a result of several interacting influences that cannot be attributed solely to the leader or the subordinates. Rather, they rest in the way the work is organized and the operations are carried out. Two questions will always reveal them. What tasks are the individuals in the group doing? Is there a basis for teamwork, or are the people being rewarded for competing with one another?

In some organizations, for example, the marketing department is re-warded for selling, the production department for manufacturing, and the finance department for carefully monitoring and controlling overall budgets and capital expenditures. What the top manager fails to realize, however, is that all three cannot succeed. One or two win at the expense

---

[4]Dale E. Zand, "Trust and Managerial Problem Solving," *Administrative Science Quarterly*, June 1972, pp. 229–239; and W. Brendan Reddy and Anne Byrnes, "Effects of Interpersonal Group Composition on the Problem-solving Behavior of Middle Managers," *Journal of Applied Psychology*, December 1972, pp. 516–517.

of the third. In particular, if finance holds down expenditures, marketing may be unable to initiate its advertising program and sales will not be greater, and production may be unable to buy new machines so the cost per unit will be higher. Finally, with a smaller marketing effort and a higher product cost, the net profit will be below the forecast. The top manager must strive to develop teamwork among his or her key people by reducing this built-in goal conflict as much as possible.

A similar situation is that of salespeople who are selling the same product line in different geographic locales. In contrast to the previous illustration in which intergroup cooperation is needed to accomplish overall goals and teamwork, however, this is a classic case of "Every man for himself." Each salesperson is given a quota and urged to meet it. There is no reward, however, for cooperation or teamwork. Danny may know of a potential customer in Sue's territory, but he neglects to convey this information to her because he may endanger his chances of being the company's top salesperson this year. In order to overcome this problem, the leader must revise the sales incentive plan so that people are rewarded for teamwork. The current sales environment does nothing to encourage team players, so it must be changed.

And the environment must be right.

Finally, there is the work environment in which people depend on others for input. Assembly-line work is an illustration. If Cary doesn't assemble the widget, Karol cannot test it. One or two slow people can reduce the line to a crawl. Here the leader must work with the informal group to induce Cary to speed up his output. The work environment cannot be redesigned, so the manager needs to concentrate on the subordinate(s) causing the problem. Remember from our discussion of informal groups that if the norms are changed, people tend to go along. The leader, therefore, must first try working through Cary's peers. This can be done if the manager has developed the proper rapport with the group. If Cary bucks this informal, social pressure, the leader should replace him. However, until the manager is sure that the group's backing has been obtained, replacement of the slow worker should have a low priority. The leader needs to strike a wedge between this person and the group, to isolate the individual, and then to remove him. Teamwork depends on group support, and if the leader moves too fast, the group may feel that such action is not only inappropriate but also threatening. ("The manager might get rid of us just as fast. We'd better fight for Cary and protect our own jobs in the process.")

Counsel wisely

A third important role of the leader is to counsel wisely. ***Counseling*** is the discussion of an emotional problem with an employee for the general objective of eliminating or decreasing it. Many people in the work place need counseling because the demands of their jobs create emotional disequilibrium.

Figure 10.4
Blocked need drive and frustration

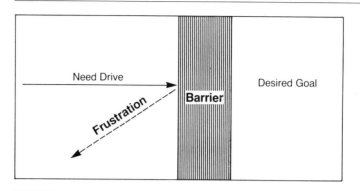

Why employees need counseling

Many factors can cause an employee to need counseling. Three of the most important are frustration, conflict, and stress.

Frustration results from blocked need drive.

Frustration   Frustration is a result of blocked need drive. We can represent it as in Figure 10.4. A person who sees his or her efforts blocked often becomes uneasy, anxious, or nervous. A worker may be unable to accomplish a task because of interference by other employees or failure of equipment.

What the manager needs to realize is that the higher the worker's motivation to reach a desired goal, the higher the person's frustration over failure; and conversely, the lower the person's motivation, the lower the frustration over failure. Since the manager wants to encourage high motivation, it is imperative that some form of counseling be given to employees who are encountering frustration reactions. Additionally, where possible the manager should use his or her power to directly reduce the barriers by, for example, personally investigating why certain raw materials have not arrived and expediting their delivery.

Conflict occurs when people disagree about an issue.

Conflict   Conflict occurs when individuals or groups in the organization clash over some issue that, at least to them, is important. Sometimes this occurs on an interpersonal basis, and at other times it takes place between groups. One person may defeat another for a promotion; one group may have new machinery installed in its department before the other gets new machines. One division may be given 15 percent more merit money than another.

Conflict is not always bad, but when it leads to a deterioration of cooperation, trust, and loyalty among the personnel, counseling is in order. This is particularly true when parties to the conflict engage in win-lose situations, in which one party's gain is the other's loss. By counseling those involved, the manager can often reduce conflicts and redirect the efforts of the personnel toward more meaningful objectives.

Stress   *Stress* is a condition that is characterized by emotional strain or physical discomfort and that, unrelieved, can impair one's ability to cope with the environment. A small amount of stress can be good. In many people it stimulates performance. If stress is increased or is maintained for an extended period, however, it can be dangerous. In the short run it can lead to a headache or upset stomach; in the long run it can result in ulcers, a heart condition, or nervous disorders.

Stress is characterized by emotional strain or physical discomfort.

Research shows that workers and managers report about the same degree of job stress. If one assumes that managerial jobs are more stressful, these findings indicate that the management selection process in many organizations apparently weeds out those least likely to withstand the pressure.[5] However, this does not negate the need for counseling. Workers must still withstand the stress associated with job insecurity, role ambiguity, role conflict, and job overload. Additionally, many employees suffer stress in their home lives and bring their pressures with them to the job. Counseling can help alleviate much of this problem.

Counseling functions

The overall purpose of counseling is to provide support to the employees in dealing with their emotional problems. The manager's objective should be that of increasing the employee's understanding, self-confidence, and ability to work effectively as a member of the team. Here are some of the most commonly accepted counseling functions.

Advice   When the manager advises the subordinate, he or she lays out a course of action to be followed. The manager takes the lead, the subordinate follows. Some professional counselors have pointed out the dangers in trying to understand another person's complicated emotions and to recommend a path of action. In spite of the possible dangers, however, this approach to counseling is widely used, because managers believe they should do it and workers expect it to be done. Many employees admit that they would rather have the manager suggest a course of action (even if it might be wrong) than ask them to plan one.

The manager must advise the subordinate.

Reassurance   Closely related to advice is reassurance. Some people, for example, encounter stress because they are unsure of how well they

Give the person reassurance.

---

[5] Vernon E. Buck, "Working Under Pressure," *Management and Organization Studies* (Seattle, Washington: University of Seattle), Autumn 1974, pp. 1–3.

are doing their jobs. The manager may tell a subordinate that he or she is doing fine and may encourage him or her to keep it up. To a worker who is experiencing job stress the manager may point out, "This is all temporary. Our busy season ends next week and everything will go back to normal." Sometimes reassurance is just what the person needs to reduce frustration or stress.

Provide a sympathetic ear.

Release of emotional tension Many times all the worker needs is a sympathetic ear. Once he or she pours out what has been bottled up inside, the tension declines. Of course, this may not solve the problem, but it often removes mental blocks and permits the worker to face the problem squarely. Few people can resolve their problems when seething with anger and tension. This counseling function can help alleviate such emotions.

Give necessary reorientation.

Reorientation Sometimes employees need to be reoriented. They require additional training for a new job, a revision of their aspirations so that they are more in line with their abilities, or a rethinking of their current goals and values vis-à-vis those of the organization. These problems can sometimes be handled by the manager, but if they are severe, it is necessary to call on professional help. If, for example, an executive becomes an alcoholic, helping him or her become reoriented can be beyond the ability of the average manager.[6] When one's subordinate has this problem, it is best to let more professional help take over.

Counseling and the modern employee

In most cases the leader's counseling role will be one of providing general guidance and advice. Sometimes, however, the leader will be dealing with a troubled employee who may be having problems with self-confidence, be suffering from depression, or be facing increased family pressures. Or the problem may go deeper and be the result of alcohol or drug abuse. The following examines how these problem areas should be addressed.

Troubled employees. Sometimes employees will be troubled over job-related or home-related problems. If the manager feels the problem is best handled by letting it go, of course, no action is required. However, if the manager believes some action is needed, three courses are available: (1) tell the employee to shape up or ship out, (2) discipline the person, or (3) discuss the problem with the employee in an effort to work out a solution. This last approach requires effective counseling or coaching by

---

[6] "Business Dries Up Its Alcoholics," *Business Week*, November 11, 1972, pp. 168–169; 173; and "More Firms, Unions Establish Programs to Fight Alcoholism," *Wall Street Journal*, October 18, 1978, p. 19.

the leader. Some of the most useful guidelines that can be employed include the following:

1. Talk to the employee early in the work week rather than just before the weekend. In this way you can follow up the next day if additional coaching or counseling is needed.

2. Talk to the employee early in the day rather than just before quitting time. This will allow you ample time to at least cover your main points and give the worker a chance to respond.

3. Talk to the individual privately, away from other workers and managers. Let the person know there are just two of you involved—at least at this stage.

4. Get to the point immediately. Describe the problem situation or behaviors you have been noticing and present them from *your* point of view rather than someone else's. For example:

Do say:
I am becoming concerned about the number of accidents you are having.

As opposed to:
You are so nervous that you are having too many accidents.

Do say:
I am upset over your failure to follow my instructions.

As opposed to:
You make me mad by failing to follow my instructions.

Do say:
I have some concerns about your work.

As opposed to:
Some concerns have been voiced about your work.

Guidelines for coaching troubled employees.

5. If the worker finds it difficult to talk, provide reassurances and let the individual proceed at his or her own pace. Acknowledge what the person says without passing judgment or giving advice.

6. When the employee is done talking, discuss how he or she can improve work performance. Let the person know you are available if assistance is needed.

7. If the individual's problem requires professional counseling, do not offer it yourself. The problem is beyond your sense of training. Help identify the problem and then have the organization's counseling service handle the matter. If no such service is available, prepare a list of community referral services to which the worker can turn. Typical examples of problems for which referrals should be made include:

recurring bouts of anger, sadness, or fear

feelings of loneliness, isolation, moodiness, or depression

suicidal thoughts

inability to concentrate or sleep

lack of self-confidence

family problems

high stress levels

constant anxiety.[7]

8. Respect the employee's confidentiality. Do not discuss his or her situation with coworkers or others who have no need to know about the matter.

Alcoholism. Frustration and stress is very common in modern organizations. In dealing with these problems, some people turn to alcohol because they believe it helps them unwind. The unfortunate fact is that alcoholism in industry has now become a major problem resulting in accidents, absenteeism, wasted time, ruined materials, and premature job termination. The annual cost to American industry is now in the neighborhood of $94 billion. Some of the specific statistics that help explain this enormous loss include: (1) each alcoholic worker costs a business over $2,500 in unnecessary expenses; (2) these employees are 2½ times more likely to be absent than their coworkers; and (3) alcoholic employees collect over three times the amount of sick-leave payments than other employees.[8]

White collar symptoms.

Blue collar symptoms.

How does a manager know when one of the workers is drinking too much? This is a difficult question to answer, but there are some signs for which the individual can remain alert. Among white-collar workers these include such things as elaborate (and often bizarre) excuses for work deficiencies, pronounced and frequent swings in work pace, avoidance of the boss and associates, and increased nervousness. Among blue-collar workers, the clues include a sloppy personal appearance, signs of a hangover, frequent lapses of efficiency leading to occasional damage to equipment or material, increased nervousness, and increased off-the-job accidents.[9] Perhaps the biggest problem managers face in dealing with alcoholics is that they are very skillful in denying the problem, especially when confronted by the boss.

Alcoholic employees have an uncanny knack for manipulating the feelings of supervisors. In many cases they sense the onset of angry outbursts and know how to play for the counterfeelings that will block

---

[7]Terry L. Smith, "Coaching the Troubled Employee," *Supervisory Management*, December 1981, p. 35.

[8]Gene Milbourne, Jr., "Alcohol and Drugs: Poor Remedies for Stress," *Supervisory Management*, March 1981, p. 40.

[9]*Ibid.*

supervisory urges to act decisively. A favorite ploy is the "whipped child" syndrome characterized by the hang-dog look and the "I can't do anything right" verbalizations. Almost invariably these behaviors tug at parental heartstrings, and suddenly a supervisor finds himself or herself comforting and supporting the alcoholic employee rather than confronting the individual. At other times outbursts of righteous indignation by an employee will frighten the supervisor and cause him or her to back off.

Alcoholics have a great deal of experience at playing these games. Unless they know what is going on, supervisors do not have a chance.[10]

Regardless of how effective they are in initially hiding their problem, however, it eventually becomes obvious to the boss. This is particularly true if the organization has trained its managers in how to identify the excessive drinker. At this point the problem worker should be sent either to the firm's medical department or personnel department for counseling or further referral. Since the manager is not likely to be an expert on alcohol rehabilitation, the individual must be careful about what he or she says. For example, it is a mistake for the manager to moralize to the employee about the dangers of drinking or try to diagnose why the person has become a problem drinker. Instead, the manager should stress that the problem will be handled confidentially and alcoholism can be successfully treated. From here it is a matter of providing assistance to the person in getting the necessary treatment. Many organizations have their own program designed to deal with alcoholism; this is the ideal situation.

According to William Dunkin, assistant director of labor management services at the National Council on Alcoholism, employee programs are the best way to treat alcoholism because of the employee's desire to keep his or her job. The costs of such programs are minimal compared to the cost of alcoholism. One small company estimated that its 102 problem drinkers cost the firm $100,650 annually, but a successful program to treat these workers cost only $11,400 a year. One consultant estimates that an effective program costs a company only 35 to 50 cents per month per employee.[11]

Drug abuse. Employee drug abuse is also on the rise. Generally people take drugs at work to reduce the boredom, tension, or anxiety that accompanies the work. The symptoms of drug abuse are similar to those of alcoholism: slurred speech, dilated eyes, unsteady walk, lack of dexterity, and uncontrollable laughter or crying. Also like alcoholism, programs have been developed for dealing with drug abusers. A typical program, in a large organization, will be designed and implemented via four stages:

[10] Donald A. Phillips and Harry J. Older, "Alcoholic Employees Beget Troubled Supervisors," *Supervisory Management*, September 1981, p. 5.

[11] Milbourne, "Alcohol and Drugs: Poor Remedies for Stress," *Supervisory Management*, p. 41.

Typical drug abuse program design and implementation.

1. A committee is formed. If there is a union, it will be adequately represented. If there is a medical department, there will be one representative in the group.

2. A policy statement expressing the philosophy of the organization toward the effect of drug abuse on job performance will be developed.

3. If there is a union, a joint labor/management policy statement recognizing the effect of drug abuse on health and behavior will be developed.

4. Supervisors and management personnel will be trained in identifying drug-related problems and the proper ways to respond in dealing with them most effectively, including monitoring rehabilitation progress as measured by job performance.[12]

Use power properly

A fourth important leadership role is that of using one's power properly. Teamwork and effective counseling both require the leader to act as a motivator without throwing his or her weight around. One of the best ways to understand how to use power properly is to begin by analyzing the various types of power the leader can hold.

Types of power

There are many types of power. Five of the most commonly cited are: reward power, coercive power, legitimate power, referent power, and expert power.[13]

Reward power involves the use of extrinsic satisfiers.

Reward power   Reward power is held by leaders who can give extrinsic satisfiers to subordinates who do their jobs well. Some of the most common forms of extrinsic reward are increases in pay, bonuses, and promotions. In human relations terms, the leader has power over the subordinates because he or she can give or withhold these rewards, depending upon subordinate performance. Sometimes this performance is measured in terms of physical output (Did Steve do all that was expected?), and at other times it is measured in less quantitative terms (Is Doris a team player or does she do whatever she wants?). Leaders who use reward

---

[12] *Ibid.*, p. 42.

[13] John R. P. French, Jr., and Bertram Raven, "The Bases of Social Power," in *Studies in Social Power*, ed. D. Cartwright (Ann Arbor, Mich.: Institute for Social Research, 1959), pp. 150–167.

power are, in their own way, employing some of the ideas we encountered in our discussion of behavior modification. By giving positive reinforcement to those who do things the way the leader wants them done and failing to reward those who do otherwise, the leader attempts to keep everyone in line. On the positive side, if the leader's reward philosophy is regarded as fair by the workers and results in attainment of organizational objectives, it may be difficult to challenge its use.

Coercive Power   Coercive power is held by those who can fire, demote, or dock subordinates who do not comply with their directives. They can also threaten to use these negative reinforcers (although they may not carry through on the threat). These leaders derive their power from the workers' expectation that they will be punished if they do not conform.

Coercive power involves the use of firing or demotions.

Legitimate Power   This form of power is vested in the manager's position in the organizational hierarchy. For example, a vice-president has greater legitimate power than a foreman, and a district manager has greater legitimate power than a unit manager. Legitimate power is often referred to as "delegated authority."

Legitimate power is vested in the manager's position.

Referent Power   Referent power is based on the followers' identification with the leader. If the followers like the leader, the leader's power is greater than if they are indifferent about the leader. Leaders with charisma, reputation for fairness, or "winning" personalities commonly hold referent power.

Referent power is based on the followers' identification with the leader.

Expert Power   Leaders have expert power when their employees attribute knowledge and expertise to them. They are regarded as knowing what they are doing. Leaders who have demonstrated competence to implement, analyze, evaluate, and control group tasks are often seen as knowledgeable in their jobs, and they acquire expert power.

Expert power is based on knowledge and competence.

Power and the leader

Depending on the individual and the situation, a leader can possess varying amounts of all the sources of power we just discussed. For example, Hellriegel and Slocum point out:

The area of rewards, punishment, and coercion power are largely specified by the hierarchical structure of the organization. For example, the first-line foreman is at a lower level in the organization's hierarchy than the vice-president for manufacturing. Consequently, the foreman's bases of legitimate, reward and punishment power are less than the vice-president's. On the other hand, some supervisors may possess per-

"*True, you were only mildly wicked. But, like everyone else, we've lowered our standards.*"

Drawing by Ed Fisher; © 1981
The New Yorker Magazine, Inc.

sonal characteristics that increase their referent or expert power, regardless of their position in the organization's hierarchy.[14]

Are there any types of power that the effective leader can rely on consistently? Are there any types that a leader should avoid using? Although any answer must be tempered by the specifics of the situation,

---

[14]Don Hellriegel and John W. Slocum, Jr., *Organizational Behavior: Contingency Views*, 2nd ed. (St. Paul, Minn.: West Publishing Co., 1979), p. 465.

research shows that coercive power brings great resistance from the subordinates but that they will comply if this power is very strong. People tend to like legitimate power better than coercive power. Additionally, they like expert power, and the leader who proves to be an expert on one task is likely to find an increase in his or her ability to exert influence on a subsequent task.[15]

More directly related to our study of human relations, however, is the relationship between a manager's power and the resulting satisfaction and performance of the subordinates. On the basis of studies of five organizations, including a branch office, a college, an insurance company, a utility company, and some production work units, one group of researchers was able to make the following conclusions[16]

1. **Expert power is most strongly and consistently related to satisfaction and performance.**
2. **Legitimate power, along with expert power, was rated as the most important basis of complying with a leader's wishes, but was an inconsistent factor in determining organizational effectiveness.**

Some conclusions about power.

3. **Referent power was of intermediate importance as a cause for complying with leader directives, while at the same time was positively correlated with organizational effectiveness.**
4. **Reward power was also of intermediate importance for complying with leader directives, but had an inconsistent correlation with performance.**
5. **Coercive power was by far the least valuable in bringing about compliance to leader directives, and it was negatively related to organizational effectiveness.**

These findings indicate that informal bases of power can have a more favorable impact on organizational effectiveness than formal bases. This means that the effective leader must be greatly concerned with persuading the subordinates to follow orders and setting a good example through demonstration of expertise and should not rely exclusively on position power. People obey orders only when they feel it is in their best interests to do so. Quite obviously, we could argue that a person who is told to "obey or else" may well choose to follow the leader's command. However, sometimes people accept the punishment rather than comply. Given this fact, it should be apparent that the effective leader tempers his or her orders with a concern for the needs of both the people and the organization. No leader is effective unless the subordinates obey. Thus we can think of power as a two-way street: the leader has power and the subordinates have the right to either comply or refuse to do so.

---

[15] John Scholler, "Social Power," in *Advances in Experimental Social Psychology*, ed. Leonard Berkowitz (New York: Academic Press, 1965), pp. 177–218.

[16] Jerald G. Bachman, David G. Bowers, and Philip M. Marcus, "Bases of Supervisory Power: A Comparative Study in Five Organizational Settings," in *Control in Organizations*, ed. Arnold S. Tannenbaum (New York: McGraw-Hill Book Company, 1968), p. 236.

Manage time well

A fifth important leadership role, which is often overlooked, is that of managing time well. No leader can afford to be so bogged down in work that he or she lacks the time to carry out managerial tasks such as planning, decision making, organizing, communicating, counseling, and developing teamwork. On the other hand, the leader must set priorities and realize that every matter cannot be given primary attention. In large part, effective leaders get things done because they know how to budget their time to address major issues and to delegate minor ones. In doing so, they have learned how to deal with each of the three different kinds of management time.

Kinds of management time

There are three different kinds of management time: boss-imposed, system-imposed, and self-imposed.

Boss-imposed time is used to accomplish those activities that one's superior wants done. The manager cannot disregard these activities, so the time needed to carry them out must be allocated.

System-imposed time is used to handle requests from other managers. Sometimes they need assistance or support in coordinating activities or planning operations. These time demands are often not as important as those imposed by the boss, but the manager must try to respond to them.

Self-imposed time is used for doing the tasks the manager originates or agrees to do personally. Much of this is often referred to as *subordinate-imposed time* and will be spent answering questions and providing assistance to group members. The remaining portion is *discretionary time*, which the manager can use in any way he or she desires.

The effective leader realizes that boss-imposed and system-imposed time demands cannot be ignored. This leaves only self-imposed time from which to take the hours necessary to carry out all remaining tasks. To use this remaining time well, the leader needs to be aware of several vital principles of time management.

Boss-imposed time is used for doing what the boss wants done.

System-imposed time is used to handle requests from other managers.

Self-imposed time is used for handling the manager's other responsibilities.

Handling the monkey

One of the primary ways a manager finds self-imposed time being used up is by subordinates who continue to drop by the manager's office and talk him or her into doing their work. Often, the approach is very subtle and the manager is unaware of what has happened until the subordinate has left. Other subordinates do not wait to get into the office; they waylay the manager in the hallway.

Let us imagine that a manager is walking down the hall and he notices one of his subordinates, Mr. A, coming up the hallway. When

they are abreast of one another, Mr. A greets the manager with, "Good morning. By the way, we've got a problem. You see . . ." As Mr. A continues, the manager recognizes in this problem the same two characteristics common to all problems his subordinates gratuitously bring to his attention. Namely, the manager knows (a) enough to get involved, but (b) not enough to make the on-the-spot decision expected of him. Eventually, the manager says, "So glad you brought this up. I'm in a rush right now. Meanwhile, let me think about it and I'll let you know." Then he and Mr. A part company.

Let us analyze what has just happened. Before the two of them met, on whose back was the "monkey"? The subordinate's. After they parted, on whose back was it? The manager's. Subordinate-imposed time begins the moment a monkey successfully executes a leap from the back of a subordinate to the back of his superior and does not end until the monkey is returned to its proper owner for care and feeding.[17]

By accepting the monkey, the manager has taken a subordinate position. It is now up to the manager to make the next move. As a result, his or her self-imposed time is being reduced.

How can the manager prevent this problem in the future? Several ground rules should be followed:

1. The manager should offer assistance but should never agree to handle the problem.

2. The manager must tell the subordinate that assistance is given only to someone who needs it—in other words, to the person who has the monkey. If the subordinate wants the manager to *take* the monkey, there is no basis for assistance.

3. When the conversation is over, the monkey should be where it was initially—on the subordinate's back.

4. In those rare instances in which the manager must temporarily accept the monkey, the next move must be worked out by both manager and subordinate together.

Some time management ground rules.

By following these guidelines, the manager can reduce the amount of self-imposed time that is taken up by others.

Time priorities and work delegation

Even if the manager can eliminate the attempts of subordinates to pass the buck upward (or the monkey over), he or she must still be concerned with the remaining duties. As we noted in the previous chapter, many subordinates want participative leadership, and most managers find their people willing to help out, especially if they have created good rap-

---

[17]William Oncken, Jr., and Donald L. Wass, "Management Time: Who's Got the Monkey?" *Harvard Business Review*, November–December 1974, p. 76.

Table 10.1
Time management chart

What Must Be Done Today	Time for Each Activity	A Must Personally Be Done	B Could Be Delegated	C Should Be Delegated
1.				
2.				
3.				
4.				
5.				
Total Time _____	= _____	+ _____	+ _____	

Develop a time management chart.

port with the group. What can be delegated and what should be handled personally?

One way of deciding this question is to develop a time management chart for either the day or the week, on which the manager can assign priorities, determine what must personally be done, and decide what can and should be delegated. Table 10.1 is an example of such a chart. Notice that at the bottom of the chart the initial total time for all the manager's daily activities is equal to the sum of Columns A, B, and C, but that the actual total time is equal to the sum of Column A and whatever in Column B the manager is willing to do.

In trying to use time effectively, most managers make three critical mistakes. First, they fail to delegate, believing that good managers assume responsibilities rather than pass them on. What they do not realize is that an effective manager is not a workaholic; he or she does not have to be doing something every minute of the day. The best managers assign the work that can be handled by the subordinates and keep only what is left. They know the importance of pacing themselves and never getting caught in these all-too-common time traps.

Second, managers fail to schedule their work time. Some of the most commonly employed techniques for scheduling include:

1. Using a calendar as a major scheduling document.
2. Scheduling on a short-interval basis—day-to-day or week-to-week.

Some scheduling techniques.

3. Not letting the activities of other departmental personnel interfere with their planned activities.
4. Not letting the schedule get filled with routine tasks when their high energy could be better utilized.
5. Reviewing objectives and priorities before finalizing the schedule.

Table 10.2
Ten rules of time management for effective leaders

1. Carry a "to do" list with you; jot down notes on those things you have to do and cross out those that you have finished.

2. When reading memos, mail, or short reports, do so standing up. You read faster in this position.

3. As you read memos and letters that call for a reply, answer each as you go along. Otherwise you will have to read each again later when you get around to formulating a response.

4. Concentrate your efforts on one thing at a time.

5. Give your primary attention to those tasks which are most important and work at delegating minor jobs to your subordinates.

6. If you have an appointment to visit someone, bring work with you so that if you are forced to wait you can put the time to good use.

7. When you finish a particularly important or difficult task, give yourself time off as a special reward.

8. Try not to work on weekends.

9. Examine your work habits for ways of streamlining your current procedures and saving time.

10. If you do not get all you wanted accomplished in a given day, tell yourself you will get to it the next day. Do not feel guilty over any failure to meet your daily work plan. As long as you are doing your best, tell yourself that this is good enough.

Third, and last, many managers do not believe that they can manage their time well. Effective managers, however, are certain that with careful planning they can accomplish their assigned goals within the allotted time. They try to devote their energies to working smarter, not harder.[18] Table 10.2 provides some of the rules they follow in doing so.

Manage stress well

Effective leaders also learn how to manage stress well: both their own and that of their subordinates. What the leader needs to remember is that most people are unable to function well on the job unless they have some stimulus to get them going. However, if this stress is allowed to continue for a long period of time, it can be dangerous to their health. This danger is most prevalent among individuals who are known as Type A people.

---

[18] For additional guides to managing time see H. Kent Baker and Stevan Holmberg, "Stepping Up to Supervision: Managing Time and Job Pressures," *Supervisory Management*, December 1981, pp. 25–32; and Larry D. Alexander, "Effective Time Management Techniques," *Personnel Journal*, August 1981, pp. 637–640.

Are you a Type A or Type B person?

Below are ten combinations of statements related to your work and personal habits. In each case read the A and B statements and decide which is most descriptive of you. If A is totally descriptive of you and B is not at all descriptive, give 10 points to A and none to B. If both statements are descriptive of you, divide the 10 points between A and B based on their degree of descriptive accuracy. If B is totally descriptive of you and A is not at all descriptive, give 10 points to B and none to A. An interpretation is provided at the end of the chapter.

Points

1. A — Even when it is not necessary I find myself rushing to get things done.

B — I seldom rush to get things done, even if I am running late.

2. A — I often get upset or angry with people even if I do not show it.

B — I seldom get angry with people if there is no real reason for it.

3. A — When I play a game or compete in an event, winning is my primary objective.

B — When I play a game or compete in an event, my greatest enjoyment comes from the social interaction and participation with others.

4. A — I am a tense, anxious person, but I try to cover this up by smiling a lot and trying to be social.

B — I am basically a relaxed, easy-going individual; I seldom get tense or uptight.

5. A — Even when I am sitting down watching TV I am usually moving around, checking my nails, tapping my foot or carrying out some similar physical activity.

B — When I sit down to watch TV, I get totally involved in the program and seldom move around or change position.

6. A — I set high goals for myself and become angry if I fail to attain them.

B — I set reasonable goals for myself and if I fail I try not to let this get me down.

7. A — I write down how I intend to spend my day and I rigidly stick to this schedule.

B — I note objectives that I want to attain during the day

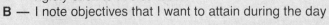

Points

_10_   but try to remain flexible; if something is not
        finished today, I will get to it tomorrow morning.

_3_   **8. A —** I hate to wait for people; it makes me edgy and
        nervous.

_7_   **B —** If I have to wait for others, I try to spend the time
        doing something relaxing like reading, talking to
        others, or quietly walking around.

_4_   **9. A —** Meals interrupt my schedule, and I often find myself
        doing work at the same time I am eating.

_6_   **B —** I enjoy meals and eat them slowly and in a relaxed
        fashion; if there is any work to do, it can wait until I
        am finished eating.

_6_   **10. A —** At the end of the day, I often find myself extremely
        tired and run down.

_4_   **B —** I like to get things done but not at the expense of
        physical exhaustion.

Type A people

In 1974 two California cardiologists proposed a nickname for achievement-oriented, competitive behavior patterns found in hard-driving individuals who strove to get more and more accomplished in less and less
time. They called these people *Type A individuals* and pointed out that
the behaviors that characterized these people could bring about heart attacks.[19] Yet it was very difficult for these high achievers to break their old
habits because for years they had trained themselves to work at a feverish
pace. Type B people can also be achievement-oriented, but they take
things at a slower pace. Are you a Type A or Type B person? Before continuing, take the quiz to find out which type you are.

If you have examined your results to this quiz, you have a fairly
good idea of what a Type A and Type B person is like. More specifically,
you can understand why Type A people are often described this way:

1. thinking or doing two or more things at the same time

2. scheduling more and more activities into less and less time

3. hurrying the speech of others

4. believing that if you want something done well, you have to do it
   yourself

---

[19] Meyer Freedman and Ray H. Rosenman, *Type A Behavior and Your Heart* (New York:
Fawcett Crest Books, 1974).

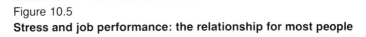

Figure 10.5
Stress and job performance: the relationship for most people

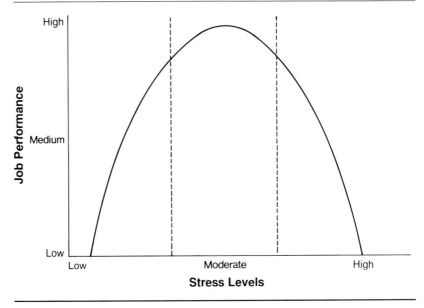

Some of the characteristics of Type A people.

5. gesticulating when you talk

6. making it a fetish of always being on time

7. using explosive speech patterns or frequent use of obscenities

8. playing nearly every game to win, even when playing against children

9. measuring your own and other's success in terms of numbers (number of articles written, patients seen, sales made, etc.)

10. becoming impatient when watching others do things you think you can do better or faster.[20]

Stress and productivity

As noted earlier, everyone needs some stress to get them going.[21] However, few people work well under high stress; this is especially true if the stress continues for an extended period of time. Figure 10.5 illustrates

---

[20] For more on this, see Jane E. Brody, "Study Suggests Changing Behavior May Prevent Heart Attack," *New York Times*, September 16, 1980, pp. C1; C3.

[21] Sandra L. Huber, "Managing Stress for Increased Productivity," *Supervisory Management*, December 1981, pp. 2–12.

this idea. For the average person a moderate amount of stress will bring about high performance. However, under high stress the individual begins to falter and fail. He or she is unable to cope with the extreme anxiety, tension, and nervousness that result.

Individuals facing this type of situation are often caught in what is called the *fight-versus-flight dilemma*. On one hand, they want to stay and fight the stress; on the other hand, they want to run away from it. In many instances, especially among up-and-coming managers, the decision is made to stay and fight. These people learn to live with the pressures and hope that their health will not fail as a result. Nor is it necessary to confine our attention exclusively to high-achieving managers to find individuals suffering the negative effects of stress. Personal life events can bring on the same results. Some of the most common of these include: the death of a spouse, a divorce, a jail term, marital separation, the assumption of a mortgage on a first house, and a change in eating habits. Some of the most serious business-related events that cause stress include: being fired, retiring from work, changing to a different line of work, trouble with the boss, and being moved to a new city by the company. All of these constitute what are called *life stressors*, which bring about tension and anxiety.

Personal and job-related events can cause stress.

Troubled employees, troubled managers

Stress is faced by both employees and managers, so the leader has two primary challenges. The first is being able to identify and help employees deal with their own stress-related problems. The second is being able to identify and deal with stress from a personal standpoint.[22]

The first of these challenges was addressed, in large part, when we discussed how to handle troubled employees. When workers are under stress, they manifest many of the symptoms of Type A people; they seem to be in a nervous hurry or they have withdrawn into themselves because the stress is too much for them. In either event, they need counseling.

Managerial stress is an even greater problem because many managers have learned to identify stress in others; they have not learned how to identify it in themselves. The result is that they push themselves too long and too hard. The eventual outcome is called **burnout**, a condition in which the manager is both mentally and physically exhausted. Levinson has provided an excellent example of managerial burnout.

Burnout can result.

A vice president of a large corporation did not receive an expected promotion so left that company to become the CEO of a smaller, family-owned business, which was floundering and needed his skills. Although he had jumped at the opportunity to rescue the small company, once

---

[22] Herbert Benson and Robert L. Allen, "How Much Stress Is Too Much?" *Harvard Business Review*, September–October 1980, pp. 86–92.

there he discovered an unimaginable morass of difficulties, among them continuous conflicts within the family owners. He felt he could not leave, but neither could he succeed. Trapped in a kind of psychological quicksand, he worked nights, days, and weekends for months trying to pull himself free. His wife protested to no avail. Finally, he was hospitalized for exhaustion.[23]

Learning to cope

How can leaders help their people cope with the negative aspects of stress? How can they, themselves, deal with these same problems? The first way is by learning to recognize its symptoms. This can be done by posing and answering stress and burnout-related questions such as those posed in the short quiz on stress, burnout and you.

Second, leaders must be willing to take these symptoms seriously. When someone begins to manifest signs of burnout, or they, themselves, feel they are working too hard and too fast, action must be taken that will slow the person down. Many times leaders let these symptoms go unaddressed, believing that they are only temporary; they won't last very long. The result is burnout.

Third, those suffering from excessive stress must learn to realign their goals. They are trying to do too much too fast. They have to reduce their objectives to a more realistic and attainable level. Here is where the leader must offer counseling to others and also be prepared to personally accept and follow such advice.

There are ways of effectively dealing with stress.

Fourth, if possible, the individual under stress should restructure his or her job so that some of the work which causes this stress is shifted to others or totally eliminated. The leader can be extremely important here in helping ensure that the employee's job is changed and made less stressful.

Fifth, those suffering from overwork should strive to keep themselves in a positive mental state. One of the most effective ways of doing so is by pampering oneself with small rewards, praising oneself for doing a good job, and telling oneself that it is all right to slow down and do less work.

Sixth, relaxation techniques should be considered. Many individuals find that by forcing themselves to take 15 minutes in the morning and again in the afternoon to do nothing but sit quietly in a chair with their eyes closed and their minds working to force their bodies to totally relax, they are able to overcome many job-created tensions. Others report that by getting involved in an active sport such as tennis, racquetball, or jogging, they are able to work out some of the stress that comes from the job.

---

[23] Harry Levinson, "When Executives Burn Out," *Harvard Business Review*, May–June 1981, p. 74.

Stress, burnout, and you

Read and answer each of the following as accurately as you can.
An interpretation is provided at the end of the chapter.

	Basically Yes	Basically No
1. Do you feel you are working harder but accomplishing less?	____	____
2. Have you lost your vim and vigor lately?	____	____
3. Is your job beginning to get you down?	____	____
4. Are you snapping at people a lot more lately?	____	____
5. Do you feel your job is taking you on a road to nowhere?	____	____
6. Is your temper getting shorter?	____	____
7. Do you have a lot of aches and pains, even though you have not been ill lately?	____	____
8. Is your job enthusiasm beginning to go downhill?	____	____
9. Do you find it is hard to laugh at a joke about yourself?	____	____
10. Are you more tired lately than you used to be?	____	____

Seventh, and finally, individuals suffering from stress and burnout need to view the fight against stress and burnout as a lifelong battle. It can never be totally won. The person must continually work to maintain a positive attitude toward self-development and self-improvement. In this way the individual not only develops antistress, antiburnout techniques but continues to use them every day.

Summary

The leader has a number of important roles to play. One of these is to represent and support the subordinates. In a manner of speaking, the individual must be a linking pin with the manager directly above. In this way the leader represents the people to his or her boss. The individual's job is also to provide supportive assistance to the subordinates.

A second important role of the leader is to develop teamwork. The three key factors in this process are the leader, the subordinates, and the environment. Each plays an important part, but of the three, the environment is often the most crucial.

A third important role of the leader is to counsel wisely. Counseling is discussing an emotional problem with an employee for the general objective of eliminating or decreasing it. Some of the major factors that cause an employee to need counseling are frustration, conflict, and stress. Counseling functions that the manager can use to help employees deal with their emotional problems include advice, reassurance, release of emotional tension, and reorientation.

A fourth important leadership role is that of using one's power properly. The most commonly cited kinds of power are reward, coercive, legitimate, referent, and expert. Use of each kind has benefits and drawbacks.

A fifth leadership role is the management of time. Since boss-imposed and system-imposed time demands usually cannot be reduced, it is up to the leader to manage self-imposed time well. Some of the ways of doing this are not letting the subordinate put the monkey on one's back, setting time priorities and delegating minor tasks, and developing a schedule for one's daily work time.

A sixth leadership style is that of managing stress. Many managers are Type A individuals characterized by a chronic, incessant struggle to achieve more and more in less and less time. Yet some stress is necessary if work is to be accomplished. The leader's primary concern should be that of identifying and dealing with the negative aspects of stress, from both a personal and employee standpoint, so that burnout does not result.

Having now discussed the fundamentals of leadership and the role of the leader, we turn to a final area of consideration—how the leader goes about evaluating and rewarding performance. This is the focus of attention in Chapter 11.

Key terms in the chapter

linking pin function
social exchange theory
counseling
frustration
conflict
stress
reward power
coercive power

legitimate power
referent power
expert power
boss-imposed time
system-imposed time
self-imposed time
Type A person
burnout

Review and study questions

1. One way of looking at a leader is as a linking pin. What is meant by this statement?

2. In what way can an understanding of social exchange theory be of value to a leader?

3. What is meant by *teamwork*? Put it in your own words.

4. There are three key factors in the development of teamwork: the leader, the subordinates, and the environment. What is meant by this statement?

5. Why do employees need counseling? Explain your answer.

6. What are some of the most commonly accepted counseling functions? Describe them.

7. How should a manager counsel a troubled employee? Describe at least five useful guidelines.

8. What do managers need to know about alcohol and drug-related employee problems? How should the individual go about dealing with these problems?

9. In your own words, define each of the following types of power: *reward*, *coercive*, *legitimate*, *referent*, and *expert*.

10. What are the three types of management time? Explain.

11. How can leaders manage their time well? Cite some principles of time management in your answer.

12. What is the relationship between stress and productivity?

13. How can a manager identify Type A people or those suffering burnout symptoms? Be complete in your answer.

14. How can leaders help their people cope with stress? How can they, themselves, learn to cope with them? Offer at least five practical steps.

Interpretation of are you a Type A or a Type B person?

Add up your total points for the A statements and the B statements.

If your total for A is:
80–100   You exhibit strong Type A behavior.
60–79   You exhibit moderate Type A behavior.

If your total for B is:
80–100   You exhibit strong Type B behavior.
60–79   You exhibit moderate Type B behavior.

Any other combination is a mixture of Type A and B behavior which does not exhibit a clear pattern.

Interpretation of stress, burnout, and you

If you answered basically yes to 8 or more of the questions, you may well be suffering from too much stress and be on the road to burnout. Should this be the case, think seriously about discussing the situation with your boss or changing to another line of work.

Hang in there

Ellen Marko has been in charge of Unit 8 for five months. In the beginning, it was difficult. Being the first female manager at the unit level put her under a great deal of stress. However, Ellen was determined to succeed—and she did. By the end of the third month, her unit's output was up 14 percent, and her boss told her how happy he was to have her in the department.

Ellen attributes much of her success to her ability to develop the unit into a cohesive team. Everyone does his or her work, helps out in a crisis, and tries to support the other members. In turn, Ellen has tried very hard to represent the group to her boss, pointing out how much they are working and how many of them would make excellent unit managers when openings occur. The boss has promised to keep her suggestions in mind.

In particular, Ellen believes that Gary Brandon has the leadership qualities necessary to be a very effective manager. However, she is not sure that Gary will remain with the company much longer. He seems to feel that promotions are slow in coming and that opportunities are better in other firms. Ellen has tried to persuade Gary to "hang in there" for two more months for a promotion before he seeks employment elsewhere. Gary has great regard for Ellen's opinion, and he seems willing to wait.

Questions

1. What accounts for the high level of teamwork in Ellen's department? Explain.
2. How should Ellen counsel Gary during the next few months? Which counseling function(s) should she perform?
3. What type of power does Ellen have over Gary? Explain, being sure to include in your answer the five types we discussed in this chapter.

Snowed under

"You must really be working Robert hard," Della said to Chris Masing. "It seems like the kids and I don't see much of him any more. Ever since he became department manager he leaves the house at 7:30 A.M. and doesn't get home before 6:00 P.M. Then he's usually got an attache case full of papers, and he works from after supper to around 10:00. Why, he's even been working on weekends lately!"

Chris listened to Della with great interest. Obviously, the company picnic was no time to go into the matter in detail. However, Della's husband had been promoted to department head six weeks earlier, and as Chris's newest manager he might be having some problems. Chris decided to talk to Robert first thing the next week.

The two men met for coffee at 10:30 Monday morning. After some small talk, the conversation turned to business. Chris gradually moved the discussion to Robert's workload.

Robert admitted, quite frankly, that there was a lot to do. "I've got so much work on my desk that I end up taking some of it home every night. I'm so snowed under, I'm even working on weekends."

Chris explained to Robert that he was working too hard. "You've got to delegate some of that stuff or you'll be snowed under indefinitely. Look, I want you to meet me again this afternoon at 2:30 with all the work that you still have to do."

Later that day, the two men sat down and put Robert's work into three categories: (1) should be delegated to others, (2) could be delegated to others, and (3) must be done personally. Fifty percent of the material went into the first category, thirty percent into the second, and twenty percent into the third. Chris then reviewed with Robert the various people in his department who could be assigned the work in the first two categories. The men agreed to meet again on Friday.

Robert explained on Friday that he had delegated three-quarters of the work he had been doing. Furthermore, he reported, the people in his department expressed a willingness to help. One of them told him, "I'm really glad you asked me to do this. When you started taking all the work home with you, I thought maybe you didn't trust us. Now I feel important and involved."

The next week, Della called Chris to thank him. "You really saved the day," she said. "Robert is excited about his job and we're seeing as much of him as we did before! Thanks for helping out."

Questions

1. What does this case illustrate about time management and the effective leader?

2. Why are the subordinates willing to accept the work Robert is delegating to them?

3. If the pressure gets too much for the people in Robert's department, what can he do to help alleviate it? Offer some recommendations for action.

Appraising and rewarding performance

11

Goals of the chapter

If a leader effectively carries out his or her role, the subordinates will be productive. However, there are two more functions, which we have not yet discussed, that the leader must perform—appraising performance and rewarding those who merit it. Without performance rewards, productive subordinates will slow their efforts; and without an adequate appraisal system, there is no sure way of knowing who should be rewarded. In carrying out these two tasks, the leader needs first to appraise performance and then to reinforce it with the proper rewards.

The first goal of this chapter is to examine the performance appraisal cycle. The second is to review five appraisal tools commonly used in employee evaluations. The third is to study some of the problems often associated with performance appraisal. The fourth is to look at some of the extrinsic and intrinsic rewards used in rewarding performance and to review the role of equity theory in this process. The final goal is to examine discipline and methods of employing it.

When you have finished reading this chapter you should be able to:

1. discuss the performance appraisal cycle
2. explain how graphic rating scales can be used in appraising performance
3. compare and contrast graphic rating scales with the paired comparison method of appraisal
4. describe how assessment centers and behaviorally anchored rating scales can be employed in appraising performance
5. explain how management by objectives can be used in performance appraisal and why this approach is so popular today

6. describe four of the major problems associated with performance appraisal

7. list the most common types of extrinsic and intrinsic rewards

8. discuss the role of equity in performance appraisal

9. examine the link between performance and rewards

10. list the types of discipline used when performance is inadequate

11. explain how the "red-hot stove rule" can be used in effectively employing discipline.

Appraising subordinates

Every effective organization wants to reward its best performers and ensure that they remain with the enterprise. How does one separate the best from the average or poor performers? The answer is through a well-designed performance appraisal process. If this process is carried out properly, and the employees realize that management intends to be equitable in its reward system, personnel morale will be high and teamwork can be both developed and nurtured by the enterprise.

So in essence, performance appraisal is more than a control process; it is a human relations tool which provides a basis for ensuring that everyone is treated fairly. Without such a process, it is quite difficult to reward performance on anything but a random basis. After all, how does management really know who deserves the most if it has no basis for evaluating contribution to organizational effort? Everything begins with the performance appraisal process.

In order to fully understand the performance appraisal process, we must examine three areas: (1) the performance appraisal cycle, which describes how the entire evaluation process should be conducted, (2) the appraisal tools that can be used in carrying out the evaluation, and (3) a knowledge of the problems that can accompany a performance appraisal and the ways to reduce or avoid them.

Performance appraisal cycle

Performance standards must be established.

Performance appraisal is a four-step process. First, there must be some *established performance standards* that specify what the worker is supposed to be doing. These standards are often quantified, i.e., the machinist is supposed to process 25 pieces an hour or the typist is expected to type an average of 60 words a minute. Such performance standards establish a basis against which to evaluate the individual.

Individual performance must be measured.

Second, there has to be a method of *determining individual performance*. To say "Barry does a good job" or "Kathleen is an asset to the department" is not a sufficient measure of individual results. The organization needs appraisal instruments that measure desired performance. In the case of the machinist, we would want to consult daily output records to see if his or her average is 25 pieces an hour; in the case of the typist

Figure 11.1
Performance appraisal in action

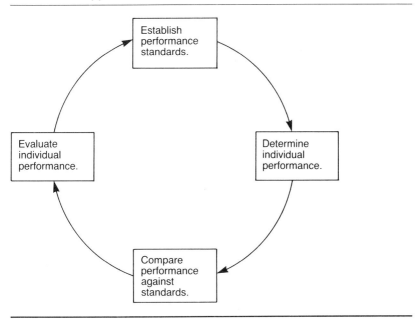

we would want to check the number of pages of material turned out in a typical day. Of course, appraisals will not be conducted on a daily basis, but if proper evaluation instruments are designed, output can be recorded periodically and can be evaluated later.

Third, there must be some *comparison of performance against standards.* At some point, usually once a year, the individual's work record should be compared with the standards set for the job.

Comparison of performance and standards must be made.

Fourth, an *evaluation of performance* should be made on the basis of the comparison. This process can take numerous forms. Sometimes the boss meets with the subordinate, reviews progress in general terms, and then announces the basic direction for the upcoming year. At other times, the manager has a detailed work report on the subordinate and is able to pinpoint strengths and weaknesses in great detail. In either case, this step is not finished before the manager has told the subordinate how well he or she is doing. The more definitive the manager is, the more useful the feedback will be in directing and motivating the subordinate. Once this fourth step is completed, the manager and the subordinate are ready to establish performance standards for the next evaluation period. Building on current successes (and sidestepping failures), the two can determine the department's needs and the subordinate's abilities and then work to mesh them. This overall performance appraisal cycle, presented in Figure 11.1, provides the primary basis for any evaluation program.

Evaluation of performance must be made.

Figure 11.2
Illustration of a graphic rating scale (partial form)

| Employee _____ | Date _____ |
| Department _____ | Rater _____ |

Rating \ Factor	1 Unsatisfactory Totally Inadequate	2 Fair Meets Minimal Requirements	3 Good Exceeds Minimal Requirements	4 Superior Always Does Above the Basic Job Requirements	5 Exceptional Is Consistently Outstanding
Quantity The Volume of Output Produced					
Quality The Accuracy and Thoroughness of the Output					
Supervision The Need for Direction, Correction, and/or Advice					
Attendance Dependability, Regularity, and Promptness					

Performance appraisal tools

Many kinds of appraisal tools can be used to evaluate employee performance. Five of the most common are graphic rating scales, the paired comparison method, assessment centers, behaviorally anchored rating scales, and management by objectives.

The graphic rating scale is the most widely used performance appraisal tool.

Graphic rating scales Graphic rating scales are the most widely used of all performance appraisal tools. One of the major reasons is undoubtedly the ease with which they can be developed and used. Figure 11.2 illustrates such a scale. In the chart the factors on which the employee is to be evaluated are identified and the degrees of evaluation are spelled out. The rater, usually the subordinate's boss, merely has to read each of the factors and then check the appropriate box. By totaling the value associated with every factor degree (i.e., from 1 for unsatisfactory up to 5 for exceptional), the rater can obtain a total score for the subordinate.

Paired comparison method is more discriminating in its approach.

Paired comparison method The paired comparison method is regarded by many managers as superior to the graphic rating scale because it is more discriminating in its approach. Rather than just giving a person an overall evaluation, in which each might end up receiving an excep-

Figure 11.3
The paired comparison method for rating employees on work quantity and quality

On the Basis of Work Quantity

As Compared to:	Personnel Being Rated				
	Anderson	Brown	Carpenter	Davis	Evans
Anderson		−	+	−	+
Brown	+		+	+	+
Carpenter	−	−		−	+
Davis	+	−	+		+
Evans	−	−	−	−	

Evans has the highest ranking for work quantity.

On the Basis of Work Quality

As Compared to:	Personnel Being Rated				
	Anderson	Brown	Carpenter	Davis	Evans
Anderson		−	+	+	+
Brown	+		+	+	+
Carpenter	−	−		+	+
Davis	−	−	−		−
Evans	−	−	+	+	

Davis has the highest ranking for work quality.

Note: A plus (+) indicates higher than, and a minus (−) indicates lower than. The individual with the greatest number of pluses is the one with the highest ranking.

tional score on all factors, this method compares each employee to every other one in the group (Figure 11.3). In this way, while everyone may be doing good work, it is still possible to determine who is best and who is poorest. It is no longer a matter of whether or not the person is doing fair or good work, but how the individual compares with all the other workers. In Figure 11.3 there are a number of different factors (in this case, quality and quantity) that can be measured; the rater may end up with five to ten paired comparison forms before compiling the scores and getting an overall evaluation for each employee. Regardless of the number of factors rated, however, only one person ranks at the top of the list when all the ratings are completed.

In recent years many organizations have turned to paired comparison rating because it relieves the pressures on the manager to give each subordinate a good rating. Now the manager has to decide who is first in the group and who is last. The American military began moving in this direction when it became obvious that commanding officers were giving all their men high ratings because low ratings were bad for their military careers. With paired comparison ratings, this is no longer possible.

Many universities are also beginning to follow this trend. With enrollments slowing up and funds for salaries hardly keeping pace with inflation, departmental chairpeople are being asked to rate their people in paired comparison terms and then to recommend the top half or top third to the dean for merit raises. As a result, the entire faculty may get an across-the-board raise of 3 percent, and those on the merit list may get an average of 3 percent more.

Assessment centers   During the last 10 years, the assessment center has become a popular form of performance appraisal. Unlike most other appraisal techniques, the assessment center focuses more on evaluating employee long-range potential than on just short-range evaluation. For this reason, it is a very useful tool for identifying managers with potential for assuming higher-level positions.

Assessment centers are currently used by many well-known organizations including IBM, GE, Merrill Lynch, J.C. Penney, and the FBI. The approach is basically the same regardless of the enterprise. It consists of six fundamental steps:

1. A series of assessment techniques are used. At least one of these must be a simulation or exercise in which the applicants are required to use behaviors related to dimensions of performance on the job. This simulation may be a group exercise, fact-finding exercise, interview simulation, etc.

2. A number of assessors must be used. These people must have had thorough training so they know exactly what to look for in the applicants.

3. The final decision regarding what to do (hire, promote, etc.) must be a result of a group decision by the assessors.

4. The simulation exercises that are used must have been developed to tap a variety of predetermined behaviors, and have been pretested prior to use to ensure that they provide reliable, objective, and relevant behavioral information.

5. The techniques used in the assessment center must be designed to provide information that can be used in evaluating the dimensions, attributes, or qualities previously determined.

6. The assessment by the evaluators must be made after the exercises are completed, not during the exercises.[1]

On the positive side, a number of organizations have reported great success from their assessment centers. At IBM, for example, 1,086 non-management employees were classified as having either potential for successful assignment beyond the first-level management or having no potential beyond this level. Of those assessed as having such potential, 20 percent achieved second-level positions. Conversely, only 10 percent of those rated first-level were promoted beyond this level. Additionally, 20 percent of those promoted against the prediction were eventually demoted in contrast to only 9 percent of those who were promoted in accordance with the prediction.[2]

On the other hand, there is some concern about the fact that most of the validation studies to date have been restricted to large business organizations. A second concern is that unless the organization knows how to carry out an assessment center, the evaluators may not really know what they are doing or why they are doing it. A third area of concern is whether these assessment centers can be defended in a court of law. In one recent case, an assessment center was used to select the deputy police chief of a large Midwestern city. While the judge upheld the validity of the process, he questioned some of the methods used.

Behaviorally anchored ratings scales In recent years a new appraisal method, known as behaviorally anchored rating scales (BARS), has been developed. Advocates of this appraisal method claim that it provides more detailed and equitable evaluations than anything else available in the field.[3] As we have just seen, the graphic rating scale requires the organization to develop a series of factors and degrees for each, and the paired comparison requires the identification of factors and the comparison of each person in the group against every other on the basis of these factors. BARS uses a different approach, usually consisting of five steps:[4]

[1]"When Is an Assessment Center Really an Assessment Center?" *Training/HRD*, March 1980, p. 24.

[2]Ron Zemke, "Using Assessment Centers to Measure Management Potential," *Training/HRD*, March 1980, p. 30.

[3]Cheedle W. Millard, Fred Luthans, and Robert L. Otteman, "A New Breakthrough for Performance Appraisal," *Business Horizons*, August 1976, pp. 66–73.

[4]Donald P. Schwab, Herbert G. Heneman III, and Thomas A. DeCotiis, "Behaviorally Anchored Rating Scales: A Review of the Literature," *Personnel Psychology*, Winter 1975, pp. 549–562.

1. People who have knowledge of the job(s) to be appraised are asked to develop specific illustrations of effective and ineffective behavior. These critical incidents serve as a foundation for the rest of the development of the appraisal form.

2. The people are then asked to cluster these incidents into smaller sets, usually of five to ten, of performance dimensions. Each of these clusters or dimensions is then defined. Illustrations of common clusters include: knowledge and judgment, operating skill, and conscientiousness.

BARS consists of five steps.

3. Another group of people who are familiar with these jobs is then given the cluster definitions and critical incidents, and asked to review and, where necessary, reassign each incident to the proper cluster, i.e., critical incidents associated with knowledge and judgment are put in one group, while critical incidents associated with operating skill are placed in another.

4. Then the second group is asked to rank the critical incident behaviors on a seven-to-nine point scale, with the value of one or two given to ineffective behavior up to seven or nine for highly effective behavior. At this point only those critical incidents which best describe effective and ineffective behavior are used.

5. The overall instrument is then constructed and used to evaluate the personnel.

Figure 11.4 is an example of a behaviorally anchored rating scale for an employment interview. Note that the performance criterion in this case is knowledge and judgment. This, of course, is only one of many that would be developed for the interviewer's job. Others would generally include job involvement, interpersonal relationships, and adaptability. As also can be seen in Figure 11.4, there is a scale for rating performance from 1 to 9. The scale is "behaviorally anchored" in that the critical incidents specify what is meant by effective and ineffective behavior.

Critics of the BARS approach point to some obvious shortcomings. First, the process can be very time consuming and expensive. Many things have to be done. A rating scale for quite a few performance criteria, such as knowledge and judgment, job involvement, interpersonal relationships, and adaptability, must be constructed. Then the rater has to evaluate each individual on each of these scales. Finally, an overall evaluation must be determined. The process may take as much as 30 to 60 minutes per employee, compared with 5 to 10 minutes for the graphic rating scale.

Disadvantages of BARS.

However, the BARS approach has a number of advantages. First, the standards of measurement are clear. The rater should have no trouble distinguishing between poor, average, good, and outstanding performance. Second, the instrument is put together by individuals who know the job and the requirements, so the evaluation form tends to be highly valid and reliable. Third, by putting together a series of five or six performance di-

Advantages of BARS.

Figure 11.4
Behaviorally anchored rating scale (partial form)

Knowledge and Judgment = familiarity, understanding, and application of information needed to meet employment needs of applicant and/or employers.

Employment interviewers and claims deputies must possess and apply job knowledge in order to perform their jobs. Some understand thoroughly the many policies and procedures, application files, and labor market information. Others do not seem to understand and to apply even what should be common knowledge about their jobs and why certain things are done.

Actions indicate possession of knowledge and judgment needed to anticipate, select, and perform appropriate employment services to meet the basic employment needs of all applicants for common job openings and of those applicants requiring special services.	— 9	You can expect this interviewer to use knowledge of labor market, jobs, and employers to perform Job Development, thereby placing applicants with special problems.
	8	Could be expected to give applicant needing guidance a summary of local labor market, suggestions for applicant to pursue, and to perform Job Development contacts.
	7	Would expect this interviewer to discuss fair labor practices legislation with an employer and explain other services the office can render.
Actions indicate possession of knowledge and judgment normally needed to select and perform appropriate services to meet the basic employment needs of applicants for common job openings.	6	This interviewer can be expected to talk with a complaining employer about present job situation, the number of job orders on file, and applicant shortages.
	— 5	Could be expected to tell an employer wanting to pay women less than men for the same work that such a request violated sex discrimination laws.
	4	Could be expected to place an unskilled applicant without recognizing need for job counseling.
	3	Could be expected often to depend on supervisor to make his/her routine decisions.
Actions do not demonstrate possession of the knowledge and judgment needed to perform appropriate employment services to meet even the basic employment needs for common job openings.	2	In order to take a break, this interviewer can be expected to stop placement activities with clients in line.
	—1	This interviewer could be expected to release confidential information to the applicant concerning applicant's release from previous job.

From Cheedle W. Millard, *The Development and Evaluation of Behavioral Criteria for Measuring the Performance of Non-Operational Employees*, Ph.D. Dissertation, University of Nebraska, 1974, p. 185.

mensions (knowledge and judgment, job involvement, and so on), the rater has a much better idea of what is being rated. This is superior to a scale on which he or she is working with just one or two factors (such as concern for work and ability to work well with fellow employees) that are so encompassing that it may be impossible to appraise the employee objectively. Finally, having five to six performance dimensions makes it much easier to point out to people where they have not performed well and how they can improve in the future.

MBO is an overall appraisal system.

Management by objectives   Management by objectives (MBO) is an overall appraisal system used at all levels of the hierarchy.[5] Many organizations prefer MBO because it is systematic, all-encompassing, and easy to understand. Because of its great popularity, we shall study it in much greater depth than the other appraisal tools. Before doing so, however, let us define the term. *Management by objectives* is a process in which the superior and the subordinate jointly identify common goals, define the subordinate's major areas of responsibility in terms of expected results, and use these measures as guides for operating the unit and assessing the contribution of each member.

How MBO works.   There are six basic steps in the MBO process. Figure 11.5 illustrates the typical cycle employed in implementing it.

First, the manager identifies the goals that his or her unit should pursue over the next evaluation period. These goals can often be expressed in terms of profit, revenues, margins, competitive position, or employee relations.

Second, the individual has to describe the organization clearly. Who is in the department? What does each person do? Having answered these questions, the manager then reviews each individual's past work, noting what can be expected of the person.

There are six steps in MBO.

Third, the superior sets objectives for the next evaluation period for the workers individually. This is done by: (1) asking each subordinate to list those objectives he or she has in mind for the next year and setting a date for discussing them, (2) making a personal list of objectives one would like to see the subordinate attain, (3) reviewing both lists and then jointly agreeing on a final set of objectives for the subordinate, (4) having two copies of the final draft of objectives typed, one for the superior and one for the subordinate, and (5) making oneself available to help the subordinate accomplish the assigned goals.

Fourth, an annual goal-setting worksheet is designed to help the subordinate reach these objectives. Figure 11.6 is an example. As can be seen in the figure, the worksheet is divided into three parts: (1) objec-

---

[5] George S. Odiorne, *Management by Objectives* (New York: Pitman Publishing Corporation, 1965).

Figure 11.5
The basic MBO cycle

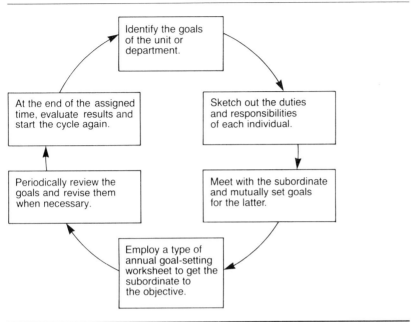

tives, (2) major steps planned for achieving the objectives, and (3) way in which progress is to be determined in evaluating performance; in short, what is to be done, how it will be accomplished, and what way(s) will be used to show how well it is being accomplished.

Fifth, during the year each subordinate's goals are checked to see if the milestones or objectives are being reached. In particular, the manager needs to know how closely the person is coming to attaining these targets, whether any of the goals need to be amended, and what kinds of assistance the person requires to reach the goals.

Sixth, results are measured against goals. Near the end of the MBO cycle, which commonly coincides with the budget year, the superior asks each subordinate to prepare a brief statement of performance. Then the two meet to review how well the subordinate has done and to establish objectives for the next budget year.

Why MBO is so popular. MBO has proved a very popular approach because it is both comprehensive and easy to understand. One of its primary advantages is the attention given to the subordinate in the goal-setting process. Rather than telling the individual what goals he or she should pursue, there is now a give-and-take process in which the subordinate has the opportunity to participate.

The subordinate participates.

Figure 11.6
An annual goal-setting worksheet (partial form)

NAME Hal Lymer	DATE January 1, 1982
POSITION Superintendent of Engine Manufacturing	SUPERVISOR Les Rodgers

Objectives	Major Steps for Achieving Planned Objectives	The Way in Which Progress Will Be Evaluated
Increase the number of production hours in the engine departments from 30,000 to 40,000.	Conduct methods study of the bottleneck operations in engine assembly and make necessary changes. Reduce machining time on the planer type mill by employing an assistant operator during peak periods. Add 3 floating foremen to give round-the-clock supervision to the bottleneck operations.	Progress will be measured in terms of shipments reported on the monthly cost control report.
Reduce supervisory overtime by cross-training foremen.	Cross-train foremen in the large machine, small machine, and engine assembly departments. Determine how general foremen can be used as substitutes for foremen and assistant foremen. Use these general foremen on at least 4 Sundays per calendar quarter.	In the first 6 months of last year foremen and assistant foremen in engine manufacturing worked an average of 20 of 26 Sundays. The target for the first 6 months of this year is to reduce this to no more than 15 of 26 Sundays.
Reduce scrap cost from 4 percent to 3 percent of production.	In conjunction with the quality assurance manager conduct a study to identify the specific causes of scrap losses. Determine ways to measure scrap and rework costs by shift. Put together a task force for determining alternative ways to reduce this scrap. Develop an incentive plan for rewarding the shift with the best scrap record. Determine the feasibility of disciplining employees who cause major scrap losses.	Measure progress in terms of scrap and rework costs reported on the monthly cost control report.

Another advantage of this approach is that MBO places a strong emphasis on quantifiable objectives that are tied to a time dimension. For example, performance standards are stated in specific, measurable terms such as percentages, dollars, ratios, costs, and quality. If a manager is going to reduce tardiness, this goal will be stated in a percentage: "We will cut tardiness by 18 percent." In addition, a period will be set for the attainment of the objective. Expanding the above statement, then, we can bring together the quantifiable goal and the time dimension in this way: "We will cut tardiness by 18 percent within the first 6 months of the upcoming fiscal year." Objectives for other major areas of organizational performance might be:

Objectives are quantifiable and tied to a time dimension.

Raise return on investment to 15 percent within the next four operating quarters.

Complete the management control reporting system for all operating decisions by December 31.

Install the new computerized information system by April 30.

Note that each objective is written in such a way that what is to be attained (the goal) and when it is to be attained (the time dimension) are clearly stated.

A third advantage of MBO is that there is a concentration on the organization's key objectives. Each manager ties his or her unit's objectives to those of the organization at large. As a result, all units are working in the same direction.

There is concentration on key objectives.

In the MBO approach, emphasis is given to working with a small, manageable number of objectives. Goals assigned to each person are usually limited to five or six. These are the key goals that must be accomplished if the manager is to be effective. Condensing all the individual's targets into a handful of goals makes it easier for the person to channel his or her energies toward goal accomplishment and for the superior to monitor progress and to review performance.

Consideration is limited to 5 or 6 goals.

MBO helps coordinate the activities of the units by linking each with those above, below, and on the same level. For example, Mary is in charge of Department B. When she meets with her boss, Ted, who is in charge of a group of departments, to determine objectives for her, Ted integrates her objectives with his own. He will do the same for the other Departments, A and C, which report to him as does Mary for Departments D, E, and F, which report to her. We can diagram the process as in Figure 11.7.

MBO helps link the organization together.

Another advantage of MBO is that it encourages the manager to delegate time-consuming activities and to devote his or her energies to overall planning and control. With MBO the manager knows what everyone is supposed to be doing. The initial delegation of authority is very systematic. Additionally, MBO helps the manager to evaluate the subordinates and to learn in the process what each can do well and what each

It encourages the manager to delegate time-consuming activities.

Figure 11.7
MBO helps coordinate departmental objectives

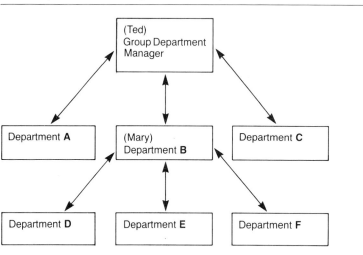

does poorly. With this information, the manager can then determine what work to delegate to each subordinate in the future. Who does Job A well? Who is best assigned to Job B? Who is the best performer on Job C? In delegating these tasks, the manager is able to pass off much of the busy-work he or she has performed in the past because now the manager knows the strength of the subordinates better. Additionally, the manager's boss will encourage such delegation. One of the primary benefits of MBO is its philosophy of delegating busy-work and concentrating one's time on "think-work." An effective top manager will not let the subordinate manager delegate work that should be handled personally while hanging onto time-consuming activities.

Overall, MBO has been well accepted in many modern organizations. In particular managers like its systematic approach and the emphasis it gives to the key managerial functions of planning, organizing, and controlling. In both public and private sectors, it holds a great deal of promise for the future.[6]

Comparison of appraisal techniques

Which of these five appraisal techniques is the best one to use? The answer depends on what the organization is looking for. Examples include a low-cost appraisal instrument, one that is easy to use, one that is of value

[6]Jack N. Kondrasuk, "Studies in MBO Effectiveness," *Academy of Management Review*, July 1981, pp. 419–430.

Table 11.1
Advantages and disadvantages of selected performance appraisal techniques

Dimension	Graphic Rating Scale	Paired Comparison	BARS	Assessment Center	MBO
Amount of time required to develop the appraisal tool	Low	Low	High	High	High
Cost of developing the appraisal tool	Low	Low	High	High	Medium
Acceptability of the technique to superiors	Low	Low	High	High	High
Acceptability of the technique to subordinates	Low	Low	High	High	High
Potential for rating errors	High	High	Low	Low	Low
Usefulness for counseling employees	Poor	Poor	Good	Good	Good
Value for allocating rewards	Poor	Poor	Good	Fair	Good
Value for identifying those who are most promotable	Poor	Poor	Fair	Good	Fair

in allocating rewards, one of use in identifying potentially promotable managers, and so on. Table 11.1 provides such a comparison.

A close look at the table shows that management usually gets what it pays for. The easier it is to develop the appraisal technique and the lower the costs involved, the higher the potential for rating errors. If management wants to increase the overall effectiveness of its evaluation process, it must be prepared to invest the time and money needed to develop a valid and reliable instrument. If it does not, several types of problems can result.

Performance appraisal problems

Performance appraisal helps the manager identify those who should be rewarded for adequate or superior performance and those who should not. However, such an approach can yield erroneous results if the appraisal form is improperly designed or the rater is biased.[7]

[7]Ann M. Morrison and Mary Ellen Kranz, "The Shape of Performance Appraisal in the Coming Decade," *Personnel*, July–August 1981, pp. 12–22.

Raters must fully understand all the factors.

Clarity of the appraisal form   One of the most common appraisal problems relates to clarity of the form. If every rater does not have an identical interpretation of what the factors and their degrees mean, uniformity is impossible. In Figure 11.2, for example, quantity, quality, supervision, and attendance are briefly defined. So, too, are the degrees of each. But how does the rater determine when a person should get a rating of fair and when he or she should be rated good? Unless the factors are defined and this information is made available to the evaluator, an employee might be rated fair by one manager and good by another. The situation is even worse if the factors or their degrees are not described at all. If each manager is using only his or her own judgment and interpretation, performance evaluations will not be uniform throughout the organization.

To overcome this problem it is necessary to describe on the evaluation form the factors and degrees on which the employee will be evaluated and to ensure that the raters have a uniform interpretation. When is an individual's performance to be considered good? When is it to be rated superior? Many organizations find it very helpful to have all the people who are rating one group of employees, such as salespeople, meet, discuss the evaluation form, and determine the ground rules for the appraisal. In this way, all employees doing similar work can be rated in uniform terms.

The halo effect can bias the rating.

The halo effect   A *halo effect* occurs when the appraiser gives workers the same rating on all factors, regardless of actual performance. For example, the manager has noticed that Paul is occasionally late for work. The manager believes that Paul does not care much for his job, and this impression carries over to the manager's rating of Paul. Regardless of how much work Paul does or how high the quality of the work output is, he continually receives a fair rating. Conversely, Mandy is always on time for work and has a very pleasant personality. This biases the manager's rating of her, and she always is rated excellent in all categories. Many firms find that a training program can alleviate this problem by helping the manager identify these built-in biases and work to correct them.

So can central tendency.

Central tendency   A second common rater-generated problem is that of *central tendency*, in which everyone receives an average rating, regardless of how effective he or she has been. For example, Andy is one of the department's poorest workers and Karl is one of the best. However, their performance ratings are always identical. The manager continually rates both as good. Such an approach helps Andy, who should be given a rating of fair, but it punishes Karl, who should be given a rating of superior.

One of the greatest problems faced by managers who rate their people this way is that the best workers begin looking for new jobs. After all, their chances for increased salary or promotion ranks are being severely limited. Another problem is that the evaluations are now useless.

The organization cannot rely on them to identify those who should be advanced and those who should be terminated. One way of overcoming this problem is to use a paired comparison evaluation or an MBO approach in which expected results are quantified or described in such terms that when they are accomplished the manager is literally required to give the person a higher rating.

Leniency   A third common rater-generated problem is that of *leniency*; some managers give all their people the highest possible rating. Here again, failure to distinguish between those doing an outstanding job and those doing a poor one results in inaccurate ratings. Many organizations in recent years have worked around this problem through use of a paired comparison evaluation.

And leniency.

Dealing with appraisal problems   The problems we have identified in this section are caused by either the rating form or the rater. By investigating the various advantages and disadvantages of each rating approach, an organization can determine which one best meets its needs. Additionally, training the raters in how to use the form can eliminate many bias problems.

Remember, two major issues must be dealt with in performance appraisal: validity and reliability. By *validity* we mean that the instrument measures what we want it to measure. If work quantity is important, then this factor should be on the rating form. If cooperation with others is of no value because the individual works alone, it should not appear on the form. By *reliability* we mean that the instrument measures the same thing over and over. If we are interested in work quality but not work quantity, we want to be sure that the raters understand this. Otherwise, the way a person is rated by two managers might differ.

Validity and reliability must both be present.

A good example of validity and reliability problems is provided by the typical true or false or multiple-choice test given in college. Since all the students are taking the same test, there is reliability. The instrument is continually measuring the students' knowledge of certain material. However, if the test has not been designed properly, a large number of questions may not really measure a student's command of the subject. Some questions may be trivial, some may be ambiguous, and some may be based on information not contained in the text. There is no validity. Some behavioral scientists have pointed out that it is much easier to obtain reliability in testing than to obtain validity. In the future, people constructing tests for the purpose of measuring knowledge will have to address the issue of validity.[8]

---

[8] Fred Luthans, *Organizational Behavior*, 3rd ed. (New York: McGraw-Hill Book Company, 1981), pp. 587–590.

Rewarding performance

The manager is in a position to reward (or not reward) a subordinate on the basis of the performance appraisal. In determining the type and degree of reward to give, it is necessary to examine three important areas: (1) extrinsic and intrinsic rewards, (2) equity theory, and (3) discipline. The first two areas are discussed in Chapter 2, but here we want to apply them directly to performance rewards. Discipline is important because sometimes the manager has to give out negative rewards.

Extrinsic and intrinsic rewards

Extrinsic rewards are external and physical, taking such forms as money, increased fringe benefits, and use of a company car. *Intrinsic rewards* are internal and psychological, taking such forms as a feeling of accomplishment, increased responsibility, and the opportunity to achieve.

Money is both an extrinsic and an intrinsic reward. In and of itself, money is extrinsic, but with it often come psychological rewards, such as esteem ("I'm important; look how much the organization is paying me"), a feeling of accomplishment ("Well, I did it: I finally made $75,000 in one year"), and a sense of achievement ("I'm good at what I do; a real achiever, that's why I'm being paid so much").

The right mix of extrinsic and intrinsic motivators must be used.

The effective leader realizes that a mixture of extrinsic and intrinsic rewards is needed. What mix will be best? This depends on the subordinate, and to be more definitive in our answer, we must apply expectancy theory to the specific situation.

Remember that expectancy theory is: Motivational force = Valence × Expectancy. Valence is the individual's preference for an outcome; for example, John may prefer a $100-a-week raise to a company car. Expectancy is the perceived probability that a particular act will be followed by a particular outcome; if John has the highest sales in the region he will be given a one-week, all-expenses paid trip to San Francisco. Knowing a person's valence and expectancy is no easy task. However, effective leaders understand their people and soon learn to know what rewards will motivate them.

Maureen Wilson is the head of advertising for a large cosmetics firm. Maureen is making more than $100,000 a year in salary and 50 percent more in bonuses tied directly to sales. The more effective the advertising program, the more likely that sales, and her bonus, will rise.

Realizing that money will not motivate Maureen very much, her boss has scheduled her to go to sales meetings in London, Paris, and Rome during the next month. The boss knows that Maureen likes to travel and that her husband, who owns a successful retail store, can get away any time he wants. The two of them can spend three weeks in Europe and the cosmetics firm will pay most of their expenses. Next year Maureen will be going to the Far East.

It is obvious that Maureen's boss knows how to motivate her. The reward schedule is designed to meet Maureen's specific needs. The boss gave her a combination of extrinsic and intrinsic rewards. The free travel saved her the cost of going to Europe on her own (her income tax bracket is very high, so if the cost of her trip were $6,000, she would have to make around $12,000 to have this amount after taxes) and also shows her how much the firm appreciates her talents.

On the other hand, some people want extrinsic rewards and are little influenced by psychological payoffs. This is especially true for people just starting their careers and raising a family at the same time.

Tony Farino is a middle manager in a manufacturing plant. He is married and has three children. He bought a house for $60,000, and his car is two years old. Tony's salary is $22,500, but with overtime, including Saturday and occasionally Sunday work, he can gross $30,000. Last month there was an opening for a manager in the purchasing department. This department has had more than its share of problems. The company's sales are growing so quickly that the department is in a constant state of turmoil trying to check on orders, verify deliveries, and see that suppliers are paid promptly.

When the department manager resigned, Tony was offered the job. The salary was $30,000 with the opportunity of making another 25 percent through overtime. Tony accepted and so far has been very happy. Although he is working harder than ever before, he feels that the higher pay more than compensates. Also, with the increased salary, he and his wife are planning to take the family on a week's vacation, something that would have been impossible with his former salary. Tony realizes that he is working long hours and not seeing very much of his family, but he feels that within 12 to 18 months, things will turn around. The car will be paid for, and the cost-of-living increase that management gives the employees will raise his salary enough to ease the burden of the house payments. Then he will be able to relax and spend more time with the children. For the time being, however, he is willing to sacrifice his leisure time for increased extrinsic rewards.

In both our illustrations, the manager knows how to motivate the subordinate, offering each what he or she wants. Involved in the two cases was the issue of equity, something that merits closer attention than we have yet given to it.

Equity theory

Equity theory relates most heavily to extrinsic rewards, especially money. The essence of equity theory is that people will compare their work/reward ratio to those of others in deciding whether they are being properly rewarded. Figure 11.8 is an illustration. If Martha is receiving the same rewards from the organization as Alfred but feels she is working longer hours, has more job experience, and puts out greater effort, she will be dissatisfied. She must feel that her input is fairly rewarded in comparison with Alfred's.

In addressing the equity issues, many leaders do more than merely

People compare their work/reward ratios.

Figure 11.8
Equity comparisons

Martha	Alfred
hours worked, job experience, effort	hours worked, job experience, effort
rewards given by the organization	rewards given by the organization

reward good performance. They also let their people know that those with less performance will not be given the same rewards. However, if the manager is lying and the subordinates discover that poor performers are getting the same reward, they will no longer trust the manager. Sometimes, the leader cannot tie rewards to performance, and he or she should make this clear. Many subordinates will be unhappy about it, but it is better to be truthful. If the organization does not give the highest rewards for the greatest performance, high producers will either slow down or seek employment with organizations that do reward high performance.

Keep one thing in mind: not all organizations reward superior performance. Many, especially in the public sector, demand a minimum degree of output but do not give rewards for superior productivity. The organizations do not have to be equitable in giving rewards; they simply accept less than maximum effort from the personnel. For many people, however, equity is an important issue, especially on an intraorganizational basis. Davis puts it this way:

> For most employees, equity comparisons within their organization tend to be more important than comparisons in the external community. Pay becomes a symbolic scorecard by which employees compare themselves with others. Since people tend to have high opinions of themselves, they often find it rather easy to conclude that pay inequities exist. One nationwide United States study of workers reported that approximately 50 percent felt that they received "less than they deserved compared to persons in other occupations."
> Even inequity in psychological rewards may affect employee demands for money. If there is a lack of psychological rewards, and employees feel that more cannot be secured, they may instead ask for more money. What they are trying to do is equalize perceived unfair provisions of their psychological contract.[9]

Linking performance and rewards

One of the most important questions in modern compensation theory is: how closely should performance and rewards be linked? From a human relations standpoint, this question relates less to the specific types of re-

---

[9] Keith Davis, *Human Behavior at Work: Organizational Behavior*, 6th ed. (New York: McGraw-Hill Book Company, 1981), p. 456.

"It's for the big shots in the front office. The tax cut has only minimal effect on those in their bracket."

Drawing by Bruce Cochran, Changing Times, April 1978.

wards that can be given than it does to the reward system itself. The system can offer three types of rewards: wages, incentive programs, and benefit programs.

Wages, incentive programs, and benefit programs Wages are agreed upon or fixed rates of pay. For an hourly employee making $6 an hour, we need merely multiply the number of hours worked by $6 to determine the person's pay for the time period under consideration. Most people, however, do not work for an hourly wage; they are salaried. Managerial personnel, in particular, are paid an annual amount, such as $26,000 a year. This salary is then broken down by pay period, i.e., $500 a week before taxes and other deductions.

Some organizations also have wage incentive programs. When offered on an individual basis, they typically take the form of production or sales incentive plans. In a production incentive plan, a worker is paid a higher rate for producing output over and above an established level. For example, a firm might pay $1 per manufactured piece per week up to 200 and $1.25 for any output in excess of 200. In a sales incentive plan, the salesperson's pay is tied to sales dollars generated. Quite often the individual receives a guaranteed draw, such as $50 a week, and a percentage of sales, such as 5 percent of all receipts generated.

There are individual incentive plans.

Table 11.2

A comparison of individual, group, and organization-wide incentives

Individual Incentive Plans	Group and Organization-Wide Incentives
Typical Characteristics of the Plan	
Rewards are based directly on what the individual produces.	Rewards are based on group performance.
Performance is determined by the individual worker.	A committee typically determines performance standards.
Rewards are provided every payday.	Performance is only indirectly controlled by employees.
Individuality and competitive spirit are encouraged.	Rewards are paid on a monthly, quarterly, semiannual, or annual basis.
The incentive relies heavily on monetary rewards.	Teamwork and unity are encouraged.
Commonly Cited Advantages	
There is a strong sense of individualism.	The incentive motivates a large number of employees.
Rewards are in direct proportion to output.	The approach can be used on a wide variety of tasks.
	All employees in the organization can be included.
	Group cooperation is encouraged.
Commonly Cited Disadvantages	
Seldom are all of the employees included in the plan.	Employees are not all rewarded according to their own productivity.
This incentive tends to be restricted to mass-produced and relatively simple operations.	Individual initiative and effort are often discouraged.
The incentive cannot be easily adapted to high-quality jobs.	
Employee grievances are a continual headache.	

Group incentive plans.

Group incentive programs can also be found in some organizations. In these cases the program is similar to the individual incentive plan. For example, the production output of the group, or the sales of the unit, are combined in determining how much of an incentive has been earned by these employees.

And organization-wide incentive plans.

Some organizations have found they can save money by instituting an organization-wide incentive program. In this case, everyone in the enterprise participates. The logic is simple. Management believes that with a joint worker-management effort increased efficiency and cost savings can be effected. Table 11.2 provides a comparison of these three different types of incentive plans.

As well as benefit programs.

Benefit programs also come in many different versions. Some of the most common include life, health, and accident insurance, sick leave, workers compensation, pension plans, and unemployment insurance. An

increasing number of organizations are also making use of "cafeteria benefits" in which each worker can pick and choose the benefits he or she
wants within a dollar limit established by the firm. This allows people to
tailor the benefit package to meet their own particular needs.

Causal link?   For the most part, managers have very little control
over how performance and rewards are to be linked, except that they
may be able to give the poorest performers only a 3 percent raise while
the best workers get 8 percent. However, if there is a union or if management is reluctant to stand up to the pressures created by those who
would receive very small raises, the difference between the largest and
smallest raises will be minimal. Of course the best performers will quit
and go elsewhere, but management may be willing to accept this loss. In
fact, this is why many organizations like pay secrecy: no one knows what
the other person is making, and this effectively reduces pay-related complaints. Can pay and performance ever be closely linked and open salaries
promoted? Cascio and Awad feel that it can but argue that this should be
done only when the following four conditions are present:

1. Individual performance can be measured objectively.

2. There is a low degree of interdependence among the individuals in
   the system.

3. It is possible to develop measures for all the important aspects of
   the jobs.

4. Effort and performance are closely related over a relatively short
   time span.[10]

*Conditions for
directly linking
rewards and
performance.*

Since these four conditions seldom exist, the pay-performance linkage is often less than ideal. This is why the manager must rely heavily on
creating an *environment* in which workers can attain psychological rewards. Given this fact, one might ask: why then do organizations want
effective performance evaluation systems? There are two reasons. First,
these appraisal systems help identify those who are not doing their job
properly, and management can follow up and have these people either
retrained or dismissed. Second, in many cases the organization wants to
promote from within and will choose those employees who are highly
qualified in their current jobs as potential candidates.

Discipline

Sometimes, instead of giving rewards to employees, it becomes necessary
for the leader to discipline some of the people. Often this is referred to as
a *negative reward*. For purposes of human relations, the two most impor-

---

[10] Wayne F. Cascio and Elias M. Awad, *Human Resources Management: An Information
Systems Approach* (Reston, Va.: Reston Publishing Company, Inc., 1981), p. 392.

tant areas of discipline are: (1) the types of discipline, and (2) the way in which discipline should be administered.

Types of discipline   Most formal disciplinary processes employ what is called *progressive discipline*, beginning with an oral warning and, if things do not straighten out, terminating with firing.

First, usually, comes an oral warning.

If an employee breaks a rule, especially a minor one, the first step is usually a clear *oral warning*, pointing out that repetition of the act will result in discipline. At this point the manager hopes that the worker will refrain from breaking the rule in the future.

Then a written warning.

If the employee breaks the rule again or if the first offense was a major one, some firms require *written warnings*. These become part of the employee's records and can be cited as evidence if it is decided to terminate the individual in the future.

Then a disciplinary layoff.

A *disciplinary layoff* is the next most severe form of discipline. In this case the person is required to not come to work for a specified period and forfeit the pay for the period. A layoff varies in length from one day to two weeks. Some organizations, however, do not believe in disciplinary layoffs, because they are unable to find a replacement for a few days or weeks. Instead, they simply fire the employee.

The discharge.

Discharge is the ultimate penalty. In recent years this approach has been used less and less, principally because the penalty is often regarded as too harsh. Unions always fight a discharge, and arbitrators are reluctant to side with the organization's decision. Why has this trend developed?

> Consider the impact of a discharge on a man of 55, with 30 years' seniority. In the first place, he may lose pension rights which would eventually be worth $60,000 or more, plus substantial vacation benefits. Few high-paying employers would be willing to hire a man of his age, especially after they check his references and discover his discharge. Certainly he can expect less pay than he was getting from the job to which his 30 years' service had carried him. Further, as a low-seniority man, he is now fully susceptible to all the winds of economic misfortune. Assuming he loses $6 an hour for the rest of his life, his financial loss may be as high as $150,000.[11]

The effective leader strives to avoid this situation by preventing rule violations. When they do occur, the individual is consistent and impersonal in employing discipline.

The "red-hot stove rule"   One of the most effective methods of employing discipline is the *red-hot stove rule*. This rule draws an analogy between touching a red-hot stove and receiving discipline. When someone touches a red-hot stove the burn is *immediate*. There was *advanced warning* in the form of heat emanating from the stove, which should have alerted the person to the danger. Anyone who touches the stove is

---

[11] George Strauss and Leonard R. Sayles, *Personnel: The Human Problems of Management*, 4th ed. (Englewood Cliffs, N.J.: Prentice-Hall, Inc., 1972), p. 221.

burned, and this *consistency* holds for everyone else who touches it. The burn is *impersonal* in that everyone touching the stove is burned regardless of who they are. These four characteristics are applied to discipline.

Discipline should be immediate. As soon as the manager knows that a worker has broken a rule, discipline should follow. If the manager waits, there is the likelihood that the worker will not associate the disciplinary action with the violation of the rule. When this happens, bitter feelings are likely to result. Consider the following example.

> **Mary Lou was taking a psychology final in the large university auditorium. The exam consisted of 100 true-false and multiple-choice questions. All answers were to be marked on a computer scoring sheet and turned in with the question booklet. Each student had been asked to bring a No. 2 pencil and an eraser. The proctor made it clear to the students that any extra pencil marks on the score sheet could result in a computer scoring error.**
>
> **During the exam a student behind Mary Lou leaned forward and asked if he could borrow an eraser. He had forgotten to bring one. Mary Lou gave him the eraser and a minute later he returned it. One of the graduate students standing nearby noticed the exchange.**
>
> **When Mary Lou and the student turned in their papers, the graduate student informed them that they had failed the exam for cheating. Both protested, but their papers were removed from the general pile of exams and placed on the side. When grades were reported both had received an F in the course.**

The error in this instance is that the graduate student waited until the end of the exam to announce the disciplinary procedure. Actually, the student should have tried immediately to find out what was going on and then should have determined whether or not there was an infraction of the rules.

By immediate discipline we do not mean hurried action. The facts of the case should be clear, and only if there is an obvious infraction of the rules should discipline be given. In many organizations a worker is suspended until the investigation is complete. In this case, both students appealed to a college review board and were given the opportunity to retake the exam. Many business firms also have review boards to investigate disciplinary actions. If a worker is suspended and found innocent, he or she is reinstated and given back pay for the suspension period. Conversely, if the worker is found guilty of the offense, the prescribed discipline is carried out.

Do not wait; discipline immediately.

There should be advanced warning. The organization should make its rules clear and the employees should know what the penalties are for breaking them. One of the most common ways of doing this is to familiarize workers with the rules during the induction period. Any future rule changes should then be communicated by the immediate superior or, if workers are unionized, should be included in the union contract.

Two important guidelines must be followed by management in giving advance warning. *Never have too many rules.* If people are given 5

*Make sure
everyone knows
the rules.*

rules to follow, they will generally adhere to them. However, if they are asked to abide by 105 rules they will generally ignore them. The degree of importance tends to decline as the number of rules increases. *Clearly state and uniformly apply the penalties for infractions.* If management does otherwise, the workers will protest disciplinary procedures. For example, if Paul, a new worker, sees people walking around the construction site without hard hats, he will feel discriminated against if the foreman disciplines him for not wearing his hat. In addition, when such cases go to arbitration, it is likely that the company will lose because disciplinary action has not been taken for previous offenses. "Why," the arbitrator will reason, "should the firm suddenly decide to start enforcing the rule now?"

Discipline should be consistent.

*Match the
discipline to
the offense.*

If two people commit the same offense, each should be given the same discipline. The biggest problem for the manager is that of identifying everyone who breaks the rules. If the manager can catch only 20 percent of the workers who violate a particular rule, those who are caught are often angry, because discipline seems to be more a matter of chance than anything else. Strauss and Sayles echo these sentiments:

> **We have heard foremen say, "I can only catch a small portion of the rule violators, but those I catch I punish severely." Is this fair? Many workers consider it a form of Russian roulette. Adventurous souls may try to see how much they can get away with, making a game of this procedure. Furthermore, scattered instances of discipline hardly constitute clear warning.**
> **If a rule is on the books, the manager should make an effort to enforce it, and enforce it uniformly. If that is impossible to do so, the rule may have to be revised or dropped altogether. Sloppy enforcement of one rule encourages employees to disregard other rules.**[12]

Discipline should be impersonal.

*Treat everyone
the same.*

The manager should make it clear to the workers that they are all on the same team but that this does not mean the workers can violate the rules with impunity. Some workers are more productive than others. Some are informal group leaders and others are followers. The manager would, quite obviously, want to cultivate the friendship of the more productive or leading workers. However, this cannot be done at the expense of either the other workers or the organization.

On the other hand, the manager should not be punitive when disciplining a worker. After ensuring that the worker has indeed broken the rule, the effective manager tries to learn why and then to work with the individual to prevent another violation.

> **Supervisor: Bill, you've been late twice this month. As you know, the rules require me to send you home immediately. Before I do so, however, I'd like to know why you've been late so that we can work**

---

[12] *Ibid.*, pp. 226–227.

to prevent this in the future. If you are late again this month, you will be given a week off, and if you are late a fourth time within a 90-day period, you'll be fired.

Worker: I think my problem is that I'm trying to carry three courses in night school. I want to graduate in 18 months and apply for a job as a management trainee.

Supervisor: A college degree is certainly going to help you get ahead in this company, Bill, but not if you can't keep your job. Remember, every time you're late it goes into your file. You need to start building a good record now. Three courses is a lot. Why not cut down to two and pace yourself a little more?

Worker: I appreciate that advice. Maybe I will. In fact, since I have the day off, I think I'll go by the college and drop one of those courses.

The supervisor used the disciplinary meeting to counsel and advise the worker. Notice that the manager kept the disciplinary aspects of the meeting on an impersonal basis, while trying to work with the worker in preventing future tardiness. If the manager handles the situation properly, it is often possible to prevent feelings from being hurt. Of course, to a large degree, the individual's success is determined by his or her negotiating ability. In fact, appraising, rewarding, and disciplining employees requires effective skills. Before concluding this chapter, take the quiz to rate how great your negotiating ability is.

How great is your negotiating ability?

Performance appraisal, the allocation of rewards, and the effective use of discipline requires a manager to be, among other things, a skilled negotiator. The individual must be able to evaluate performance diplomatically and effectively and withstand the pressures that come about when subordinates complain that they are being treated unfairly. How great is your negotiating ability? In each of the following 20 statements, decide whether the statement is basically true or basically false in describing you.

	Basically True	Basically False
1. When I need to get someone or some group to do something, I can do so.	____	____
2. I really like to be liked.	____	____
3. I get a real kick out of going out to shop where prices are fixed and manage to get a discount on what I buy.	____	____
4. I am not a very good listener, but I am an excellent talker.	____	____

	Basically True	Basically False
5. I try not to do formal preparation for any negotiation because it detracts from my spontaneity and creativity; I prefer to play things by ear.	____	____
6. I am not really much of a compromiser; I know what I want and I fight to get it all.	____	____
7. Under pressure, I can really handle myself well.	____	____
8. People who know me well find me to be both tactful and diplomatic.	____	____
9. I do not like taking short-range losses even at the price of long-range gains.	____	____
10. I find that most things in life are negotiable.	____	____
11. No matter what salary increase is offered to me, I try to get more.	____	____
12. I take what people say at face value.	____	____
13. Whenever possible, I try to avoid conflict and confrontation.	____	____
14. I do not care how the other side feels about the results of my negotiation efforts; that is their problem not mine.	____	____
15. I am willing to work long and hard to gain a small advantage.	____	____
16. I do not like to haggle with people over prices; I pay what is asked or walk away from the deal.	____	____
17. A person's facial expressions often tell me more about what the individual is saying than do his or her words.	____	____
18. I am not particularly adept at expressing my point of view.	____	____
19. In most cases I am not willing to compromise on issues.	____	____
20. I find it easy to smile even when engaged in a serious discussion.	____	____

The interpretation of your self-assessment can be found at the end of the chapter.

Summary

In this chapter, we deal with the issue of evaluating employees. Performance appraisal is a four-step process: (1) performance standards are established, (2) individual performance is determined, (3) a comparison of individual performance and performance standards is made, and (4) overall performance is evaluated. When this fourth step is completed, the cycle starts again.

Many kinds of appraisal tools can be used to evaluate employee performance. The simplest is the graphic rating scale in which all the factors (and degrees of each factor) on which the employee is to be evaluated are listed. The manager's job is then to check the appropriate degree of every factor and total the value associated with each to arrive at an overall score for the individual.

The paired comparison method of evaluation requires the manager to compare each employee in the group with every other. Often there are five to ten factors on which all are compared. On the basis of the comparisons on all factors, the manager is able to rank the workers from the best to the poorest.

Assessment centers are used for evaluating employee long-range potential as well as short-range performance. Employing a series of assessment techniques as well as a number of assessors, the employee is required to use behaviors related to dimensions of actual performance on the job. The final decision regarding what to do (hire, promote, etc.) is the result of a group decision by the assessors.

Behaviorally anchored rating scales (BARS) rely heavily on an identification of critical incidents that represent effective and ineffective behaviors. After these behaviors are put in clusters, they are used to develop a rating scale for a particular cluster or dimension. The rating usually extends from 1 (ineffective behavior) up to 7 or 9 (effective behavior).

Management by objectives (MBO) can be used at all levels of the hierarchy. The MBO process consists of six steps: (1) identifying the goals of the unit or department, (2) describing the duties and responsibilities of the personnel, (3) meeting with the subordinate and mutually setting goals for the latter, (4) employing a goal-setting worksheet to help the subordinate work toward the objective, (5) periodically reviewing the goals and revising them where necessary, and (6) evaluating the results and starting the cycle again.

In every performance appraisal, the manager must be aware of problems. The most common problems are attributable to: (1) lack of clarity of the form itself, (2) the halo effect, (3) central tendency, and (4) leniency. While noting ways in which these problems can be overcome, we stress the need for validity and reliability in performance appraisal instruments.

The last part of the chapter is devoted to the issue of performance rewards. After reviewing common types of extrinsic and intrinsic rewards, we discuss equity theory. The essence of equity theory is that people will compare their work/reward ratio to those of others to determine whether they are being properly rewarded.

Another important part of equity theory is the link the organization establishes between performance and rewards. Some organizations attempt to do this through the use of incentive payment plans; others make strong use of performance appraisal. In most cases, the reward-performance linkage is not very great, and the manager must rely most heavily on providing an environment in which workers can attain psychological rewards.

The manager must also be able to exercise discipline, sometimes referred to as a *negative reward*. Most formal disciplinary processes employ progressive discipline, beginning with an oral warning and moving to a written warning, a disciplinary layoff, and, ultimately, discharge. In carrying out discipline many managers use the *red-hot stove rule*. Effective discipline has four characteristics: (1) it should be immediate, (2) there should be advance warning of discipline penalties, and if the individual still violates the rule, the discipline should be (3) consistent and (4) impersonal.

Key terms in the chapter

performance appraisal cycle
graphic rating scales
paired comparison method
assessment center
behaviorally anchored rating
   scales
management by objectives
halo effect
central tendency
leniency
validity

reliability
extrinsic rewards
intrinsic rewards
equity theory
incentive payment plans
oral warning
written warning
disciplinary layoff
discharge
red-hot stove rule

Review and study questions

1. How does the performance appraisal cycle work? Be sure to discuss all four steps.

2. How does the graphic rating scale help the manager appraise subordinates?

3. In what way is the paired comparison method similar to the graphic rating scale? How is it different?

4. Why do some organizations prefer paired comparison to the graphic rating scale?

5. How do assessment centers work? Explain.

6. How are behaviorally anchored rating scales constructed? Explain.

7. What are some of the major advantages of a BARS appraisal method? List three.

8. In your own words, what are the six steps in the basic MBO cycle?

9. Why is MBO so popular? Explain.

10. What are some of the major performance appraisal problems? Cite three.

11. Can the paired comparison method help eliminate central tendency? Leniency? Why or why not?

12. What is meant by *validity*? *Reliability*? Which is more difficult to attain? Explain your answer.

13. When it comes to rewarding performance, which is more important, extrinsic rewards or intrinsic rewards? Explain.

14. What is equity theory? How does it influence motivation?

15. Should pay and performance be linked? What role can incentive payment plans play in this process?

16. What are the four stages of progressive discipline? Explain each.

17. According to the red-hot stove rule of discipline, what are the four characteristics of discipline? Explain each.

Interpretation of How great is your negotiating ability

Take your answers to the self-assessment quiz and compare them to those below. For each one you have that is identical to the scoring key presented here, give yourself one point.

1. Basically true	11. Basically true
2. Basically false	12. Basically false
3. Basically true	13. Basically false
4. Basically false	14. Basically false
5. Basically false	15. Basically true
6. Basically false	16. Basically false
7. Basically true	17. Basically true
8. Basically true	18. Basically false
9. Basically false	19. Basically false
10. Basically true	20. Basically true

Your score, assuming your self-evaluation is correct, provides some insights regarding your ability to negotiate well. The following is a general breakdown regarding how effective you are:

17–20	Excellent. You are a true negotiator.
14–16	Good. You have real negotiating potential.
11–13	Average. You do not see yourself as that much of a negotiator.
Less than 11	Below average. You do not see yourself as a negotiator.

How can you improve your negotiating ability? The best way is by examining your incorrect responses and trying to change your behavior appropriately.

University evaluations

Mildred Dandridge is a state senator and chairperson of the State Education Committee. During some educational budget hearings held recently, Mildred became very interested in how the largest state university evaluates the performances of its faculty members. The president of the university, who was appearing as a witness, told Mildred that the university system had adopted a rating scale similar to the paired comparison method. At the beginning of each academic year the chairperson and each faculty member decide together what the professor is going to do. Their objectives are written on a sheet of paper and transferred to a formal memo of which both have a copy. On the memo, the relative amounts of time to be allotted to teaching, research and writing, and community service are designated. At the end of the academic year, the chairperson meets with each professor to review progress. Then the chairperson makes an overall evaluation of the faculty member, compares this rating to that given to all the other members of the department, and rates the professors from first to last. The members with the highest ratings are given merit increases, while the others share only in the cost-of-living increase given to everyone.

Mildred likes this idea of paired comparison and the identification of the best and poorest performers. However, a few things concern her. If all the people in one department are only marginal, while those in another are outstanding, why are half of both groups being given merit increases? Being somewhat familiar with the area of performance appraisal, she is also wondering why the university does not develop a BARS approach to rating the faculty. Also, she wants to know what type of performance appraisal system is used for evaluating chairpeople and administrators.

Responding to her questions in order of presentation, the university president has answered that it would be very difficult to evaluate faculty on any basis other than performance as judged in each department. He sees no way of preventing the best performer in a weak department from getting merit money, nor does he believe it possible to do much for the poorest performer in a very strong department. He feels that the establishment of a BARS evaluation program would be time consuming and expensive; he has suggested MBO as an alternative. The president acknowledges that it is difficult to evaluate the performance of top administrators in the university system, but he says that this is a problem with which everyone has to live. This is true for top managers in any organization. The higher up the line you go, the less able you are to evaluate performance objectively.

Mildred is not sure she agrees with the university president on any of his answers. She has indicated that the education bill will be tied up in her committee for at least six more weeks while further investigation is made into the appraisal of university personnel at all levels. "I think we need to run a tighter ship if the taxpayers are to get their money's worth. I'd like to look into this matter a great deal more before we decide how much money to allocate to higher education for next year," she said, just before adjourning the hearing.

Questions

1. Is the paired comparison method a fair way to evaluate university faculty? Explain.
2. How would you resolve the dilemma of merit pay? To whom would you give it, and whom would you bypass? Be specific in your answer.
3. Is there any way to evaluate university administrators? How would you do it? Be complete in your answer.

Clock-in time

Fred Winslow is a shop steward in a New York City manufacturing firm. He is well liked by the management and the workers. The management feels that Fred is particularly helpful in working out union-management grievances before they reach arbitration. Several times, Fred has served as an intermediary and has always been able to establish harmony between the disagreeing factions.

Last month, for example, one of the unionized employees was charged with stealing some supplies. The supervisor laid the man off immediately and recommended that he be fired. Fred, as the shop steward, came to the man's defense and said that the punishment was too great for "accidentally" walking off the job with $10 worth of supplies. After talking to the man and getting his side of the story, Fred approached the supervisor and suggested a compromise. The worker would admit that he accidentally took some supplies from the premises and would submit to punishment of five days off without pay. The supervisor agreed that the compromise was fair, and everyone was pleased.

In the last two weeks, however, the supervisor, who also happens to be Fred's boss, has encountered a problem. There is a company rule that says anyone who comes in late must be docked an hour's pay for any tardiness less than 60 minutes, two hours' pay if the lateness extends into the second hour, and so on. In addition, a worker who is late twice in one week is laid off for one week. If a worker is late three times in a four-week period, the penalty is a layoff of two weeks. Finally, if the worker is late four times in any four-week period, he is dismissed.

Two weeks ago, Fred was late 30 minutes one day and was docked an hour's pay. He said that the train had been delayed. Earlier this week Fred was again late by 30 minutes and was docked an hour's pay. The supervisor is worried, however, because Fred was late again today. He came in at 8:15 A.M. and immediately went to his work station. The supervisor noticed this, because he had been waiting since 7:30 to talk to Fred. At 7:55, when he had gone to check for Fred's time card, it had not yet been punched.

When the supervisor finally saw Fred enter the work area, he immediately went over to talk to him. The supervisor said nothing about Fred's tardiness, although Fred said that he was sorry he was late getting to his work station but that he had been talking to one of the men in another part of the plant about a union matter.

What has the supervisor concerned is this: Fred has to clock in by 8:00 A.M. regardless of union activities, although he is allowed to go then to other parts of the plant on union business. If he is late, the supervisor feels, Fred should be penalized regardless of his position in the union and his value to management in helping solve union-company problems. The actual proof, of course, is the time card, which should have Fred's actual arrival time on it. The supervisor went over to get the card after talking to Fred. It showed a clock-in time of 7:58 A.M. Now the supervisor is unsure of what to do, for he is certain that Fred was not in the building before 8:15.

Questions

1. If you were the supervisor, what would you do first?
2. If you found Fred to be guilty of tardiness, what would you do?
3. If you were the supervisor's boss and he came and told you that he had proof that Fred was late but wanted your advice before doing anything, what would you recommend? Explain.

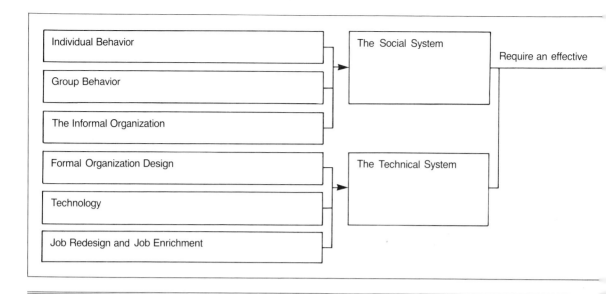

Individual Behavior		The Social System		Require an effective
Group Behavior				
The Informal Organization				
Formal Organization Design		The Technical System		
Technology				
Job Redesign and Job Enrichment				

Behavioral effectiveness

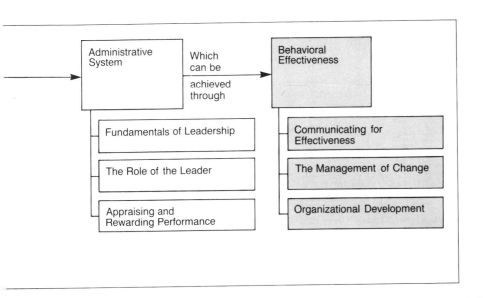

Parts II through IV examined the social system, the technical system, and the administrative system. However, we have not yet attempted to address the question, "What does the organization do to prevent problems from occurring, and what does it do if it is unsuccessful in this attempt?" In Part V, we answer this question by examining the three most important areas for ensuring behavioral effectiveness: (1) communication, (2) the management of change, and (3) organizational development.

In Chapter 12 we study how modern organizations go about communicating for effectiveness. We define *communication*, describe the communication process, discuss major communication flows, and examine some of the common barriers to effective communication, including perception, inference, language, and status. Then we study how organizations try to overcome or prevent such problems through understanding the four steps in the communication process, and employing simple and repetitive language, using empathy, learning how to understand body language and to receive and give feedback, developing effective listening habits, and improving writing skills.

In Chapter 13 the subject of attention is the management of change. In addition to defining *change* and discussing how the change process works, we attempt to answer the question, "Is resistance to change bad?" Then we describe some of the important factors that influence an individual's evaluation of a proposed change, explain the four most common responses to change, cite some of the common reasons for resisting change, describe the three dimensions of change, list the five basic steps in the change process, and explain why time is an important factor in implementing change. Finally we discuss the role of participation and communication in the change process, describe how balance theory can help the manager in introducing and implementing change, and discover why removal of anxieties is so important in the management of change.

In Chapter 14 we study organizational development. When organizations attempt to introduce change and manage it properly, they commonly have a strategy. This is where organizational development comes in. In this chapter we define *organizational climate*, compare and contrast the formal and informal aspects of the organizational iceberg, define *organizational development* (OD), discuss the eight major characteristics of most OD programs, and describe some of the most common OD interventions. Then we outline the conditions necessary for optimum success in an OD program and address the issue of whether organizational development is an effective approach to the management of organizational resources.

When you are finished reading this part of the book, you should have a solid understanding of the communication process, of how modern organizations attempt to manage change, and of the role of OD in this process. You should also understand the importance of behavioral effectiveness and should know how communication, the management of change, and OD help to ensure this result.

Communicating for effectiveness

12

Goals of the chapter

One of the most common causes of organizational inefficiency is poor communication. In this chapter we study ways in which managers can communicate effectively. The first goal of this chapter is to study the communication process. In particular we are interested in how messages are put together, transmitted, and interpreted. The second goal is to study downward, upward, lateral, and diagonal communication flows. The third goal is to examine some of the common barriers to communication, including perception, inference, language, and status. The final goal of the chapter is to study ways of achieving effective communication: knowing the steps in the communication process; using simple and repetitive language; using empathy; learning how to get and give feedback; and developing effective listening habits.

When you are finished reading this chapter you should be able to:

1. define the term *communication*
2. describe the communication process
3. discuss major communication flows (downward, upward, lateral, and diagonal)
4. explain why perception is a major barrier to communication
5. explain how inference, language, and status can also lead to communication breakdown
6. outline the four steps in the communication process and describe how an understanding of them can help a manager improve his or her communication skills
7. describe the importance of using simple, repetitive language and using empathy in achieving effective communication

8. cite some of the ways of understanding body language and receiving and giving feedback

9. list some of the listening habits valuable to effective communication

10. discuss how to improve your writing skills.

The communication process

Communication is the process of transmitting meanings from sender to receiver. These meanings are conveyed through a medium such as a telephone call, a memorandum, or a conversation. In this process there are five essential elements: (1) the sender, (2) the message being transmitted, (3) the medium used to carry the message, (4) the receiver of the message, and (5) the interpretation given to the message. In conveying meanings from sender to receiver, three functions must be performed. First, the message has to be encoded, or put into a form that will be understood by the receiver. Second, it has to be conveyed through the proper medium or channel. Third, it must be decoded, or interpreted properly by the person to whom it was directed. These functions are described in Figure 12.1.

Encoding

First, the message must be encoded.

Before a message can be sent from one person to another it has to be ***encoded***, or expressed in a code (words, facial expressions, gestures) that is intelligible to the receiver. For example, if a top executive is flying from New York to London to attend a corporate meeting with his counterpart in the United Kingdom, he might call the British executive and say, "I'm arriving on Wednesday at 7 A.M. on Pan Am Flight 201. My secretary tried to get an earlier flight but everything here is booked up because of the heavy tourist travel to your country. Would you be kind enough to have someone meet me at the airport so I won't be late for our meeting at 9:30?" However, if the executive is unable to reach his coun-

Figure 12.1
The communication process in action

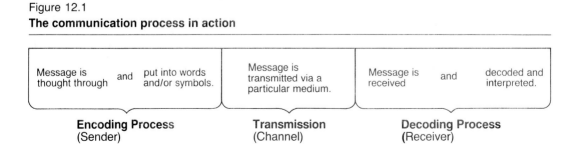

| Message is thought through | and | put into words and/or symbols. | Message is transmitted via a particular medium. | Message is received | and | decoded and interpreted. |

Encoding Process
(Sender)

Transmission
(Channel)

Decoding Process
(Receiver)

terpart by phone, he might send a telegram. In this case the message will be encoded differently. Telegrams are much briefer and leave out a lot of the window dressing. The executive's telegram might read "ARRIVING EARLIEST POSSIBLE FLIGHT WED PANAM 201 STOP WILL REQUIRE TRANSPORTATION STOP." It is up to the British manager to work out the details such as arrival time and transportation.

Note that in the encoding process there are two important steps: First, the sender thinks through the ideas to be communicated. Second, the sender translates these ideas into some code or symbol, which in this case was words.

Medium

In describing the encoding process, we have already noted two of the most common forms of communication media: the telephone and the telegram. Other forms include conversation, pictures, diagrams, figures, and charts. For example, when one is advertising a product, one frequently uses pictures to convey the idea, as in newspaper ads and billboards. Diagrams, figures, and charts are often used when managers communicate with each other. Much business data is conveyed in these forms.

Then a communication medium must be chosen.

In addition, we need to consider nonverbal forms of communication. For example, there is body language.[1] People transmit meanings by their facial expressions, eye movements, and how close (or far away) they sit or stand in relation to other people. Even the way they walk tells us something about them.

How you walk, for instance, is often a strong indicator of how you feel. When you have a problem, you might walk very slowly with your head down and your hands clasped behind your back. You may even pause to kick a rock on the ground. On the other hand, when you feel especially proud or happy, you might walk with your chin raised, your arms swinging freely, and your legs somewhat stiff—with a bounce in your step.[2]

Even the physical environment in which people live has an influence on their communication. Dentists' offices have comfortable chairs and pleasant decor in the waiting rooms so that patients will be less nervous. Restaurants have dim lighting and soft music, which encourage people to talk softly and stay longer. Even the colors of the room can have an effect on people's mood, resulting in a particular communication pattern. Table 12.1 lists the moods commonly associated with certain colors. If the boss

---

[1] Julius Fast, *Body Language* (New York: Pocket Books, 1971); and Michael B. McCaskey, "The Hidden Messages Managers Send," *Harvard Business Review*, November–December 1979, pp. 135–148.

[2] Larry L. Barker, *Communication* (Englewood Cliffs, N.J.: Prentice-Hall, Inc., 1978), p. 79.

Table 12.1
The association of moods with colors

Mood	Color
Exciting, stimulating	Red
Secure, comfortable	Blue
Distressed, disturbed, upset	Orange
Tender, soothing	Blue
Protective, defending	Red
Despondent, dejected, unhappy, melancholy	Black
Calm, peaceful, serene	Blue
Dignified, stately	Purple
Cheerful, jovial, joyful	Yellow
Defiant, contrary, hostile	Red
Powerful, strong, masterful	Black

From Lois B. Wexner, "The Degree to Which Colors (Hues) Are Associated with Mood-Tones," *Journal of Applied Psychology*, December 1954, pp. 433–434.

is going to communicate important news to a subordinate and has him or her wait in the orange room, the subordinate may feel the news is bad (orange tends to create a distressed, disturbed mood), but if the subordinate is waiting in a yellow room, he or she might begin to expect good news (yellow tends to create a cheerful, jovial mood).

Finally, we have to consider that the medium is also used in directing the message toward certain people and away from others. This selective process is examined in Chapter 5 in the discussion of informal communication networks and the high degree of selectivity that exists among organizational personnel. Some people are passed information and others are deliberately bypassed.

Decoding

Finally, the message must be decoded.

The last phase of the communication process involves a ***decoding*** or interpreting of the message by the sender. In understanding how this decoding process works, we must consider three areas: the sender's meaning, the receiver's interpretation, and the degree of overlap between them. Let us consider an exaggerated example of very little overlap.

Eddie Jones spent two weeks in South America consulting for the local branch office. The branch manager assigned him a secretary and an office. A few days before his assignment was over, Eddie told the branch manager that he wanted to show his gratitude to the secretary for a job well done. He planned on getting her a small present on his last day there. The branch manager told Eddie that the secretary would appreciate such a gesture. Following up on his promise, Eddie brought the secretary a dozen roses.

Imagine his surprise when the office manager came by to tease him later. "When you said you were going to get her a gift I thought you were going to buy her something for her home. I should have asked

Figure 12.2
A major decoding problem

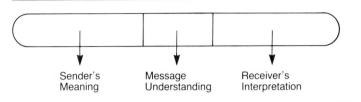

| Sender's | Message | Receiver's |
| Meaning | Understanding | Interpretation |

Figure 12.3
A minor decoding problem

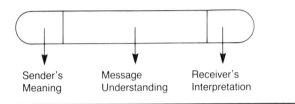

| Sender's | Message | Receiver's |
| Meaning | Understanding | Interpretation |

you before hand what you wanted to get. You see, giving flowers in this country is a sign of *romantic* interest!"

In this case we can diagram the decoding of the message between Eddie (the sender) and the branch manager (the receiver) as in Figure 12.2.

Let us take another example.

The hospital administrator told Roy Jones, his associate administrator, that the board of directors would be visiting the hospital the next day and would be looking at the new wing that had just been built. The wing had seven stories and the top five stories contained patients' rooms. "The beds and other furniture arrived yesterday and we should get them put into the rooms as soon as possible," the administrator told Roy, "so the board members can see what the rooms look like when they're furnished." Roy rounded up all the help he could get on short notice and began moving the furniture and arranging the rooms. It took until 1:00 A.M. just to get all the furniture up in the rooms, but by the time the board members arrived at 9:00 A.M., everything was ready. The members examined the first two floors of the building, took the elevator to the third floor to look at some of the patients' rooms, and then returned to the main part of the hospital for lunch.

Later, the hospital administrator said to Roy, "I didn't realize that you were going to furnish all the rooms. I should have told you that they would only be looking at one of the patients' floors! All of them are the same, so there was really no need for them to go on up any farther. Nevertheless, it's better to have done too much work than too little. We would have had to put all the furniture in those rooms later in the month anyway."

In this case, we can see that there was more than adequate information conveyed. We can diagram the decoding process as in Figure 12.3.

Figure 12.4
Communication flows

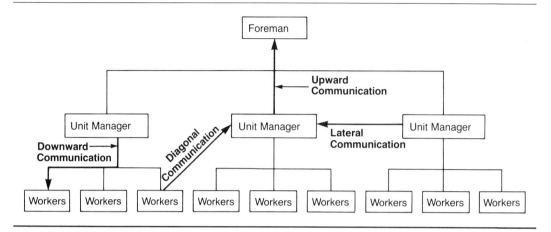

Communication flows

The communication process carries messages in four basic directions: downward, upward, lateral, and diagonal. Figure 12.4 illustrates each direction of flow.

Downward communication

Downward communication provides direction and control.

Downward communication travels from the superior to the subordinate. The most common purposes of this communication flow are to transmit information and instruct employees in the performance of their jobs. Some of the most typical downward communication channels include written directives, face-to-face conversations, use of public address systems, bulletin boards, and company newspapers.

For human relations study, downward communication is important because it provides direction and control for the employees. Remember from the discussion of informal organizations that if there is a lack of information it will be filled by rumor, gossip, or other grapevine activity. Effective downward communication can prevent confusion and distortion.

Additionally, it is important to note that orders coming down the line tend to be expanded in terms of interpretation and impact. A top manager tells a subordinate, "Find out how many people we have working in our San Francisco branch. I know the president is going to ask for this information during our meeting Friday, and I want to be prepared." The subordinate passes the message to a secretary, who calls the San Francisco branch and tells the secretary there, "The president has asked for a complete list of everyone who works in your branch. We need it all

---

Figure 12.5
Operation Halley's Comet

A Colonel Issued the Following Directive to His Executive Officer:

"Tomorrow evening at approximately 2000 hours Halley's Comet will be visible in this area, an event which occurs only once every 75 years. Have the men fall out in the battalion area in fatigues, and I will explain this rare phenomenon to them. In case of rain, we will not be able to see anything, so assemble the men in the theater and I will show them films of it."

Executive Officer to Company Commander:

"By order of the Colonel, tomorrow at 2000 hours, Halley's Comet will appear above the battalion area. If it rains, fall the men out in fatigues, then march to the theater where this rare phenomenon will take place; something which occurs only once every 75 years."

Company Commander to Lieutenant:

"By order of the Colonel be in fatigues at 2000 hours tomorrow evening, the phenomenal Halley's Comet will appear in the theater. In case of rain, in the battalion area, the Colonel will give another order, something which occurs once every 75 years."

Lieutenant to Sergeant:

"Tomorrow at 2000 hours the Colonel will appear in the theater with Halley's Comet, something which happens every 75 years. If it rains, the Colonel will order the comet into the battalion area."

Sergeant to Squad:

"When it rains tomorrow at 2000 hours the phenomenal 75-year-old General Halley, accompanied by the Colonel, will drive his comet through the battalion area theater in fatigues."

From a speech by Dan Bellus of the Santa Monica firm of Dan Bellus and Associates. Reprinted in the DS LETTER, Vol. 1, No. 3 (1971). Published by Didactic Systems, Inc., Box 457, Cranford, N.J. Reprinted with permission.

within two days." The branch secretary then expands the message by telling the branch manager that the president wants personnel records of all the branch employees sent as soon as possible. Within two hours, five people are assigned to the task. The data arrives at the main office early the next morning in four large boxes shipped air freight.

This is message expansion. A simple order is distorted as it comes down the line. The top executive merely wanted the subordinate to come up with the number of employees, i.e., 137 people. Instead, the order is turned into a major project involving 10 people. In downward verbal communication, we often find that the number of links often determines the extent of message distortion. The more people (links) there are in the chain, the greater the likelihood of communication expansion and distortion (Figure 12.5). To overcome this problem, managers must strive to forge the shortest link between themselves and the person who will carry out the order.

Figure 12.6
Upward communication in action

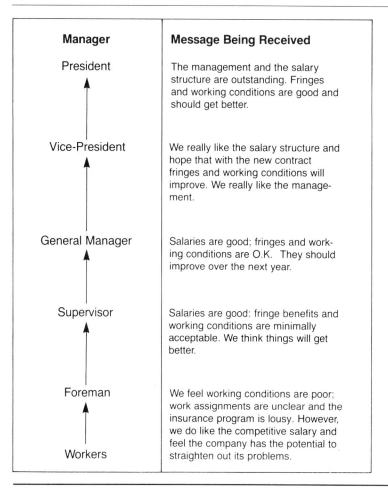

Manager	**Message Being Received**
President	The management and the salary structure are outstanding. Fringes and working conditions are good and should get better.
Vice-President	We really like the salary structure and hope that with the new contract fringes and working conditions will improve. We really like the management.
General Manager	Salaries are good; fringes and working conditions are O.K. They should improve over the next year.
Supervisor	Salaries are good; fringe benefits and working conditions are minimally acceptable. We think things will get better.
Foreman	We feel working conditions are poor; work assignments are unclear and the insurance program is lousy. However, we do like the competitive salary and feel the company has the potential to straighten out its problems.
Workers	

Upward communication

Upward communication provides feedback.

Upward communication travels from subordinate to superior. The most common purpose of this information flow is to provide feedback on how well things are going. It also provides the subordinates' superior with the opportunity to represent the subordinates to his or her own boss.

Whereas downward communication tends to be expanded, upward communication tends to be contracted. As information flows up the line it is compiled, examined, reduced, and passed on. Figure 12.6 illustrates this contraction. Note that good news tends to rise, but bad news is filtered out. This is particularly true when managers do not like to hear bad news from their subordinates. Realizing this, the subordinates simply screen out or reduce the amount of bad news they pass on. This often leads to insulation of the top manager, who may make erroneous decisions as a result. The only way to overcome this problem is to make it clear that *all* information, good and bad, is to be conveyed upward. Additionally, top managers must refrain from being critical of subordinates who give them this feedback, for once it becomes obvious that a manager dislikes bad news, selective filtering will occur.

Lateral and diagonal communication

Lateral communication takes place between people on the same level of the hierarchy. The most common reason for this communication flow is to promote coordination and teamwork. For example, the manager in Department A needs to know when the materials from Department B will arrive so that none of the members of Department A will be sitting around doing nothing. In communicating with the B manager, the A manager uses lateral communication.

Lateral communication provides teamwork.

Diagonal communication occurs between people who are *neither* in the same department *nor* on the same level of the hierarchy. For example, an advisor to the president calls the head of Department A to ask when the prototypes of the new consumer appliance product will be ready for inspection, or the head of Department B calls the vice-president of personnel to complain about errors in the computation of some employees' paychecks. In each case, someone communicates either downward or upward with someone in another functional area.

Diagonal communication facilitates efficiency.

Drawing by Ziegler; © 1982
The New Yorker Magazine, Inc.

Figure 12.7
Fayol's gangplank theory

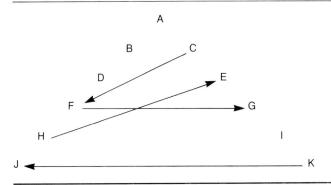

Some students of human relations believe that it is wrong for managers to use either lateral or diagonal communication because it violates the chain of command by cutting across the organizational structure. While this is true, this form of cross-communication is widely used in organizations today because it facilitates efficiency. Introduced in 1916 by Henri Fayol, this justification is often referred to as *Fayol's bridge* or *gangplank theory.*[3] In Figure 12.7, diagonal communication is being used by Manager C to talk to Manager F, by Manager F to talk to Manager G, and by Manager K to talk to Manager J.

Obviously, both lateral and diagonal communication can be dangerous because they cross the organizational structure and sidestep the long, formal line of command. However, this form of communication should be promoted as long as anyone initiating the communication follows two simple rules:

1. Obtain permission from one's direct supervisor before undertaking the communication.

2. Inform the direct supervisor of any significant results of the cross-communication.

Barriers to communication

All communication flows are subject to barriers that prevent the receiver from getting the sender's meaning. Some of the most common barriers are: (1) perception, (2) inference, (3) language, and (4) status.

---

[3] Henri Fayol, *Industrial and General Administration*, translation by J. A. Coubrough (Geneva: International Management Institute, 1929), p. 28.

Figure 12.8
A communication continuum

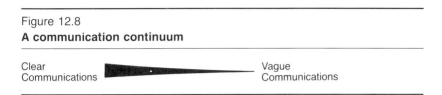

Clear
Communications

Vague
Communications

Perception

As noted in Chapter 3, *perception* is a person's view of reality. Since no two people have the same experiences and training, no two people see things exactly the same way. However, for effective communication, it is not necessary for them to have the same perception. One person needs to transmit sufficient information for the other person to take appropriate action. The major question for the manager is, "What constitutes 'sufficient' information?" Some messages may be well thought out and still may be misunderstood by the receiver. Other messages may be vague but the receiver may have no trouble understanding them.

Perception is a person's view of reality.

These two ideas—clear and vague—can be placed on a communication continuum as in Figure 12.8. The messages on the left deal with ideas that are easily understood and do not involve matters of opinion or issues that are open to interpretation.

"George, beginning tomorrow you are to occupy Ralph's office. He is being transferred to the Denver office, and you are next in line in seniority so the office is yours." This is a clear message. We can expect George to clean out his desk and move the contents into Ralph's office tomorrow. We would be surprised if we found that George moved into his boss's office, because that would indicate quite a deviation from the originally transmitted message.

"George, if you do well in your current position, you can expect a promotion to the Denver office as well." This message is much more vague than the previous one. Note that the sender of the message does not make clear what is meant by "if you do well." It is implied that George knows, but does he?

Degrees of perceptual difficulty   As one moves across the communication continuum in Figure 12.8, there is some point after which the messages become extremely difficult to comprehend. However, it is erroneous to believe that all clear communiques are error-free. Often, people see and hear what they want or expect to see and hear. When this happens, communication breakdown can occur. Let us take an example. After this paragraph there is a sentence containing all capital letters. Read this sentence slowly and carefully so that you understand its entire meaning. When you are finished, go on to the paragraph that follows.

FINISHED FILES ARE THE RESULT OF YEARS OF SCIENTIFIC
STUDY COUPLED WITH THE EXPERIENCE OF MANY YEARS.

Before reading further, you may read the above sentence one more
time. When you have finished, and *only* when you have finished, continue reading down this page.

The capitalized sentence that you have read consists of seventeen
words. It is a somewhat long although not particularly difficult sentence
containing a handful of ideas. Within this sentence there are a number of
different letters: fourteen E's, four A's, and so on. Count the number of
times another letter appears in the above sentence, with the following
ground rules. First, you may not use your finger, pen, or pencil in reread-
ing the capitalized sentence; you may use only your eyes. Second, you are
to read the sentence as quickly as possible, taking no more than 10 seconds to do so. (If possible, time yourself.) When you have finished reading the sentence, you may continue to the next paragraph. Ready? Okay.
Begin reading the capitalized sentence and count the number of times
the letter F appears. Go!

How many times did you find the letter F in the sentence? The most
common answers are two, three, four, five, six, and seven. Was your answer one of these? The right answer is included in this list. Regardless of
the number you arrived at the first time, go back to the sentence and read
it *slowly* and *deliberately*, counting the number of F's very carefully.

If you have counted three—no more, no less—you are typical of
most people. Actually, there are six F's in the sentence, in *finished, files,
scientific*, and the three *of*'s. Most people miss these last three because
they are accustomed to reading past short words, skimming over them
too quickly to notice the spelling. This exercise demonstrates that even
when it comes to "clear" messages people make errors because they do
not perceive what actually is there.

Let us take another illustration, this time using a vague message. Below this paragraph are nine dots. After studying them for a minute, connect all nine dots with four straight lines. Here are the rules:

1. You may not take your pen or pencil off the paper.

2. If you retrace a line by, for example, going from left to right and
   then back again to the point of departure, you have used *two* lines.

3. The lines must indeed be straight; do not curve them in any way.

•   •   •

•   •   •

•   •   •

After you have finished this exercise (take no more than five minutes with it), you can check your answer with the solution given at the end of the chapter. As you will see, the puzzle can be solved *only* by going outside the perimeter formed by the nine dots. If you try to stay within this square area, you cannot solve the problem without using at least five straight lines.

When managers communicate, they often believe that their messages are clear. Often, however, they are vague, and the receiver ends up asking, "What did the boss mean by that?"

Inference

Another common communication problem, closely associated with perception, is inference. An *inference* is an assumption made by the receiver of a message. Inferences are most often present in messages that are very long or that involve a large number of facts. In interpreting their meaning, the receiver is often forced to make assumptions, since the facts are not all clearly transmitted. The following story is an illustration.

An inference is an assumption.

A matter of inference

Instructions   Read the following story very carefully. You may assume that everything it says is true, but be aware that parts of the story are deliberately vague.

You can read the story twice if you desire, but *once you start reading the statements that follow, do not go back to either the story itself or any previous statements.* Simply read each statement and decide if it is true (the story said so), false (the story said just the opposite), or inferential (you cannot say whether it is true or false; you need more facts). Write your answer (T for true, F for false, I for inferential) on the line after the statement. When you are finished, check your results with the answers given at the end of the chapter.

The story   Bart Falding is head of the research and development department of a large plastics firm located in New England. Bart has ordered a crash R&D program in hopes of developing a new process that will revolutionize plastics manufacturing. He has given five of his top R&D people authority to spend up to $250,000 each without consulting him or the R&D committee.

He has sent one of his best people, Mary Lou Rasso, to a major Midwestern university to talk to a Nobel Prize winner there who has just applied for and received a patent that Bart believes may provide the basis for a breakthrough in the plastics field. Three days after Mary Lou left for the university, Bart received a call from her. Mary Lou was very excited and said she and the scientist were flying in to see Bart the next day, although she declined to discuss the matter over the phone.

Bart believes that he will have very good news for the company president when they meet for their biweekly lunch early next week.

The statements

1. Bart is head of the research and development department of a large plastics firm. _____
2. The company is located in Los Angeles, California. _____
3. Bart received orders from the president to engage in a crash R&D program. _____
4. Bart's R&D budget is in excess of $1 million. _____
5. Bart assigned five of his best people to work on developing a new process for revolutionizing plastics manufacturing. _____
6. Mary Lou was sent to talk to a Nobel-prize-winning professor. _____
7. Mary Lou works for the plastics manufacturing department. _____
8. Mary Lou was authorized to spend up to $250,000 without approval from the R&D committee. _____
9. Bart's company wants to buy the patent from the university professor. _____
10. Bart believes that Mary Lou has already offered the professor a deal and the latter is prepared to accept it, but first wants to discuss the matter with top management. _____
11. Mary Lou has agreed to pick up all the scientist's expenses if the latter will consent to come and talk to Bart in person. _____
12. The scientist must be interested in some type of financial or business arrangement with Bart's firm, or the scientist would not have agreed to fly in and meet with Bart. _____
13. The scientist received the Nobel prize for work he did in the area of plastic processes. _____
14. Bart and the company president have lunch on a biweekly basis. _____
15. Bart believes that he will have good news for the president for he is sure that the scientist will agree to sell the patent to the company if the firm makes a sufficiently high offer. _____

How well did you do? Check your answers with those at the end of the chapter. Most people get no more than eight right.

Inference occurs whenever the sender of the message fails to communicate clearly and completely. In face-to-face communication many of these problems can be overcome, since the listener can quickly stop the conversation and ask a question. However, with written messages this is more difficult, because the receiver is forced to use his or her own best judgment in deciding what the message really means.

Language

Language is used to convey meanings in the communication process. This is as true in written as in verbal communication. However, sometimes language proves to be a communication barrier. One of the most common reasons is that people have different meanings for the same words. For example, in engineering firms the word *burn* often means to photocopy. Imagine the surprise of a manager in such a company when he or she tells a new secretary to burn a copy of the original blueprints and then finds that they have to be redrawn!

Every profession has its own meanings for words. In the medical profession *OD* stands for overdose, an excessive amount of a drug. However, in the field of management, *OD* signifies organizational development, a strategy used to introduce planned change. Or consider *OB*, which in the medical profession stands for obstetrics but in the management profession signifies organizational behavior, an academic discipline taught in accredited schools of business. Communications theorists like to point out that meanings are not in words but in the people who use them. When we employ language for communication purposes, we sometimes do not have the same meaning for a word that the receiver does, and communication breakdown is all but inevitable.

Meanings are in people, not in words.

Another common language-related problem is that of reading. Many schools no longer teach students to read and write properly. Grammar, sentence construction, and reading skills all go unstressed. Students now enter the work force unprepared to communicate effectively (Figure 12.9).

Figure 12.9

E can't read what they won't let ir

Still another reason why Johnny can't read: The Broward County School Board, already using excesses of him-or-her and he-or-she phraseologies in its official documents in an ongoing effort to purge itself of institutional sexism, this week went a step further and banished pronouns altogether.

Flagrantly offensive buzz-words such as "he" and "she" and "him" and "her," along with similarly sexism-reeking terms that have been putting wrong ideas into the heads of our children all these years, are no longer in the official School Board vocabulary. We quote from the introduction to the newly issued "Program Guide For Gifted Education":

"Alternative language has been developed for this guide to insure non-discrimination on the basis of sex. The symbols 'e' (he/she) and 'ir' (him, his/her) were designed to incorporate the common or uncommon elements of the pronouns; thus they refer to both male and female gender."

For example, objectives of the program guide include "learning about the speed of ir learning, whether e needs outside motivation or is self-motivated."

Board chairperson Estella Moriarty, asked what e thought about all this, said there was nothing e could do about it, shrugged ir shoulders and returned to ir work.

Reprinted by permission from the *Miami Herald*, May 26, 1978, p. 1.

Status

Status is a person's relative rank.

Status, as defined in Chapter 4, refers to the relative ranking of an individual in a group. In the formal organization, those at the top tend to have much higher status than those at the bottom. When people communicate, status affects the process, because they often monitor what they say or write on the basis of who is going to receive the message, and they distort what they hear by judging its accuracy according to who said it.

Management may regard a complaint it receives from the union as nothing more than union rhetoric. However, if a member of management tells the president that the complaint is accurate, the union's message takes on a higher degree of credibility. Conversely, if a union employee is late for work and is laid off for three days, the shop steward may fight to have the punishment reduced. However, if people in the employee's area tell the steward that the employee is always late for work, falls down in assignments, and altogether is more of a hindrance than a help, the shop steward may not argue the employee's case very hard. The steward has been given two messages by the other unionized employees: the worker got what he deserved, and we're happy to see him laid off for a few days, if only to keep him out of our hair.

One of the ways to motivate people is to give them status symbols. The personnel may want equality, but most people want just a little bit more for themselves than the average person is getting. In short, status is important. We all want to feel that we are special. As a result, the organization cannot remove status symbols, so it must learn to adjust to the problems that accompany them, including communication breakdown.

Achieving effective communication

The barriers we have just examined can prevent the sender from conveying his or her meaning to the receiver, but this need not happen. There are ways to overcome the barriers and achieve effective communication. Some of the most useful are: (1) knowing the steps in the communication process, (2) using simple, repetitive language, (3) using empathy, (4) understanding body language, (5) learning how to get and give feedback, (6) developing effective listening habits and (7) improving writing skills.[4]

[4] In addition to the material in this section, other useful suggestions can be found in: Russell W. Driver, "Opening the Channels of Upward Communication," *Supervisory Management*, March 1980, pp. 24–29; Paul Hersey and Joseph W. Ralty, "One-On-One OD Communications Skills," *Training and Development Journal*, April 1980, pp. 56–60; Edward L. Levine, "Let's Talk: Tools for Spotting and Correcting Communication Problems," *Supervisory Management*, July 1980, pp. 25–37; and George Miller, "Management Guidelines: Being a Good Communicator," *Supervisory Management*, April 1981, pp. 20–26.

Knowing the steps in the communication process

If a manager knows the steps in the communication process, many of the breakdowns we have just discussed can be avoided. There are four steps in communication: (1) attention, (2) understanding, (3) acceptance, and (4) action.

Attention   Attention is possible only when the listener has screened out all the disturbances or other distractions that can interrupt his or her concentration. The sender can help in this process by remembering that many listeners are confronted with message competition. There are other things on their minds—telephone calls that must be returned, memos and reports that need to be read, people who have asked them for assistance and are awaiting replies. If the sender does not keep the message interesting and informative, there is a good chance that the receiver will begin to daydream or ponder some of the other messages competing for his or her attention.

Message competition must be overcome.

Understanding   Understanding requires a comprehension of the message. The receiver must get the meaning. In trying to accomplish this step, many managers ask their people, "Do you understand what I'm saying?" However, this is the wrong approach. One should never ask people *if* they understand, because all the pressure is on them to answer, "Yes." Rather, the manager should ask them *what* they understand. In this way, the listener is forced to restate the message in his or her own words, and the manager can judge the accuracy of understanding. Following is an illustration.

Always ask what, not if.

> Manager: Doris, we need this report typed up and sent to the division manager. I want you to get to it as soon as possible.
>
> Doris: Uh, okay. I'll get to it as soon as possible.
>
> Manager: Are you sure you understand?
>
> Doris: Sure.
>
> Manager: What are you going to do?
>
> Doris: Well, I'm going to drop that rush job I'm working on and get going on this report for the division manager.
>
> Manager: No, Doris, that's not what I meant to say. I want you to finish that rush job and *then* do the report for the division manager.
>
> Doris: Oh, okay. I misunderstood. I'm sorry.
>
> Manager: That's all right, Doris. The important thing is that we now understand each other. In the future if you have any questions about what I meant, don't hesitate to ask.

Note that the manager initially asked *if* the subordinate understood, but avoided a problem by then asking Doris *what* she understood. The manager also encouraged her to ask questions in the future to ensure continued understanding.

Acceptance requires compliance.

Acceptance   Acceptance occurs when the receiver is willing to go along with the message. Only in rare cases do subordinates refuse to comply with directives from the boss. They usually obey without giving the matter much thought. However, people balk if they think the order is detrimental to their best interests.

> **Manager: Jack, I've just gotten a phone call from Morris, and they're shipping over the supplies we ordered last week. They'll be here in about 40 minutes. I'd like you to wait, sign for the supplies, and put them in the storeroom.**
>
> **Jack: Sir, I've got a night class at the university that starts at 6 P.M. If I don't leave right now, I'll miss it.**

Obviously, the manager can try to force Jack to stay. However, if the boss reads the feedback signs, he should be able to see that Jack's acceptance will at best be slow in coming. The manager must be aware of these negative vibrations and either press for acceptance or ask someone else to wait for the supplies. In this case, asking someone else appears preferable.

Action requires the receiver to do what was expected.

Action   Action requires the receiver to follow up and do what was requested. A purchase order may have to be placed, a report filed, or a meeting held. It would appear that, if the sender gets to this action stage, the communication process will attain completion with no further problems. However, this is not always so. Sometimes the receiver will encounter unforeseen difficulties. The purchase order may not be filled because the supplier is temporarily out of raw materials; an executive secretary may be on vacation so a particular report may have to wait to be filed until she returns; a vice president may be on an extended business trip so a meeting may have to be delayed until he or she returns. In all these cases, the message will not get through the action stage.

Other common causes can be found in the receiver, who may be incapable of carrying out the order. For example, if Mary tells Bob to fill out Report A and send it to the comptroller, but Bob has never been told how to do it, the report may be done wrong or not at all. The message may not reach the stage of completed action. Or, if Bob asks Mary for help and she is too busy to see him, he will fill it out as best as he can, with the same result.

If the action stage is to be completed, the sender must be available to answer questions and provide assistance to the receiver. If a problem develops, the receiver then has someone to turn to. The action stage ensures that there is feedback in case of trouble. Remember, the sender's communication responsibility does not end until the desired action is completed.

Using simple, repetitive language

The simpler a message, the more likely it will be understood and acted on properly. Consider the advertisements you see in the daily newspaper. Research shows that the shorter the ad, the higher the reader rate, and the greater the likelihood that the material will be remembered.

Unfortunately, many managers do not carry this simple rule to the work place with them. They tend to communicate long messages in hurried-up fashion. The receivers are unable to follow everything said, but the sender is in such a rush that they are afraid to interrupt either to ask questions or get the sender to repeat the more difficult portions of the message. If the message is in writing, the sender tends to use vague terms and incorporate too many ideas into one sentence. When the receiver has read the memo, only part of the message has been properly decoded.

Simple messages often get the best results.

Effective managers know that every message should be understandable. If the subject matter is complex, the communication should be done in "small bites," giving the listener the opportunity to ask questions or seek clarification. In addition, the sender should, from time to time, recap part of the message so that the listener finds it easier to follow the flow of information. We illustrate how this can be done further on in the chapter.

Using empathy

Empathy means putting oneself, figuratively, in another person's place. In so doing one begins to see things as the other person does. Barker has put it this way:

> **Empathy means deep understanding of other people, identifying with their thoughts, feeling their pain, sharing their joy. Such empathy is typical of strong, healthy relationships. Indeed, empathetic communicators know each other so well that they can predict the responses to their messages. For example, Mario says to himself, "I know if I tell May that I'm not crazy about her new dress, she'll be hurt. So instead I'll say, 'May, that dress looks great on you, but I think the green one is even more becoming.'"[5]**

We know that successful managers empathize with their subordinates. They know when to be task-oriented and when to be people-oriented, because they are capable of putting themselves in a subordinate's place and answering the question, "What kind of direction does this person need?"

Successful managers are empathetic.

Empathy is particularly important at two stages of the communication process: acceptance and action. When the manager gives an order

[5] Barker, *Communication*, p. 151.

that the subordinate is reluctant to accept, the manager should be tuned in to pick up the hesitancy. Apparently the subordinate does not understand how important the matter is and how significant his or her role will be. The manager needs to further clarify the situation and explain why the subordinate is being asked to handle the task. If a manager lacks empathy, it is likely that he or she will ignore the hesitancy. The astute manager knows that the problem or issue should be dealt with immediately and laid to rest.

Empathy also helps in the action stage. When the subordinate has trouble carrying out a directive, the empathetic manager is quick to give assistance. He or she realizes immediately that help is needed and does not let the subordinate down. Conversely, the manager who lacks empathy does not check on worker progress and, when he or she learns that the subordinate is having trouble, lets the subordinate work it out alone. Research shows that empathetic managers are more effective than managers who lack empathy.

Understanding body language

Body language is one of the most important forms of nonverbal communication. People use this communication form to pass messages to each other, although in many cases they are unaware they are doing so. Common examples of body language include the way a person moves his or her eyes, where an individual stands in a room in relation to others there, the way a person shakes hands or touches another on the shoulder, and the way people dress.

Eye movement is important.

In regard to eye movement, many managers believe that if people are lying, they will not look the listener in the eye. This is untrue. Effective liars often do look their listeners right in the eye; they know such eye contact increases their credibility. However, there are things managers can learn by looking at the other person's eye movements. In particular, it is possible to tell when the other party is under stress or emotion. For example, right-handed people tend to look to the left when they are trying to deal with an issue on an emotional level, and they tend to look to the right when they are unemotional or rational. The reverse is true for left-handed people. In addition, notes Preston:

. . . when an individual is excited or aroused, the pupils of the eyes will dilate. When haggling over price, a buyer will unconsciously signal an alert seller that a particular price is acceptable. By watching for such a signal, the dealer knows when to stop haggling and begin closing the deal. Candid, slow-motion movies of people in grocery stores showed various eye pupil dilation levels when individuals looked at different colors, shapes, and designs of packages on the store shelves. Some colors or shapes caused more excitement than others, and the reaction registered in the shopper's eyes. With this research information, marketing people redesign their products to better appeal to buyers in a competitive environment. Good poker players watch the eyes of their

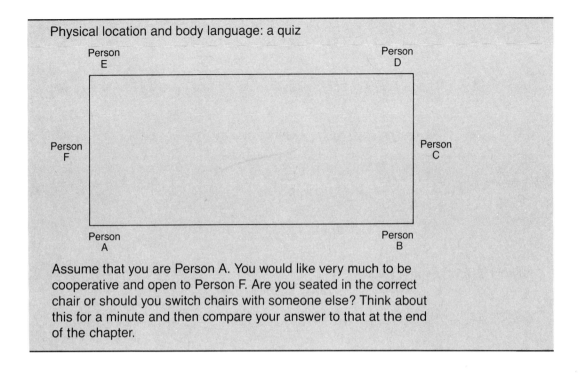

Physical location and body language: a quiz

Person E

Person D

Person F

Person C

Person A

Person B

Assume that you are Person A. You would like very much to be cooperative and open to Person F. Are you seated in the correct chair or should you switch chairs with someone else? Think about this for a minute and then compare your answer to that at the end of the chapter.

fellow players as new cards are dealt. The pupil dilation very often will show if the card being dealt improves the player's hand.[6]

Touch is another important body language sign. When people shake hands, a vigorous handshake (by a man) or a firm one (by a woman) is often regarded as a sign of self-assurance. Touching is used to define power relationships. A manager who wants to emphasize an order will grasp the employee's arm while issuing the order. If the individual wants to congratulate the employee, he or she will pat the person on the back.

So is touch.

Physical location is a third important form of body language. As we saw in Chapter 2, the way furniture is placed in a room communicates something about the person who occupies it. The same is true regarding where an individual stands or sits in relation to others.

Physical location.

Clothing also conveys messages, fashion experts believe. For example, Molloy, discussing how men should dress in his book, *Dress for Success*, writes that:

And dress.

The most authoritative pattern is the pinstripe, followed in descending order by the solid, the chalk stripe and the plaid. If you need to be more authoritative, stick with dark pinstripes. But if you are a very large man or if you already have a great sense of presence or if you have a

[6] Paul Preston, *Communication for Managers* (Englewood Cliffs, N.J.: Prentice-Hall, Inc., 1979), p. 161.

gruff or swarthy appearance, it is best to trim down your authority so that people will not be frightened by you. This can be accomplished by wearing lighter shades of blue and gray and beiges.

Body language is something that managers learn over time. The most effective way of doing so is by remaining alert to the way in which others conduct themselves and continually ask the question: what is this person saying to me? In answering the question, the manager must take both the other person and the environment (the room, where the person is sitting or standing, and how the person is dressed) into account.

Learning to receive and give feedback

The primary way for any manager to improve in communication ability is by learning when his or her messages are being transmitted poorly and working to overcome the breakdown. One way to do so is to solicit feedback. To do so, there are a number of effective openers. Some are:

Solicit communication feedback.

"Could you give some more information about . . . ?"

"You've given me some things to think over. I'd welcome any other ideas you might have about . . ."

"I think the proposed reorganization plan is a good one. What do you think?"

Notice that in each of these opening remarks, the sender is encouraging the receiver to give feedback. The channel is being opened.

In discouraging feedback, the sender closes the channel by either threatening or belittling the receiver. In those cases the receiver is likely to say nothing. The following are illustrations:

"Let me say straight off that there is no way that I'll go along with any recommendation other than the one that J. R. proposed yesterday."

"While you may not be aware of all the constraints I'm working under . . . ."

"Of course, that may be the way you see it, but let's look at the facts."

In each of these statements the sender is closing down the feedback channel. In the first example, the sender is apparently backing up a top manager and daring the receiver to argue the point. In the second, the sender seems to be saying that he or she is overworked and does not want any disagreement or argument from the receiver. In the last example, the sender appears to be labeling the receiver as stupid. Unless the

---

[7]John T. Molloy, *Dress for Success* (New York: Warner Books, 1975), p. 46.

receiver is looking for an argument with the manager, there is little chance that he or she will say anything in response.

Once the manager starts getting feedback, it is important to sustain the flow of information. Numerous stock phrases or statements can be used for this. Here are some of the most effective:

"Could you tell me more about . . . ?"

"I see."

"Right, right. Go on."

Sustain the flow of information.

"I appreciate your saying that."

"Am I going into sufficient detail?"

"What else?"

Finally, we need to consider the subject of giving feedback. Sometimes the subordinate will not ask questions about matters that merit further discussion or explanation. At these times the effective manager needs to know how to introduce feedback into the process. Some of the best opening lines are:

"Would you be interested in my reactions to . . ."

"You may be at a good point right now for me to give you some feedback on . . . ."

"I like what you did. What sets it apart is . . . ."

In each of these instances the sender (manager) has approached the feedback issue from the standpoint of the receiver (subordinate). Each comment conveys something of help or value to the receiver. For example, in the first opening, the manager is going to give reactions to some matter that apparently involved the subordinate. Note, however, that the manager did not attempt to give these reactions unsolicited. The manager asked if the subordinate would be interested in them. If the subordinate feels feedback will be of little value, he or she can say so, but the opportunity for feedback is there if the subordinate wants it. In the second and third openings, it is obvious that the subordinate is going to be given feedback that is important and, in the last case, laudatory.

Give subordinates feedback.

These effective openers contrast significantly with ineffective openers that commonly lead the subordinate to tune out the message. Some common examples are:

"You really ought to know better than to . . . ."

"How many times do I have to tell you not to . . . ?"

"Now, Bob, you're just too critical of . . . ."

In each case the listener is not really being given feedback as much as being criticized for particular behavior. The most common response is to ignore it.

How does a manager overcome these common pitfalls and learn how to both receive and give feedback? The answer rests in analyzing one's messages and putting oneself in the receiver's shoes (empathizing).

Developing effective listening habits

Listening is difficult business. Research reveals that most people speak approximately 125 words a minute but are capable of listening to over 600 words a minute. This leaves the brain a great deal of slack, which can be used for such things as daydreaming or thinking up responses to issues that the speaker raises. Instead of really listening to what the person is saying, the listener is trying to formulate a response.[8]

Fortunately, the skills of effective listening can be developed. The best way to do so is by creating a motivation to hear, to understand, and to remember. Some of the most useful techniques are:

1. Do not label the speaker as either boring or uninteresting merely because you dislike his or her delivery. Listen to *what* is being said rather than *how* it is being said.

2. Tell yourself that the speaker has something to say that will be of value or benefit to you. Give him or her a chance to communicate.

3. If the speaker starts talking about something you find boring, ask a pertinent question to influence him or her toward more interesting subject matter.

4. If the presentation becomes too technical or difficult to understand, fight the tendency to tune out the speaker by increasing your determination to listen, to learn, and to remember.

Ten ways to develop effective communication.

5. Note the techniques used by the speaker to determine if you should adopt any of them yourself. Did he or she use a lot of facts? Was an emotional appeal ever employed? When? Were either of these approaches effective in presenting the message? Could you use these techniques yourself to improve your own communication skills?

6. Evaluate the relevance of what is being said. Are any new or useful data being communicated that can be of value to you?

7. Listen for intended meanings as well as for expressed ideas. Are there any hidden messages that the speaker is trying to convey?

8. Integrate in your mind what the speaker is saying so that it all fits into a logical composite. If any information does not fit into this overall scheme, place it on the sidelines but seek to integrate it later.

---

[8] Ralph G. Nichols, "Listening, What Price Inefficiency?" *Office Executive*, April 1959, pp. 15–22.

9. Be a responsive listener by maintaining eye contact with the speaker and giving him or her positive feedback, such as nods and facial expressions.

10. Be willing to accept the challenge of effective listening by telling yourself that it is something you need to develop.

Are you a good listener? One way of finding out is by taking the quiz that follows.

Are you a good listener?

Read the 14 statements below and rate yourself on each by using the following scale:

A = Always
B = Almost always
C = Usually
D = Sometimes
E = Rarely
F = Almost never
G = Never

1. Do you let the speaker completely express his or her ideas without interruption by you? _____

2. Do you become upset or excited when the speaker's views differ from your own? _____

3. Are you able to prevent distractions from disrupting your ability to listen? _____

4. Do you make continuous notes on everything the other person says? _____

5. Are you able to read between the lines and hear what a person is saying even when there are hidden messages being conveyed? _____

6. When you feel that the speaker or topic is boring, do you find yourself tuning out and daydreaming about other matters? _____

7. Are you able to tolerate silence by sitting quietly and allowing the speaker time to gather his or her thoughts and go on with the message? _____

8. As you listen, do you find yourself trying to pull together what the speaker is saying in way of determining what the person has said and where the individual seems to be headed with the message? _____

9. As you listen to the speaker, do you note that person's body language and try to incorporate this into your interpretation of the person's message? _____

10. If you disagree with what the individual is saying, do you provide the person with immediate feedback by shaking your head no? _____

11. Do you move around a great deal when listening, changing your posture, crossing and recrossing your arms and/or legs, and sliding back and forth in your chair? _____

12. When you listen, do you stare, intensely into the other person's eyes and try to maintain this direct contact throughout the time the individual is speaking? _____

13. When the other party is done speaking, do you ask pointed and direct questions designed to clarify and amplify what was said? _____

14. If the other person has been critical of you, do you try to put the individual in his or her place before addressing the substantive part of the message? _____

The interpretation of your answers is at the end of the chapter.

It is not always easy to follow these ten guidelines. In fact, many effective managers report that when they first decided to become better listeners they had to force themselves to follow these guidelines. Effective listening is not simply "doing what comes naturally"; for, as Preston has noted, "everyone has learned to talk, but no one has learned to listen."[9] Listening is a developed skill. This is why, in many organizations today, managers are being given effective listening courses in which they are being taught how to become active listeners. In large degree, listening is starting to be regarded as partly a science (rather than a total art) which can be improved through training and practice.

Improving your writing skills

Whenever communication is discussed, talk usually centers on reading, speaking, and listening; writing typically is given a low priority. Why is this so? Perhaps the main reason is that most managers do not write well and they hate to be reminded of it. Yet written communication is an important part of their job as seen by the fact that managers are always writing memos, reports, evaluations, and so on.

---

[9] Preston, *Communication for Managers*, p. 52.

How can you improve your own writing skills? There are a number of steps you can take. First, force yourself to write and rewrite material. If you do this long enough, you are going to become much more effective in written skills. Professional writers admit that writing is difficult work, but you can get better at it if you make yourself do it.

Second, make it a point to write at least three drafts of everything you do. The first draft is for the gathering of ideas. The second draft is for assuring that the material is accurate. The third draft is for polishing and making the material read smoothly and interestingly.

There are a number of useful steps.

Third, see if you can get someone in your organization to review your written work and comment on it. There may be four or five problems that account for 90 percent of your inability to write effectively. Once you identify the problems you can anticipate them in your writing.

Finally, if possible, sign up for a course at a nearby college or university and force yourself to learn more effective writing skills. If this is either too time consuming or threatening, put together your own checklist of the most important things to look for in written communiques and compare your written work with this checklist. Figure 12.10 provides a written performance inventory that can be useful. If you look closely at the figure, you see that it addresses the four most important areas of written material: readability, correctness, appropriateness, and thought. Use this figure as a point of departure until you have developed one of your own that more closely addresses your particular needs.

Summary

One of the best ways to achieve behavioral effectiveness in the work place is to communicate properly. In this chapter we review the ways in which effective communication can be attained. First we examine communication, which is the process of transmitting meanings from sender to receiver. In this process there are five essential elements: (1) the sender, (2) the message, (3) the medium, (4) the receiver, and (5) the interpretation given to the message. In conveying the message, three functions must be performed: encoding of the message, choice of a communication medium, and decoding of the message.

In an organization, communication has one of four basic directions: downward, upward, lateral, and diagonal. Each of these can play an important role in conveying messages throughout the hierarchy. However, many barriers can prevent effective communication, including perception, inference, language, and status. *Perception* is a person's view of reality. Since no two people have the same experiences and training, no two people see things exactly the same. For this reason there are degrees of perception, and what is crystal clear to the sender may be very vague to the receiver. *Inference* is an assumption made by the receiver of a message. Whenever messages are long, involved, or unspecific, there is a good chance that inference will be made. *Language* is a barrier whenever two people have dif-

Figure 12.10
Written performance inventory

1. Readability

Reader's Level
☐ Too specialized in approach
☐ Assumes too great a knowledge of subject
☐ So underestimates the reader that it belabors the obvious

Sentence Construction
☐ Unnecessarily long in difficult material
☐ Subject-verb-object word order too rarely used
☐ Choppy, overly simple style (in simple material)

Paragraph Construction
☐ Lack of topic sentences
☐ Too many ideas in single paragraph
☐ Too long

Familiarity of Words
☐ Inappropriate jargon
☐ Pretentious language
☐ Unnecessarily abstract

Reader Direction
☐ Lack of "framing" (i.e., failure to tell the reader about purpose and direction of forthcoming discussion)
☐ Inadequate transitions between paragraphs
☐ Absence of subconclusions to summarize reader's progress at end of divisions in the discussion

Focus
☐ Unclear as to subject of communication
☐ Unclear as to purpose of message

2. Correctness

Mechanics
☐ Shaky grammar
☐ Faulty punctuation

Format
☐ Careless appearance of documents
☐ Failure to use accepted company form

Coherence
☐ Sentences seem awkward owing to illogical and ungrammatical yoking of unrelated ideas
☐ Failure to develop a logical progression of ideas through coherent, logically juxtaposed paragraphs

3. Appropriateness

A. Upward Communications

Tact
☐ Failure to recognize differences in position between writer and receiver
☐ Impolitic tone — too brusque, argumentative or insulting

Supporting Detail
☐ Inadequate support for statements
☐ Too much undigested detail for busy superior

Opinion
☐ Adequate research but too great an intrusion of opinions
☐ Too few facts (and too little research) to entitle drawing of conclusions
☐ Presence of unasked for but clearly implied recommendations

Attitude
☐ Too obvious a desire to please superior
☐ Too defensive in face of authority
☐ Too fearful of superior to be able to do best work

B. Downward Communications

Diplomacy
☐ Overbearing attitude toward subordinates
☐ Insulting and/or personal references
☐ Unmindfulness that messages are representative of management group or even of company

Clarification of Desires
☐ Confused, vague instructions
☐ Superior is not sure of what is wanted
☐ Withholding of information necessary to job at hand

Motivational Aspects
☐ Orders of superior seem arbitrary
☐ Superior's communications are manipulative and seemingly insincere

4. Thought

Preparation
☐ Inadequate thought given to purpose of communication prior to its final completion
☐ Inadequate preparation or use of data known to be available

Competence
☐ Subject beyond intellectual capabilities of writer
☐ Subject beyond experience of writer

Fidelity of assignment
☐ Failure to stick to job assigned
☐ Too much made of routine assignment
☐ Too little made of assignment

Analysis
☐ Superficial examination of data leading to unconscious overlooking of important pieces of evidence
☐ Failure to draw obvious conclusions from data presented
☐ Presentation of conclusions unjustified by evidence
☐ Failure to qualify tenuous assertions
☐ Failure to identify and justify assumptions used
☐ Bias, conscious or unconscious, which leads to distorted interpretation of data

Persuasiveness
☐ Seems more convincing than facts warrant
☐ Seems less convincing than facts warrant
☐ Too obvious an attempt to sell ideas
☐ Lacks action-orientation and managerial viewpoint
☐ Too blunt an approach where subtlety and finesse called for

Source: John Feldon, "What Do You Mean I Can't Write," *Harvard Business Review*, May–June 1964, p. 147. Reprinted with permission.

ferent meanings for the same word. *Status* is a problem whenever people modify messages according to who is receiving or sending them.

These barriers can lead to communication breakdown, but there are ways of overcoming them. Some of the most helpful are: (1) knowing the steps in the communication process, (2) using simple, repetitive language, (3) using empathy, (4) understanding body language, (5) learning how to receive and give feedback, (6) developing effective listening habits, and (7) improving writing skills. Of these ways, the two that warrant most consideration are the first and the last. By knowing the steps in the communication process, it is possible for the manager to be aware of breakdowns and to work to overcome them. By being an effective listener, the manager ensures a closed loop in the communication process. The subordinate sends back a message to the manager, and the manager can use it to correct any problems that have occurred in the communication process.

Key terms in the chapter

communication process
encoding
decoding
downward communication
upward communication
lateral communication
diagonal communication
Fayol's gangplank theory

perception
inference
attention
understanding
acceptance
action
empathy

Review and study questions

1. What is meant by *communication*? Put it in your own words.
2. What are the five essential elements in the communication process? Explain each.
3. Even the colors of the room can have an effect on one's mood, resulting in a particular type of communication pattern. What is meant by this statement?
4. What is the purpose of downward communication? Upward communication? Lateral communication? Diagonal communication?
5. In what way can perception be a communication barrier?
6. Most communication experts believe that there are degrees of perceptual difficulty that account for communication problems. Do you agree or disagree with this conclusion? Explain.
7. What is an *inference*? In what way is it a communication barrier?
8. How can language lead to a breakdown in communication? Explain.

9. Is status a communication barrier? How? Explain.

10. What are the four steps in the communication process? Describe each.

11. How can a knowledge of the steps in the communication process help the manager achieve more effective communication?

12. How can empathy on the part of the manager help achieve effective communication?

13. In what way can simple, repetitive language lead to more effective communication? Explain.

14. What does a manager need to know about body language? Cite some specific examples.

15. What are some of the most effective ways of getting feedback? Giving feedback? Give some examples.

16. What are some of the important ways to develop effective listening habits? List at least six.

17. How can managers improve their writing skills? Offer at least three useful suggestions.

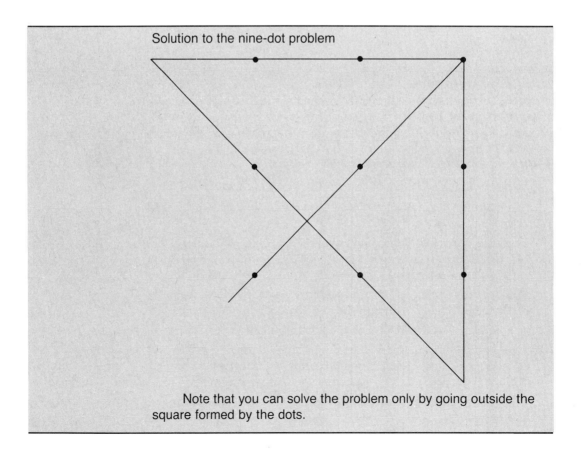

Solution to the nine-dot problem

Note that you can solve the problem only by going outside the square formed by the dots.

Answers to a matter of inference

1. **True**—the first sentence of the story says so.

2. **False**—although we are never told *exactly* where the firm is located, we do know that it is in New England.

3. **Inference**—we are never told who gave Bart the order to engage in the crash R&D program.

4. **Inference**—we are never told the size of Bart's budget. The $250,000 he has allowed his top R&D people to spend might be coming from a special fund created for this purpose by the president of the firm and so may not be included in his regular budget.

5. **Inference**—we do not know what the five people are supposed to be doing with the money. They may be working to develop a new process or they may be trying to buy the process from someone else. The story is unclear on this point.

6. **Inference**—we do not know that the individual Mary Lou is talking to is a professor. The story refers to the person as a scientist, who may not hold a professorial rank.

7. **False**—the story says that Mary Lou is one of Bart's best people, so she is in the R&D department, not the plastics manufacturing department.

8. **Inference**—we do not know whether Mary Lou is one of the five people authorized to spend up to $250,000 or a sixth member of Bart's department.

9. **Inference**—we do not know that the company wants to buy the patent. Even if they do want it, they might be interested in giving the scientist stock in the firm and a position that pays about what the scientist is currently receiving but offers better fringe benefits. In short, they may want to trade for the patent, not to buy it.

10. **Inference**—Bart may believe this. However, he may also believe that the scientist is wavering and needs to be convinced by someone in higher authority who can spell out the terms of an agreement. Even this conclusion, however, is inferential.

11. **Inference**—we do not know why the scientist is coming with Mary Lou. Additionally, he or she may have decided not to accept any reimbursement of expenses so that there is no implied obligation to go along with the company's offer.

12. **Inference**—again, we do not know for sure why the scientist is coming to see Bart. Could it be that Mary Lou has told him or her that the firm will build a special research facility far better

than that at the university and that this is motivating the scientist to fly in and talk to Bart?

13. Inference—we do not know in what area the scientist received the Nobel Prize. Nor do we know that the scientist is a man.

14. True—the story says that Bart and the president have lunch on a biweekly basis.

15. Inference—we do not know the basis for Bart's belief that he will have good news for the president. Can it be that the president assigned Bart to another project, which is coming along so well that Bart knows the president will be pleased?

Answer to physical location and body language

You are seated in the correct chair. Individuals seated at an angle to each other are more likely to engage in cooperative interaction than are those seated either side by side or completely opposite each other. You and Person F can move closer to each other or farther away, making the corner position the ideal one for the two of you.

Interpretation of are you a good listener?

Take your answer to each question and, using the scoring key below, determine the total number of points you earned.

Points Earned For Answer

Question	A	B	C	D	E	F	G	Score
1.	7	6	5	4	3	2	1	_____
2.	1	2	3	4	5	6	7	_____
3.	7	6	5	4	3	2	1	_____
4.	1	3	5	7	5	3	1	_____
5.	7	6	5	4	3	2	1	_____
6.	1	2	3	4	5	6	7	_____
7.	7	6	5	4	3	2	1	_____
8.	7	7	6	4	3	2	1	_____
9.	7	6	5	4	3	2	1	_____
10.	1	2	3	4	5	6	7	_____
11.	1	2	3	4	5	6	7	_____
12.	1	3	5	7	5	3	1	_____
13.	7	6	5	4	3	2	1	_____
14.	1	2	3	4	5	6	7	_____

Bonus point   +2

Grand total   _____

Scoring interpretation

90–100	Excellent. You are an ideal listener.
80–89	Very good. You know a great deal about effective listening.
70–79	Good. You are an above average listener.
60–70	Average. You are typical of most listeners.
Less than 60	Below average. You need to work on developing more effective listening habits.

Scheduling problems

Gary Langler is the registrar at a large Midwestern university, where total enrollment last semester was 22,619. Eight weeks before the semester began Gary received all the class schedules from the various departments. The new chairperson of the English Department had scheduled 20 sections of Composition I. However, during early registration all sections were filled to their limit of 35 students each, and 14 students who tried to pre-register were turned away.

Gary called the department chairperson and explained the situation. The chairperson told Gary, "Go ahead and schedule some more classes to handle the overflow." Gary scheduled three more on the basis of his estimate that 75 more students would enroll during late registration. The three sections were to be offered on Monday, Wednesday, and Friday at 8:30 A.M., 10:30 A.M., and 3:30 P.M. Gary sent the proposed schedule back to the chairperson for notification and told his assistant to add three sections for Composition I. The chairperson, meanwhile, assigned the 3:30 class to a professor and gave the other two to doctoral students.

On the first day of class, the three new sections presented problems for the chairperson. The 8:30 class had only 6 students, while the 10:30 class had 60. It seems that Gary failed to tell his assistant to limit the classes to 35 students each. The chairperson had to help the doctoral student transfer 25 students to the 8:30 section, and this was accomplished only after a great deal of argument with some of those chosen for transfer. Finally, the professor who agreed to teach the 3:30 class found that it had been scheduled to meet on the other side of campus from his office because no classrooms were available in any of the nearby buildings. The professor was furious. "I'm not going to walk halfway around the world to teach this class," he told the chairperson. The matter was resolved when a special seminar room was found to be available in a neighboring building and the class was moved there.

Last week the English Department chairperson was making out the schedule for the next semester, enrollment for which was estimated at 23,100. When she was done, the chairperson called Gary Langler. "Gary," she said, "I'm sending over my class schedules for next semester. If the enrollment is as high as this semester, we'll need to open some more classes. Before we do so, however, let's sit down and discuss the specifics. I don't want the foul-up we had last semester." Gary agreed.

Questions

1. What communication barrier caused Gary's assistant not to limit the classes to 35 students? Give your reasoning.
2. What communication barrier resulted in the professor's class being scheduled on the other side of campus? Explain.
3. How can the chairperson and Gary ensure that these problems do not occur again next semester? Explain your answer.

The rush order

Jean Schell, vice president of sales, received a call last week that spelled trouble. National Widget's biggest customer was on the line telling Jean that it needed its order of widgets within 24 hours. The widgets had been ordered a month ago and should have been sent out six days ago. Apparently there was an unforeseen delay in production.

As soon as Jean finished talking to the customer, she called Steve Wilson, vice president of production, and explained the situation to him. Steve said that he would look into the matter immediately and get in touch with her when he had details.

Upon calling Andre Beumont, the head of manufacturing, Steve learned that the order was just being completed and would be sent to shipping within the hour. To ensure that there were no foul-ups, Andre called George Sampson, the foreman who was in charge of seeing that the order was sent to shipping. George assured Andre that the order was just being finished and that if there were any delays, he would call back immediately. Andre emphasized how important the order was and said that it was to be shipped RUSH. George said that he would make sure the order went out right away.

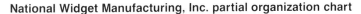

National Widget Manufacturing, Inc. partial organization chart

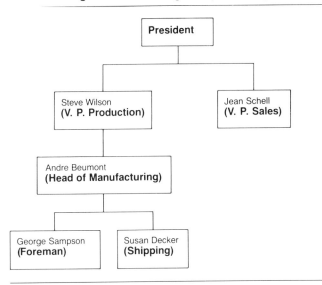

As soon as the order was finished, George took it over to Susan Decker, head of shipping. "This has to be handled RUSH," he told her. Susan took the package and said she would take care of it. However, after he left, Susan realized that she was confused. What did George mean by RUSH? There was a new order from the vice president of finance saying no orders were to be sent by air. After pondering the matter for a while, Susan sent the widget order out by truck. It arrived two days later. In the interim Jean Schell received a telegram from the company's large customer saying that the widgets had not arrived within the 24-hour period so the company had purchased them elsewhere. The truck shipment was refused when it arrived and was sent back to National Widget.

When Jean learned of the order cancellation, she was very angry and she fired off a memo to Steve Wilson. She also mentioned the order cancellation to the president. Steve called Andre Beumont into his office and bawled him out.

Andre met with George Sampson and Susan Decker and told both of them, "This mess was uncalled for! If you people don't know how to do your jobs, I'll replace you with someone who does!" As they left the office, George told Susan that she should have sent the order out by air because it was a special RUSH order and that in these cases it was not necessary to comply with the finance vice president's directive. Susan was so upset over the incident that she quit her job the next week.

Questions

1. Why did this communication breakdown occur?

2. In your opinion, who was responsible for the problem? Explain.

3. In order to ensure that this does not happen again, what would you recommend be done? Be explicit in your answer.

The
management
of change

13

Goals of the chapter

As discussed in Chapter 12, one of the most important duties of the manager in achieving behavioral effectiveness is that of communicating well; however, this alone will not ensure overall effectiveness. Sometimes the manager may be able to communicate a message well but the workers will not accept it or they will resist it. One of the most common illustrations is that of change. Whenever change is introduced, for whatever reason, there is the possibility of resistance. Sometimes an organization has to introduce change if it is to remain effective. New machines may be needed in the production area, even though they will displace 20 percent of the workers, because the competition has installed similar equipment and will be able to offer better prices. In this case, there is a very strong likelihood that the workers will fight the change. Thus, sometimes what is good for the organization is not good for the people. As a result, the management of change continues to be a topic of great concern to the field of human relations. Before reading on, test yourself and see how much you know about the change process by taking the quiz (following).

 The first goal of this chapter is to define *change* and examine how it takes place. The second goal is to answer the question, "Is resistance bad?" The third goal is to analyze human response to change, with specific consideration of rejection, resistance, tolerance, and acceptance. In particular, we study the main reasons why people choose to resist change. In the last part of the chapter we examine how to introduce and manage change properly. Our goal here is to study the dimensions of change, the steps in the change process, the importance of the time factor in introducing change, the value of participation and communication in this process, the usefulness of balance theory, and ways to remove anxiety brought about by the introduction of change. When you have finished reading this chapter, you should be able to:

1. define *change*

2. discuss how change occurs, relying on force-field analysis to describe the process

3. answer the question, "Is resistance to change bad?"

4. describe the importance of psychological factors, personal factors, and the social situation on one's attitude and evaluation of a proposed change

5. explain the four most common responses to change: rejection, resistance, tolerance, and acceptance

6. cite some of the most common reasons for resistance to change

7. discuss the three dimensions of change and their importance to the manager who is trying to bring about a particular change

8. describe the five basic steps in the change process

9. explain why the time factor is so important in the implementation of change

10. discuss the role of participation and communication in the change process

11. describe how balance theory can help the manager in introducing and implementing change

12. tell why removal of anxieties is so important in the management of change.

The nature of change

Change alters the status quo.

Change, which is any modification or alteration of the status quo, sometimes results in resistance from those who are encountering the change. Before examining the importance of change in the field of human relations, however, let us look at the nature of change by studying how it occurs and by answering the question, "Is resistance to change always a bad thing?"

How change occurs

When change takes place, three things happen: (1) there is a movement from one set of conditions to another; (2) some force(s) cause(s) the change to come about; and (3) an effect or consequence results from the change. The first two of these can be explained with Kurt Lewin's ***force-field analysis***, a constructive technique of analyzing a change situation. In this analysis, there are two types of forces, those favoring the change and those opposing it. If the forces pushing in both directions are equal in strength, as seen in Figure 13.1A, there will be no change in the status quo.

Ways of achieving change.

The only ways of achieving a change are to: (1) increase the forces favoring the alteration of the status quo so that they drive back the resist-

How much do you know about the change process?

Before studying the management of change, take a minute to examine how well you understand the change process. Presented below are a dozen statements that relate to change. Read each carefully and then check whether it is basically true or basically false. Answers are given at the end of the chapter.

	Basically True	Basically False
1. Because change is so much a part of everyday life, most modern workers like new work procedures and policies.	_____	_____
2. Most work changes lead to an immediate increase in productivity.	_____	_____
3. Many employees like the status quo; change scares them.	_____	_____
4. If a computer designed to help them do their work were available, most employees would try to learn how to use the machine as quickly as possible.	_____	_____
5. Most organizational changes that are introduced are truly designed to increase efficiency.	_____	_____
6. If their friends at work are opposed to a change, most workers will also oppose the change.	_____	_____
7. Most people who resist change do so because they enjoy giving the organization a hard time.	_____	_____
8. People prefer to be told about new changes just before they are to be implemented.	_____	_____
9. People tend to be more supportive of changes they helped fashion than of those forced upon them.	_____	_____
10. Most managers tend to overrate the time needed to implement changes effectively.	_____	_____
11. Change always results, if only in the short run, in an increase in work output.	_____	_____
12. Unions tend to reject new work changes.	_____	_____

Figure 13.1
Force-field change analyses

A. Current and Desired Situations

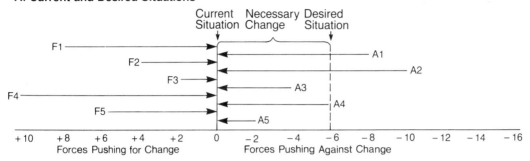

B. Change Accomplished through an Increase in the Factors Pushing for Change

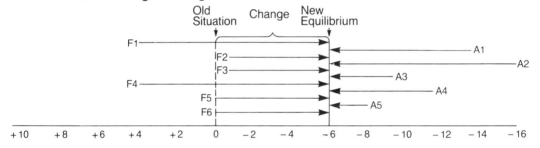

C. Change Accomplished through a Decrease in the Factors Resisting Change

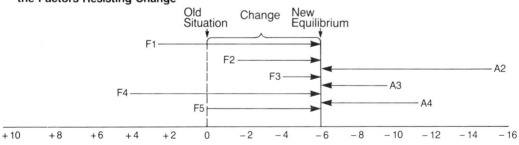

ing forces and create the desired equilibrium; (2) reduce the forces opposing the change; or (3) some combination of the two. Figure 13.1B is
an example of the first method. In this figure, in contrast to Figure 13.1A,
the forces favoring the change have increased in strength (F_1 has an
increase in strength of +1, F_2 has increased by +1, F_3 has increased by
+3, and a new force, F_6, has been added). Together these forces have

pushed back the resisting forces and the desired new equilibrium has been established.

In Figure 13.1C the strengths of the forces pushing for change are the same as they were in Figure 13.1A, but the forces pushing against change have been significantly reduced. For example, A_1 and A_5 have been eliminated.

Although we have not presented an illustration in which the forces pushing for the change gain strength while those pushing against lose strength, it would be a combination of Figures 13.1B and C. Sometimes the manager will find that this is the best alternative, because the forces pushing for the change, by themselves, will be unable to generate the strength to push back the resisting forces. However, by gathering some strength among the change forces and working to reduce the strength of the resisting forces, the manager can achieve the desired equilibrium.

Is resistance bad?

Some people believe that resistance to change is inevitable. In many cases this is true, for when the organizational employees weigh the benefits associated with the status quo against those they believe will result from the change, they opt for things the way they are. As a result, they resist any alteration of the status quo.

Such resistance is not necessarily bad. There are several important functions served by it. First, resistance forces those supporting the change to build a case against the status quo, thereby providing management a chance to weigh the pros and cons. Let us take an example:

Resistance is not always bad.

> The vice president of computer operations of a large Eastern manufacturing firm recently suggested to the president that the firm buy a larger computer and have it handle more of the paperwork functions throughout the firm. The heads of the other major departments objected to this recommendation, saying that it would be far more costly to have such information keyboarded and computer-processed than to do it by hand. After calling in an expert to evaluate the two arguments, the president learned that the computer would indeed be too costly, and he vetoed the suggestion from the vice president.

Another benefit of resistance to change is that it encourages the organization to look before it leaps. By limiting the degree of change, resistance provides a stabilizing influence. Thus, while it is dangerous to be too conservative in a dynamic environment, it is equally dangerous to be overly flexible.

> During the 1960s some private universities expanded their operations, began offering a greater variety of courses, and hired an increasing number of teachers to staff the classes. As student enrollments grew, so did university administrative budgets. It took more and more money to break even, and this could only be obtained through still further increases in enrollment. During this period, many other private institutions fought the compelling desire to expand and accommodate what

they saw to be a "short-lived" market. When the military draft ended and the inflation of the 1970s roared in, the universities that had over-extended themselves suffered major financial setbacks. Some of them were forced to close their doors.

In this case we see how change can lead to problems. Unless careful planning accompanies the change and the organization is aware of the problems that can occur, it may be very difficult for the organization to respond appropriately. Thus, resistance is not bad. We have to examine the situation and on the basis of the examination to determine: (1) whether there should be a change, (2) if so, what type of change is required, and (3) how the change should be implemented.

Change and the employees

In many cases, contrary to the evidence of our two examples (and whether the personnel like it or not), change is good for the whole organization. For example, a computer can often do computational work faster and more efficiently than any human being. Additionally, while some workers decry the advent of the computer, claiming that it causes unemployment, research indicates that this is usually not so.

One reason why computerization has not resulted in vast unemployment is that the kind of work most likely to be affected—that done by clerical workers—has been growing year by year. In fact, some companies say that they had to computerize some of their paperwork operations because they could not get enough people to handle them at the salaries they could afford to pay. When one considers that in some firms it may be necessary to process as many as a million documents within a short period, it appears that this may very likely be true. . . .

All this is not to say that eventually computerization may not cause some serious unemployment among clerical workers, but to date it has not done so.

As for managers and technical employees, the need for them has been growing fast enough to offset, or more than offset, any trend toward abolishment of the jobs they have been doing. Some surveys have shown, in fact, that the number of management jobs actually grew after computerization.[1]

Response to change

Response to change is often varied.

Despite findings such as these, the introduction of change tends to frighten many people, and they will fight it even after it has been introduced. However, not everyone is against each change. People's reactions will depend on what they see in change for themselves. If they believe they stand to profit from the change, they will support it; if they feel they will

---

[1] Ernest Dale, *Management: Theory and Practice*, 4th ed. (New York: McGraw-Hill Book Company, 1978), pp. 539–540.

Figure 13.2
Stimulus-response-outcome-effect brought on by change

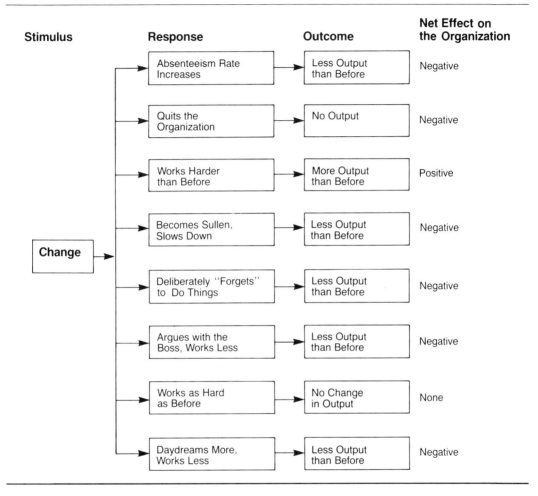

Stimulus	Response	Outcome	Net Effect on the Organization
	Absenteeism Rate Increases	Less Output than Before	Negative
	Quits the Organization	No Output	Negative
	Works Harder than Before	More Output than Before	Positive
	Becomes Sullen, Slows Down	Less Output than Before	Negative
Change	Deliberately "Forgets" to Do Things	Less Output than Before	Negative
	Argues with the Boss, Works Less	Less Output than Before	Negative
	Works as Hard as Before	No Change in Output	None
	Daydreams More, Works Less	Less Output than Before	Negative

lose status, prestige, earning power, or the job itself because of change, they will fight it. If we think of change as a stimulus, numerous responses can be made by the personnel, with varied outcomes and effects on the organization. For example, in Figure 13.2, 10 workers are being subjected to the same change. As you can see, there are many responses: increase in absenteeism, resignation, working harder than ever, slowing down, arguing with boss, and so on. Overall, however, there is a negative effect on the organization. In this case, we may conclude that most of the workers do not like the change or that it was not properly introduced.

In examining the situation further, we need to take a closer look at the stimulus (change) and response (outcome) relationship. We can

Figure 13.3
Analysis of response to change

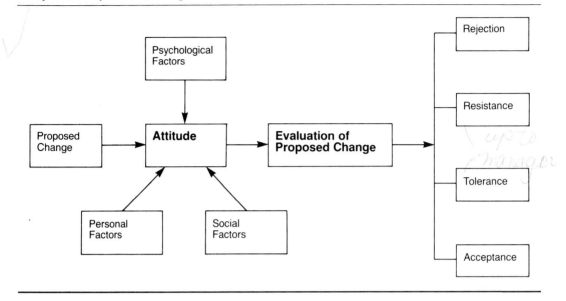

view the change or stimulus as a *causal* variable, and the response or outcome as an *end-result* variable. For human relations purposes, however, we need to investigate why different people respond in different ways to the same stimulus.

Some psychologists believe the answer can be found in the individual's attitude toward the stimulus. A person's attitude is a reflection of psychological factors, personal factors, and social factors. These factors will result in a particular evaluation of the change. In turn, the evaluation will lead to one of the four reactions: rejection, resistance, tolerance, or acceptance (Figure 13.3).

Reaction to stress is a determinant.

One of the most important psychological factors affecting attitudes is the individual's reaction to stress, a topic discussed earlier in the text. Some workers are rather comfortable under stressful or high-anxiety-producing conditions, but other employees shun stress and seek a calm environment.

So is personal experience.

One of the most important personal factors is experience; people who have encountered similar changes in the past draw on the results of those changes to evaluate the current or pending change. For example, if the last time a company changed work procedures it tried to increase output requirements by 15 percent, the workers will probably fight the management's new attempt to change work procedures again. They are likely to believe that if they give in the management will once more increase output requirements. Conversely, we can take the example of the organization that introduced a new hospitalization plan to save the employees' money; the next time the company announces a change in the hospitalization plan, there is likely to be warm support for the move because the employees had a good experience with a similar change.

The social factors refer to the group in which the individual works. If there is a great deal of cohesion in the group, all the members will tend to stick together. If the proposed change conflicts with the norms and values of the informal group, it will not go along with management's attempt to introduce change. Conversely, if the change is supportive of its norms and values, the group will accept the change. Keep in mind that when we talk about group acceptance, one of the primary norms is always group unity. If the management makes any reorganizational changes that will break up the group, the members will oppose plans.

And the norm of the work group.

As a result of psychological, personal, and social factors, an employee will form an attitude regarding the change. This attitude will assist him or her in evaluating the impact of the change to determine whether it is acceptable. On the basis of this evaluation, the employee will reject, resist, tolerate, or accept the proposed change.

Rejection   Rejection occurs when the change is perceived as potentially destructive. Those being subjected to the change view it as totally unacceptable. In this case, it is not uncommon to find workers resigning their jobs or going on strike. At best, management can expect to encounter increased turnover, alienation, and dramatic reductions in productivity and job satisfaction. The Lordstown strike is one of the best examples in recent history.

Rejection can lead the workers to quit.

The strike of the 7700 member work force of the Lordstown Vega factory was called on March 3, 1972, and lasted for 22 days. The union membership voted 6350 to 200 to walk out. The pro-strike vote was the largest in any local election in the UAW's history. The strike cost GM over $100 million in lost production and slowed their battle to compete with foreign imports.[2]

Three issues led the union to strike: (1) recognition of seniority and transfer rights under a newly determined organizational merger, (2) rehiring of laid-off workers, and (3) settlement of all grievances associated with the first two issues.[3]

As you can see, these three issues were so important to the workers that they were unwilling to continue working until the matters were resolved. They rejected the changes being imposed on them by the organizational merger.

Resistance   Whenever workers feel threatened by or extremely anxious about a particular change, they are likely to resist. The resistance can

When workers feel threatened, resistance is likely.

---

[2] Richard M. Hodgetts, *The Business Enterprise: Social Challenge, Social Response* (Philadelphia: W. B. Saunders, 1977), p. 174.

[3] *Ibid.*

be either overt or covert. ***Overt resistance*** is observable; management can see it. Work slowdown, the setting of lower informal production norms, and outright sabotage are examples. ***Covert resistance*** is not readily observable because it is done under the guise of working as usual. For example, the management has brought in a group of consultants to study operations and make efficiency recommendations. The work force is concerned that some of them will lose their jobs or will be transferred to other departments. In an effort to thwart the consultants' efforts, the workers use veiled resistance. When the consultants ask for some data on a particular topic, a worker hands them a massive report containing the information. However, it will take two or three hours to find the material. In short, the workers are not refusing to go along; they are simply making it more difficult for the consultants to do their job.

If workers feel neutral, they will often tolerate change.

Tolerance   If the workers are neutral about the change or have equal positive and negative feelings, they will often tolerate the change. For example, management decides that in future all people who work in Section D must wear safety equipment when they are in the work area. Because of the particularly high noise factor created by the machinery there, management wants every worker to wear plastic earmuffs that will screen out the noise and prevent damage to hearing. Many of the workers admit that they are not particularly anxious to wear the earmuffs, but they can understand management's point of view, so they will go along with management's request. They have no particularly strong feelings either way.

If the change is viewed positively, it will be accepted.

Acceptance   Sometimes the positive factors favoring the change are weighed much more heavily than the negative ones. In these cases the workers will gladly accept the change. For example, instead of asking the workers to wear regular plastic earmuffs, the management has a set specially wired for each person. Through the set music can be piped so that workers can listen to music and do their jobs at the same time. Changes like this have been widely accepted in many industrial settings. Printing companies, especially large newspaper firms, often give this kind of earmuff to their pressmen, who, according to research, like the changed environment.

Muzak's studies indicate that worker productivity usually reaches its low point in midmorning and midafternoon and picks up just before people go to lunch or leave for the day. To boost productivity when the "blahs" set in, Muzak pipes in music. Is this approach really beneficial to productivity? "Bing" Muscio, president of Muzak, seems to think so. He claims that music has definite physiological and psychological effects on people. "It affects," he said, "the heartbeat and blood pressure, and moderates tenseness and anxiety." And an AT&T division manager agrees, pointing out that telephone operators report they are more relaxed with music by Muzak than they were prior to its installation.

There are many other companies using Muzak's services, including **Black & Decker** and **American Machine & Foundry Inc.**, who support these findings.[4]

Why is there resistance to change?

In most cases, workers do not reject change outright nor do they accept it. Rather they tend to either resist it or tolerate it. In our study of human relations, resistance is the reaction of greatest interest to us. After all, if the workers tolerate a particular change, there is really nothing for the manager to be concerned about. However, if they resist, the manager should find out why and then should determine how this resistance can be reduced or eliminated. Let us discuss in detail the most common causes of resistance to change.

Obsolescence of job skills   A bookkeeper who has worked for the same company for 20 years and learns that bookkeeping functions are going to be transferred to a computer will fight the change. An assembly-line welder who learns that the company has just bought automatic welding machinery that will weld things faster and more efficiently than can be done by hand will oppose the change. Additionally, while organizations will attempt to find these people other positions in the firm, the meaningful alternative jobs require special training that the displaced workers lack. These people have been on the job for so long doing the same thing day after day that their knowledge about other work is obsolete. Also, they do not qualify for the jobs being given to college-educated engineers and business specialists. In short, they have no real marketable skills, so they fight for the status quo.

Machinery may replace people.

Fear of economic loss   Another reason for resistance to change is fear of economic loss. Sometimes workers are replaced or fired or find themselves in dead-end jobs. Technology often plays a key role here, turning rather demanding jobs into simple ones that can be done by anyone. When this occurs, the lower demands of the job are often reflected by a new pay rate, and the people now find that salary raises are much less than before. After all, who needs highly paid people if the job is automated so anyone can do it?

The workers may lose money.

Ego defensiveness   Sometimes a change will make a person look bad, so he or she will fight it. For example, Roberta has an idea for expanding the market effort out of the eastern part of the country and into the western states. If things go well there, the effort will then be ex-

Or the change may be ego-deflating.

[4] Richard M. Hodgetts, *Management: Theory, Process, and Practice*, 2nd ed. (Philadelphia: W. B. Saunders, 1979), p. 18.

panded to the national market. However, her boss, Chuck, is reluctant to go along with her suggestion because it will make him look bad with his colleagues, who will all realize that Roberta was the one who thought up the new sales effort. Rather than allow this to happen, Chuck continually claims that he needs to develop the market in the east more fully before considering expansion.

Many people like routine.

The comfort of the status quo   To put it simply, change is disturbing to many people. They feel more comfortable working in established routines and procedures than taking risks by entering into new ventures or undertakings. Any attempt to alter this status quo is met with resistance.

The long run scares them.

Shortsightedness   Many people know what is going to happen in the short run but not the long run. Therefore, they only look at the short-run effects of any change. We can illustrate this through an analysis of the impacts of autocratic and democratic-participative leadership. In the short run, if a manager changes from autocratic to participative leadership, his or her department will often suffer short-term decreases in productivity (Figure 13.4). This will not last indefinitely, however; long-term increases will eventually follow. Research reveals that it takes time for such a change to bring about increased productivity. Unfortunately, many managers are not interested in riding out the short-run declines in order to reap long-run benefits and so are not interested in changing their leadership style.

Their peers oppose the change.

Peer pressure   Many times people refuse to accept change because their peers are unwilling to go along with it. Remember, as noted in the discussion of group cohesiveness, if there is high cohesion, the group will stay together. If change is introduced, therefore, the group may collectively agree to resist it.

They do not fully understand it.

Lack of information   Whenever people do not know what is going to happen, they are likely to resist the change. The unknown scares them. Consider how you would feel if a doctor told you that you were very sick and had to have an immediate operation. Not knowing what is wrong with you, what kind of operation you need, or what the effect of the operation will be, you would probably be very nervous, and unless you were convinced that the operation was indeed warranted, you would resist the doctor's advice.

Social relationships may be disturbed.

Social displacement   Whenever changes are introduced, it is possible that work groups will be broken up and social relationships will be disturbed. People usually enjoy working with their fellow employees, and when these friendships are interrupted, a psychological letdown oc-

Figure 13.4
From autocratic leadership to participative leadership—an illustration

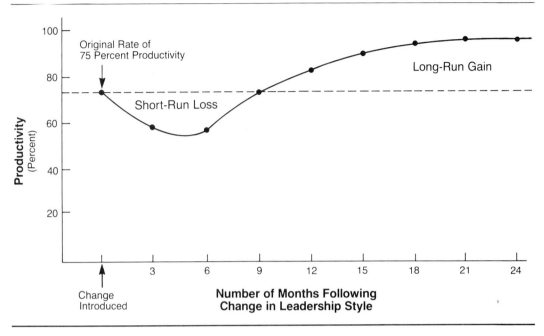

**Number of Months Following
Change in Leadership Style**

curs. Research shows that in combat situations soldiers often fight the tendency to make friends among the other members of their platoon, because if one is killed or injured, the effect on the others can be disastrous. They would not be totally prepared to do their jobs and could be injured or killed themselves. When social relationships have been developed, people tend to want to maintain them and to fight *social displacement*.

Introducing and managing change properly

Until now, we have been discussing how people respond to change and why they often resist it. Now we consider how the manager should introduce and manage change properly. Admittedly, change causes problems, but if the manager analyzes the situation properly, follows some basic steps, and remains aware of the important areas of implementation, he or she can effect many changes to the benefit of both the personnel and the organization. In particular, the manager needs to: (1) understand the three dimensions of change, (2) know the basic steps in the change process, (3) consider the time factor, (4) be aware of the importance of participation and communication, (5) know the impact of management atti-

Figure 13.5
Dimensions of change

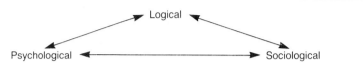

tudes on change response and the value of balance theory in this process, and (6) be aware of the need to remove anxieties both before and after the change is introduced.

The dimensions of change

One of the first things a manager must know is the three ***dimensions of change***. (See Figure 13.5.)

Is the change needed?

First there is the *logical dimension*, which is based on technological and scientific reasons. Why is the change needed, from an organizational standpoint? The logical answer is found in responses such as increases in profit, productivity, or efficiency, and decreases in cost, worker fatigue, monotony, or machine down time.

Is it in accord with worker values?

Then there is the *psychological dimension*, the logic of the change in terms of the workers who would be affected. Do these people feel the change will be good for them? Is it in line with their values? If the answer is affirmative, the psychological dimension has been satisfied.

Is it consistent with group norms?

Finally there is the *sociological dimension*, which refers to the logic of the change in terms of the work group. Will the change be consistent with the norms of the group? Will it help maintain teamwork? Will the group members be able to live with it?

Unless the manager considers all three of these dimensions, implementation of the change will be less than ideal.

The basic steps in change

If the three dimensions of change have all been adequately considered, attention can then be focused on the basic steps in change. There are five basic steps in securing effective change, and each is vital to maximum effectiveness.

Weigh the benefits and costs.

First, the manager must answer the question, "Is this change *really* necessary?" The benefits and costs must be weighed. If the manager has examined the dimensions of change we have discussed, the answer to this question must be affirmative before further consideration of the change process is undertaken.

Second, the manager must consider whether the proposed change is the right one. In many cases there are alternative changes, any one of which might accomplish the desired result. The manager must choose the one that will provide the best results for both the organization and the personnel.

Examine alternative changes.

Third, and often most important, the *impact* of the change must be evaluated. What will be the effect of the change in the short run? In the long run? These may be difficult questions to answer, but the manager should attempt some investigation in order to compare the impact of various proposed changes.

Evaluate the full impact.

Fourth, the manager must work to *secure acceptance* of the change. In this case, workers most directly affected by the change hold the key to success. Their anxieties and fears must be calmed if the company hopes to effect a successful change. Some of the steps for doing this are dealt with in the discussion of the importance of increasing forces pushing for the change, decreasing those pushing against the change, or both.

Get worker acceptance.

Fifth, there must be some *follow-up*. After the change is implemented the manager has to obtain information on how well things are going. Has the change been accepted and implemented properly? More importantly, is it doing what was desired or was it a waste of time? Let us take an example.

Follow up and evaluate the outcome.

A large university decided to experiment with its introductory economics course by changing the basic format. In all, there were to be three versions of the course offered. The first was to be the standard course, in which students came to two lectures a week and attended a lab section with a graduate student. The second was a videotaped presentation of economic topics twice a week followed by a lab section with a graduate student. The third was a "book only" course, in which the students read the text but attended no lecture or lab sections. At the end of the semester, all three groups were given a standardized, objective (multiple-choice) test. It turned out that none of the three sections scored better on the exam (statistically speaking) than the others. The department, therefore, polled the students and found that there was greatest support for teaching the course the way it was always taught: two lectures and one lab section a week. As a result, the faculty voted to return to the traditional format.

Considering the time factor

Another crucial issue in the implementation of change is the *time factor*. There is a general rule of change: the greater the degree of change, the more advance notice the company must give. If the organization plans on building a new warehouse across the street and moving some of the warehouse personnel to this facility, a one-month notice may be appropriate. However, if the company plans on establishing a new branch office 500 miles away, it may be necessary to give at least six months' notice to the employees who will be transferred there. They have to sell their homes, find new ones, move their families, and locate schools and other

Give advance notice of change.

Table 13.1

Extent to which superiors and subordinates agree about whether superiors tell subordinates in advance about changes

How Often Superiors Tell Subordinates in Advance about Changes Affecting Them or Their Work	Top Staff Says about Its Own Behavior (percent)	Foremen Say about Top Staff's Behavior (percent)	Foremen Say about Their Own Behavior (percent)	Workers Say about Foremen's Behavior (percent)
Always	70	27	40	22
Nearly always	30	36	52	25
Always or nearly always (total)	*100*	*63*	*92*	*47*
More often than not		18	2	13
Occasionally		15	5	28
Seldom		4	1	12

Adapted from Rensis Likert, *New Patterns of Management* (New York: McGraw-Hill Book Company, 1961), p. 52. Reprinted with permission.

services (doctor, accountant, lawyer) that they will need in order to settle into a comfortable life in the new location.

Research shows that most managers tend to underrate the time needed to implement change effectively. In many cases, managers believe that they communicate change in advance, but subordinates report that this is not the case. Additionally, while the problem exists at the upper levels of the organization, it is also present at the lower levels of the hierarchy, and the lower the level of the organization, the more the problem is magnified. In Likert's survey, for example, as shown in Table 13.1, 100 percent of the top staff said that they always or nearly always told their subordinates in advance about work changes, but only 63 percent of the foremen agreed. However, when asked the same question, 92 percent of the foremen said they always or nearly always told subordinates in advance about work changes, but only 47 percent of the workers agreed. Unless managers are aware of statistics such as these, they are likely to fall into the trap of believing that their workers are both aware of and in agreement with the impending change.

Participation and communication

Allow employee participation.

Participation is important in the change process because, as we know from research, people will be more supportive of changes that they helped bring about than of changes that were either assigned to them or forced upon them. Additionally, if some problem occurs with implementation of a change they have assisted with, the workers will help eliminate or work around the problem. However, if they have had no input regarding the change, they will sit on the sidelines and let management figure out how to solve the problem.

"Thanks for asking, but I assure you that you are not going too fast for me."

Drawing by Modell. © 1981
The New Yorker Magazine, Inc.

Research also reveals that although many managers believe they involve their people in the change process, workers do not think so. Table 13.2 supplies statistics gathered by Likert about whether or not superiors use their subordinates' ideas and opinions in solving job problems. As you can see, 70 percent of the top staff said that they always or almost always consult their subordinates, but only 52 percent of the foremen agreed. Likewise, although 73 percent of the foremen said that they practice a participative approach, only 16 percent of the workers agreed.

Much of the problem rests with the different ways managers and workers perceive the managers' actions. Sometimes the workers do not

Table 13.2

The extent to which superiors and subordinates agree about whether superiors use subordinates' ideas and opinions in solving job problems

How Often Superiors Use Subordinates' Ideas and Opinions in Solving Job Problems	Top Staff Says about Its Own Behavior (percent)	Foremen Say about Top Staff's Behavior (percent)	Foremen Say about Their Own Behavior (percent)	Workers Say about Foremen's Behavior (percent)
Always	70	52	73	16
Often	25	17	23	23
Sometimes or seldom	5	31	4	61

Adapted from Rensis Likert, *New Patterns of Management* (New York: McGraw-Hill Book Company, 1961), p. 53. Reprinted with permission.

regard attempts by the manager to get them involved as inviting participation. At other times, the workers may give the manager a suggestion for a change that will increase productivity, and after thinking over the matter, the manager will decide to go ahead and implement it. Because the manager gives them no feedback, the workers are unaware that they generated the idea, and they tend to believe that the management is forcing the change on them.

We can make another rule of change on the basis of these statistics: never surprise the subordinates with a change; always give them plenty of notice of what you are doing and keep them informed as you go along. This is where communication comes into the picture.

Let us examine an example involving both participation and communication to see how things can get fouled up if the manager does not keep everyone informed about what is going on.

On Friday afternoon, the plant manager told Fred that he would be getting new machinery in his department. Fred had been after the top management to buy this machinery for almost a year. Now he was informed that the machines would be arriving the first thing Monday morning.

In order to have room for the new equipment, however, the old machines would have to be dismantled, packaged, and moved off the floor. They were to be sold, the plant manager told Fred, to a firm in another part of the country.

The good news was a big surprise to Fred and he was delighted. He hurried down to the plant floor and told his people to start dismantling the old machinery. However, he did *not* tell them why they were doing this. Fred decided to let them enjoy the surprise on Monday morning.

However, things did not go according to Fred's plan. As soon as he reached his desk on Monday, he received a call from the plant manager telling him that the Personnel Department had called and said that six of the fifteen workers in Fred's department had quit and three more had called in sick. Fred promised to get the matter straightened out.

He immediately called one of the workers who had resigned. "George, this is Fred. I was just talking to the plant manager and he tells me you're quitting. Why?"

"Listen, Fred," George answered. "I'm not going to sit around waiting to be fired. I spent all day yesterday looking through the want ads and there are plenty of jobs available for machinists. I have an interview in about an hour with another firm."

"But why do you want to quit?" Fred exclaimed. "What makes you think you'll be fired?"

"Are you kidding? Why were we dismantling those machines and packaging them, if the firm weren't getting ready to lay us off? There's nothing left for us to do. I know someone's getting ready to lower the ax on me."

"But that's not it at all, George! We have new machines coming in to replace those old ones. That's why we were packaging the old ones and shipping them out. We were making room for the new ones. I didn't tell you about the new machines because I wanted to surprise you," Fred explained.

"Well, you sure surprised me!" George promised to cancel his interview and come to work.

Fred spent the next hour calling the rest of the men and explaining the situation. By noon all of them were back in the plant helping assemble the new machinery.

Remember the discussion in Chapter 5 of the informal organization? People who work near each other tend to be on the same grapevine, and when there is incomplete information about something, they begin to construct rumors to explain the situation. They will give the matter their own interpretation rather than live with uncertainty or ambiguity. This is what happened in Fred's department. However, with participation and communication, the manager can overcome these dysfunctional results.

Management attitudes and balance theory

When it comes to change, very few things will get the manager in more trouble than to have a negative personal attitude toward the change. If the manager does not agree with the proposed change ordered by the boss, he or she should voice opposition as soon as the order is issued. However, if the company is determined to implement the change, the manager's job is to help do so. If the proposed change conflicts with the manager's values or morals, he or she should transfer to another department or resign. In introducing the change to the workers, the manager cannot take the stance, "This is the proposed change. I personally disagree with it, and wouldn't blame you if you did, too. However, they told me to implement it, so I'm going to have to do just that." The manager should have a positive attitude toward the change at all times. Additionally, he or she should find out *why* the change can be beneficial to the workers and should use these positive features as selling points to obtain worker acceptance.

Have management support for the change.

In balance theory, there are three critical elements.

One way of looking at management attitudes toward change and the strategy that can be used in bringing it about is through **balance theory**. In balance theory terms, change has three critical elements: (1) the manager, (2) the worker, and (3) the proposed change. A balance is needed among all three.

Let us examine Figure 13.6, a simple illustration of balance theory in action in which the relationship among the elements is positive. The manager has a positive attitude toward the change, the worker has a positive attitude toward the manager, and the worker has a positive attitude toward the change. We have a balanced triad.

Now let us examine an unbalanced triad, as presented in Figure 13.7. Here the manager is positive toward the change, the worker is negative toward the change, and the worker is positive toward the manager. We have two pluses and a minus, and in such a case there is imbalance. How can balance be restored? There are two ways: (1) have three pluses or (2) have two minuses and a plus. What should the manager do to obtain balance? Obviously, if the worker has a positive attitude toward the manager, the manager should try to get the worker to change his or her attitude toward the change. The manager should point out why he or she is personally in favor of the change. Now the worker has two options. He or she can say, "I like and respect you, and if the change is agreeable to you, it's okay with me." Then we have three pluses in the triad and balance is established. On the other hand, the worker may say, "I disagree with you. The change is a bad idea. I will not alter my attitude toward it." How can the worker have a positive attitude toward the manager and still disagree with the manager's point of view? The worker cannot do so, at least in the long run. So he or she will begin to reason, "The manager is not my friend. All he wants to do is manipulate me into accepting the change. I'm not going to do it, and I'm not going to trust him either." In this case we have two minuses and a plus. The manager has a positive attitude toward the change, and the worker has a negative attitude toward both the change and the manager. There is balance. However, it is the *wrong* kind. In short, the manager in this case must try to alter the worker's attitude toward the change. Otherwise we have a balanced triad that is anti-change. The only acceptable solution to this problem in balance theory terms is three pluses.

Let us take a last illustration, this time involving a manager who does *not* like the change. The situation is depicted in Figure 13.8. As you can see, the manager has a negative attitude toward the change, the worker has a positive attitude toward the manager, and the worker has a negative attitude toward the change. Here we have a balanced triad (two minuses and a plus), but it is a dangerous balance. The worker and manager like each other and both dislike the change. The only way to establish a different balance in the triad is for the manager's boss to convince him or her to be positive toward the change. If this does occur, of course, we will have (at least for the moment) an unbalanced triad. The manager will like the change, and the worker will like the manager and dislike the

Figure 13.6
A balanced triad

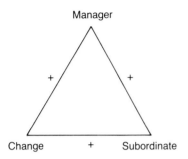

Figure 13.7
An unbalanced triad

Figure 13.8
A balanced triad

change. The situation can now be rectified if the manager shows the worker how the change can be good. If the manager is successful in this attempt, we will then have three pluses and a balanced triad.

In our recommended solution to this problem it is important to remember that the successful manager is interested in both the company

Table 13.3
Relationship between management's appraisals and workers' views of superiors

Management's Appraisal of Supervisor	Workers' View of Supervisor (percent of workers)			
	Pulls for the Company	Pulls for Himself	Pulls for the Workers	Pulls for the Company and the Workers
Immediately promotable	4	21	0	75
Promotable and/or Satisfactory-plus	23	11	9	57
Satisfactory	22	10	10	58
Questionable and/or Unsatisfactory	30	21	9	40

Adapted from Rensis Likert, *New Patterns of Management* (New York: McGraw-Hill Book Company, 1961), p. 19. Reprinted with permission.

and the workers, and he or she does not support either one over the other. This is clearly illustrated in Table 13.3, which summarizes the results of another study. Note that the supervisors whom the management considered immediately promotable were seen by the employees as pulling for *both* the company and the workers. This is in contrast to the supervisors who were rated as questionable or unsatisfactory by the management; they were seen by the employees as much more interested than the immediately promotable managers in pulling for the company alone (30 percent versus 4 percent) than for both the company and the workers (40 percent versus 75 percent). If you compare these two groups closely, you can see that the greatest difference between them was whether they were seen as pulling for the company alone or for both the company and the workers. This is the deciding factor in distinguishing the most successful from the least successful.

Balance theory shows how to manage change.

Balance theory is valuable because it shows how to manage change. If you construct your own examples and apply them to the triad, you can also work your own solutions. The only thing you must keep in mind is that the changes in attitudes must be logical. For example, it is unlikely to have a balanced triad in which the manager and the worker like the change but the worker dislikes the boss. People who dislike each other seldom have the same opinion about changes. The worker will think, "If the boss likes this change, and I don't like the boss, I'd better not like it. He's always out to get me, so this change must be something I should oppose." If you keep this concept of logic in mind, you can run through various examples of changes and determine how the manager should handle each situation.

Removing anxieties

Consideration of the time factor, the importance of participation and communication, and the balance theory are all important tools by which the manager can reduce the anxieties that are so natural in the change process. Although these do not constitute all the things a manager needs to do in managing change properly, they are the most important for they help deal with anxiety, which is the major problem associated with change. In fact, this topic is so important that it warrants separate consideration.

Remember, as we stress throughout the chapter, that as people get ready to leave an environment in which they feel comfortable and familiar, they tend to become fearful and anxious. What will the new situation be like? This fear of the unknown can be a source of stress. As we noted earlier, it is often also a cause of resistance. The worker is concerned about how long it will take to learn the new skills and techniques being introduced, wondering what new criteria will be used to evaluate performance. The manager needs to pay close attention to these anxieties because they are the biggest factors in causing resistance to change. Herbert suggests ways to deal with such problems:

Change often creates anxiety.

> **Fears and anxieties may be allayed through removing penalties for failure in an experimental period. The change may be tried without measurement of individual failure or performance; those affected by the change may become familiar with what is involved in it and how they may adapt to it. Linking the goals of the change to the goals of the individuals and groups involved can also help to eliminate built-in conflict.[5]**

Also, although acceptance of the change is important, there must also be a *follow-up* program to see that everything is going well. (See Table 13.4 regarding important dos and don'ts of dealing with change.) If people accept change, they want to believe that they were right. An ideal example of this is the consumer who is persuaded by advertising to switch brand names and buy a different company's product. The consumer often begins to have second thoughts, so some of a company's budget has to be directed toward post-purchase advertising. In this way the consumer is assured that his or her decision was the right one and is encouraged to buy the product again. This process works for subordinates who have accepted some change. The company needs to reassure them that they made the right decision. Most commonly, the manager can do so by telling them what a good job they are doing because they have accepted the change.

See that everything is going well.

The accounting department of a retail chain recently requested that all stores begin submitting some of their sales data on specially designed forms. These forms would help the accounting department tabulate the information more quickly and give feedback to the stores regarding cost and budget information. While the store managers were initially reluctant to ask their people to adopt the new forms, they did go along with the request. In turn, the head of the accounting department made it a special point to call each store manager to thank him or her for helping out and to explain how the newly submitted data would help the store get faster feedback for decision making. Made aware of

---

[5] Theodore T. Herbert, *Dimensions of Organizational Behavior*, 2nd ed. (New York: Macmillan Publishing Co., Inc., 1981), p. 360.

Table 13.4

Managing change: some dos and don'ts

Dos	Don'ts
Do realize that most people like the status quo.	Do not assume that employees will automatically accept change simply because you explain why it is useful to them.
Do give advance notice regarding the change.	
Do explain the reason for the change.	
Do relate how the change will be helpful to the employees.	Do not embarrass or ridicule those who question the change.
Do weigh the costs and benefits of the change.	Do not threaten to fire or punish those who resist the change.
Do be frank and honest regarding any changes that will take place in the salaries or job tenure of the employee.	Do not believe that employees always fight change because they enjoy giving management a hard time; usually it is economic and social issues that cause resistance.
Do realize that any change affecting group norms will probably be opposed by the workers.	Do not assume that because the change makes sense to you, it will also be accepted by the employees.
Do keep employees aware of when and how the change will be implemented.	Do not underrate the impact of informal group pressures on the acceptance of change.
Do praise and encourage those who support the change.	Do not underrate the importance of being open and honest with the employees.
Do follow up and address any problems that still exist after the change is implemented.	Do not overlook the fact that most employees are more concerned with the short-run effects of a change than with the long-run effects.
	Do not be afraid to compromise if the situation warrants such action.
	Do not create lasting animosities over the change; remember that you have to work with these people in the future.

the value of the new forms, the store managers began to urge their people to fill out the reports as completely as possible and get them in on time. The accounting department manager was thus able to sell the store managers on the change and keep them sold. In turn, the store managers did the same with their people.

Summary

Change is any modification or alteration of the status quo. When change takes place, three things occur: (1) there is a movement from one set of conditions to another, (2) some force(s) cause(s) the change to come about, and (3) an effect or consequence results from the change. In analyzing the change process in action, it is helpful to think of two types of forces at work: those favoring the change and those opposing it. The former push in one direction, the latter in the opposite. In bringing about change, management usually employs one of three strategies: (1) the forces pushing for change become so strong that they shove the opposing forces back, (2) the forces opposing change are weakened and can no longer stand up to the forces encouraging the change, or (3) some combination of the two.

Some people believe that resistance to change is inevitable. While this may be true, there are some very good reasons for resistance. One is that it compels the pro-change forces to build a case against the status quo. Another is that it encourages the organization to look before it leaps.

How do most people react to change? There are many responses, but most can be put in one of four categories: rejection, resistance, tolerance, and acceptance. Of these, the most common is resistance to change. Why does a worker resist change? The most common reasons include: (1) obsolescence of job skills, (2) fear of economic loss, (3) ego defensiveness, (4) the comfort of the status quo, (5) short-sightedness, (6) peer pressure, (7) lack of information, and (8) social displacement.

Despite the various pressures and tendencies to resist change, it is possible to alter the status quo if the change is introduced and managed properly. One of the first things the manager must do is to be aware of the three dimensions of change: logical, psychological, and sociological. Additionally, the manager should know the five basic steps in the change process: (1) make sure that the change is really necessary, (2) determine whether the proposed change is the right one, (3) evaluate the probable impact of the change, (4) secure acceptance of the change, and (5) follow up to be sure things are going according to plan. A third important consideration is the time factor. The greater the change, the longer in advance the notice must be given. Furthermore, participation by and communication with the workers to be affected by the change will help ensure acceptance. No one likes to be kept in the dark about a development that will change something important about his or her job. In addition, the manager needs to have a positive attitude toward the change and to know how to use balance theory to secure both acceptance and implementation of the change. Finally, the manager must discover any subordinate anxieties that have not yet been dealt with and work to overcome them. This can often be handled through a follow-up program that reassures the workers that the change was good for them and they were right in accepting it.

In this chapter we examined how the change process works. When is change necessary and what are some of the specific programs that can be used for implementing it? These questions are a natural consequence of what we have discussed here, and we address them in the next chapter.

Key terms found in the chapter

change
force-field analysis
causal variable
end-result variable
rejection
overt resistance

covert resistance
tolerance
acceptance
dimensions of change
balance theory

Review and study questions

1. In your own words, what is change?

2. How does change take place? Explain by using Kurt Lewin's force-field analysis.

3. Is resistance to change bad? In your answer, be sure to make a case both for and against resistance.

4. One of the most common reactions to change is that of rejection. What happens when workers reject change?

5. Under what conditions will workers tend to tolerate change? Give an illustration.

6. Are there any changes that workers will accept? Give an example.

7. One of the primary reasons for resistance to change is the fear of economic loss. What is meant by this statement?

8. When will ego defensiveness result in resistance to change? Cite an illustration of ego defensiveness in action.

9. How can lack of information result in resistance to change? Give an example.

10. Social displacement is a key cause of resistance to change. What is meant by this statement?

11. What are the three dimensions of change? Why are they important to the manager in the change process?

12. What are the five basic steps in the change process? Describe each.

13. In what way is consideration of the time factor important in implementing change? Explain.

14. Is participation really of any importance in the introduction of change? How? Explain.

15. What is balance theory? Explain, incorporating in your answer an explanation of how this theory can be useful to the manager in bringing about acceptance of change.

16. The major problem associated with change is anxiety. What is meant by this statement?

Answers to How much do you know about the change process?

1. Basically false—most changes scare people and they, at least initially, tend to dislike them.

2. Basically false—most changes take time to be accepted so, if anything, there is an immediate decrease in productivity.

3. Basically true—as explained in number one above.

4. Basically false—they would regard it with fear or concern, wondering if the machine would have them do more work or even replace them.

5. Basically true—this is usually the objective of all organizational changes.

6. Basically true—workers tend to stick together, especially when change is involved.

7. Basically false—people resist because they are afraid of losing their jobs.

8. Basically false—advance notice is crucial, and the greater the change, the more the advance notice that should be given.

9. Basically true—participation in the change process is one of the most effective ways of ensuring successful implementation of the change.

10. Basically false—they tend to underrate the time needed to implement change effectively and end up pushing the change too quickly. The result is resistance from the workers.

11. Either answer can be right here so take one point regardless of your response—if the change is a positive one, it often results in a short decline in work output before things turn around and vice versa.

12. Basically true—unions usually fight change because they are afraid of the effect of the change on worker employment.

Add up your right answers. How well did you do? Use the following to measure your current knowledge of the change process:

11–12 right:	Excellent
9–10 right:	Above average
7–8 right:	Average
6 or less right:	Below average

Regardless of how well you did, you will find the answers to these questions in the chapter. So take heart and read on.

For and against

As part of her assignment for the human relations course she is taking, Paula Fayer recently visited a nearby manufacturing firm. Her assignment called for her to identify, describe, analyze, and solve a human relations problem involving the change process. Her uncle Ted, who works for this company, arranged for her entry to the plant and an interview with Edward Styner, one of the supervisors.

Ed was a good target for this investigation because his department is about to receive new machinery. Most of the present machines are quite old, and management is going to replace them with more efficient ones. As a result, 10 percent of the workers will be transferred to other departments, because they will no longer be needed in Ed's department. Most of the people to be transferred are support help who assist the machinists in various ways. The new machines will make their jobs obsolete.

The workers in the department are divided in their reactions to the new machines. Some are for the change and some are against it. Ed recommended that Paula interview the departmental personnel and get their opinions firsthand.

When she finished this phase of her investigation, Paula found there were five arguments (or forces) against the change and five arguments favoring it. Paula listed the arguments and numbered them according to how strong she thought they were.

Against the change
- −1 The workers are familiar with the old machines but will have to learn new procedures and techniques before using the new ones.
- −2 The management has already indicated that there will be an increase in the work quotas once the new machines are up and running.
- −3 These new machines will require much greater attention to feed and speed.
- −4 Transfer of 10 percent of the department will destroy some of the social networks.
- −5 If the workers do not fight this change, there will be even more changes in the future; it's better to fight now and hold the line.

For the change
- +1 With a minimum amount of training, the workers can become familiar with these new machines.
- +2 There will be increases in work quotas, but they can be met

with the new machines with no increase in physical effort or fatigue for the workers.

+3 While there will need to be greater attention to machine feed and speed, the amount of down time and preventive maintenance will be greatly reduced.

+4 The group will be able to form new social relationships, and the 10 percent who are being displaced will be given jobs elsewhere in the firm.

+5 There is no proof that this is the beginning of massive change; besides, management communicated the change well in advance of its happening.

Paula has concluded that there is a standoff. There are five forces of equal weight on each side.

Questions

1. In terms of Kurt Lewin's force-field analysis, what would these forces look like if drawn as a figure? (Hint: use Figure 13.1 as an aid.)

2. What kinds of issues are most important to those opposing the change? What do the issues have in common?

3. How should the manager go about gaining acceptance for the change? Explain.

Success and failure

City Hospital has been having trouble keeping control of its costs and expenditures. As a result, a new monthly cost control report has been devised. This report is specially designed to provide information to central accounting as well as feedback to the various departments.

Now that the reports have been in use for three months, it has become evident that some departments understand the report, fill it out completely, and use it as a source of feedback for controlling their own costs and expenditures. Other departments, however, seem confused about the report, do not know what to put into it or leave out, and do not appear to be using the data to control their own costs and expenditures.

Bob Bradley, the head of central accounting, decided to check out the situation for himself by visiting one of the departments that was filling out the form properly and one that was not doing so. The first department was run by Pat Rodgers, and after talking to both Pat and her personnel, Bob realized that Pat's people were familiar with the form, knew the kinds of information that were supposed to go into it, and were aware of how to use the data for control purposes. Much of their awareness stemmed from a meeting Pat had held with her people at which they had discussed the report at length. By the end of the meeting, everyone in the department was familiar with the format of the report and was prepared to provide the necessary data.

Conversely, Paul Heckman's department was having all sorts of problems with the report. All three times it was submitted both incomplete and late. Additionally, Paul's department was currently 11 percent over budget. Upon talking to the department personnel, Bob learned that Paul had not discussed the report with his people. Rather, he had sent a Xeroxed copy of the form to each person announcing that in the future the report was to be submitted monthly to accounting. He told his people that he wanted them to decide what they thought should go into the report and submit the data to his secretary. Then Paul would take the information and put it into the monthly cost control report. Bob realized that this way of introducing the report undoubtedly accounted for most of the problems Paul's department was having with it, but he was unsure of how to begin discussing the matter with Paul.

Questions

1. How important is participation and communication in effecting change?
2. Has Pat's approach helped reduce the anxiety that often accompanies change? Has Paul's approach?
3. What would you recommend that Bob say to Paul? Explain.

Organizational development

14

Goals of the chapter

In Chapter 13, we have studied the management of change. Most of our discussion, however, has been general. We have not really dealt with specific problem areas nor have we attempted to outline steps that the organization might take in resolving the dilemma. Now, however, we are going to fill this gap by examining the area of organizational development. A successful organization introduces change by means of careful strategy. This is particularly true when the organization is having problems and needs to solve them by introducing an effective behavioral program that will get everyone working in harmony. The term given to this entire area is *organizational development*, or *OD*. It is the overall goal of this chapter to study how OD works since, sooner or later, every human relations manager will need to use one or more OD techniques and/or be aware of the value they have for improved organizational effectiveness. To a large degree, modern managers do not practice OD: this is a specialized area often handled by outside experts skilled in psychology and/or sociology. However, managers do need to know what OD is all about and how it can lead to improved efficiency and effectiveness.

The first goal of this chapter is to define the term *organizational climate* and discuss what makes up this climate. The second goal is to discuss what organizational development is all about. The third goal is to study the most common interventions used by OD specialists. The fourth goal is to review the conditions necessary to success of these programs. The fifth goal is to answer the question, "Is OD an effective approach to managing organizational resources, or is it a lot of hocus-pocus?"

When you have finished reading this chapter you should be able to:

1. define *organizational climate*
2. compare and contrast the formal and informal aspects of the organizational iceberg
3. define *organizational development*
4. describe the eight major characteristics of most OD programs
5. explain how the following OD interventions work: role playing, sensitivity training, team building, survey feedback, System 4 management, and grid training
6. discuss the conditions necessary for success in an OD program
7. address the issue of whether OD is an effective approach in the management of organizational resources.

Organizational climate

In Chapter 13 we discussed the management of change. Why is change needed? There are many answers, but most of those we examined in the chapter related to developments in the external environment that necessitated an organizational response. However, change is sometimes required because the organization is having internal problems. For example, if the employees are angry because management has been unresponsive to certain human relations problems, there needs to be a change on the part of management. Likewise, if two work groups are continually fighting each other and efficiency is suffering because of it, some changes are necessary to rectify the intergroup conflict. And if some people in a work group do not know what they are supposed to be doing and are slowing everyone else up, corrective measures need to be taken.

How can an organization know when its managers or personnel need human relations training? The answer is that it cannot always know. However, one way of getting some feedback on the organization at large is to examine its *organizational climate*. While this term has been defined in many ways, Williams has offered a terse, yet complete definition:

Organizational climate **is a set of attributes of a particular organization that are identifiable in the collective attitudes, perceptions, and expectations of its members. For instance, organizational climate is in part determined by how members perceive their organization's leadership, products, pay, employee benefits, discipline, policies, and goals.**[1]

The organizational iceberg

The formal aspects are observable.

In measuring organizational climate, what one is really interested in learning about is the informal organization, which is analogous to the part of an iceberg that rests under the water. Figure 14.1 depicts the orga-

---

[1] J. Clifton Williams, *Human Behavior in Organizations*, 2nd ed. (Cincinnati, Ohio: South-Western Publishing Co., 1982), p. 315.

Figure 14.1
The organizational iceberg

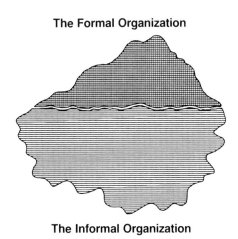

The Formal Organization

Formal Aspects
Job Definitions
Job Descriptions
Forms of Departmentalization
Spans of Control
Organization's Goals
Operating Policies
Efficiency Measures

These are readily observable and oriented to structural considerations.

Informal Aspects
Power and Influence
Interpersonal and
    Group Relations
Group Norms and Sentiments
Perceptions of Trust
    and Openness
Value Orientations
Personal Superior-
    Subordinate Relations
Employee Satisfaction

These are hidden from view and oriented to social-psychological process and behavioral considerations.

The Informal Organization

nizational iceberg. The formal aspects of the iceberg are those that are *readily observable*. Job definitions, forms of departmentalization, organizational goals, and efficiency measures are all examples. We can see these things, and they are oriented toward structuring the organization. On the underwater part of the organizational iceberg are the informal aspects. These are *hidden from view* and are oriented to social-psychological processes and behavioral considerations. They include power, influence, interpersonal and intergroup relations, group norms, perceptions of trust and openness, value orientations, and employee satisfaction.

The informal are not.

The major differences between formal and informal organizational aspects are that the formal aspects are visible, and also that if there is something wrong with the formal aspects, we can adjust them. If someone is inefficient, we can find out why and try to deal with the problem. However, if there is a lack of trust and openness in the organization, how does one identify this problem before it begins to create trouble? One is seldom able to do this. Usually we do not know what is going on in the informal organization until problems begin. However, there are ways of measuring organizational climate and dealing with a trouble situation before it becomes too serious. The catchall term used to describe this process is *organizational development*.

Drawing by Bo Brown, *Changing Times*, December 1980.

Organizational development

OD defined.

Organizational development, or *OD*, has been defined in many different ways. In general terms, it is *an effort to improve an organization's effectiveness by dealing with individual, group, and overall organizational problems from both a technical and a human standpoint.* At the heart of organizational development is a concern for improving the relationships among the organization's personnel. This is often accomplished

There are numerous types of interventions.

through what we call **OD interventions**, which take such forms as sensitivity training, role playing, team building, survey feedback, and grid training. These activities are called *interventions* because they are behavioral science techniques used to intervene in or interrupt a situation for the purpose of improving it. For example, when two work groups are in conflict with each other, an intergroup team-building intervention is often used to resolve the problem. The intervention interrupts the situation for the purpose of resolving the conflict.

The individual who carries out or leads the intervention is often referred to as an **OD change agent**. The agent's job is to introduce the intervention, get the personnel involved, and show them how the particular intervention can help them deal with the problems they face. For example, the intergroup team-building intervention is designed to help members of both groups resolve differences and work in harmony. The techniques used in the intervention, therefore, would be geared to attaining this particular goal. In short, OD is a practical, application-oriented approach to introducing and managing change.

The change agent manages them.

Characteristics of OD

There are eight major characteristics of most OD programs.

First, OD is *an ongoing, dynamic process*. The approach is not a quick, easy solution to an organization's problems; it involves a considerable investment of time and money.

Can be time consuming.

Second, it *applies behavioral science knowledge*. OD change agents rely heavily on psychological and sociological ideas in developing and using their interventions. For example, if the organization has a motivation problem, the change agent will investigate how other organizations have solved similar problems.

Uses psychosociological ideas.

Third, the change agent believes that there is a need for everyone involved to be *open and trusting* with everyone else. The purpose of the intervention is to provide reeducation to do things differently. If everyone expresses his or her fears and concerns, the change agent can be aware of how meaningful change can be introduced with the least number of problems.

Calls for mutual trust.

Fourth, OD takes a *systems view* of the organization. The person leading the intervention knows that a change in the work procedures of one group may lead to problems in other areas. For example, if one group is subjected to a team-building intervention and their output goes up, other groups may also want to have a team-building session. You cannot change one part of the organization without affecting other parts.

Takes a systems approach.

Fifth, OD interventions are *data-based*. By this we mean that the change agent does not act on what he or she believes the problems of the organization might be; nor does the individual let top management make this decision. Instead, research is conducted in the form of attitude surveys, for example, and from such methods of collecting data, decisions are reached regarding the organization's problems and how they should be handled.

Relies on research data.

Sixth, OD depends heavily on people's *experience*. In fact, it is common to hear OD interventions referred to as *experiential assignments*, because they require the participants to experience something. The interventions that are used directly involve the participants and are, at the same time, designed to shed light on the problem under analysis. For ex-

Is experience-based.

ample, if the OD change agent is working with a group to improve intra-group communication, the intervention will involve a group activity through which the members will obtain insights into developing effective communication skills.

Emphasizes goal setting and planning.

Seventh, OD emphasizes *goal setting and planning*. The change agent sets goals with the group and together they all strive to achieve them. There is some purpose or direction to the intervention.

Works with intact groups.

Eighth, OD focuses on on-going or *intact work groups*. OD practitioners believe that working with such groups provides the most effective means of achieving organizational goals. People therefore remain with their work groups throughout the OD training.

OD interventions

Many types of interventions can be used by OD change agents. Some of these are directed toward the individual; role playing is the most popular example. Others are more group-oriented, as in the case of team building. Still others, such as survey feedback, System 4 management, and grid training, are comprehensive. Let us examine each of these in detail.

Role playing

Spontaneous acting out of a real-life situation.

Role playing is one of the most common forms of training used in organizational development. It consists of the spontaneous acting out of a realistic situation that involves two or more people. The purpose of the training is to acquaint one or more of the participants with the proper way of handling a given situation. For example, one person may be told that he or she is a plant supervisor and that absenteeism and tardiness at the plant have been increasing dramatically. The supervisor's job is to reduce these irregularities by sending everyone home who comes late, thereby penalizing him or her a day's pay. Another person is to play the role of a late worker who is trying to talk the supervisor out of sending him or her home. As the two people begin acting out their roles, the rest of the participants watch. When the scene is over, the trainer and the participants all have the opportunity to give their analysis of what each said and did. Then the trainer gives the participants and the other members of the group some *do*'s and *don't*s for handling similar situations.

The benefit of role playing is that it puts the participant in a situation that he or she is likely to face in the future, gives him or her a chance to react to the situation, and then provides feedback on performance. When the person returns to the real work environment and faces a similar situation, he or she experiences less tension and anxiety regarding how to handle the matter because for all practical purposes, he or she has been in that situation before.

Team building

Currently, the most popular form of OD consists of approaches directed toward improving the effectiveness of regular work groups. The overall term given to these approaches is *team building*, and there are a number of different team-building interventions. Some of these focus on intact, permanent work teams and others are directed toward special teams or newly constituted work groups. Common objectives pursued by team-building interventions include:

1. Increasing task accomplishment by improving the group's problem-solving ability, decision-making skills, and goal-setting approaches, and/or defining the roles and duties of the individual managers.

2. Building and maintaining effective interpersonal relationships, in-cluding boss-subordinate relationships and peer relationships.

Common objectives of team building.

3. Understanding and managing group processes and intergroup relations.

4. Improving intergroup relations and resolving interpersonal and/or intergroup conflict.

5. Developing more effective communication, decision-making, and task-allocation skills, both within and between groups.

One of the most popular methods of team building consists of having two work groups who are having trouble working with each other adjourn to separate rooms and draw up: (1) a list of those things it dislikes about the other group, and (2) a list of those things it believes the other group will say it dislikes about them. Then the two groups are brought together and each reads its first list. The only questions permitted are those that allow the person reading the list to clarify what the group means by a listed item. When both groups are finished, each then reads its second list (what it believed the other group would say about it).

Having now identified their real and imaginary problems, the two groups begin discussing the issues. Some issues are disposed of very quickly, because they had been caused by lack of communication or simple misunderstandings. From here, a list of the major problems that still exist between the two groups is constructed, and ways of solving the problems are identified. Then the groups put together a timetable for solving the problems and list the specific steps that will have to be taken to deal with them. Having developed an action plan, the two groups then work together and follow the timetable to overcome their mutual problems. In most cases, the OD change agent checks back with the two groups to see whether they are making progress in resolving the problems or whether further meetings are needed to revitalize their efforts.

Evaluation Most OD practitioners have great faith in team building, which undoubtedly helps account for the approach's current popularity.

However, there are some common problems with the intervention. The major difficulty is that one work group may fail to be honest with the other group, holding back feelings because it is afraid of being too forthright with people it has learned to distrust. However, this problem can be overcome early in the intervention if the change agent keeps everyone honest.

The early stages of these interventions—making lists and sharing them and using the fishbowl technique—lead the participants to *experience feelings of success in dealing with the other group*. Feelings of anxiety, apprehension, and hostility start to give way to feelings of competence and success as the early stages of the interventions produce better communication and understanding than the participants had expected. Nothing succeeds like success, and the early stages are usually perceived as a success experience by both groups. This leads to the optimistic realization that "We *can* work together with those people." Participants are watching for subtle cues of defensiveness, resistance to the data, stubbornness, and the like, and the controlled nature of the process makes most of these unnecessary. This starts building momentum for feelings of competence and success.[2]

If carried out competently, team building can be very beneficial to both the personnel and the organization.

Survey feedback

Another important and widely used intervention is that of *survey feedback*, a comprehensive OD intervention. The technique entails three distinct steps: (1) a systematic collection of data on the current state of the organization, usually obtained through questionnaires, interviews, or both, (2) a feedback of the findings to the organizational personnel, and (3) the development of an action plan for dealing with the problems that have been identified.

Information is gathered.

Gathering the data   Data in the survey feedback intervention are often gathered by means of an objective-subjective questionnaire like that illustrated in Figure 14.2. The survey is usually designed by a specialist in attitude measurement and is administered to the total organization, to a department, or to a representative sample of either. However, survey feedback also attempts to gather *subjective* information to supplement the questionnaire data.

Feeding back the information   After the information is collected and analyzed, the results are revealed to the survey participants. In a

[2] Wendell L. French and Cecil H. Bell, Jr., *Organizational Development*, 2nd ed. (Englewood Cliffs, N.J.: Prentice-Hall, Inc., 1978), p. 137.

Figure 14.2
Sample survey feedback questions

	Strongly Agree	Agree	Un-decided	Disagree	Strongly Disagree
There is a lot of teamwork in my work group.	____	____	____	____	____
Very few people in this organization listen to each other.	____	____	____	____	____
Management is as interested in the people as it is in the work.	____	____	____	____	____
Most important decisions are made by management and then announced to the workers without any input from the latter.	____	____	____	____	____
This organization is a good place in which to work.	____	____	____	____	____

In your opinion, what are the three biggest problems currently facing the firm? Write your answers in the space below, and use the back of the page if necessary.

nutshell, the OD change agent is saying, "Here's an overall view of what you told me about the organization. These are the things that everyone seems to like. These are the things that most people feel need to be corrected. Let us look at this information and decide what should be done about the situation."

Fed back to participants.

Developing an action plan The last phase of the survey feedback involves the development of an action plan. This plan is formulated by individuals at all levels of the group(s) that participated in the original survey. Often included in the action plan is a time limit for following up to see that the proposed plan is implemented. The follow-up prevents the OD effort from becoming only a short-lived, interesting experience.

And an action plan is developed.

Several months after the OD survey is conducted, a check should be made to determine if the action plans developed in the earlier stages are being implemented. In one company an action plan was developed to realign the wage scale of first-line supervision. A three-month checkup revealed that nothing had been done. Prodding by the OD consultant and a representative from first-line supervision helped management begin some long-needed changes.[3]

Evaluation Survey feedback has proven to be an effective change technique. Bowers, for example, has reported that a study evaluating the effects of different change techniques in 23 organizations revealed that survey feedback was a more effective change strategy than many other

[3] Andrew J. DuBrin, *Human Relations: A Job-Oriented Approach* (Reston, Va.: Reston Publishing Company, Inc., 1978), p. 274.

types.[4] However, in keeping these results in perspective, we should note that these survey feedback programs may have been better rated because they were more comprehensive than other programs. The positive results may reflect the superiority of more comprehensive programs to less comprehensive ones. On the other hand, some researchers have also noted that survey feedback is a cost-effective means of implementing a comprehensive program, making it a highly desirable change technique.[5]

System 4 management

The survey feedback approach is closely related to a larger theory of management developed by Rensis Likert called *System 4 management*, another comprehensive OD intervention. Likert classifies management philosophies in four categories: System 1 (exploitive-autocratic), System 2 (benevolent-autocratic), System 3 (consultative-democratic), and System 4 (participative-democratic). An example of the profile is shown in Figure 14.3.

Of what value is the Likert profile in organizational development? It can give an organization a look at what is going on under the surface of organizational activity. If the management believes that it is operating under a System 4 philosophy but the workers filling out the profile indicate that they are being managed under a System 2 philosophy, the organization had better start examining the implications of these findings. Apparently things are not as rosy as they believe. It may be time to identify some potential problems and decide how to solve them.

Many organizations use System 4.

Likert has found that the most effective organizations have System 4 characteristics and the least effective organizations have System 1 and System 2 characteristics. A number of organizations have employed System 4 with very good results. For example, a comprehensive organizational change project involving the Weldon Company, a sleepwear manufacturing firm, has been well documented.[6] In this project, substantial changes were made in the organization's work flow, training programs, leadership styles, incentive and reward systems, and use of employees as a source of expertise. The results were both impressive and significant. There were improvements in all aspects of the organization's functioning that were maintained over an extended period.

System 4 is often better.

System 4 management has also been used in a General Motors assembly plant. Dowling has reported that training sessions on Likert's theory, team-building sessions starting at the top of the organization and

[4] David G. Bowers, "OD Techniques and Their Results in 23 Organizations: The Michigan ICL Study," *Journal of Applied Behavioral Science*, January/February 1973, pp. 21–43.

[5] French and Bell, *Organizational Development*, p. 156.

[6] For a complete account of the program see: Alfred J. Marrow, David G. Bowers, and Stanley E. Seashore, *Management by Participation* (New York: Harper & Row, 1967).

Figure 14.3
The System 4 approach

	System 1	System 2	System 3	System 4
Extent to which subordinates have confidence and trust in the superior	Have no confidence and trust in the superior	Have subservient confidence and trust, such as a servant has to the master	Substantial but not complete confidence	Complete confidence and trust
Extent to which superiors behave so that subordinates feel free to discuss important things about their jobs with their immediate superior	Subordinates do not feel at all free to discuss things about the job with their superior	Subordinates do not feel free to discuss things about the job with their superior	Subordinates feel rather free to discuss things about the job with their superior	Subordinates feel completely free to discuss things about the job with their superior
Attitudes toward other members of the organization	Subservient attitudes toward superiors coupled with hostility; hostility toward peers and contempt for subordinates; distrust is widespread	Subservient attitudes toward superiors; competition for status resulting in hostility toward peers; condescension toward subordinates	Cooperative, reasonably favorable attitudes toward others in the organization; there may be some competition between peers with resulting hostility and some condescension toward subordinates	Favorable, cooperative attitudes throughout the organization with mutual trust and confidence
Satisfaction derived	Usually dissatisfaction with membership in the organization, with supervision, and with one's own achievements	Dissatisfaction to moderate satisfaction in regard to membership in the organization, supervision, and one's own achievements	Some dissatisfaction to moderately high satisfaction in regard to membership in the organization, supervision, and one's own achievements	Relatively high satisfaction throughout the organization in regard to membership in the organization, supervision, and one's own achievements
Amount of cooperative teamwork that is present	None	Relatively little	A moderate amount	Very substantial amount throughout the entire organization
Are there forces to accept, resist, or reject goals?	Goals are overtly accepted, but covertly they are resisted strongly	Goals are overtly accepted but often covertly resisted to at least some degree	Goals are overtly accepted but at times with some covert resistance	Goals are fully accepted both overtly and covertly
Extent to which there is an informal organization present and supporting or opposing goals of the formal organization	Informal organization is present and opposing the goals of the formal organization	Informal organization is usually present and partially resisting formal goals	Informal organization may be present and may either support or partially resist the goals of the formal organization	Informal and formal organization are one and the same; all social forces support efforts to achieve organization's goals

moving to lower levels, improved information and communication flows to the hourly employees, changes in the job of the first-line foremen, increased participation of hourly employees in job changes, and new approaches to goal setting were all used in this program. The results were improved operating efficiency and decreases in grievances and waste costs.[7]

Evaluation   Many managers like the System 4 approach to human relations. It seems intuitively to be the right method of managing people. Because it draws heavily on a human resources philosophy of management and views the personnel as important assets that must be treated properly, most practicing managers admit they can find little fault with the approach. It must be kept in mind that System 4 may not be the best management approach for *every* individual. Overall, however, it does appear to be superior to the others. French and Bell have commented:

> **We believe that Likert's theory is basically correct, that it can be translated into organization development intervention and programs, and that it represents a significant contribution both to management theory and to the theory of planned change. A theory-guided approach to organization development allows organization members and practitioners alike to have a cognitive map or model of the change process and the change goals.[8]**

Grid organization development

Grid organization development, or *grid training* as it is often called, is another approach to change. It encompasses *all* levels of the hierarchy. In fact, much of what we have already studied in this book is incorporated in the grid approach, including concerns for the individual, the group, and the organization structure.

The grid approach is most closely associated with Robert Blake and Jane Mouton.[9] At the heart of the approach is the *managerial grid*, depicted in Figure 14.4. This grid, a model that serves to describe different ways of managing, was also discussed in general terms in Chapter 9 (see Figure 9.4).

The managerial grid   The managerial grid consists of two dimensions: *concern for production* and *concern for people*. As can be seen in Figure 14.4, there are 9 gradients or degrees associated with each dimension, so there are 81 possible combinations of concern for production

[7]William F. Dowling, "At G.M.: 'System 4' Builds Performance and Profits," *Organizational Dynamics*, Winter 1975, pp. 23–28.
[8]French and Bell, *Organizational Development*, pp. 157–158.
[9]R. R. Blake and J. S. Mouton, *The Managerial Grid* (Houston, Tex.: Gulf Publishing Company, 1964).

Figure 14.4
The managerial grid

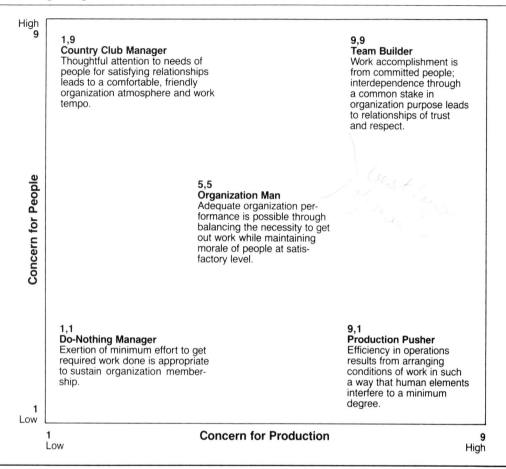

High
9

Concern for People

1,9
Country Club Manager
Thoughtful attention to needs of
people for satisfying relationships
leads to a comfortable, friendly
organization atmosphere and work
tempo.

9,9
Team Builder
Work accomplishment is
from committed people;
interdependence through
a common stake in
organization purpose leads
to relationships of trust
and respect.

5,5
Organization Man
Adequate organization performance is possible through
balancing the necessity to get
out work while maintaining
morale of people at satisfactory level.

1,1
Do-Nothing Manager
Exertion of minimum effort to get
required work done is appropriate
to sustain organization membership.

9,1
Production Pusher
Efficiency in operations
results from arranging
conditions of work in such
a way that human elements
interfere to a minimum
degree.

1
Low

1   **Concern for Production**   9
Low   High

and concern for people. A 1 represents low concern for the dimension
and a 9 represents high concern.

Rather than try to direct attention to all 81 combinations, grid development practitioners tend to focus on 5 critical combinations. The
combinations are usually referred to by number, and when people become familiar with the grid they know what the numbers mean. Although
they are briefly described in Figure 14.4, let us examine each combination in more detail.

The 1,1 managerial style is used to describe the *do-nothing manager*. This individual tends to put people in jobs and then leave them
alone. He or she does not check up on their work (concern for produc-

tion) or try to interact with them by offering praise and encouraging them to keep up the good work (concern for people).

The 9,1 managerial style describes the *production pusher*. This manager has a high concern for production and a low concern for people. He or she plans the work and pushes to get it out. Little interest is shown in the workers; if they cannot keep up, they are replaced by others who can.

The 1,9 managerial style has been called *country club management* because of high emphasis given to concern for people's feelings, comfort, and needs. The manager is interested in obtaining loyalty from the subordinates and tries to motivate them to do their work without putting pressure on them.

The 5,5 managerial style typifies the *organization manager*. This person assumes that there is an inherent conflict between the concerns for production and people. Therefore, he or she tries to compromise and balance the two dimensions.

The 9,9 managerial style is used by the *team leader*. It is regarded by many as the ideal style, as the one that both managers in particular and the organization in general should employ. This style focuses on people's higher-level needs, involves subordinates in decision making, and assumes that the goals of the people and the goals of the organization are in harmony. As a result, the 9,9 manager believes that maximum concern for both dimensions will result in the greatest overall efficiency.

Which of these basic styles is best? The answer will depend on the needs of the subordinates, the manager, and the organization. As noted in Chapter 9 in our discussion of leadership styles, there are effective managers with 9,9 styles, with 1,1 styles, with 1,9 styles, with 9,1 styles, and so on. *There is no such thing as the ideal style.* This can be made clear by giving you the opportunity to choose a leadership style on your own.

Identifying your style   A modern manager must perform many functions. Four of the most important are: planning, decision making, leading, and controlling. In carrying out these functions, various degrees of concern for both people and work can be employed. In Figure 14.5, we have listed for each of these functions five leadership behaviors that can be used to implement them. Read the five behavior descriptions that accompany each function and place a 1 next to the behavior that you feel is *most* descriptive of you. Put a 2 next to the second most descriptive behavior, and so on, to a 5 for the *least* descriptive. If you are not currently a manager, imagine that you are in a managerial position while you take the test.

When you have finished assigning numbers to all of the behaviors, write your answers in the columns of the table below Figure 14.5. Be sure to enter the numbers properly. If you assigned a 3 to alternative b in the Planning part, put a 3 in Column I in the table. If you gave a 5 to alternative d in the Planning part, put a 5 in Column II. Then add each column and put the total on the bottom line of each.

Figure 14.5
Management style identification test

Planning

a _____   I sit down with my people, review the whole picture, and get reactions, ideas, and commitments from them. Schedules, goals, responsibilities, and control points are developed during this interaction period.

b _____   I plan the work for each of my people after discussing such things as targets and schedules with the person. I then make individual assignments but also ensure that each person knows to check back with me whenever further assistance is needed.

c _____   I suggest steps and offer assistance to my people in arranging their activities.

d _____   I let my people have planning responsibilities for their own parts of the job.

e _____   I plan for my people, set quotas where they are needed, and assign steps to be followed. I also establish check points that can be used for measuring performance.

Decision Making

a _____   I make decisions, and after they are made, I stick with them.

b _____   My decisions follow the thinking of my boss; I think as he (or she) does.

c _____   I discuss decisions with those who will be affected by them, give them the facts from my point of view, and, in turn, get facts from them. After evaluation of alternatives, decisions are reached based on mutual understanding.

d _____   I sit down with each person who is affected by the decision and listen to the person's point of view. Then I make the decision and communicate it to those who will be affected, along with my reasons for making that particular decision.

e _____   I try to get a picture of what the subordinates want and use it as a basis for my decisions.

Leading

a _____   Once assignments and plans have been clearly explained, I keep up with each person's performance and review their progress with them. If someone is having difficulty getting the job done, I lend assistance.

b _____   After assignments have been given to the people, I prefer to take little on-the-spot action. I think it is best for people to solve their own problems.

c _____   Once upcoming assignments are discussed, I keep in touch with my people in order to show that I am interested in how each is getting along.

d _____   Once plans have been determined, I keep up with the progress of the subordinates. I contribute time and effort as required by defining problems and removing roadblocks.

e _____   After I have set out plans and instructions, I keep a close eye on the subordinates' work performance and make changes as necessity dictates.

Controlling

a _____   As work progresses, if any problems or changes need to be made, I make them on the spot. When the job is completed, I evaluate everyone's performance, correct those who have done a poor job, and give recognition to those who have performed well.

Figure 14.5 (continued)

b _____   I sit down with my subordinates and review progress in detail, and when the job is totally finished I study how the entire operation was handled. Correct decisions, good work, errors, and misjudgments are all noted and examined in detail so that the former can be reinforced and the latter can be prevented in the future. When deserved, recognition for contribution is given on both a joint and an individual basis.

c _____   When I receive a reaction to their work, whether it is praise or a complaint, I pass this information on to the respective subordinates.

d _____   I compliment my subordinates when they do a good job and invite their discussions for improvements. I believe that criticism tends to arouse tension and make people defensive.

e _____   I point out weaknesses as well as strengths to each subordinate. Each person then gets a chance to introduce his or her own suggestions for improvements.

	I	II	III	IV	V
Planning	b _____	d _____	e _____	a _____	c _____
Decision Making	d _____	b _____	a _____	c _____	e _____
Leading	a _____	b _____	e _____	d _____	c _____
Controlling	e _____	c _____	a _____	b _____	d _____
TOTAL	_____	_____	_____	_____	_____

The short survey quiz is designed to determine the type of leadership style you use in carrying out each of the four functions we discussed. Which overall leadership style is your favorite? That will depend on the total scores of the columns. Remember, the *lower* the total the *higher* your support for that leadership style. (You gave a 1 to your favorite choice and a 5 to least preferable.)

Column I reveals your preference for the 5,5 style. Column II measures your preference for the 1,1 style. Columns III, IV, and V measure preference for the 9,1 style, the 9,9 style, and the 1,9 style, respectively. Which is your most preferred style? Your least preferred style? Could you have predicted this, or are the findings a surprise to you?

This type of quiz shows where you currently are in management thinking, and this is one of the objectives of the managerial grid. A second objective is to ask managers, "With which of the five basic styles would you be most effective?" If a manager says that he or she should use a 9,9 style, but the initial evaluation shows that the manager tends to employ a 9,1 style, the OD intervention will be directed toward getting the manager to become more people-oriented. The manager is as concerned for production as he or she should be but is not paying close enough attention to the human element.

Implementation of the managerial grid   Changing a manager's style involves a six-phase program. The grid approach to OD can be quite complex, and it often takes three or four years for an organization to complete all the phases. A short summary of each phase follows.

Phase I: laboratory-seminar training.   Phase I typically lasts one week and is designed to introduce the manager to the grid philosophy and objectives. The seminar starts with an evaluation and review of each participant's managerial style in the areas of production and people. Then there is as much as 50 hours of problem-solving assignments focusing on situations involving interpersonal behavior and its influences on task performance. Each group regularly assesses its problem-solving performance, and the immediate, face-to-face feedback sets the stage for the next phase.

Phase II: work-team development.   This phase is designed to assist the participants in applying what they have learned in the first phase to their specific situations. The purpose of Phase I and Phase II is to provide conditions that:

. . . enable managers to learn Managerial Grid concepts as an organizing framework for thinking about management practices;
. . . build improved relationships between groups, among colleagues at the same level, and between superiors and subordinates;
. . . make managers more critical of outworn practices and precedents while extending their problem-solving capacities in interdependent situations. Words like "involvement," and "commitment" become real in terms of day-to-day tasks.[10]

Phase III: intergroup development.   This phase involves group-to-group working relationships and focuses on building group roles and norms that go beyond the single work group. Situations that result in intergroup tension are identified and discussed by the group members. The objective of this phase is to move the groups away from the typical problem-solving situation in which one group succeeds at the expense of the others and toward a joint problem-solving approach.

Phase IV: development of an organization blueprint.   Phase IV is directed to constructing an ideal of what the organization should become. There is a decreased emphasis given to "what is" and an increased emphasis given to "what should be." As a result of this phase, it is typical to find statements and understanding of changes in and new development of organization strategies, objectives, policies, and structures.

Phase V: implementation of the blueprint.   During Phase V the group attempts to bridge the gap between "what is" and "what should be." This

---

[10] Robert R. Blake, Jane S. Mouton, Louis B. Barnes, and Larry E. Greiner, "Breakthrough in Organization Development," *Harvard Business Review*, November–December 1964, p. 137.

is usually the longest phase, sometimes lasting two to three years. While there are many ways of designing this phase, one of the most common is to form a planning team in each area of the organization. It is the responsibility of these teams to conduct conversion studies to determine how their areas are to change and what specific changes need to be made. Meanwhile, any organizational areas that will not be covered by the various planning teams are assigned to an overall planning team of top executives.

Phase VI: stabilization.   The objective of the last phase is to prevent any slipping back. During this phase, an overall evaluation is made of the organization's progress and insights as to the need for new changes and plans are developed.

Evaluation   Many organizations have used and liked the grid approach to OD. Commenting on one implementation of the approach, Blake has reported:

> **Specific advantages have been shown in the gain in dollar savings. Plant-wide practical application of cooperative effort toward greater effectiveness is shown by: decreased time of plant units' tasks, such as unit shutdowns; increased use of capacities and energies of plant personnel through union-management agreed-upon arrangements . . . ; and a greater personal interest and involvement in the work.**[11]

In all fairness, we must consider that the grid approach has not been subjected to rigorous analysis. We cannot say with certainty what its greatest advantages and disadvantages are. Many practicing managers like this approach because it is both comprehensive (from an organizational standpoint) and structured (in terms of the six phases). As a result, this organizational development technique will probably continue to be used throughout both the public sector and the private sector.

Conditions for optimal success

There are many things that can go wrong in an OD program. However, in most cases these problems can be either avoided or rectified through *careful planning*. Additionally, eleven conditions are generally accepted as necessary for *optimal* success of an OD program.[12]

1. *Top managers and/or other key people must be aware that the organization has a problem.* If this condition does not exist, it is

---

[11] Robert R. Blake, Jane S. Mouton, Richard L. Sloma, and Barbara Peek Loftin, "A Second Breakthrough in Organization Development," *California Management Review*, Winter 1968, p. 78.

[12] French and Bell, *Organizational Development*, pp. 177–187.

highly unlikely that the necessary time, effort, and money will be invested in an OD program.

2. *A behavioral science consultant must be brought into the picture.* Quite often this person comes from outside the organization. It is the consultant's job to diagnose the problem(s).

3. *There must be initial top-level management support or involvement.* No OD program can succeed unless it has top-level management support. Very few departments or units are going to give serious attention to an OD program that does not have the backing of higher management. If we follow this logic up the line, it becomes evident that the top executives must stand behind the effort from the beginning.

4. *Action research must be used.* The change agent needs to make a preliminary diagnosis, gather data, feed it back to the personnel, and develop a plan of action for follow-up. This process provides data on which to base the change while simultaneously getting the organizational members involved.

5. *The process must start slowly and gain momentum through its own successes.* There is no sense in committing the organization to a five-year or ten-year OD effort. Rather, the management, in collaboration with the change agent, should make commitments to reasonably sized "chunks" of activities. Then, as success is achieved in the initial OD effort, the company can move on to more ambitious undertakings.

6. *The organizational members should be educated about OD.* The personnel are likely to feel that they are being manipulated if they do not fully understand the reasons for the change. Therefore, every effort should be made to familiarize them with what is going on and why.

7. *Relationships with current good management practices should be made clear.* The change agent should give every indication that the OD effort will be congruent with the better managerial practices already in existence in the organization. Managers who are currently effective must be made to realize that the OD effort will complement, not oppose, what they are doing.

Conditions for optimal success.

8. *The OD effort should involve the personnel people and should be in line with current personnel policies and practices.* These people have important input for any OD program, and their expertise should be relied upon.

9. *The organizational personnel must build on what they learn from the OD change agent.* The effective change agent strives to work himself or herself out of a job by showing the organization how it can begin to implement change effectively. As the regular personnel begin to take over many of these functions, the change agent can begin slowly to exit from the scene.

10. *The OD effort must be carefully monitored.* As the effort proceeds, the change agent and the organizational personnel must communicate with each other so that all understand where the organization is heading. If the personnel begin to slip, the change agent can jump in and show them where they are making mistakes. If things go well, the organization can begin to phase out the agent, using him or her only on a periodic monitoring basis.

11. *The OD effort, in order to be truly successful, must be monitored in terms of checking on the personnel attitudes regarding what is going on and determining the extent to which the problems that are identified are being resolved.* Data on results provide both the change agent and the managers with important feedback on the organization's efforts, thereby serving as a closed loop to keep things from slipping back.

Evaluation of organizational development

Before concluding our discussion of OD we need to address the issue of *evaluation.* Is OD an effective approach to managing organization resources or is it a lot of hocus-pocus? This is an important question, because it forces us to examine the difficulties associated with implementing and evaluating the respective intervention. Herbert comments:

> As a rather new approach, OD suffers the same types of difficulties of other emerging disciplines: lack of research, lack of documentation, far more heat than light. It operates under another substantial handicap, the difficulty of defining its processes and results in verifiable, measurable terms. How does one define the organization's "climate?" How does one measure the extent of interpersonal "openness and trust?" In what ways may traditional management development methods be compared with OD in terms of comparative task effectiveness or dollar savings? These are some of the many difficulties inherent in evaluations of OD. Another perspective on these difficulties may be found in a perusal of the OD literature: few OD authors agree on what OD is, let alone what composes its inventory of intervention methodologies.[13]

Some critics question whether OD is really as scientific as its practitioners would have us believe.[14] Others attack the value of overall or integrated OD programs such as System 4 management and grid training. How does one measure the quantitative changes that occur when these interventions bring about higher levels of trust, opening of communication channels, increases in participation by subordinates and delegation by superiors, mutual goal setting by all parties, and reduction of conflict?

[13] Theodore T. Herbert, *Dimensions of Organizational Behavior*, 2nd ed. (New York: Macmillan Publishing Co., Inc., 1980), p. 483.

[14] Patrick E. Connor, "A Critical Inquiry into Some Assumptions and Values Characterizing OD," *Academy of Management Review*, October 1977, pp. 635–644.

The answer is that one cannot always quantify results of OD programs or state with certainty that when an OD program is introduced and things begin to improve, the program itself was the cause.

Nevertheless, a great deal of work has been done in organizational development, and many practitioners would attest to the success of their work.[15] For a definitive statement about the advantages of the approach, let us turn to French and Bell, two of the best known authorities in the field. They have stated:

> There are many problems associated with such field research and experimentation, but progress is being made on a number of fronts. Selected research examples were examined in some detail to determine what effects, if any, various OD treatments had on individual, work group, and total organization functioning. It appears, from these examples of research, that *there is considerable evidence to suggest that OD works.*[16]

Summary

In this chapter we examine the broad area of organizational development. *Organizational climate* is the attitudes and perceptions the personnel have about the organization at large. The climate can be thought of as an iceberg; some of it can be seen and the rest remains hidden from view. It is the hidden part that can cause problems.

Organizational development (*OD*) is an effort to improve an organization's effectiveness by dealing with individual, group, and overall organizational problems from both a technical standpoint and a human standpoint. At the heart of OD is a concern for improving the relationships among the organization's personnel. This is often accomplished through *OD interventions*. The person who carries out or leads the intervention is often referred to as an *OD change agent*. Some of the common characteristics of OD programs are: an application of behavioral science techniques, a systems view of the organization, data-based interventions, an emphasis on goal setting and planning, and a focus on on-going or intact work groups.

---

[15] See for example: Larry E. Pate, Warren R. Nielsen, and Paula C. Bacon, "Advances in Research on Organization Development: Toward a Beginning," in Robert L. Taylor, Michael J. O'Connell, Robert A. Zawacki, and D. D. Warrick, eds., *Academy of Management Proceedings '76* (Proceedings of the 36th Annual Meeting of the Academy of Management, Kansas City, Mo., August 11–14, 1976), pp. 389–394; David G. Bowers, "OD Techniques and Their Results in 23 Organizations: The Michigan ICL Study," *Journal of Applied Behavioral Science*, Vol. 9, No. 1 (1973), pp. 21–43; John R. Kimberly and Warren R. Nielsen, "Organization Development and Change in Organizational Performance," *Administrative Science Quarterly*, June 1975, pp. 191–206; Jacob E. Hautaluoma and James F. Gavin, "Effects of Organizational Diagnosis and Intervention on Blue-Collar 'Blues,'" *Journal of Applied Behavioral Science*, Vol. 11 (1975), pp. 475–496; and William F. Dowling, "The Corning Approach to Organization Development," *Organizational Dynamics*, Spring 1975, pp. 16–34.

[16] French and Bell, *Organizational Development*, p. 252 (italics added).

There are many kinds of OD interventions. Some relate exclusively to the individual and seek to improve behavioral skills. One of these is role playing. Other OD interventions, such as team building, are designed to improve intragroup and intergroup performance. Finally, there are overall or comprehensive interventions. Some of the most popular are survey feedback, System 4 management, and grid training.

Certain conditions must obtain for optimal success of an OD program. The most important of these conditions include: top-level support for the program, use of action research, involvement of the organizational members in planning and carrying out the program, and careful monitoring of the entire change effort.

Is OD an effective approach to managing organizational resources? While noting that there are several problems, including the difficulty of defining organizational climate, measuring openness and trust, and putting a dollar saving on the entire program, we must emphasize that there is considerable evidence to suggest that OD does indeed work.

Key terms in the chapter

organizational climate
organizational iceberg
organizational development
OD intervention
OD change agent
experiential assignment
role playing
team building
survey feedback

System 4 management
grid organization development
managerial grid
1,1 managerial style
9,1 managerial style
1,9 managerial style
5,5 managerial style
9,9 managerial style

Review and study questions

1. In your own words, what is *organizational climate*?

2. When the organizational iceberg concept is discussed, there is reference to formal aspects and informal aspects of the iceberg. What are the formal aspects? What are the informal aspects? How do they differ?

3. In your own words, what is *organizational development*?

4. OD specialists try to improve the relationships among the organization's personnel through the use of OD interventions. What is an OD intervention? How does it work?

5. The individual who carries out or leads the intervention is often referred to as an OD change agent. Exactly what does this person do?

6. What are the eight major characteristics of most OD programs?

7. Role playing is one of the most common forms of training used in OD. How does role playing work?

8. How does a team-building intervention work? Why are these interventions so well liked by OD practitioners?

9. What are the three distinct steps in survey feedback? How effective is this OD approach? Explain.

10. In what way is System 4 management as much a philosophy as it is an OD intervention? What is the objective of System 4 management?

11. In your own words, explain what is meant by each of the following: 1,1 management; 9,1 management; 1,9 management; 5,5 management; 9,9 management.

12. What are the six phases used for implementing the managerial grid? Explain each.

13. It is commonly accepted that 11 conditions are necessary for optimal success of an OD program. What are they?

14. Does OD work or is it just a lot of hocus-pocus? Explain your answer.

What's it all about?

A large private hospital has been having a lot of trouble in the past year. It has lost money for the first time in 25 years, and even the hospital administrator has heard rumblings of discontent among the staff. Following the advice of one of his associates, the administrator has agreed to bring in a team of consultants to look the situation over and offer operative recommendations for solving the problems.

The first thing the consultants did was to make an overall analysis of the hospital. They wanted to find out what the organizational climate looked like. In this regard they gave a random sample of hospital personnel the Likert profile (see Figure 14.3). They then asked each of the respondents to put an X on each continuum to designate where they thought the hospital was in regard to each organizational characteristic. They also asked each person to put an asterisk (*) on each continuum to designate where they would like the organization to be on each organizational characteristic.

In every case, the X was to the left of the asterisk. The consultants concluded that the hospital was operating under System 2 management and that most of the personnel preferred a System 4 management. From their interviews with the workers, the consultants also concluded that there was little trust in top management, communication flows were mostly downward, and the personnel felt that the administration was more interested in the efficiency of the hospital than in the well-being of its employees. At the end of their report, the consultants indicated that they had only identified the tip of the iceberg. They then made recommendations for solving the problems:

What we have here is an institution that is in need of organizational development. Why are the workers discontent with conditions? Why do their responses to the Likert profile show that there is a great desire for System 4 management when the organization is operating under System 2? Why is the hospital losing money? All these problems are interrelated. The only way to get to the bottom of the situation is to carry out some OD interventions, identify the major causes of these problems, and then develop methods for solving them.

The hospital administrator is reading the report with a great deal of interest, for he is determined to straighten out the situation and put the institution back into the profit column. Also, the board of directors has made it perfectly clear to him that if things continue to go downhill, they will begin looking for a new administrator. In short, it is to his advantage to get moving on the problems. However, he has some important questions. What is OD all about? How do OD interventions work? Most importantly, would they be effective? In his own mind, the administrator is unable to see any relationship between OD interventions and improvement of personnel efficiency. He has decided that he will have to talk to the consultants about what they want to do and how they can bring about improved organizational efficiency. For the moment, however, he is confused.

Questions

1. What does the organizational climate in the hospital look like? Defend your answer.
2. What are OD interventions all about? Explain.
3. If you were one of the consultants, how would you answer the administrator's questions? Be complete in your answer.

An all-out effort

A large electronics firm in a major West Coast city has been having what its board chairman calls "human relations problems." These problems are not confined to any one level of the organization, but rather seem to be everywhere. For example, at the upper levels there is vicious fighting among the senior vice presidents. Each is trying to attain departmental goals at the expense of the others. There is little communication or trust among the executives.

The same attitude and managerial philosophy is found in the middle levels of the structure. Additionally, middle managers put a strong emphasis on the work aspect of operations and give little concern to the people side of the business. This has resulted in interdepartmental friction and lack of coordination. For example, some orders are running as much as 60 days late because the head of the purchasing department does not like the manager of production operations and has been late in placing orders for parts and materials.

At the lowest levels of the hierarchy there is a great deal of confusion. The workers know that the managers are fighting among themselves and they are uncertain how to react. Some managers are encouraging their personnel to work harder so their output records will look good and other departments and managers will be blamed for the company's current problems. Other managers are having their people slow up while claiming that their departments or units cannot work any faster because they don't have the requisite support from other departments.

When the Likert profile was given to the organizational personnel two years ago, the results showed that the organization was operating under System 3 management. When the instrument was given again last month it showed that the organization is now operating under a System 2 management, and 30 percent of the workers feel they are working under System 1 management.

The board chairman and the president have examined these results and believe that the company needs an overall OD effort. As a result, they are going to bring in a team of change agents next week to implement grid organizational development. The chairman's memo explained the decision to the board this way:

We brought in OD people to help us with the Likert profile survey and then had a meeting with our top managers. After going over the results we realize that we need a *total* OD effort. A piecemeal approach will be ineffective.

After consulting with these OD people, we opted for grid training because it will address all our problems. It is a long-range, systematic approach that will help us deal with planning, organizing, coordinating, communicating, decision making, motivating, leading, and controlling. We need help in all these areas.

The program will begin at the top of the hierarchy and will be implemented in stages, gradually working its way to the bottom. We are going to give it our full support because we believe this OD effort will get us back on the straight and narrow. We have great faith in this approach and I don't think we'll be disappointed.

Questions

1. In what way is grid training an overall effort? Explain.

2. What are the steps involved in grid training? List them.

3. Given the problems described in this case, is grid training a good choice? Defend your answer.

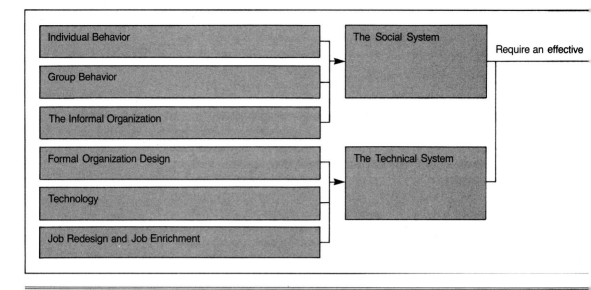

Looking to the future

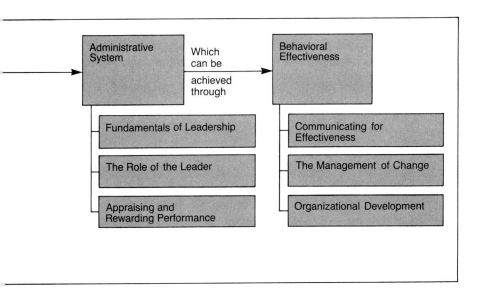

| Administrative System | Which can be achieved through | Behavioral Effectiveness |

| Fundamentals of Leadership | | Communicating for Effectiveness |

| The Role of the Leader | | The Management of Change |

| Appraising and Rewarding Performance | | Organizational Development |

VI

In this book we have examined the areas that are of primary importance to the manager who wants to improve his or her human relations skills and abilities. We began by noting the significance of motivation, because the effective manager must be able to galvanize people so that they are willing to strive toward goal attainment. Then we studied the social system of organizations, which consists of individual behavior, group behavior, and the informal organization. The social system can be thought of as the people who work for (or in) the organization.

Next we studied the technical system, which is composed of formal organization design, technology, and job redesign and enrichment. The technical system represents the structure of the organization; it is the environment in which the people carry out their jobs.

Then we examined the organization's administrative system. To a large degree this consists of the way in which the management directs its day-to-day activities, with specific emphasis given to the human element. Of particular importance in this area were the fundamentals of leadership, the leader's role, and how the leader appraises and rewards performance of subordinates.

Finally, we turned our attention to behavioral effectiveness. There may be problems in the social system, the technical system, or the administrative system. How does the organization deal with these problems? By seeking to achieve behavioral effectiveness. This involves communicating for effectiveness, managing change properly, and using organizational development interventions where appropriate.

So far in this book, we have studied the entire field of human relations, which, as you will remember from Chapter 1, we defined as a process by which management brings workers into contact with the organization in such a way that the objectives of both groups are achieved.

Now we consider the question, "How can you use your human relations knowledge to help you obtain employment and move ahead in your chosen career?" In answering this question, we begin by setting forth key areas in which a self-evaluation must be conducted. We also offer human relations tips related to writing an effective resume and carrying out a successful job hunt. Guidelines for managing a career effectively are also suggested. The final part of the chapter describes the characteristics that successful executives must have in the future and discusses the challenges that face the human relations-oriented manager of the 1980s.

Human relations and you

15

Goals of the chapter

Having studied what the field of modern human relations is, we now turn our attention to the ways in which you can use human relations to help you obtain employment and move ahead in your chosen career. The first goal of this chapter is to discuss the ways of choosing a career including how to make a self-evaluation.

The second goal is to study the ways of actually finding a job. In doing so, particular attention will be devoted to writing an effective resume and carrying out a successful job hunt.

The third goal is to identify some of the most important steps in managing your career effectively. Consideration will also be given to the role and value of a mentor and the importance of dressing for success and organizing your office properly.

The final goal of this chapter is to examine the responsibilities and challenges for the modern manager. Here the focus is on the conditions you will face in carrying out your managerial tasks.

When you have finished reading this chapter you should be able to:

1. set forth the key questions that should be asked in carrying out a self-evaluation
2. know something about your own degree of creativity
3. write an effective resume
4. carry out a successful job hunt
5. describe some of the major steps you should follow in managing your career effectively
6. discuss the role and importance of a mentor

7. set forth some of the basic rules regarding both how to dress for success and organize your office properly

8. describe the characteristics that successful executives must possess in the future

9. discuss the challenges that face the human relations-oriented manager of the 1980s.

Choosing a career

The value of human relations is not confined to the management of others. It can also be used in choosing a career and succeeding in that choice. When applied this way, human relations concepts can be employed in making an accurate self-evaluation and a successful job hunt.

Self-Evaluation

The most important initial step in applying human relations concepts to your career is that of evaluating yourself. What do you do well? What do you do poorly? In conducting this evaluation, some of the most important questions are the following:

1. What do you do best?
2. What do you like to do?
3. What do you dislike doing?
4. Do you work well with others or do you work best by yourself?
5. Do you know your own talents and abilities? What are they?
6. What do you think you would like to do for a living? Has your education prepared you for this career, or is further training necessary?
7. How hard are you willing to work?
8. What are your work habits? Do you work at a steady pace or in short bursts of intensive effort?
9. Have you sought any information or professional advice regarding your career choice(s)? What have you learned?
10. How will you go about beginning your career employment search?

These questions require you to apply many of the ideas you have studied in this book to your own career development. Included in this group are such concepts as: motivation, personality, values, group behavior, job design, leadership, communication, and your ability to deal with change. This type of self-analysis is helpful because it provides basic direction in assessing where you are and where you would like to go.

Figure 15.1

Assumed distribution of employee ability and job requirements based on ability

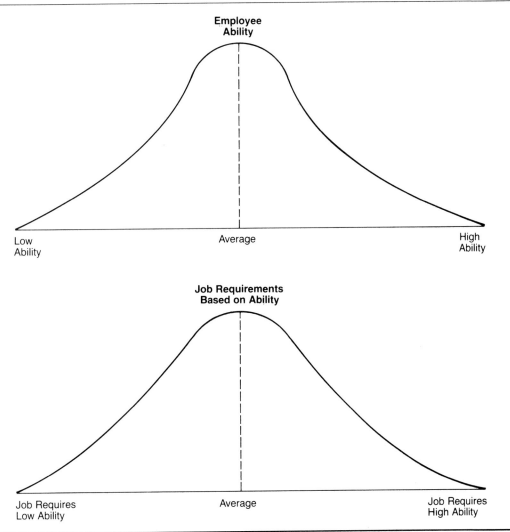

Employee
Ability

Low
Ability

Average

High
Ability

Job Requirements
Based on Ability

Job Requires
Low Ability

Average

Job Requires
High Ability

Do not underrate your ability   In your self-analysis, be sure not to underrate your ability. Otherwise you will be selling yourself short. One way of approaching this subject is to keep in mind that you not only possess ability, but you probably have more than enough to do most jobs. This idea is illustrated in Figures 15.1, 15.2 and 15.3. Notice from the first figure that many people assume that both employee ability and job requirements can be depicted as a bell-shaped curve. Some employees

Figure 15.2

Actual distribution of employee ability and job requirements based on ability

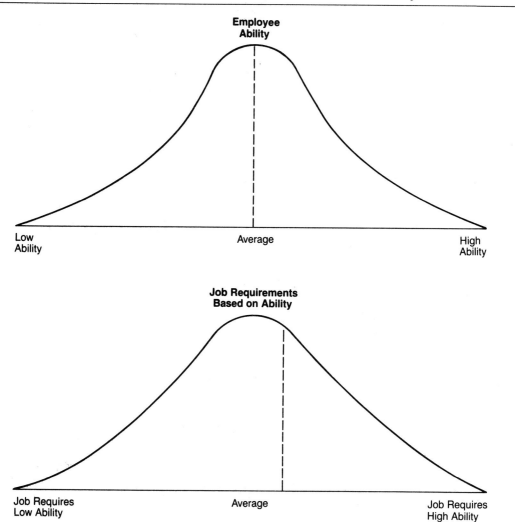

have low ability, most have average ability, some have high ability. Like-wise, some jobs require low ability, most require average ability, some call for high ability. However, as seen in Figure 15.2, this is *not* an accu-rate depiction of job requirements based on ability. The result, as pre-sented in Figure 15.3, is human resource waste. People often have more ability than is required by the job.

If you do feel you are above average in ability, be sure to take this into consideration. What may be an interesting or challenging job for the average person could prove quite boring to you.

Figure 15.3
Job requirements distribution superimposed on ability distribution

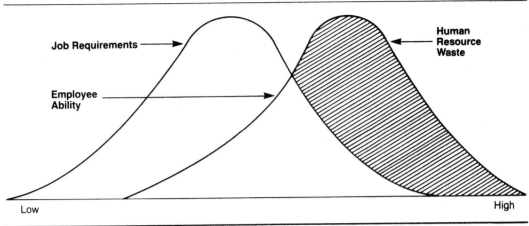

The creativity issue Many individuals also fail to examine their creativity. They believe that only geniuses are creative. Actually, as noted in Chapter 9, creativity is very common, and individuals in the general population possess varying degrees of it. Some of the characteristics of these people include:

1. Creative people tend to be bright rather than brilliant. Extraordinarily high intelligence is not required to be creative, but creative people are good at generating many different ideas in a short period of time.

2. Creative people tend to have a positive self-image; they feel good about themselves.

3. Creative people are emotionally expressive and sensitive to the world around them and the feelings of others.

4. Creative people, almost by definition, are original in their thinking.

5. Creative people tend to be interested in the nature of the problem itself; they are motivated by challenging problems.

Characteristics of creative people.

6. Creative people usually suspend judgment until they have collected ample facts about a problem. Thus they are more reflective than impulsive.

7. Creative people are frequently nonconformists. They value their independence and do not have strong need to gain approval from the group.

8. Creative people lead a rich, almost bizarre, fantasy life. They are just "crazy" enough to serve their creative ends.

"I took an aptitude test once and after that I never looked back."

Drawing by Smilby, *Changing Times*, January 1977.

9. Creative people tend to be flexible and not authoritarian. Faced with a problem, they reject black and white (categorical) thinking and look for nuances.

10. Creative people are more concerned with meanings and implications of problems than with the small details.[1]

Are you very creative? You can obtain some insights to your own creativity by taking the quiz to find out how creative you are. Use the results as a gauge in helping you decide on the best type of job. Remember, do not sell yourself short.

[1] Andrew J. DuBrin, *Human Relations: A Job Oriented Approach* (Reston, Va.: Reston Publishing Company, Inc., 1978), pp. 53–54.

How creative are you?

The following statements are designed to provide input about your own creativity. Answer each as objectively as you can.

	Basically True	Basically False
1. I read more than 10 hours a week.	✓	
2. I have very strong convictions: right is right and wrong is wrong.	✓	
3. I really do not care why people are nice to me as long as they are nice.		✓
4. If I work long enough and hard enough, I can find the answers to most problems.	✓	
5. I really do not take rules and regulations too seriously.	✓	
6. I prefer to read nonfiction books; fiction is a waste of time.		✓
7. I do not like getting vague instructions; it makes me nervous.		✓
8. Sometimes I'll take a different route to work to break up my everyday routine.	✓	
9. Detective work has some appeal for me.		✓
10. It is more important to me to please myself than to please others.	✓	
11. When I write, I try to avoid the use of unusual words or word combinations.		✓
12. I always dress well; I hate to look shabby.	✓	
13. I have a standard rule of the road: business before pleasure.	✓	
14. I like doing things that are fun, but if there is no monetary payoff, I spend very little time doing them.		✓
15. I never read the latest best-selling novels, but I do try to read the most current business-oriented literature.	✓	

The interpretation of your answers can be found at the end of the chapter.

Finding a job

After your self-analysis, the next step is finding a job. This requires you to do two things. First, you have to write a resume that attracts attention and points you out as someone whom the organization should pursue. Second, you have to conduct yourself properly during the job hunt, especially the interview.

The effective resume

Regardless of the job you are seeking, you should put together a ***resume*** or summary of your education, work experience, training, and references. The resume is typically the first step to the interview. After reviewing resumes of job applicants, an organization will choose those that look most promising and extend them an interview. Without an effective resume, you will never get to the interview stage.

If you are just starting out in a career, your resume should be simple, straightforward, and factual. A good general rule is to make it only one to two pages long, and, if you are looking at one organization only, gear it specifically to that enterprise. Otherwise, it can be more general. Some of the most important guidelines you should follow in putting together your resume are the following:

1. Group your information into 4–6 categories such as personal data, employment objective, education, work experience, special interests, and references.

2. Start by listing your name, address, telephone number, and other personal information; then move on to your education and job experience, listing your most recent degree or job first and working backwards.

3. If you do have a specific employment objective, state it, but avoid the use of generalities such as "wanting a challenging position" or a "desire to work with people." These do not really tell the reader a great deal.

4. Use a format that is easy to read, has eye appeal, and provides a positive impression about you and your goals. If you feel it is necessary or useful, underline some words or capitalize them.

5. Have duplicated copies of your resume if you intend to interview with more than a handful of firms; these should be made up by a professional printer so that each copy looks identical to the original.

6. If you want to send along a picture of yourself, do so. However, attach it to the resume; do not have it printed as part of the resume. In this way if the organization is prohibited by state law from requiring pictures or simply does not want them as part of the resume, the picture can be removed.

7. References are optional. If you are just starting out, it is useful to list them. If you have been working for a number of years, you may not want anyone to contact your references without your approval; in this case, simply state that these are available on request.

Notice that the seven suggestions all draw upon human relations concepts, and they help you present yourself in a positive light. Figure 15.4 provides an illustration of a resume that follows these suggestions.

Figure 15.4
A sample resume

MARTHA VELAZQUEZ

HOME ADDRESS:	1345 Antigua Way Coral Gables, Florida 33134	Phone: 305-442-1110
PERSONAL:	Age: 21 U.S. citizen Language Proficiency: English and Spanish	Height: 5′ 6″ Weight: 120
CAREER OBJECTIVES:	Sales assignment in Latin or South America with the opportunity for marketing management experience and position within the next five years.	
EDUCATIONAL BACKGROUND:	B.S. in Marketing, Florida International University, June 1982. Major GPA 3.75/4.0, overall GPA 3.61/4.0. Specific areas of study have included consumer behavior, marketing research and forecasting, international marketing, international management, import-export marketing, sales management, advertising, and physical distribution management.	
EMPLOYMENT HISTORY:	Part-time assistant buyer for South American Imports, Inc. Duties involved weekend travel to Caracas, Quito, and Lima to assist in negotiation of imported goods through the port of Miami for sale throughout the continental United States. Also served as interpreter to company executives who did not speak Spanish and assisted them in negotiating both price and quantity contract terms.	
PROFESSIONAL ASSOCIATIONS:	Member, Marketing Club, Florida International University, 1980–1982. Member, International Marketing Club, Florida International University, 1980–1982.	
REFERENCES:	Dr. William Gladue, (Professor), Marketing Department, Florida International University, Tamiami Trail, Miami, Florida 33199 Mr. Robert Ramirez, President, South American Imports, Inc., P.O. Box 1197, Miami, Florida 33137 Mr. Julio Contreras, Vice President, First National Bank, 111 Miracle Mile, Coral Gables, Florida 33134	

The successful job hunt

If you have written an effective resume, the next step is to get it into the right hands. One of the easiest ways, if you are about to graduate, is by signing up at the college placement office with prospective employers who will be recruiting on campus. Another way is to contact organizations directly that have job openings and send them your resume. If things go your way, you will be interviewed and hired. From a human relations standpoint, however, there are eight things you need to know.

Silence can be golden. If you already have a job and are looking for another, do not advertise this fact to everyone. Keep your search quiet, seeking help only from friends or business associates who can provide leads or introductions. If your boss will hit the ceiling or jeopardize your career should he or she find out you are looking for other employment, ask all potential employers to treat your application confidentially.

Sometimes it is best to say nothing.

On the other hand, if this is your first career job, you should go out of your way to advertise it. Interview with all campus recruiters who have job openings similar to your career objectives. Give all of your major professors a copy of your resume for distribution to any employer they may meet who is looking for someone with your qualifications.

Don't answer every employment ad. Many firms place help-wanted ads in newspapers and trade journals. Most identify themselves and describe their job openings; some merely provide a brief explanation of the individual they are seeking and a coded box number to which one can send a resume. The former ads, which seem to offer those opportunities you are seeking, are worth pursuing; the latter are not. In most cases, blind ads, as these are known, do not result in responses. The organization is usually trying to gauge the labor supply in the field or determine salary levels for certain types of jobs; so you may be wasting your time by applying.

Know how to be interviewed. When you get an interview, you are halfway toward your goal of a job offer. Now you want to be sure that you do not flub your chance. The first thing you should do is bone up on the company. What goods or services does it produce? How much did it gross last year? What is its reputation? If you know about the company, this is likely to impress the interviewer and improve your chances of a job offer. However, do not stop here. Develop some questions that demonstrate your knowledge of your field. Let the interviewer know that you know what you are talking about. Be prepared to go on the offensive.

Be positive in your approach.

Also keep in mind that the interviewer is checking to see if there could be personal chemistry between you and the organization. How you dress, act, and talk are all important. Keep things on a positive note. If you are asked about your ability to interact well with others, talk about your personality strengths. If you are asked why you are leaving your current job, discuss your desire for increased responsibility and challenge. Do not talk negatively either about yourself or your current employer. Such discussion casts a pall over the interview and can result in your losing the job.

Downplay salary. How do you answer the question, "What salary do you want?" If possible, sidestep the question by explaining that salary is only one of your considerations and you would prefer to learn more about the job. If you are pushed into an answer, cite a range such as $18,000–$20,000 rather than a single figure, such as $19,200. If the employer is willing to pay $18,700 for the job, you are in the ballpark with a salary range answer but too high with a set number. Additionally, because they really do want the job, some people will drop their asking price to a lower level, such as $18,200. In this case, they have given up $500 since the employer is seldom inclined to pay more than is necessary.

Talk opportunity not salary.

If you are just starting out, you really do not have to be concerned with knowing how much to request. Most employers have a specific salary range for positions and, if they do not, you can compare starting salaries and job requirements at interviews before deciding which job to take.

Strive for originality. Most organizations will be interviewing more than one person for each job opening. If you are a typical candidate, you will do all of the usual things: write an interesting resume, dress well, act properly. However, if possible, try to do something different. Look for a way to distinguish yourself from the others. While this requires some degree of creativity, it does not have to be truly unique. The following is an example:

Try to be different.

> Career counselor John C. Crystal tells of one of his students, a high school teacher, who wanted to become a personal financial planner and counselor. He embarked on an ambitious exploration of the field. "He visited 55 financial planners across the country," says Crystal. "When he called for interview appointments, he told each one what he was doing—surveying those in the field to learn about the business. After his first visits he could tell successive planners that he had just talked to so-and-so, and that opened doors for him. By the time he had completed his research, he had received eight unsolicited job offers."[2]

Do not lose hope. As you get into your job search, you may discover yourself sending out 30 resumes and getting 15 responses of which only 10 express any interest. You may also find yourself interviewing with seven of these firms and only two make you an offer, neither of which you feel is truly competitive. As a result, you may decide to start the process all over and send out resumes to new organizations. The im-

Keep a positive attitude.

[2] "Eight Ways to Flub a Job Hunt," *Changing Times*, December 1981, p. 78.

portant thing to remember is do not despair. Keep a positive attitude. You will eventually get something that will satisfy you.

To find a job you must sell your capabilities, and tired or unenthusiastic salespeople don't make sales. You can't let the stress of the job hunt lead you to undervalue your potential or restrict your options. There is no logical reason to despair. You know the kind of work you are capable of doing. The big catch is meeting the person who needs someone like you to do a job. Logic says that will happen sooner or later.[3]

Getting ahead

After you have secured a job, there are still ways in which human relations knowledge can help you. These include ways of managing your career effectively, getting a mentor, dressing the part, and organizing your office properly.

Manage your career effectively

After you have secured employment, your challenge becomes one of managing your career effectively. The most successful people do not allow their career paths to develop randomly. They take steps to ensure that things go their way; and when they do not, these people know how to adjust their career course. Some of the major steps they employ are discussed below.

Master your work.

Know your job. In every job there is a basic set of skills that need to be mastered. For engineers these skills are technical in nature; for personnel specialists they are behavioral in content; for managers they are a combination of technical and behavioral. Find out those skills that are most important to your job and learn and master them as quickly as possible.

Know the formal evaluation criteria.

Know how you will be judged. Most people are judged on two types of criteria: formal and informal. Formal criteria tend to be measurable and often take such forms as volume of work output or productivity, sales increases, and/or profit. Those who do well in these areas receive greater raises or faster promotions than those who do not. Your performance on formal criteria is measured by some document or evaluation instrument. If you are determined to win the career promotion game, you must concentrate on doing well on these formal criteria and let other things go. On the other hand, if you find that formal criteria include

---

[3]*Ibid.*, p. 79.

the above-stated objectives as well as less quantitative criteria, such as personality, interpersonal skills, leadership styles, and work attitudes, you must broaden your attention and address these as well. Sometimes you will find that most people do quite well in pursuing the quantitative objectives, and it is the qualitative ones that separate the most promotable from the others. In this case, concentrate the bulk of your attention on the qualitative side. Here is where your current career progress will be decided.

Informal criteria are more difficult to describe. They are determined by your boss. Typical examples include the way you dress, whether you seem interested in your job, and whether you fit in as a member of the work group. The best way to meet these challenges is by watching the other successful members of your department or group and seeing how they do things.

And the informal evaluation criteria.

Keep a hero file.   The formal evaluation system is used by the organization to reward you for your contributions. However, at some point during your career you may decide to move to another enterprise. How will you be able to show your new prospective employer how good you are? One way, of course, is by pointing to your past promotions and current salary. A second way is by having your boss write a letter of recommendation for you (assuming he or she would comply). A third way, and best of all, is to keep a hero file which contains all of your accomplishments. Typical examples include memos congratulating you on your work, awards given to you by the organization, and samples of your work (a major report you wrote, an advertisement you designed, a financial analysis you conducted) that show the quality of your performance. Remember, modesty has its place, but sometimes it pays to blow your own horn!

Develop alliances.   Very few loners succeed in modern organizations. You have to be able to get along with others if you are going to advance. This requires the development of alliances. In doing so, begin with your subordinates by creating an effective work relationship with them. This will show others that you are qualified in your job and begin to open doors at the management level. Next you should begin developing your peer-group relationships with others on the same level in the hierarchy as you. Finally, you should seek ways of developing work relationships with higher-level managers. If you violate this "from the bottom up approach," you may find it very difficult to develop meaningful alliances. Your peers will regard you as an apple polisher or someone who is trying to succeed at their expense; when possible, they will look for ways to undercut your performance and your reputation. Your subordinates will look on you as someone who is more interested in his or her own career than in helping them to get things done. They will retaliate by giving you minimum performance and helping create a reputation for

Create effective work relationships.

you as someone who is not very effective in managing work teams. Since both of these groups can be just as harmful to you as they can be helpful, it is best to win their support and create an alliance with them as soon as possible.

Show that you are a star.　Strive to prove that you are a star on the rise. There are a number of ways that you can do this. One is by turning in top-notch performance. When your work is outstanding, this gets around. People begin to notice you.

A second way is by realizing the truth in the cliché that great performance is 99 percent perspiration and 1 percent inspiration. In modern organizations most people succeed because of hard work; it is still the key to great performance.

Let them know you are a winner.

A third way is by making yourself a crucial part of the work team. The more your boss relies on you, the greater your chances for success. As your supervisor goes up the chain of command, he or she is likely to take you along. Of course, you may find that your boss is at a dead end. A classic example of the Peter Principle, he or she has risen to their level of incompetence. In this case—get out. Find another position in the organization or look elsewhere. Your mobility is limited. How do you know when your boss is no longer a fast-track manager? Simply compare the average time between promotions for other managers and for your boss. Typically, managers get promoted every 3–5 years. If your boss has been in the same position for 7 years, he or she is probably not going anywhere. If you remain in the department, the same is true for you.

A fourth way is by getting continuous feedback on how well you are doing. Stay alert to comments from your boss on what you are doing well and where you need improvement. Treat this feedback as a source for personal action. Sure it may hurt when the individual tells you, "Your report was incomplete," or, "Jones tells me that you were late for the meeting yesterday afternoon," or, "I want you to start paying closer attention to the cost data I'm sending you; your work group's efficiency is falling down." However, you are getting feedback on how to improve your performance. Accept it in a positive light and use it to help correct your shortcomings.

A fifth way is by standing out from the crowd. Do something that sets you apart. Take an assignment that provides you the opportunity to present your findings to the board of directors. Agree to serve on a committee that has representatives from all management levels and go out of your way to impress them. Volunteer for extra assignments that you feel you are qualified to handle and no one else wants. As you try to separate yourself from the crowd, remember that your strategy has its risks. If you fail, your career may be jeopardized. So be somewhat conservative and do not bite off more than you can comfortably chew.

Train your replacement.　If you are a rising star, you will leave a void when you are promoted, unless you have a replacement. In some cases your promotion may be delayed until there is someone to take your place. You can speed up your career progress by training your replacement early. If you are being promoted to another department or unit, your boss will be reluctant to let you go because he or she will be left without adequate assistance—hence, the need for a replacement.

Have someone ready to step into your shoes.

Periodically reassess your career.   As you begin to learn your job and show those around you that you are capable of higher tasks, continually reassess your career. Sometimes there will be little chance for you to be promoted in your current organization. If your boss is five years younger than you are and it appears that the individual, in all likelihood, is content with the organization, you are not going to get promoted over him or her. You are either going to have to go around him or her by finding a job elsewhere in the organization, or seek employment in another enterprise. In deciding exactly what you should do, periodically reassess your career. Set some objectives for yourself, and if you do not attain them, consider moving. Typical objectives include: (1) if you do not receive two promotions in the first five years, you will leave; (2) if you do not receive an average raise of 10 percent each year for the first three years, you will leave; (3) if you are not in a middle-management position, with a group or unit of at least seven subordinates within five years, you will seek employment elsewhere; and (4) if you feel you are not going to be in top management by the time you are 45, you will leave. All of these are examples; none is meant to serve as a definitive guideline. However, they are representative of the types of goals high-achieving people set for themselves in reassessing their careers.

Set goals and assess your performance annually.

One final note: if you do decide to leave, do so at your convenience and on a good note. Kleiner puts it this way:

If your company lost an important government contract and you know there will be a lot of pink slips coming in the next few months (and you'll probably get one of them through no fault of your own), the time to find a job is now while you enjoy the status of being fully employed. It's amazing how much lower your market value can become once the other company knows you have been terminated by your last employer. It's not fair, because you have the same skills, but that's frequently the way it is. If the new company asks you why you are looking for another job while you are presently employed, just truthfully tell them that you are seeking to work for a company that will provide you with better prospects for advancement.[4]

Furthermore, regardless of why you leave, stay on good terms with everyone. Bosses tend to remember your last days on the job more vividly than they do most other days. So if you need them to say something about you in the future, you want them to be positive and complementary responses.

---

[4]Brian H. Kleiner, "Managing Your Career," *Supervisory Management*, March 1980, pp. 20–21.

Get a mentor

Another important aspect of getting ahead is to get a mentor. A *mentor* is a person who coaches, counsels, teaches, and/or sponsors others. While it is possible to succeed in a large organization without having a mentor, it is easier to do so if you have one. One researcher, reporting on a survey he conducted among top executives mentioned in the "Who's News" column of the *Wall Street Journal*, found that mentor and protege relationships are quite common in the business world today. More specifically, he reported that:

1. **Nearly two-thirds of the respondents had a mentor or sponsor and one-third of them had two or more mentors.**
2. **Mentor relationships seem to have become more prevalent during the last twenty years.**

Mentoring is popular.

3. **Executives who have had a mentor earn more money at a younger age, are better educated, are more likely to follow a career plan, and, in turn, sponsor more proteges than executives who have not had a mentor.**
4. **Those who have had a mentor are happier with their career progress and derive somewhat greater pleasure from their work than do those who have not had a mentor.**[5]

What, in particular, makes a mentor so useful? The primary answer is the individual's willingness to share knowledge and understanding with younger managers, helping them develop into effective leaders. The mentoring process is particularly important to individuals between the ages of 25–40. These people are still in the learning and growing period of their career.

Mentors and women executives. Hennig and Jardim, writing about the managerial woman, have reported that mentors are particularly important to the success of female executives.[6] Recent research continues to support these findings. Statistically speaking, women are more likely to have mentors than their male counterparts and tend to have more of them. Additionally, reports Roche:

Out of every 10 women respondents, 9 formed relationships with their mentors in the work setting, the majority during the sixth to tenth years of their career. Since that is the period when many women decide to pursue a "career" rather than simply "work," it may be that those who form mentor relationships during these years are the ones who feel they can succeed and thus choose careers.[7]

---

[5] Gerald R. Roche, "Much Ado about Mentors," *Harvard Business Review*, January–February 1979, pp. 14–15.

[6] Margaret Hennig and Anne Jardim, *The Managerial Woman* (New York: Anaheim Press/Doubleday, 1977).

[7] Roche, "Much Ado about Mentors," p. 24.

Trends. Today the trend toward mentoring continues. Approximately 75 percent of all executives under the age of 40 have a mentor. As these people continue their climb up the ladder, they eventually lose their need for a mentor but begin taking on proteges of their own. So mentoring begets mentoring.

To a large degree this process is inevitable. Given today's complex and rapid-paced environment, increased demands are being put on managers. One of the best ways to meet these demands is by seeking out individuals from whose experience one can learn. Of course, you can succeed in any organization without a mentor, but it will help if you have one (or more) who can provide you assistance and advice along the way. A mentor cannot guarantee you will succeed, but he or she can give you that extra push that will help you move out from the pack.

And these trends will continue.

Dress the part

Successful managers dress the part. Face it, if you are well groomed, your hair is properly cut and combed, your clothing is well pressed and neat, and your shoes are shined, you are going to make a much better impression than someone who is a casual, and basically sloppy, dresser. There are a number of ways of going about dressing correctly. One of the easiest is to buy your clothing from a quality store (and you should) where the salesperson can help you look your best. He or she is used to dressing people for success. A second, and complementary way, is to watch how people in your organization dress and emulate those who are known as "up and coming." A third is to pick up a good book on how to dress. Just remember that you want to look the part of a successful winner. Figure 15.5 provides some useful information for both men and women who wish to do so.

Dress for success.

Organize your office properly

Another important success variable is the way you organize your office. If you do have an office, you can employ psychological principles that will help you most effectively organize and arrange it. The first rule is: no matter how small it is, make your office look spacious and uncrowded by arranging the furniture appropriately. This should be done by giving initial priority to the desk. If the office is small, keep the desk fairly small or it will crowd the rest of the room. Conversely, if the office is spacious, get a fairly large desk that takes up more room. If at all possible, have a wooden desk or one that looks like wood. In contrast to metal desks, wood connotes power and authority and will help increase your status.

The size of the desk chair should be dictated by your own physical dimensions. If you are a tall or large person, a small chair will make you look like an ogre. If you are a short or slender person, a large chair will

---

Figure 15.5
Selling yourself through clothing

Do clothes really make the person? Some individuals believe they do, including John T. Molloy, an acknowledged expert of how to dress for success. Some of the tips that he offers to men and women who want to look their best include the following:

For Men

1. If you have the choice, dress affluently.
2. If you are unsure of how to dress, it is better to err on the side of conservatism.
3. Always dress as well as the people to whom you are selling.
4. Do not wear green.
5. Do not wear sunglasses or glasses that change tint as the light changes; people must see your eyes if they are to believe you.
6. Always carry a good pen and pencil.
7. If the choice is available, wear an expensive tie.
8. Do not take off your suit jacket unless you have to; it weakens your authority.
9. If it is part of your business equipment, always carry a good attache case.
10. Never wear anything that might be considered feminine.

For Women

1. Tailor your clothing to the demands of your job and your company.
2. Carry an executive gold pen.
3. Wear upper-middle class clothing.
4. Never be the first in your office to wear a fashion; fashion fades.
5. Do not carry a handbag when you can carry an attache case.
6. Wear neutral-color pantyhose to the office.
7. Wear a coat that covers your skirt or dress.
8. Do not take off your jacket in the office.
9. Have a neuter rather than a masculine or feminine office.

John T. Molloy, *Dress For Success* (New York: Warner Books, 1975), p. 147; John T. Molloy, *The Woman's Dress For Success Book* (New York: Warner Books, 1977), pp. 185–186.

---

dwarf your appearance. Choose a chair proportional to your size and, if possible, one which has a back that comes up to the back of your head.

If you have your choice of chairs, get two that match your desk chair. Some of the most acceptable colors for these chairs are natural leather, rich brown, or deep maroon. Black, the most commonly manufactured color, is not as effective, because it lacks the richer look of these other colors.

Visitors' chairs should be placed in front of your desk. Do not put any of them on the side of your desk because this reduces your power and authority in relation to other people.

If there is room, you can put a couch, coffee table, and/or easy chairs in this area. When this is done, the room is divided in two. The part with the desk is for business. The part with the couch and/or coffee table is for small group work or conferences.

Finally, for maximum psychological results, you must try to set up the office so that it draws attention to you. You have to "frame yourself" so that when people enter your office they are directed toward you—the central person there. There are two ways of accomplishing this. One way is by placing your desk in front of a window. The second, if you do not have a window, is by placing a picture on the wall directly behind your chair. In either case, the desk should be positioned symmetrically in front of the window or picture. Otherwise, visitors will feel that your desk is off center or the picture is askew.

Frame yourself.

A final test of your office's effectiveness is to take a picture of it and take pictures of several friends' offices who are in the same line of work. Give these pictures to other managers (outside your organization) and ask them to rate the importance of the office holder based on the office arrangement. This will give you a good idea of how your office compares.

See what others think.

Meeting new challenges

In keeping your career on track, you must understand and meet new challenges. First, you will have to continually review your assumptions about the employees. Second, you will have to possess specific characteristics in order to be successful—and these characteristics are likely to change profoundly during the 1980s. Third, you will have to learn to live with ambiguity, as indicated by the rise of adhocracy. Finally, you will have to learn how to give career counseling to your personnel.

A new set of assumptions

As we noted earlier in the book, most managers are soft Theory X types. They do not adhere rigidly to Theory X tenets, but they have some faith in them.

If you hope to be effective, you will have to learn that high job satisfaction and high output occur most frequently in organizational climates in which there is a great deal of trust and mutual concern. When workers are nervous or afraid of the organization, they regard it with suspicion, and they do only what is required by organizational directive. Additionally, department and organization cliques make covert power plays, people try to manipulate each other for personal gain, and a great deal of an employee's energy is used to "cover tracks" so that if any error is found, he or she can claim to have followed the rules to the letter. These activities use up a lot of an organization's time and effort and accomplish very little in the way of attaining its goals.

On the other hand, if you can develop high trust and low defensiveness among the personnel, open and supportive behavior often emerges.

For this to happen, of course, you must lead the way. Maslow has suggested managerial assumptions necessary to create the environment for such development;[8]

Everyone can be trusted.

People need to know as many facts and truths as possible regarding what is going on.

People want to do a good job and they have a drive to achieve.

If given the chance, everyone in an organization can identify with the goals of the enterprise.

In a healthy organization there is good will among all the members, in contrast to enterprises where rivalry and jealousy abound.

Healthy people are able to admire the capacities and skills of themselves and others.

People need to be able to carry out their own ideas.

Everyone is capable of enjoying teamwork and friendship.

Managerial assumptions for effective leadership.

Most people can take the rigors of organizational life; they are a lot stronger than we give them credit for.

People need to like their boss.

People have a tendency to improve things, to make them better.

People like to work rather than to sit back and loaf.

All people prefer meaningful work.

Most people make wise choices.

Everybody likes to be treated fairly and justly, especially in a public setting.

Most people would rather create than destroy.

People get more satisfaction out of loving than hating.

People would rather be interested than be bored.

People can become better than what they are; they are improvable.

Everyone wants to feel important, useful, needed, proud, and successful.

These 20 assumptions are reflected by Table 15.1, a description of the managers of today and tomorrow. They also embody the type of organizational behavior we have been discussing throughout this text. Most importantly, they point out the role of the manager in attaining the right organizational climate.

---

[8] Abraham H. Maslow, *Eupsychian Management* (Homewood, Ill.: Richard D. Irwin, Inc., and The Dorsey Press, 1964), pp. 17–33.

Table 15.1
How managers of the future will differ from those of today

Characteristics of Successful Executives	Today			1990		
	Not Important	Important	Very Important	Not Important	Important	Very Important
Highly creative	X					XXX
Visionary/Futuristic	X					XXX
Able to handle complexity	X					XXX
Desires to improve the environment	X					XXX
Innovatively effective	X					XXX
Energetic		XX				XXX
Assertive		XX				XXX
Proven administrator		XX			XX	
Logical			XXX		XX	
Good contact personality			XXX		XX	
Good communicator			XXX		XX	
Traditionalist			XXX	X		

Source: Frank Feather, "The Executive of the Future: A Creature of External Environment," *Business Tomorrow*, Spring 1978, p. 5. Published by the World Future Society, 4916 St. Elmo Avenue, Washington, D.C. 20014. Reprinted with permission.

New demands for success

You will also have to possess or develop characteristics in sharp contrast to those required of today's or yesterday's managers. Table 15.1 lists some of the differences. Note that some characteristics will increase in importance, others will diminish somewhat, and the need to be traditional will decline significantly.

From the data in this table it is obvious that the successful executive of the future must place a premium on creativity, futuristic thinking, and innovation. Also, he or she will have to be able to handle complexity and improve the environment. Feather has put it this way:

Executives of the future will not toe the party line. They will speak their minds and scream for innovation. They'll spend long hours worrying about what's going on outside in the whole, wider world of political and social action. Why?

Because the executive of the future who fails to heed the changing moods of the outside world will not be an executive for long.

Traditionally, executive thinking and professional habits were conditioned first by formal training and later by company policies and style. This was essentially an internal process.

In contrast, the executive of the future will be a creature of the external environment. The old internal influences will still exist, but their importance will fall considerably in favour of the new political and social pressures that are squeezing the business community on all sides.[9]

---

[9] Frank Feather, "The Executive of the Future: A Creature of the External Environment," *Business Tomorrow*, Spring 1978, p. 5.

How will a concern with the external environment help the manager of the future cope with the human relations problems that arise in the organization? Without an understanding of the external environment and its influences on the workers, the manager will be unable to understand the workers' values, which they bring with them to the work place.

Workers will also be putting a premium on satisfaction of higher-level needs and so will managers. Workers will want "think" work, and managers must be able to handle this kind of work if they are to be successful. Workers will become more futuristic in terms of handling their own careers, and managers will have to echo this concern. Like other employees, managers will have to strive to be innovatively effective.

At the same time, however, the manager will have to be a good communicator, a good contact personality, and a logical thinker when dealing with the employees. These characteristics will not be as important in the future, however, because of the changing environment and the need of the executive to keep up with what is going on *both* inside and outside the organization.

Dealing with adhocracy

You are also going to have to learn to live with uncertainty, of which the current rise of adhocracy is a harbinger. **Adhocracy** refers to a *temporary* organization structure. As with ad hoc committees, its purpose is to carry out a particular job, after which it is disbanded.

The most common type of temporary organization design is the *matrix structure*. In contrast to the permanent types of departmentalization studied in Chapter 6, the matrix design is used when an organization has a project it wants to accomplish within specified time, cost, and quality limitations. The person assigned to supervise the undertaking is known as the ***project manager***, whose job is to coordinate all activities associated with the project by *cutting across functional lines*. Figure 15.6 illustrates how this is done. Note that there are five functional departments reporting to the president. Personnel from each department have been assigned to various groups. Project Manager A is responsible for coordinating all activities associated with Project A. To do so, the manager must communicate with and secure cooperation from the heads of the other functional departments—research and development, design, purchase, manufacture, and test and control. The same approach is used by the other project managers in coordinating the activities for their respective projects.

When we examine the type of authority held by the functional managers who head the functional departments and the project managers who supervise the respective projects, a very distinct difference warrants our attention. The functional managers all have line authority and are able to give orders to their subordinates in the various groups beneath them. However, the project managers have only ***project authority***,

Figure 15.6
A matrix structure

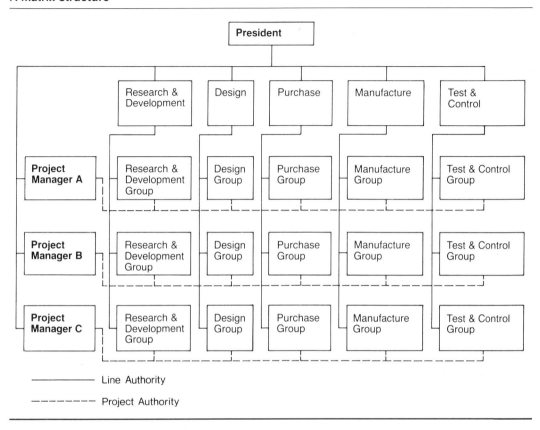

which means that they give orders to the people assigned to them *only* on project matters and that if there is a problem of cooperation, they must work through the functional department heads to resolve it. For this reason, we say that the functional department manager's authority flows *vertically*, while the project manager's authority flows *horizontally*. The functional manager is an order giver, whereas the project manager is a coordinator.

Additionally, the project manager has some major problems to overcome. One is the fact that responsibility often outweighs authority. The manager is responsible for many things but has only limited power to carry them out. As a result, the project manager needs to be exceptionally good at human relations, since he or she must rely so heavily on cooperation from the functional department heads. How can this be done? Research shows that he or she must use four important human relations techniques: (1) negotiating with the functional department heads,

Project authority flows horizontally.

(2) having the personality or persuasive ability to secure favors and support from the functional heads, (3) being competent because functional department heads are much more likely to provide support and assistance, and (4) encouraging reciprocity—making sure that functional managers believe that if they do the project manager a favor, he or she will return the favor sometime.[10]

The project manager must also use the proper human relations approach with the subordinates who participate in the project. Some typical ways of doing so are:

Human relations techniques for project managers.

1. **Make the team members feel that their efforts are important and have a direct effect on the outcome of the program.**
2. **Educate the team regarding what is to be done and how important their role will be.**
3. **Provide credit to project participants when they do a good job.**
4. **Work closely with the team members to create an overall sense of esprit de corps.**
5. **Get to know the people on the team and make them understand that they are an indispensable part of the team.[11]**

Finally, it is important to note that once the project is completed, the workers will be returning to their functional departments where they will be reassigned to other projects. There is thus a great deal of impermanence associated with project organizations. People spend most of their time moving from one project to another with no real permanent home in the organization. This, of course, can create problems for both the manager and the subordinates. Yet this type of organization structure is being used more and more, and the manager of the future will have to learn how to manage in this kind of environment. One way of doing so is to show a genuine concern for the well-being of the personnel by helping them address an issue we discussed earlier in the chapter, namely career planning.

Assisting with career planning

A final aspect of human relations that you will have to know about is how to assist the employees in planning their careers. The assistance can be reduced to answering two simple questions: Where is the employee at this point of his or her career? Where does the employee want to be in the next 10 years (or 20 years, or by the end of his or her career)? The approach often used to answer these questions involves the employee and the manager doing the following things:

[10] Richard M. Hodgetts, "Leadership Techniques in the Project Organization," *Academy of Management Journal*, June 1968, pp. 215–216.
[11] *Ibid.*, p. 217.

1. making an assessment of life and career paths up to this point in time, noting the individual's highlights, particularly important events, strengths, and deficiencies.
2. formulating goals and objectives related to both the individual's desired life style and career path. These are both future-oriented goals.
3. developing a realistic plan for achieving the goals and moving systematically toward accomplishing them. In this phase the goals are specified, action steps are outlined, a schedule of target dates is established for measuring progress, and control of the entire process is undertaken.[12]

Evaluation of an employee's career.

There are a number of ways this can be done. One of the most popular is for the employee to draw a horizontal line from left to right on a piece of paper representing his or her life span and indicating how long the employee expects to live. He or she then indicates present position on the line, the important things that have recently happened, and peak experiences that he or she hopes to have before ending the career. Finally, the employee is asked to write his or her own obituary.

From this experiential assignment, you should be able to determine a number of things about the employee. Most important, you should be able to identify where the employee is currently and what he or she would like to have happen between now and the end of his or her career. You are now in a position to determine if the employee can attain these desired objectives. Will everything he or she is hoping for come true? If the answer is yes, you can help start planning the employee's career. If the answer is no, you have a responsibility to point this out, help the employee decide what success he or she might have by remaining with the firm, and what the chances for success are in another organization.

Followed by sound advice.

Some people believe that the manager's job should be one of keeping the organizational personnel. However, if the employee has a better chance for promotion or advancement with another organization, you have a responsibility to help him or her move in this direction. Remember, your job is to use people well by helping them attain satisfaction of upper-level needs. People strive for the chance to achieve, to be competent, and to self-actualize. Your job should be one of blending the needs of the individual and those of the organization. Career planning is an important step in this process.

Human relations challenges will remain.

Let us make one final point: the demands on the manager of the future will change. However, the practice of human relations will remain a constant challenge. We defined human relations in Chapter 1 as a process by which management brings workers into contact with the organization in such a way that the objectives of both groups are achieved. This will be as true in 1990 as it is today.

---

[12]Wendell L. French and Cecil H. Bell, Jr., *Organization Development*, 2nd ed. (Englewood Cliffs, N.J.: Prentice-Hall, Inc., 1978), p. 147.

Summary

Our overriding objective in this chapter has been to illustrate how human relations concepts can be of value to you personally. The first part of the chapter discusses how to go about choosing a career; particular attention is given to self-evaluation and how to determine whether you are very creative.

The next part of the chapter addresses the issue of finding a job. Specific steps for writing an effective resume are provided. Then a series of eight steps designed to improve your chances of a successful job hunt are outlined.

This is followed by a discussion of how to manage your career effectively. At this point attention is directed at both succeeding in your current position and knowing when to move on. Associated topics such as mentors, the importance of dressing well, and the way to organize your office properly are addressed.

The last part of the chapter focuses on the new responsibilities and challenges that face the manager of the 1980s. Managers are going to have to change their assumptions about the workers. They must also develop different characteristics from those that were necessary to a successful manager of the 1970s. Finally, they will not only have to learn to live with ambiguity, as manifested in the rise of adhocracy, but they will also have to learn to provide career counseling for the personnel. Yet their overall objective, from a human relations standpoint, will remain the same: Future managers will have to bring the workers into contact with the organization in such a way that the objectives of both groups are achieved.

Key terms in the chapter

creative person
resume
mentor
adhocracy

matrix structure
project manager
project authority

Review and study questions

1. What types of questions should a person ask when conducting a career-related self-evaluation?

2. When comparing employee ability and job requirements based on ability, how closely do the two actually mesh? Of what importance are the results of this comparison?

3. What are some of the characteristics of creative people? List five.

4. In conducting a successful job hunt, what are five things the applicant should know? Identify and describe each.

5. A friend is preparing a resume which she would like to be as effective as possible. What are some suggestions you would offer her? Be complete in your recommendations.

6. What are five major steps that everyone should follow who is interested in managing their career effectively? Be specific in your descriptions.

7. What is a mentor? Of what value are mentors? Explain. Will their use increase or decline during the decade of the 1980s? Explain.

8. Your best friend has just been hired by a large corporation and wants to make a good impression. What recommendations would you give your friend regarding how to dress? What would you tell the individual regarding how to organize his office? Be complete in your answers.

9. What are some of the career guidelines currently being recommended to young managers? Cite and explain six.

10. What assumptions will the manager of the 1980s have to have in order to lead successfully?

11. Will the characteristics of successful executives change much between now and 1990? Explain your answer.

12. How does a matrix structure work? What challenges will it present for the manager?

13. How can the human relations manager help the personnel plan their careers? Explain.

Interpretation of How creative are you?

There are basic responses given to these statements by creative people. Compare your answers to those below and for each one you have correct, give yourself one point.

1. Basically true	6. Basically false	11. Basically false
2. Basically false	7. Basically false	12. Basically false
3. Basically true	8. Basically true	13. Basically false
4. Basically false	9. Basically true	14. Basically false
5. Basically true	10. Basically true	15. Basically false

Highly creative people have scores of 13–15. Above average creative people have scores of 10–12. Average people have scores of 7–9. How well did you do? Regardless of your score, however, remember that creativity can be nurtured and developed. You are probably much more creative than you think. So if your score was lower than you would have liked, review the answers above and examine the philosophy and logic behind them. Start learning how to think more creatively. You can do it!

Joe's strategy

When Joseph MacQuillan finished two years at the local community college, he did not know what he wanted to do. However, within one semester at North University, he had made up his mind to major in marketing. He liked his professors and found they were able to explain marketing in such an interesting and applicable way that the whole field came alive for him. Since then Joe has taken a total of seven upper division courses in marketing and is going to graduate in three months.

Beginning next week, Joe hopes to start interviewing with a number of national and local firms, all of which will be on campus to recruit new graduates. Joe is trying to get everything in order. He is roughing out a resume that he can give to each recruiter. He has also obtained a list of the first six firms that will be on campus looking for marketing majors. Four of these companies look very promising, and Joe has signed up to be interviewed by them.

Joe is also looking into other job sources, including newspaper ads, both local and national. He has clipped five employment ads, including one blind ad, and intends to send each a copy of his resume.

Another avenue Joe has pursued is that of faculty contacts. Two of his professors have given him names of individuals in personnel departments to whom he can write, inquiring about employment and asking for an interview. Joe intends to follow up on these just as soon as his resume is typed and photocopied.

Joe realizes that the interview can be the most important part of the job hunt. In getting ready for this phase of the job search, he and two of his friends are practicing being interviewed. One of them plays the role of the interviewer and asks typical recruitment-related questions. One of them plays the role of the interviewee, fielding questions and responding to queries. The third takes the role of an onlooker and offers advice and suggestions to the person being interviewed. Joe believes that the mock interviews have helped him get a feel for the real thing.

Based on these initial preparations, Joe believes he is ready to talk to recruiters about a job. He intends to devote the time remaining before the first interview to getting his resume in shape and buying a new suit.

Questions

1. Review the job hunting steps presented in this chapter and compare them to the ones being used by Joe. In what areas is Joe doing well? Where is he not?

2. What would you recommend that Joe do in addition to what he is currently doing? Be complete in your answer.

3. What recommendations would you make to Joe regarding how to dress for the interview and on the job? Be as specific as possible.

A case of career planning

Jeanette Powers has just graduated from State University. She is currently interviewing with a number of large organizations in New York City. One in particular has impressed her. It is a finance firm, and its growth rate over the last 20 years has been phenomenal. The organization has offices in 108 locations throughout the United States, and from what she can determine from her extensive interview, it is very interested in hiring Jeanette to work in the home office. This is convenient for Jeanette, because her family lives nearby and she would like to stay in the vicinity.

During her interview Jeanette was introduced to a number of different managers. The one for whom she would be working if she takes the job is Carl Klathers, an up-and-coming young executive. Carl has been with the company for five years and has been promoted every year. He is currently in charge of one of the larger offices in the company's headquarters, and everyone has tagged him as top-management timber.

Carl and Jeanette chatted for over 30 minutes during her interview. Additionally, she had the opportunity to speak with some of the personnel in Carl's department. It seems that Carl is not only on the way up, but he is taking some people with him. One man and one woman have been with him for the last five years. Carl appears to be their mentor, and he has told Jeanette that if she works out well in the department, he will take her along with him, too, as he is promoted.

Jeanette also likes the fact that this company would put her in a position where she will be interacting with the public rather than just staying in the office all day handling paperwork assignments. The job promises to be not only challenging but also personally rewarding. Therefore, while Jeanette is also considering three other offers from firms in the area and has two more interviews scheduled, she is convinced that she will be going to work for Carl's firm.

Questions

1. If you were advising Jeanette, what would you tell her about managing her career? In addition to what she already knows, what other things does she need to be aware of?

2. Does Carl meet the requirements of a good boss in terms of helping Jeanette with her career, or should she turn to another company and look for a different kind of boss? Explain and defend your answer.

3. Assuming that Carl is indeed a very successful manager, what assumptions do you think he has about the workers? What executive characteristics does he possess? How capable is he of living with ambiguity? If Jeanette becomes disenchanted with her job after the first year, what recommendations would you give Carl regarding how to assist her in further career planning?

Glossary of Terms

The following glossary contains definitions of many of the concepts and terms used in this book. For the most part, the terms correspond to those given in the text and represent words that the reader is most likely to encounter in the business world. In addition, a few extra definitions not included in the book have been added in order to provide the most comprehensive and most useful glossary possible.

Acceptance.   The third step in the communication process, which involves getting the receiver to agree to comply or accept the directive. The term also refers to willingness to go along with a change because one sees more to be gained from the new conditions than will be lost by them.

Acceptance theory of authority.   Popularized through the writings of Chester I. Barnard, this theory holds that the ultimate source of authority is the subordinate, who chooses to either accept or reject orders given by the superior.

Achievement.   The desire to accomplish things. High achievers tend to want not only to get things done but also to receive concrete feedback on their performance so they can tell how well they have done (*see* High achiever).

Action.   The last step in the communication process, which involves a duty on the part of both the receiver and the sender to follow up and do what was expected or see that it is done.

Ad hoc committee. A committee that is appointed for a specific purpose and disbanded upon completion of the job.

Adhocracy. The formation of temporary organization structures as found in the case of matrix designs used by project managers (*see* Matrix structure).

Administrative skills. Abilities that help a manager understand how all parts of an organization or department fit together. These skills are very important for top managers, who must be able to operate the enterprise as an integrated unit.

Adult ego state. A psychological state in which a person deals objectively with reality. Problem solving and rational thinking are products of this state.

Aesthetic value. A principle characterized by interest in form and harmony. Artists have high aesthetic value.

Affection need. The urge to establish and maintain satisfactory relations with others in respect to love and friendship.

Affective component. The emotional feeling attached to an attitude.

Assertiveness training. Human relations training designed to teach individuals how to determine their personal feelings, learn how to say what they want, and learn how to get what they want without being abusive or obnoxious.

Attention. The first step in the communication process, which involves screening out all disturbances or other distractions that can interrupt one's concentration.

Attitude questionnaire. A survey instrument that measures a person's feelings, opinions, and other intervening variables that make up attitudes.

Attitudes. A person's feelings about objects, activities, events, and other people.

Authoritarian leadership. A leadership style that tends to be heavily work-centered with major emphasis given to task accomplishment and little to the human element.

Authority. The right to command.

Automated technology.   Technology in which assembly-line machines are linked together and integrated in such a fashion that many functions are performed automatically without human intervention.

Autonomy.   The degree to which a job provides freedom, independence, and discretion in scheduling the work and determining how to carry it out.

Balance theory.   A theory used to explain how people react to change. In essence, the theory places primary attention on the consideration of three relationships: (1) the attitude of the worker toward the change, (2) the attitude of the manager toward the change, and (3) the attitude of the worker toward the manager.

Behaviorally anchored rating scales (BARS).   A performance evaluation method that consists of developing a series of critical incident behaviors, ranking them on a scale, and then using the scale to evaluate the personnel.

Behavioral scientist.   An individual highly skilled in one of the behavioral sciences (psychology, sociology, anthropology) who applies such training to the study of human behavior in organizations.

Behavior modification.   A system of motivation that tries to change an individual's responses by rewarding the individual for proper responses and failing to reinforce him or her for improper ones.

Boss-imposed time.   Time that is used to accomplish the activities that one's superior wants done.

Bureaucracy.   An organization structure that makes heavy use of rules, policies, procedures, and other structural variables while having a distinct lack of concern for the personnel.

Burnout.   A condition that often occurs among Type A people, it is the result of excessive mental and physical work and is manifested by exhaustion and/or withdrawal from the work situation.

Causal variable.   A factor that determines the results that will be achieved. Management decisions, business strategies, and leadership behavior are all illustrations (*see* Intervening variable and End-result variable).

Central tendency.   A problem generated by the evaluator in which everyone receives an average rating, regardless of effectiveness.

Change.   Any modification or alteration of the status quo.

Child ego state.   A state in which the individual does things the way he or she did when a child. Common facial expressions, for example, include twinkling eyes, mischievous winks, and broad grins.

Classical model.   A descriptive model that presents the worker as an individual who is lazy, works only for money, and needs to be supervised and controlled and that holds that if the work is simple enough and the people are closely controlled, they will produce up to standard.

Cluster chain.   A grapevine network in which people selectively pass information to other members of the informal organization. In this process, some people are given information and others are deliberately bypassed. This is the most common grapevine network.

Coercive power.   Power held by those who can fire, demote, or dock a subordinate who does not comply with their directives.

Cognitive component.   The beliefs a person has about the object or event.

Cognitive dissonance.   A mental state that occurs when there is a lack of consistency or harmony between an individual's cognitions (attitudes, beliefs, perceptions) and the data he or she is receiving from the environment. The former is out of line with the latter. The individual must, therefore, change his or her cognitions or reject the environmental information being received.

Cohesiveness.   The closeness or interpersonal attractions that exist among group members.

Collaboration.   A conflict resolution approach in which all parties try to iron out their differences, realizing that without full cooperation all of them will fail.

Communication process.   The process of transmitting meanings from sender to receiver.

Complementary transaction.   An exchange between two people that progresses along expected lines. For example, the first person assumes the adult ego state when speaking and the second person answers as an adult (*see* Crossed transaction).

Completed staff work. Staff work whose completed recommendation or solution can be either approved or disapproved by a line executive without the need for further investigation.

Compromise. A conflict resolution approach that involves each party giving something with no one of them being the clear winner.

Competence. Control over environmental factors. This is often revealed in the form of a desire for job mastery and professional growth.

Conflict. The result when individuals or groups in the organization clash over some issue that, at least to them, is important. Sometimes this occurs on an interpersonal basis and at other times it takes place between groups.

Conformity. Willingness to comply with the norms and/or sanctions of other individuals. Conformity, within bounds, is required if one hopes to remain a member of the informal organization.

Confrontation. Problem solving on a face-to-face basis.

Contingency organization design. A design enabling an organization to accommodate the specific needs of the situation.

Continuous reinforcement schedule. A reinforcement schedule in which the individual is given a reward every time he or she performs a desired behavior.

Control group. A group that is not subjected to any change. Its purpose is to serve as a comparison to the test group (*see* Test group).

Control need. The urge to establish and maintain a satisfactory relationship with people in respect to power and authority.

Core job dimensions. Characteristics that job-enrichment experts attempt to design into the work so as to increase worker motivation. The five most important are: skill variety, task identity, task significance, autonomy, and feedback.

Counseling. The discussion of an emotional problem with an employee for the general objective of eliminating or decreasing it.

Covert resistance. Resistance that is not readily observable because it is done under the guise of working as usual. Illustrations include "forgetting" to file reports or providing more information than is required in the hopes of swamping the reader and slowing up his or her progress.

Creative person. An individual who is bright (but not necessarily brilliant), has a positive self-image, is emotionally expressive, is interested in challenging problems, is often a nonconformist, and tends to be flexible and interested in solving problems in new and unique ways.

Crossed transaction. An exchange between two people that does not progress along expected lines, because the second person is not choosing the appropriate ego state. For example, the first person assumes the adult ego state when speaking and the second person answers as a parent to a child (*see* Complementary transaction).

Cybernated technology. Technology in which machines run and control other machines.

Decentralization of authority. A system of management in which a great deal of decision making is done at the lower levels of the hierarchy.

Decoding. Interpreting the message that one has received from a sender (*see* Encoding).

Delegation of authority. The process a manager employs in distributing work to his or her subordinates.

Diagonal communication. Communication that occurs between people who are neither in the same department nor on the same level of the hierarchy.

Dimensions of change. Characteristics of a change in policy or procedure. They are: (1) the logical dimension, based on technological and scientific reasons for the change, (2) the psychological dimension, the logic of the change in terms of the individuals affected, and (3) the sociological dimension, the logic of the change in terms of the work group.

Discharge. The ultimate discipline penalty which calls for a separation of the individual from the organization.

Disciplinary layoff. A severe form of discipline that calls for the individual to leave the organization for a period of time and forfeit the pay for these days.

Division of labor.   Work specialization that often brings about maximum efficiency.

Downward communication.   Communication that takes place between superior and subordinate.

Economic value.   A principle characterized by interest in what is useful. This value is of great interest to the average American business person.

Elaboration.   Taking part of a message or story that is received through the informal organization and building it up to fit one's own point of view.

Empathy.   Putting oneself, figuratively speaking, into another person's shoes. In so doing, one begins to understand the other person's point of view.

Encoding.   Translating a message into a code (words, facial expression, gestures) that will be intelligible to the receiver (*see* Decoding).

End-result variable.   A factor that reflects the result of a causal variable. Some common illustrations are profit, productivity, and output (*see* Causal variable and Intervening variable).

Equity.   Fairness in the distribution of rewards for work. Equity plays a key role in expectancy theory. In particular, expectancy theorists like to point out that rewards must be commensurate with contribution, but also the individual must feel that what is given to him or her is fair or equitable.

Equity theory.   A theory holding that people will compare their work/reward ratio to those of others in determining if they are being properly rewarded.

Esteem needs.   The need to feel important and to have self-respect. These needs are often satisfied by attaining prestige or power.

Expectancy.   A person's perception of the probability that a specific outcome will follow from a specific act.

Expectancy theory.   A motivation theory that holds that motivation is a force equal to the product of valence and expectancy (*see* Valence and Expectancy).

Experiential assignment.   An exercise that requires the participants to get involved or experience something to obtain a better understanding of it. For example, in teaching people how to be more effective communicators, the OD change agent may use an assignment that involves some of the participants and excludes the others. Then, concentrating on the latter, the individual asks, "How did you feel when you were left out?" After they say they did not like it, the individual tries to show them the relationship between how they feel and how subordinates feel when they are excluded from the communication process.

Expert power.   Power held by a leader because of knowledge and expertise. Leaders who have demonstrated competence acquire expert power.

Extinction.   A learning strategy in which the individual is not reinforced for a specific behavior, thereby reducing the likelihood that he or she will perform the same act again in the future.

Extrinsic rewards.   Rewards that are external to the work itself. Common examples are money, increased fringe benefits, and a company car.

Fast-track manager.   A manager who is aggressive, bright, self-confident, and capable of setting difficult but attainable objectives. These managers are often identified by the amount of decision-making authority they have and the high salaries they command.

Fayol's gangplank theory.   A theory of communication that holds that it is all right for the manager to use either lateral or diagonal communication as long as he or she obtains permission from his or her direct supervisor before undertaking the communication and informs the direct supervisor of any significant results of the cross-communication.

Feedback.   The degree to which the work required by a job results in the individual receiving direct, clear information about his or her performance effectiveness.

Fiedler's contingency model.   The best-known contingency model of leader effectiveness, which holds that the best leadership style will be the result of three situational variables: leader-member relations, the task structure, and the leader's position power.

FIRO.   A way of studying interpersonal relations by examining an individual's need for such things as inclusion, control, and affection.

5,5 managerial style.   Often referred to as a middle-of-the-road management philosophy, which assumes that there is an inherent conflict between the concerns for production and people. This manager tries to compromise and balance these two dimensions.

Fixation.   Behavior that is characterized by the use of the same behavioral pattern over and over again, even though experience has shown such behavior to be ineffective.

Flat structure.   An organization structure in which there is a wide span of control with only a small number of levels in the hierarchy (*see* Tall structure).

Force-field analysis.   A technique for analyzing a change situation involving a determination of those forces pushing for the change and those pushing against it in order to choose the proper strategy for bringing about the change.

Fringe group.   Those who are seeking admission to the informal organization.

Frustration.   The thwarting or blocking of an attempt at need satisfaction.

Functional authority.   Authority in a department other than one's own, as in the case of the comptroller who can order production personnel to provide him or her with cost-per-unit data.

Functional departmentalization.   An organizational arrangement in which people are grouped on the basis of the jobs they perform. In a manufacturing firm, for example, it is common to find marketing, production, and finance departments reporting directly to the president.

Functional group.   A group composed of workers all performing the same basic tasks. In a manufacturing firm, for example, it is common to find major functional groups or departments such as marketing, production, and finance.

Future shock.   The effect of enduring too much change in too short a time.

Geographic departmentalization.   An organizational arrangement in which people are grouped on the basis of territory. An example is the company with four major operating divisions: Eastern division, Midwestern division, Western division, and Foreign division.

Goal conflict. Conflict that occurs whenever someone is asked to pursue two goals that are not in harmony. The term also refers to a power struggle that takes place between groups, in which one or more may win only at the expense of the others.

Gossip chain. A grapevine network in which one person passes information to all the others in the informal organization. This is one of the less frequently used grapevine networks.

Grapevine. The name given to the communication network used to carry information among members of the informal organization.

Graphic rating scales. The most widely used of all performance appraisal tools, it is a list of factors and degrees of each factor on which the individual will be rated. The evaluator reads every factor and then checks the degree of each that applies to the person being evaluated.

Group. A social unit consisting of two or more interdependent, interactive individuals who are striving to attain common goals.

Group think. Social conformity to group ideas by members of the group.

Halo effect. A performance evaluation error caused by the rater's giving the ratees the same rating on all traits, regardless of actual performances.

Handicraft era. The first phase of technological development during which people made things by hand.

Hawthorne effect. The novelty or interest in a new situation that leads, at least initially, to positive results.

Hawthorne studies. Important behavioral studies that provided the impetus for the human relations movement.

High achiever. An individual who tends to like situations in which he or she can take personal responsibility for finding solutions to problems, is a moderate risk taker, and likes concrete feedback on performance to evaluate how well he or she is doing.

Human relations. A process by which management brings workers into contact with the organization in such a way that the objectives of both groups are achieved.

Human resources model. A descriptive model that presents the worker as an ambitious individual who has self-direction, self-control, and creativity and who, if managed properly, will contribute to the extent of his or her talents.

Human skills.   Abilities that help an individual interact with other people. These skills are very important for middle-level managers, who must lead other managers.

Hygiene factors.   Identified by Frederick Herzberg in his two-factor theory of motivation, these are factors that will not motivate people by their presence but will cause dissatisfaction by their absence. Some he identified include money, security, and working conditions.

Incentive payment plans.   Wage incentive schemes designed to reward increased efficiency by individuals, groups, or the organization at large.

Inclusion need.   The urge to establish and maintain a satisfactory relationship with people in respect to interaction and association.

Industrial democracy.   A formal, usually legally sanctioned arrangement of worker representation in the form of committees, councils, and boards at various levels of decision making in the organization.

Inference.   An assumption made by the receiver of a message. Inferences are most commonly made about messages that are very long and involve a very large number of facts.

Interest-friendship group.   A group formed on the basis of common beliefs, concerns, or activities. These groups are sometimes found within departments and in other instances cut across departmental lines.

Intermittent reinforcement schedule.   A reinforcement schedule in which the individual is given a reward on a variable or random basis for performing a desired behavior.

Interpersonal needs.   As presented by FIRO, these include the need for inclusion, control, and affection (*see also* Inclusion need, Control need, and Affection need).

Intervening variable.   A factor which reflects an individual's internal state. Loyalty, attitude, and motivation are all illustrations (*see* Causal variable and End-result variable).

Intrinsic rewards.   Rewards that are internal to the work itself. Common examples are a feeling of accomplishment, increased responsibility, and the opportunity to achieve.

Isolation.   A psychological condition that results when individuals become detached from society. Technology is causing this state in some people, who are fleeing the big city and trying to raise their families in the relaxed, slower-paced life of rural areas.

Job description.   A statement (or series of statements) that lists the duties and functions to be performed by the person holding the job.

Job enlargement.   A job redesign technique that involves giving the worker more to do and, hopefully, increasing his or her job motivation.

Job enrichment.   A job redesign technique that attempts to build psychological motivators into the job. In particular, it is common to find the worker being given more authority in planning the work and in controlling the pace and procedures.

Job profile chart.   A device used to measure the degree of each core job dimension possessed by a particular job.

Job redesign.   Any activities that involve work changes whose purpose is to increase the quality of the worker's job experience and/or improve his or her productivity.

Job rotation.   Moving a worker from one job to another for the purpose of reducing boredom.

Laissez-faire leadership.   A leadership style characterized by a lack of concern for either the people or the work.

Lateral communication.   Communication that takes place between people on the same level of the hierarchy. The most common reason for this communication flow is to promote coordination and teamwork.

Leader-member relations.   The relationships that exist between the leader and the subordinates.

Leader position power.   The authority vested in the leader's position.

Leadership.   The process of influencing people to direct their efforts toward the achievement of some particular goal(s).

Leadership characteristics.   Characteristics possessed by effective leaders. The most commonly cited include drive, originality, persistence, and the tolerance of stress.

Leadership dimensions.   Dimensions or concerns central to the process of influencing people to direct their efforts toward the achievement of some particular goal(s). There are two, concern for work and concern for people, and they are independent dimensions. Someone can be low on one without having to be high on the other.

Least-preferred coworker scale.   A questionnaire that asks the leader to describe the person with whom he or she can work least well. The instrument is used by Fiedler in his contingency model.

Legitimate power.   Power vested in the manager's position in the organizational hierarchy. For example, a vice president has greater legitimate power than a district manager, who in turn has greater power than a unit manager.

Leisure ethic.   A philosophy of work held by individuals who work as either an unfortunate obligation or as a totally undesirable or punishing experience.

Leniency.   A rater-generated problem in performance evaluation in which the manager gives all the people the highest possible rating.

Life positions.   Ways in which people go about relating to others. The most desirable one is, "I'm OK—You're OK."

Line authority.   Direct authority, as that of a superior who can give orders directly to a subordinate.

Linking pin function.   Representing one's subordinates to one's superior and thereby serving as a link between them and higher management. If all groups in the organization are linked together, the entire enterprise will function effectively.

Management by objectives (MBO).   An overall performance appraisal system used at all levels of the hierarchy entailing six steps: (1) identifying the goals of the unit or department, (2) sketching out the duties and responsibilities of each individual, (3) meeting with the subordinate and mutually setting goals for him or her, (4) employing an annual goal-setting worksheet to push the subordinate toward the objective, (5) periodically reviewing the goals and revising them where necessary, and (6) at the end of the assigned period evaluating the results and starting the cycle again.

Matrix structure. A hybrid form of organization structure that contains characteristics of both the project and functional structures. It is typical to find both line and project authority in a matrix structure, the former employed by the functional department head and the latter used by the project manager.

Meaninglessness. A condition occurring when employees are unable to determine what they are doing or why they are doing it.

Mechanistic structure. An organization structure that is often effective in a stable environment in which technology does not play a significant role.

Mechanistic technology. Technological era during which interchangeable parts and job simplification were introduced on a wide scale.

Mechanization era. A phase of technological development that was characterized by machine labor replacing man labor.

Mentor. A person who coaches, counsels, teaches, and/or sponsors others.

Motivating potential score (MPS). An approach for identifying the motivating potential of a particular job that encompasses the five core job dimensions. The formula is:

$$\left[\frac{\text{Skill variety} + \text{Task identity} + \text{Task significance}}{3}\right] \times \text{Autonomy} \times \text{Feedback}$$

Motivation. A psychological drive or force that directs someone toward an objective.

Motivational force. A mathematically computed motivational drive equal to the product of valence and expectancy (*see* Valence and Expectancy).

Motivators. Identified by Frederick Herzberg in his two-factor theory of motivation, motivators are those factors that will build high levels of motivation and job satisfaction. Some he identified are recognition, advancement, and achievement.

Motive. A "why" of behavior consisting of needs, drives, wants, and impulses within the individual.

Need mix. A term that refers to the fact that people tend to be partially satisfied and partially unsatisfied at all levels of the hierarchy simultaneously. It is never an all-or-nothing situation.

Negative reinforcement. Reinforcement that increases the frequency of a behavior while bringing about the termination of some condition.

9,9 managerial style. A managerial style referred to as "team management," regarded by many as the ideal management style. The manager has high concern for work and high concern for people.

9,1 managerial style. A managerial style in which the manager has a high concern for production and a low concern for people. The manager plans the work and pushes to get it out. Little interest is shown in the workers. If they cannot keep up, they are replaced by others who can.

Normative reality. Interpretive reality, in which there is no right answer. Matters of opinion related to personal taste, politics, religion, and other areas where there is no one correct answer are examples.

Normlessness. A condition, brought about by technology, that occurs when human behavior is no longer guided by the norms of society because technology sets the rules instead.

Norms. Rules of conduct that are adopted by group members.

Nucleus group. Those who are full-fledged members of the informal organization.

OD intervention. A catchall term used to describe the behavioral science techniques used to intervene in a situation for the purpose of improving it.

1,9 managerial style. A managerial style in which the manager tends to have a high concern for people's feelings, comfort, and needs and low concern for getting the work out.

1,1 managerial style. A managerial style in which the manager tends to put people in jobs and then leave them alone. The manager does not check up on their work or try to interact with them by offering praise or encouraging them to keep up the good work. There is a low concern for both work and people.

Oral warning.   Usually the first step in the disciplinary process, which involves verbally pointing out that repetition of a particular act will result in discipline.

Organic structure.   An organization structure that is often effective in a dynamic environment, where such things as technology play a significant role.

Organizational climate.   The overall favorability of member attitudes and perceptions with reference to specific activities and features of an organization. The climate may be quite favorable for, say, good communication but relatively unfavorable for rapid change or tough-minded decision making.

Organizational development.   An effort to improve an organization's effectiveness by dealing with individual, group, and overall organizational problems from both a technical and human standpoint.

Organizational iceberg.   The formal and informal aspects of the organization. The formal consist of structural considerations that can be readily observed, including job definitions, job descriptions, and forms of departmentalization. The informal are social-psychological processes and behavioral considerations that cannot be seen, including power, influence, interpersonal relations, and employee satisfaction.

Outer group.   Those who have been rejected for membership in the informal organization.

Overt resistance.   Resistance that is observable. Illustrations include worker slowdown, setting low informal production norms, and outright sabotage.

Paired comparison method.   A performance evaluation method, involving comparing each individual who is being rated against every other individual on a number of different bases, including work quality and work quantity.

Parent ego state.   A psychological state in which the individual acts the way his or her parents acted. The parents serve as the role model for the individual's behavior.

Parity of authority and responsibility.   A principle of organizing that holds that the person who is given responsibility for a job must have the accompanying authority to get the work done.

Participative leadership.   A leadership style characterized by high concerns for both people and work.

Participative management.   An informal style of face-to-face leadership in which management and the workers share decision making in the work place. It is an example of shop floor democracy.

Paternalistic leadership.   A leadership style that tends to be heavily work-centered but has some consideration for the personnel as well.

Path-goal theory of leadership.   A leadership theory holding that: (1) the leader can improve subordinate motivation by making the rewards for performance more attractive, (2) if work assignments are poorly defined, motivation can be increased by providing helpful supervision and goal clarification, and (3) if the work is already structured, the leader should concentrate on the personal needs of the individuals by giving them attention, praise, and support.

Perception.   A person's view of reality.

Performance appraisal cycle.   A four-step process used in appraising individuals, it consists of: (1) establishing performance standards, (2) determining individual performance, (3) comparing performance against standards, and (4) evaluating individual performance.

Personal characteristics.   Personal attributes often possessed by effective leaders. The most commonly cited include superior mental ability, emotional maturity, and problem-solving skills.

Personality.   A relatively stable set of characteristics and tendencies that determine similarities and differences between one person and another.

Physiological needs.   Basic requirements such as food, clothing, and shelter.

Political value.   A principle characterized by an interest in power. Politicians have high political value.

Positive reinforcement.   Reinforcement that comes in the form of a reward and serves to strengthen the likelihood of the individual performing the same act in the future.

Postindustrial society. A society characterized by a service-oriented work force, dynamic growth of workers in professional and technical jobs, an increase in the importance of theoretical knowledge, and an interest in planning and controlling technological growth.

Power. The ability to influence, persuade, or move another to one's own point of view.

Powerlessness. A psychological condition that occurs when workers feel that they are at the mercy of technology. Workers on assembly lines, for example, report feelings of powerlessness because they are forced to keep up with the speed of the line. The technology controls them.

Prestige. The respect, status, and influence an individual has among other people.

Probability chain. A grapevine network in which people randomly pass information to other members of the informal organization.

Product departmentalization. An organizational arrangement in which people are grouped on the basis of product line. General Motors, Ford Motor, and RCA all use product departmentalization.

Profit-maximizing management. A management era during which all decisions were directed toward making the greatest amount of money possible. Self-interest and the free market system were used in determining the most efficient allocation of resources. Although many businesses do not use this approach any longer, it is still typical to find these basic values and philosophies among small entrepreneurs.

Project authority. Authority exercised by the project manager over the personnel assigned to the project. In contrast to functional authority, project authority flows horizontally.

Project group. A group consisting of individuals from many different areas or backgrounds, the purpose of which is to attain its objective within predetermined time, cost, and quality limits. The group is disbanded when the goal is attained, and everyone goes back to his or her original department.

Project manager. An individual in charge of a project (*see* Adhocracy and Matrix structure).

Quality circle. A group of 5–10 well-trained employees and a team leader that study job-related problems and make recommendations for improvements.

Quality-of-life management. An emerging management era characterized by emphasis on cooperation between management and personnel and the redesign of work so that it meets some of the demands workers bring to the work place.

Rationalization. Behavior characterized by looking for excuses. For example, "The reason why Andy got a higher grade than me in the human relations class was that the professor liked him a lot better."

"Red-hot stove rule." A system of employing discipline that holds that all disciplinary practices should: (1) be immediate, (2) offer advance warning, (3) be consistent from person to person, and (4) be impersonal.

Referent power. Power based on the followers' identification with the leader.

Regression. Behavior characterized by a reversion to childlike behavior, as when a manager throws a temper tantrum when annoyed at a worker who asks too many questions.

Rejection. Refusal to accommodate some condition or change because it is perceived as potentially destructive.

Reliability. A measurement quality of a performance evaluation technique that refers to whether or not the instrument measures the same thing over and over.

Religious value. A principle characterized by an interest in unity. Members of the clergy have a high religious value.

Resignation. Behavior characterized by the decision, after frustration, to withdraw from the situation. For example, Mary has asked the boss for a promotion to the Eastern office on three different occasions and has been turned down each time, so she has decided not to ask again.

Resume. A summary of your education, work experience, training, and references. This form is used when applying for a job.

Reward power. Power held by leaders who can give extrinsic satisfiers to subordinates who do their jobs well.

Risky-shift phenomenon. The tendency to take greater risks in a group than when acting alone.

Role. An expected behavior.

Role ambiguity. A role-related condition that occurs when job duties are unclear and the person is unsure of what to do.

Role conflict. A condition that occurs when an individual faces a situation in which he or she must assume two roles and the performance of the first precludes the performance of the second.

Role playing. A common form of training used in organizational development consisting of the spontaneous acting out of a realistic situation involving two or more people. The purpose of the training is to acquaint one or more of the participants with the proper way of handling a given situation.

Rumor. The unverified or untrue messages of the grapevine. Considered the most undesirable feature of the informal organization and often defined as "interest times ambiguity."

Safety needs. Lower-level needs such as those of survival and security.

Satisficing behavior. Behavior in which individuals accept results or payoffs that are satisfactory or good enough in contrast to choices that would maximize outcomes.

Scientific management. A system of management, popularized by Frederick W. Taylor and others in the early twentieth century, that sought to develop: (1) ways of increasing productivity by making work easier to perform, and (2) methods for motivating workers to take advantage of these labor-saving devices and techniques.

Scientific method. An objective approach for identifying a problem, gathering information on it, analyzing the data, arriving at a tentative answer, and testing it.

Selective filtering. The screening of rumors so that part of the story is maintained and the rest is discarded.

Self-actualization need. The urge to maximize one's potential, often satisfied through attainment of competence and a feeling of achievement.

Self-estrangement. A condition that occurs when an individual can no longer find intrinsic satisfaction in what he or she is doing. The work becomes a mere means to earn a living, and if the individual could go elsewhere and make more money, he or she would do so.

Self-imposed time. Time used for doing the things that the manager originates or agrees to do personally.

Sensory reality. Physical reality as characterized by objects such as an automobile, a house, or a car.

Single strand. An informal grapevine network in which each person receives information from one individual and passes it to another. The flow of information moves down a line. This is the least frequently employed grapevine network.

Skill variety. The degree to which a job requires the completion of different activities, all of which involve varying talents and capabilities.

Social exchange theory. A theory that holds that the organization consists of individuals who are exchanging supportive behaviors by doing things for others and expecting reciprocity.

Social need. The urge for interaction with others for the purpose of meaningful relationships.

Social network. Informal structures created by people in the work place and used for interaction and social exchange on the job.

Social value. A value characterized by love of people. Social workers have a high social value.

Sociogram. A schematic drawing that shows the social relationships existing among members of a group. It provides information regarding informal group behavior.

Sociotechnical systems. The relationship of technology to the people at work.

Span of control. A principle of organizing that holds that there is an optimum number of subordinates a superior can effectively manage. When not used as a principle, the term simply refers to the number of subordinates who report to a given superior.

Staff authority. Auxiliary authority as held by individuals who advise, assist, recommend, or facilitate organizational activities. An example is the company lawyer who advises the president on the legality of contract matters.

Standard. The amount of work expected from each worker every day. This concept was popularized by the scientific managers.

Standing committee. A committee that exists for an indefinite period of time.

Status. The relative ranking of an individual in an organization or group.

Status discrepancy. Conflict that occurs when people do things that do not fit with their status in the group. Union representatives can negatively affect their status by becoming too friendly with company supervisors, and so can managers who eat lunch with their subordinates.

Status incongruency. A discrepancy between a person's supposed status and the way he or she is treated.

Status symbol. Signs that help us understand where the individual ranks in the organization. Common status symbols include desks, big offices, rugs, and a key to the executive washroom.

Stereotyping. Generalizing a particular trait or behavior to all members of a given group.

Stress. A condition characterized by emotional strain and/or physical discomfort which, if it goes unrelieved, can impair one's ability to cope with the environment.

Stroking. Any act implying recognition of another's presence.

Structured interview. An interview in which specific questions are asked in a predetermined manner.

Survey feedback. An overall or comprehensive OD intervention that entails three distinct steps: (1) a systematic collection of data on the current state of the organization, usually obtained through questionnaires and/or interviews, (2) a feedback of the findings to the organizational personnel, and (3) the development of an action plan for dealing with the problems that have been identified.

System-imposed time. Time used to handle requests from other managers.

System 1.   An exploitive-autocratic management style in which management has little confidence in the subordinates and makes wide use of threats and punishment in getting things done.

System 2.   A benevolent-autocratic leadership style in which management acts in a condescending manner toward the subordinates and has little trust in them.

System 3.   A consultative-democratic leadership style in which management has quite a bit of confidence and trust in the subordinates, decision making tends to be delegated to some degree, and there is some confidence and trust between superiors and subordinates.

System 4.   A participative-democratic leadership style in which management has complete confidence and trust in the subordinates, decision making is highly decentralized, communication flows up and down the hierarchy, and the formal and informal organizations are often the same.

System 4 management.   A comprehensive OD intervention that consists of identifying the current state of management in the organization through determining which of the management systems is being used, System 1, 2, 3, or 4.

Tall structure.   An organization structure in which there is a narrow span of control with a large number of levels in the hierarchy (*see* Flat structure).

Task concept.   Planning the work of every individual at least one day in advance so that the individual receives complete written instructions describing what he or she is to accomplish as well as how the work is to be done.

Task identity.   The degree to which a job requires completion of a whole or identifiable piece of work.

Task significance.   The degree to which a job has a substantial impact on the lives and work of other people.

Task structure.   The degree to which the leader's job is programmed or specified in step-by-step fashion.

Team building.   A popular OD intervention that consists of working with intact, permanent work teams in an effort to improve the relationships that exist among them.

Technical skills.   Abilities that help an individual determine how things work. These are very important for lower-level managers such as foremen.

Test group.   People who are subjected to some behavioral change and then studied to see the effect of this change (*see* Control group).

T-group.   Small-group interaction that takes place in an unstructured setting. In this setting, individuals meet in groups, focus on the "here and now" behavior taking place in their own group, and attempt to enhance their awareness of themselves and of the social processes.

Theoretical value.   A principle characterized by interest in truth, system, and the ordering of knowledge.

Theory X.   A set of assumptions that holds that people: (1) dislike work, (2) have little ambition, (3) want security above all else, and (4) must be coerced, controlled, and threatened with punishment in order to attain organizational objectives.

Theory Y.   A set of assumptions that holds that: (1) if the conditions are favorable, people will not only accept responsibility, they will seek it, (2) if people are committed to organizational objectives, they will exercise self-direction and self-control, and (3) commitment is a function of the rewards associated with goal attainment.

Theory Z.   A management approach that blends Japanese and American management practices in arriving at a modified-American approach that uses consensual decision making, lifetime employment, slower evaluation and promotion, informal control, a moderately specialized career path, and holistic concern for the employee.

Tolerance.   Putting up with change. This usually occurs because the workers have no particular positive or negative feelings toward the change; they are basically neutral about it.

Transactional analysis.   The study of social exchanges between people.

Trusteeship management.   A management era during which the owners are no longer the managers and the organization becomes much more interested in its interface with society at large. Most organizations today operate within the confines of this type of management philosophy.

Type A person. An individual aggressively involved in a chronic, incessant struggle to achieve more and more in less and less time.

Understanding. The second step in the communication process, which involves getting the receiver to comprehend the meaning of the transmission.

Unity of command. A principle of organizing that holds that everyone should have one and only one boss.

Unity of management. A principle of organizing that holds that there should be one manager and one plan for all operations having the same objective.

Universal design theory. Organization theory consisting of a series of principles that can be used in organizing any enterprise. Today this theory is regarded as only partially accurate.

Unstructured interview. An interview in which the interviewer may have a general direction or objective, but the questions are not predetermined and the interview is allowed to develop spontaneously.

Upward communication. Communication that takes place between subordinate and superior.

Valence. A person's preference for a particular outcome.

Validity. A measurement quality of a performance evaluation technique that refers to whether the instrument is measuring what it is intended to measure.

Value. Something that has worth or importance to an individual.

Vertical dyad linkage theory. A theory of leadership that investigates the formation of direct superior-subordinate relationships and the effect of these dyads on group performance.

Vertical loading. A job enrichment principle that involves closing the gap between the "doing" and "controlling" aspects of the job.

Work. The use of physical and/or mental effort that is directed toward the production or accomplishment of something.

Workaholic. An individual who obtains deep satisfaction from work but carries this interest to an extreme, which can be both physically and psychologically dangerous.

Work ethic.   A philosophy of work held by individuals who believe that one should work hard, take pride in the job, and strive for advancement and promotion.

Worth ethic.   A philosophy of work held by individuals who work because of the self-esteem or personal and intangible rewards they receive from doing the job.

Written warning.   A form of discipline that involves placing a warning in the employee's file that can be cited as evidence if it is decided to terminate him or her in the future.

name index

subject index